WITHDRAWN
HARVARD LIBRARY
WITHDRAWN

The United Synod
of the South

Recent Titles in
Contributions to the Study of Religion
Series Editor: Henry W. Bowden

Facing the Enlightenment and Pietism: Archibald Alexander and the Founding of Princeton Theological Seminary
Lefferts A. Loetscher

Presbyterian Women in America: Two Centuries of a Quest for Status
Lois A. Boyd and R. Douglas Brackenridge

Marchin' the Pilgrims Home: Leadership and Decision-Making in an Afro-Caribbean Faith
Stephen D. Glazier

Exorcising the Trouble Makers: Magic, Science, and Culture
Francis L. K. Hsu

The Cross, The Flag, and The Bomb: American Catholics Debate War and Peace, 1960-1983
William A. Au

Religious Conflict in Social Context: The Resurgence of Orthodox Judaism in Frankfurt Am Main, 1838-1877
Robert Liberles

Triumph over Silence: Women in Protestant History
Richard L. Greaves, editor

Neighbors, Friends, or Madmen: The Puritan Adjustment to Quakerism in Seventeenth-Century Massachusetts Bay
Jonathan M. Chu

Cities of Gods: Faith, Politics and Pluralism in Judaism, Christianity and Islam
Nigel Biggar, Jamie S. Scott, and William Schweiker, editors

Theodicies in Conflict: A Dilemma in Puritan Ethics and Nineteenth-Century American Literature
Richard Forrer

Gilbert Tennent, Son of Thunder: A Case Study of Continental Pietism's Impact on the First Great Awakening in the Middle Colonies
Milton J Coalter, Jr.

Lighten Their Darkness: The Evangelical Mission to Working-Class London, 1828-1860
Donald M. Lewis

The United Synod of the South

The Southern New School Presbyterian Church

Harold M. Parker, Jr.

A Publication of the Presbyterian Historical Society
Contributions to the Study of Religion,
Number 20

Greenwood Press
New York • Westport, Connecticut • London

Library of Congress Cataloging-in-Publication Data

Parker, Harold M.
  The United Synod of the South : the Southern New School Presbyterian Church / Harold M. Parker, Jr.
    p. cm.—(Contributions to the study of religion, ISSN 0196-7053 ; no. 20)
  "A publication of the Presbyterian Historical Society."
  Bibliography: p.
  Includes index.
  ISBN 0-313-26289-6 (lib. bdg. : alk. paper)
  1. United Synod of the South—History. 2. Presbyterian Church in the U.S.A. (New School)—History. 3. Presbyterian Church—Southern States—History—19th century. 4. Southern States—Church history—19th century. I. Presbyterian Historical Society. II. Title. III. Series.
285'.13—dc 19   87-37564

British Library Cataloguing in Publication Data is available.

Copyright © 1988 by The Presbyterian Historical Society

All rights reserved. No portion of this book may be reproduced, by any process or technique, without the express written consent of the publisher.

Library of Congress Catalog Card Number: 87-37564
ISBN: 0-313-26289-6
ISSN: 0196-7053

First published in 1988

Greenwood Press, Inc.
88 Post Road West, Westport, Connecticut 06881

Printed in the United States of America

The paper used in this book complies with the Permanent Paper Standard issued by the National Information Standards Organization (Z39.48-1984).

10 9 8 7 6 5 4 3 2 1

Contents

	Preface	vii
	Abbreviations	xv
1.	The Great Division of 1837-1838	1
2.	The Years of Decision in the South	25
3.	Southern New School Ecclesiastical Development	55
4.	The New School Denomination Emerges, 1840-1857	73
5.	The Southern New School Develops	95
6.	The New School Deals With Slavery	111
7.	The Division of 1857	138
8.	The Richmond Convention	157
9.	The Knoxville Meeting and Aftermath	177
10.	The United Synod Polity and Leaders	195
11.	The United Synod at Work Antebellum	210
12.	The Years of the War	222
13.	Reunion With the Old School	249

14.	Postwar Reactions to the Union	269
15.	Results of the Union	286
16.	The United Synod of the South: An Appraisal	291
	Appendix A: Address of Protest	307
	Appendix B: Declaration of Principles of the United Synod	312
	Appendix C: Proposed Terms of Union With the Old School Assembly by the United Synod of the South	318
	Selected Bibliography	321
	Index	340

Preface

There have been numerous works on American Presbyterianism in general and the New School Presbyterian Church in particular. The account of the New School in the South, however, has been neglected in these studies, save for a footnote here or an occasional line or two there. This study is a narrative account of the New School Presbyterian Church in the South, which in 1858 led to the formation of the United Synod of the Presbyterian Church in the United States of America--more popularly known as the United Synod of the South. After a separate existence as a denomination, seven years later the Church united with the Presbyterian Church in the Confederate States of America--better known as the Southern Presbyterian Church.

The 1983 reunion of the former United Presbyterian Church in the United States of America and the Presbyterian Church in the United States (the official name of the "Southern Presbyterian Church") brought together the two largest American bodies in the American Presbyterian/Reformed tradition. Few Presbyterians are aware that historically, at least, the United Synod was an earlier source for that reunion.

The study of the United Synod has engaged me for a number of years. It was part of a larger interest I have had in the six successful organic unions that the Southern Presbyterian Church experienced between 1863 and 1874. The union of the United Synod with the Southern Church, however, was by far the largest and most contributive union in which the latter Church participated during that decade.

A Church such as the United Synod does not suddenly appear. It has roots and history--some kind of background. This study begins by reviewing those causes which led to the Old School-New School schism of 1837-1838. The next two chapters trace the development of the New School, particularly as that development related to the South. During the period 1838 to 1852 the New School emerged as a true denomination, having organized its own agencies for carrying out the mission of the Church. Chapter 4 interprets the significance of that development as it related to the southern wing of the Church, and Chapter 5 discusses how the southern governing bodies of the Church--synods and presbyteries-- developed their own programs.

The major social issue of this era in American history was that of domestic slavery. No Church in America faced this issue with greater intensity than did the New School Presbyterians. Chapter 6 is essentially a commentary on the way the New School grappled with the issue from 1839 to 1857. The culmination of the Church's efforts to work out an accommodation on slavery reached its climax at the General Assembly of 1857. Chapter 7 examines in detail those factors that precipitated the withdrawal of the six southern New School synods that year from the New School Presbyterian Church.

All this has been preliminary. With Chapter 8 and the presentation of the 1857 Richmond Convention, at which time the plans for the formal organization of the United Synod were developed, the study begins its focus on the emergence and development of the United Synod of the South. Chapter 9 treats that formal organization in Knoxville on 1 April 1858. The varied reactions to this ecclesiastical creation among southern New School ministers, churches, presbyteries, and synods are examined. The next three chapters discuss the manner whereby the United Synod organized itself to carry out its mission in the antebellum years and the period of the Civil War.

In 1863 the Southern Presbyterian Church approached the United Synod in respect to Church union. Chapter 13 details the various circumstances that ultimately brought the two Churches into organic union in 1864. Chapter 14 examines some of the negative reactions that emerged after the union had been consummated, particularly in East Tennessee and Missouri. Chapter 15 assays the contributions resulting from the union, and the last chapter examines and interprets reasons why the southern New School/United Synod failed to grow and reach its potential as did other Presbyterian Churches in that day. The chapter thus serves as a postlude to the United Synod.

Although the history of the United Synod is presented in a chronological narrative manner, there are certain themes in the account that emerge from time to time. By noting these in advance, the careful reader may find this study more interesting. Certainly, one of the most interesting facets to the story was the monistic mentality that characterized the southern wing of the New School. It had left the Old School over one issue and one issue only: protest to the manner by which the Old School majority in 1837 had exscinded four northern New School-dominated synods and a presbytery without the trial required by the Church's Constitution. This monistic frame of mind was also the immediate cause for the withdrawal of the southern synods from the New School and the formation of the United Synod of the South: slavery will not be discussed on the floors of the governing bodies of the Church. Nothing else contributed to its existence. This posture was the Church's distinguishing mark, separating it from all other Presbyterian bodies in the United States.

A second theme presented is the manner by which the northern New School element of the Church treated the southern constituents. The larger northern portion of the Church became increasingly dominated by radical abolitionists who showed no concern whatsoever for the difficulties the members in the South were experiencing over the slavery issue. The annual debates in the General Assembly over the slavery issue became increasingly one-sided. Further, although the southern men were leaders of considerable ability, their northern brothers never recognized them as being able to lead or head any portion of the Church's structure or mission. Yet the ability of the southern leaders later to erect a well-organized Church following their separation from their northern brethren belied the disdain by which the northerners viewed them.

A third theme was the late attempts of the New School to structure its own denominational agencies. For almost a decade and a half after the division of 1837-1838, the New School worked through the voluntary interdenominational agencies, such as the American Home Missionary Society, rather than develop its own denominational boards for conducting mission work, publications, support of students for the ministry, and similar programs. The results of this lengthy lack of denominational structure cast a long shadow over the southern portion of the Church. The various interdenominational agencies increasingly abandoned the South because of the presence there of the institution of domestic slavery.

Closely associated with this lack of denominational institutions and philosophy was the refusal--or inability--of the southern New School to develop a program of financial support for both the local church program as well as the denominational programs. When suddenly cut off from the New School, the United Synod did organize itself as a denomination; the structures, however, were not adequately funded. This lack of fiscal responsibility substantially weakened the numerous efforts the United Synod planned but could never get off the drawing board.

Another thread which this study develops is the doctrine of the spirituality of the Church. For many years Presbyterian historians have traced this "peculiar" tenet of Southern Presbyterianism to its Old School heritage. However, there is sufficient evidence to indicate that the basis of this theological structure was developing also in the southern New School. The epitome of the Church's position on the spirituality of the Church was its insistence that the issue of domestic slavery would never be permitted to come to the floor of any of its governing bodies. Slavery was viewed as a political, not a spiritual or religious matter.

A sixth theme this study develops is the theological heterogeneity which embraced the southern New Schoolmen. This doctrinal status made the ministers theologically suspect to the southern Old School group. Further, it hampered the development of those institutions the United Synod needed to erect. The large majority of the ministers in the Synod of Tennessee were advocates of Hopkinsianism; and other individual clergy held positions which were not in accord with more normative Presbyterian theology.

The closing chapters develop the hypothesis that the Civil War contributed dramatically to the demise of the United Synod. Prior to 1861 the Church had made encouraging progress in developing its institutions and mission. The war, however, struck the fragile Church and its plans, forcing it to pull back from implementing its programs. This turn of events made the offer of unity with the Southern Presbyterian Church a most welcome proposal.

The reader will note that references to women in the United Synod are very, very few. The paucity of such references does not indicate that women were not making their own contributions, but rather that the story of women in the United Synod simply has not been uncovered and told.

Every effort has been made to use the term blacks for such expressions as "Negroes" and "colored persons." When the latter two terms are used in direct quotations, they are retained; in secondary sources and in narrative accounts the term blacks has been used. When this has not been done, it does not reflect a racist position, for the three terms were used synonymously and interchangeably in the nineteenth century.

Apart from an article published in 1897, no study has appeared on the United Synod as such. This book, then, has required considerable research for material both primary and secondary on the subject. One of the major sources utilized was the *Christian Observer*. Its weekly columns carried considerable, extensive, and varied information touching the Church. Through its files one gains an abundance of information regarding detailed developments in the New School/United Synod history. The complete file of the *Christian Observer* for years 1835-1866 was read.

Primary sources abound. The major depository for such materials is the Historical Foundation of the Presbyterian and Reformed Churches, Montreat, North Carolina. The Foundation houses an extensive collection of manuscript records of sessions, presbyteries, synods, and supreme governing bodies of the Presbyterian Churches in the South. In addition to its excellent collection of primary materials, its staff was a dedicated asset to me. I am especially indebted to the late Dr. Thomas H. Spence, Jr., Curator of the Foundation, and his successor, Dr. Kenneth J. Foreman, Jr., for their invaluable, unspeakable guidance and counsel, assistance and encouragement. Mrs. Mary Lane rendered valuable assistance by her prompt response to my correspondence, particularly in those places where my note-taking had been less than thorough. The Presbyterian Historical Society in Philadelphia contains splendid files of pamphlets and materials from the numerous organizations of the period. Both Mr. William B. Miller, the Manager of the Society, and the Rev. Gerald W. Gillette, Research Historian, provided services that transcended the call of duty. Through the years superior supporting staffs have been assembled and trained at both Montreat and

Philadelphia, and each staff is indeed a vital element to the researcher for assistance rendered.

The research for this study embraces a period of over thirty years. Thus the names of specific librarians who gave valued assistance have frequently been forgotten. I would be remiss, however, did I not at least tender my appreciation to the following institutions for the willingness to let me research in their libraries and for the gracious assistance granted me: the library of Tusculum College; the staff of the McClung Room of the Lawson McGhee Library, Knoxville, Tennessee; Murrell Library of Missouri Valley College; Lamar Memorial Library, Maryville College; Western Kentucky Library and Museum, Bowling Green, Kentucky; Ernest Miller White Library, Louisville Presbyterian Theological Seminary; The Historical Room, Huntsville, Alabama, Public Library; and the Department of Archives and History, State of Mississippi, Jackson. I am particularly indebted to colleagues at the Leslie J. Savage Library, Western State College of Colorado for the numerous discussions we had and for the many times they went out of their way to buy, beg, or borrow materials that were helpful to me. I refer especially to Mr. Adrian Dortzweiler, Mr. John Garralda, and Mrs. Frances Jacobson.

Numerous individuals and personal friends upon learning of my research encouraged me in many ways. They loaned me books from their personal libraries, entertained me in their homes, or contributed toward my expenses. My thanks are extended to Mrs. James G. Rollins, Knoxville; Mrs. S. W. Plauche, Jr., Lake Charles, Louisiana; Dr. and Mrs. Lawrence R. Conley, Otis, Oregon; Dr. and Mrs. Calvin Fisher, Colorado Springs; and Mr. and Mrs. Herman Smith, Amarillo, Texas.

I am also indebted to congregations I have served during my years of research--Inskip Presbyterian Church, Knoxville; First Presbyterian Church, Winfield, Kansas; Community Presbyterian Church, Lake City, Colorado. They frequently gave me time off to engage in research in addition to being kind enough to listen to many illustrations in my sermons about the United Synod. My appreciation is also extended to former President of Western State College, Dr. Harlan Bryant, for approving my request for the sabbatical leave that enabled me to wrap up my research.

As I wrote, I felt the necessity of having my material read and critiqued by knowledgeable scholars who know that they can "come down hard" in their comments and yet remain friends. I am grateful to the following who read the manuscript in various stages and who made numerous corrections as well as helpful criticism: Dr. L. C. Rudolph, Indiana University; Dr. L. Gordon Tait, The College of Wooster; Dr. James Smylie, Union Theological Seminary in Virginia; Dr. Barbara MacHaffie, Marietta College; and Dr. Dwyn Mecklin Mounger, First Presbyterian Church, Valdosta, Georgia. Two of my colleagues at Western State College in the English Department assisted me in the areas of grammar, syntax, and logic--Dr. Zelda Jeanne Rouillard and Dr. Ralph I. Johnson.

It is one thing to write out a manuscript; it is quite another to get it through the stage of publication. I am very grateful for the assistance which Mr. David Young of Greenwood Press gave me in his capacity of Publications Editor. His support, guidance, and encouraging comfort always came at the right times!

Finally, a word of thanks to my wife, Barbara, and our son, Harold Malin. When on travels during the Sabbatical, they were willing to seek their own amusement while I labored in the halls of research to find the material necessary for this book. When the time came to type out the manuscript in camera ready condition, both pitched in--typing, proof-reading, making last minute corrections, and learning from square one how to work with all the intricacies of the computer. For their efforts I can only say, "Greater love hath no man . . . ." Even with all the help I received, there are probably errors of fact, of judgment, of mechanics which I alone must bear. I can only testify that without the assistance of many wonderful people--historians, friends, librarians, colleagues, loved ones--those errors would be even more numerous.

Gunnison, Colorado

Pentecost, 1988

Abbreviations

ABCFM	American Board of Commissioners for Foreign missions
ABS	American Bible Society
AES	American Education Society
AHMS	American Home Missionary Society
AHR	*American Historical Review*
AMA	American Missionary Association
ASSU	American Sunday School Union
CH	*Church History*
CO	*Christian Observer*
GAPCCSA	General Assembly, Presbyterian Church in the Confederate States of America
GAPCUS	General Assembly, Presbyterian Church in the United States
GAPCUSA	General Assembly, Presbyterian Church in the United States of America
JPH	*Journal of Presbyterian History*

Abbreviations

JPHS	*Journal of the Presbyterian Historical Society*
LPTS	Louisville Presbyterian Theological Seminary
MVHR	*Mississippi Valley Historical Review*
NS	New School
OS	Old School
PCCSA	Presbyterian Church in the Confederate States of America
PHF	Presbyterian Historical Foundation, Montreat, North Carolina
PHS	Presbyterian Historical Society, Philadelphia
SAS	Southern Aid Society
SSPH	*Studies in Southern Presbyterian History*
USS	United Synod of the South

1
The Great Division of 1837–1838

In 1837, following a decade of internal acerbity, the Presbyterian Church in the United States of America suffered a division. From that schism two denominations emerged. Although both carried the same ecclesiastical nomenclature, they are better known as the Old School and New School Presbyterian Churches. Many years would pass before they would be reunited. Officially the division came in 1837 when the Old School majority at the General Assembly exscinded four synods and a presbytery of New School sentiments. In 1838 the exscinded members arrived at the General Assembly, hoping to be readmitted. Such was not their fate. The doors were closed to them. They then withdrew to another church nearby and proceeded to organize themselves formally into a separate Church.[1]

The division of the Presbyterian Church did not suddenly occur. The causes embraced a spectrum of factors as well as a considerable period of time. Some see the origins of the 1837 schism emerging as early as 1706, when ethnically disparate groups formed the first presbytery in America. The Scotch and Irish Presbyterians possessed and inculcated those principles that were to mark the Old School, whereas the English Presbyterians were characterized by those traits that would surface in the New School.[2] These same groups became involved in the Old Light-New Light controversy and division of the mid-eighteenth century, and not all the embers from that conflagration had been completely extinguished by 1837.

The first murmurs between the two groups were heard in 1826, when the Synod of Pittsburgh made known its apprehensions to the General Assembly regarding the admission of ordained ministers into the Presbyterian Church from other denominations who had not assented to its doctrines.[3] The Finney revivals of 1828 poured additional fuel on the smoldering coals. At the same time, considerable controversy developed across the Church regarding the alliance of the New School party with the numerous voluntary benevolent associations as the vehicles for conducting the work of the Church, in contrast to the boards that the Church had erected for the operation of its various missionary and benevolent programs.[4]

The first congregation to experience a division within its ranks was the church at Lynchburg, Virginia. After hard feelings had been engendered by the discussion of the doctrines of each party, on 20 April 1830, the New School adherents withdrew to form their own congregation, and presented a petition to presbytery for that purpose. Only one of the elders in the church remained with the Old School party.[5]

The first use of the terms *Old School* and *New School* appeared in the *Christian Advocate* in 1824. This journal, edited by Dr. Ashbel Green, employed the terminology to differentiate theological stances, particularly in regard to the doctrine of the Atonement.[6] The annual meetings of the General Assembly of the 1830s simply reflected and contributed to the divisiveness that characterized the Church's party strife. That period has been described as

> a time of storm and stress, a period of controversy and conflict....There was scarcely a single phase of life that was not infected. As if by some preconcerted signal the souls of men in most divisive groups and relationships suddenly became sensitive and combative.[7]

There were numerous factors which arose in the period of the 1820s and 1830s that contributed to the division. If interpreters agree on any one fact, it is that the factors for the schism must be interpreted pluralistically. Nor is it possible to rank the causes in order of their weight. The schism cast a dreadful pall over American Presbyterianism for several decades. And while in later years both ministers and members were unable to cite any singular reason for the division, there were unknown, precise reasons at the time that were sufficient to foster and support the schism. Slavery, theology, polity, the Plan of Union, revivalism, doctrinal conformity, voluntary mission societies, heresy trials--historians have emphasized one or more of these in their interpretation of the OS-NS division.[8] The analysis of Andrew E. Murray of the multiplicity of causes for the schism of 1837 is thus quite appropriate:

> The variety of interpretations of the schism of 1837 show [sic] how different it is to weigh the relative value of social and theological factors of the Presbyterians of that day. We simply do not know enough about the complex problems of human motivation to give the final answer to this question.[9]

One may generalize, however, on the differences between the two parties. The Old School was essentially conservative, underwriting a strong Calvinistic theology and maintaining a tenacious unwillingness to interfere in the institution of domestic slavery. It accepted the existing order as right, decrying anything novel, particularly the "new measures" that characterized the revivalistic techniques used by Finney. It adhered to the strict principle of denominational autonomy in all activity, requiring that all missionary and benevolent enterprises be under the control of the Church.

The New School, on the other hand, was liberal in the sense of representing new theological principles or religio-social policies. It assumed an uncompromising stance toward slavery. In its revivalism it accepted new methods of reaching the unchurched. Its polity stood for the interdenominational voluntary societies in the conduct of the Church's mission.[10] While there were some minor, local exceptions to these categories, for the most part they represent the essential positions of each party.

One leading cause for the division was the Plan of Union of 1801. Many of the other causes actually fall under the umbrella of the plan, parts of the larger whole. C. W. Grafton correctly assessed the role of the plan when he urged that through a "careful study of the history of that early period we find the source of all their trouble was in the Plan of Union . . . ."[11] Essentially, the Plan of Union was an attempt by Presbyterians and Congregationalists to meet the increasing need for churches on the western frontier at the beginning of the nineteenth century by eliminating ecclesiastical duplication of effort and permitting a considerable degree of interdenominational cooperation. A rather free flow of ministers between the two denominations was encouraged.[12] For Presbyterians, however, this practice meant the admittance into their governing bodies of Congregational ministers and committeemen who had made no formal subscription to the Westminster Standards, as Presbyterian ministers and elders were required to do.

There were numerous instances in which ministers who had been denied ordination in the Presbyterian Church were ordained in the Congregational Church, then entered the Presbyterian Church through accommodations permitted by the Plan of Union. Committeemen, who had never subscribed to the Presbyterian Constitution, voted in the General Assembly. In some instances presbyteries in New York had been founded on the basis of the Plan of Union and sent delegates to the General Assembly who were not even committeemen.[13] At the time of the Division there was no animosity toward the Congregationalists per se, but the Plan of Union was viewed as a "Trojan horse," of introducing into the Church "many who were unfriendly" to its doctrines and government, thus making it "necessary in self-defense, to free the church from this improper and . . . ruinous connection."[14]

Congregational missions were conducted on a voluntary basis, outside the Church's control. At first the American Board of Commissioners for Foreign Missions (ABCFM) was designed for the purpose of conducting missions *on behalf of the Church*. It embraced not only Congregationalists, but also Presbyterians and Reformed bodies of various stripes. Similar conditions obtained for conducting home missions, with the erection of the American Home Missionary Society (AHMS). The American Education Society (AES) performed a similar interdenominational work in raising funds for ministerial candidates.

However, as Presbyterians began forming their own boards to conduct such programs *by* the Church, conflicts inevitably set in. There was a tendency for the supporters of the Plan of Union to drift toward the New School position--with its emphasis on a weak ecclesiasticism--operated and controlled boards gravitated toward the Old School. The latter labored for the promulgation and defense of the Gospel as set forth in the doctrinal and polity standards of the Church, whereas the former were devoted to the spread of the undefinable principles of "liberal Presbyterianism."[15]

That the Plan of Union was a major cause for the division is verified in the action by which the Old School-dominated General Assembly in 1837 exscinded commissioners from four synods whose origins could be traced directly to the Plan of Union--Geneva, Genesee, Utica, and Western Reserve. The first three lay wholly within New York. Thus "the Church was rent, not on charges of doctrinal heresy, but simply on the charge that the Plan of Union was unconstitutional."[16] Its unconstitutionality consisted in the fact that the Plan itself had not originally been referred to the presbyteries for their consideration and approval.

Pragmatically, the Plan had operated to the benefit of the Presbyterians. Presbyterian polity appealed to many Congregationalists, particularly the Connecticut portion, which functioned more like Presbyterians than did their Massachusetts kin. Under the Plan many congregations that were Congregational in origin moved sympathetically into presbyteries. However, their theological baggage "introduced inharmonious elements" into the Presbyterian body--pastors and teachers who were more in touch with New England doctrinal movement.[17] If there was anything unconstitutional about the Plan, however, such revelation staggered the New School. They pondered why the revelation of unconstitutionality had not surfaced when the Constitution of the Presbyterian Church had been revised and adopted, a score of years after the Plan had been set in operation.[18]

The Plan of Union played no direct role in the South prior to the division, because there were very few Congregational churches in that region. But its impact on some of the southern churches and presbyteries was evidenced by the reaction that developed in response to the Old School actions. These had resulted in exscinding synods, presbyteries, elders, ministers, and church members without the trial required by the Constitution. In this respect, the dissolution of the Plan of Union--more than any other cause--laid the foundation for the southern New School Presbyterian Church. Its importance, hence, cannot be overestimated.

A second major cause for the disruption, and clearly connected with the Plan of Union, was the issue of how the Church should conduct her missionary functions: through voluntary societies or through Church-dominated boards? The differences that gradually emerged proved to be a basic factor in the Division of 1837.[19] Old School conservatives were both jealous and apprehensive of the success of New England's recruiting, training, and commissioning of ministerial candidates. Many of these young men were sent out through the missionary societies over which Presbyterians had no firm control. They were partially supported by Presbyterian funds, but they would organize Presbyterian churches and infiltrate presbyteries and synods.[20] After the 1837 General Assembly the Old School took on the voluntary societies with vehemence.

Whether a church member participated in any voluntary missionary/benevolent enterprise was optional to those convinced that such participation in missionary work was a matter of choice. Those willing to join and support interdenominational societies were probably more numerous than those who believed that all Church members were *ipso facto* members of a missionary society--a position the Old School advocated.[21] To that party the missionary imperative was binding on the corporate Church; to the New School, however, the missionary command was given to individuals who unite in voluntary missionary organizations. The two views were incompatible, particularly when held in the matrix of other divisive factors. The loosely constructed ecclesiasticism of the New School echoed considerable Congregational polity.

> The New School could better be identified as including not simply Congregationalism as such, but also those who, though themselves endorsing Presbyterian principles, felt no impropriety about the presence of Congregationalists and congregational government in the Presbyterian Church.[22]

The Old School held that it was error to permit non-Presbyterians to function within the Presbyterian system.

The two societies which particularly concerned the Old School the most were the AHMS and the AES, and in that order.[23] These two voluntary agencies were in direct rivalry with the Presbyterian boards that had been established for the same purposes, but under Presbyterian control. The issues of mission philosophy, benevolent support, and church polity were intricately and intimately interwoven, even transcending doctrinal issues.[24] In fact, the General Assembly of 1837 could justify its complete break with the two societies on grounds that both the operations and the organizations were viewed as "exceedingly injurious to the peace and purity of the Presbyterian Church."[25] The Old School emerged from that Assembly unanimous in its stand on Church-supported and - controlled missions. It withdrew the financial support that its congregations had been giving to the voluntary associations. For the New School, on the other hand, the action of the Old School destroyed the "Presbygational" unity that had formed the basis for the organizations.

In regard to the doctrinal differences between the two parties, the Old School position was to maintain the constitutional character of the Church. Through faithful adherence to the provisions of the Constitution--which required subscription by all ministers to the Church's confessional Standards, examination of ministers when transferring from one presbytery to another, and denominational control of its missionary work--the purity of the Church was secured, and with it a cohesive unity. This structured ecclesiasticism contrasted with the confusion that had prevailed in the days prior to the division:

> Here was this vast body of Congregationalists . . . denying our standards, rejoicing and scoffing at our form of goverment, and in no wise subject to our discipline . . . yet participating in our counsels, voting upon our questions of faith or doctrine, and actually inflicting upon us the discipline of a code whose authority upon themselves they utterly denied.[26]

> The tendency to water down Calvinism was much more apparent in Congregationalism than in Presbyterianism. This bred doctrinal controversies which led to heresy trials. In fact, of all the frontier religious bodies Presbyterians were the most torn by controversies and divisions.[27]

Thus some historians would place the doctrinal differences first among the causes for the division.[28]

Nevertheless, others have questioned the importance of the role of theology in the Old School-New School controversy. Robert Ellis Thompson, for instance, saw more emotion than reason in the issue. He failed to discern any evidence that New Haven theology had "extensively pervaded" the Church. Rather, the peculiarities of its doctrines were "nothing but a temporary phase in the theological speculation of New England, and in some respects a distinct approach to Calvinistic orthodoxy, as compared with Hopkinsianism." Had not the entire period been heated up with other issues as well, Thompson urged that the doctrinal differences would have been treated with that "wise patience" that had characterized earlier Assemblies. He further noted that the ministry of that day was not equipped with a knowledge of historical theology to be able to distinguish "between the original and essential features of Calvinistic teaching and the later accretions."[29] George P. Hays likewise tended to play down the role of theology as a factor in the schism. Had such been so, he argued, the New School would have rewritten the Confession of Faith. He concluded his argument by noting that "various men, on the different sides, used different words and expressions and illustrations in stating the same doctrine."[30]

Just as it is difficult to pull out a single thread without damage to the entire cloth, so it was with the relationship of theological differences to the total factors that resulted in the division. For instance, the New School apologete, Absalom Peters, correlated theology and mission when he commented, "We differ from them no more than they differ from us; and we appreciate our manner of explaining the truth, and our modes of operation for the advancement of religion and the conversion of the world, as highly as they do or can appreciate theirs."[31]

There were those, however, who understood the division as essentially brought about by theological differences. The Old School defender, Samuel J. Baird, hypothesized, "The New School controversy arose from the introduction into the Church of new doctrines, which threatened the overthrow of the whole system of saving faith, contained in our standards. Strictly and fundamentally, the issue was doctrinal."[32] Earlier, another Old School apologete, James Wood, presented the case for doctrinal differences as being the primary cause for the schism: "It is not true . . . that the controversy has little or no respect to doctrines. On the contrary, the principal and primary ground of it, has been a discrepancy in doctrinal sentiments."[33]

As early as 1833, Princeton's Samuel Miller had accused the New School party of Pelagianism, particularly with respect to the denial of original sin and the assertion of human ability. He commented, however, that neither Pelagius nor his followers had gone as far as some of the New School advocates in pushing these two doctrines. "To attempt to persuade us to the contrary," he concluded, "is to be supposed that the record of the published language and opinions of those ancient heretics is lost or forgotten."[34]

More recent studies have placed considerable emphasis on the role of theology in the schism. Elwyn A. Smith urged that "the most cursory survey of the literature of the Old School-New School division . . . suffices to reveal the prominent role of doctrinal debate." George M. Marsden stated that "the consensus . . . is weighted heavily toward the conclusion . . . that theology was the primary issue." Earlier, William Warren Sweet had declared that "no religious body ever took such heroic measures to rid the church of what was considered heresy as did the Presbyterian body in 1837."[35]

While students of the period may differ as to the import of theological differences in the division, all agree that the rift may be largely attributed to a sermon preached by Yale's Nathaniel W. Taylor in 1828, "Concio ad Clerum."[36] The ideas propounded by Taylor had a powerful attraction for many clergy in the theology department where Taylor taught. And since through the Plan of Union and the operation of the AHMS, young clergy could enter the Presbyterian Church from Yale-trained Congregational associations, one can readily ascertain the New Haven theology as the major source for discoloring the pure stream of Old School Calvinism.[37]

Though Calvinists, Congregationalists had no complete system of doctrine around which the denomination could rally, since each congregation usually had its own confessional statement, which it had drawn up. These creeds varied in content. No two agreed word for word, and frequently a church would alter the terms of its doctrine. This procedure was quite in contrast to Presbyterians, who held tenaciously to the Westminster Standards and did not relish such a desultory element gaining a foothold in their Zion--well established on the two fold system of theology and discipline.[38] Even among the New School party, individuals differed in their understanding and promulgation of those doctrines wherein they were at odds with the Old School. This variance among the New School group in theology was symptomatic of the entire movement's heterogeneity, quite in contrast to the homogeneity which marked the Old School.

In the New School south, not only were the basic tenets of New School theology interpreted differently through slight modifications, but many of the men retained Old School theology. Others, such as Isaac Anderson of Maryville and his coterie of students, were avowed Hopkinsians, and Andrew H. H. Boyd had been infected with New Haven theology and Scottish common sense philosophy. Points of fundamental importance in the view of some New School adherents were regarded as less important by others. At the same time, there was considerable diversity in the mode of explaining doctrines among those who agreed in the manner of stating them. This doctrinal subjectivism provided an easy target for the solid front of objectivism that bound the Old School together.

Subscription--a minister pledging to accept and teach the doctrines of the Church as contained in the Confession of Faith--was closely related to the issue of theology. Two difficulties arose here. The first treated the issue of Congregational ministers coming en masse into presbyteries without being examined. Further, as doctrinal aberrations began to emerge in Presbyterian ranks, those of the Old School persuasion insisted that ministers stand examination in doctrine by the presbytery into which they sought admission. Those who were not in accord with the Westminster Standards could be screened out. The case of Albert Barnes, called to the First Presbyterian Church of Philadelphia, but whose examination in theology was not sustained, is an example. The problem created in this instance was solved by erecting a presbytery of like minds-- Third Philadelphia Presbytery--so that Barnes could assume the pulpit of that prestigious congregation. This practice was referred to as "elective affinity."[39]

The second issue that subscription raised treated the definition of subscription. Did it mean that every doctrine was to be subscribed to by the letter, or that one received the entire system of doctrine in its essentials? The Old School insisted on the former interpretation, the New School on the latter. The inability of the Church to resolve this difficulty permitted two increasingly divergent theological systems to develop until finally the schism occurred.

Both parties insisted that they were Calvinists. Both tended to deny the claims of the other. The Old School held to the traditional Calvinistic doctrines, including predestination, man's complete moral inability in salvation, and original guilt. For more practical reasons the New School, influenced by contemporary developments in revivalism, modified its Calvinism to accommodate the individual's freedom and his subsequent moral responsibility for his acts.

The two groups differed theologically in four areas. The first related to original sin--its extent, its imputation to the race, the fact and nature of human depravity, and the measure of ability and the responsibility of guilt remaining in the sinner. The second area related to the eternal purpose of God respecting human deliverance and salvation--the nature and purpose of election, and the extent and application of the atonement as it relates to the redemption of all who believe. The third area involved the issue of justification--its essential elements of pardon, acceptance, and adoption; the imputation of Christ's righteousness; and the manner in which faith receives and appropriates the justification provided. The last area of disagreement sprang logically from the other three. It treated the manner of the sovereignty of the Holy Spirit in the application of these divine provisions--its supremacy in regeneration, the quality of the individual experience, the responsibility of the sinner in the matter of his own salvation, and the nature of the new life implanted in the believing soul.[40]

While there was many a hue and cry that arose from the New School ranks over the manner by which the four synods were exscinded from the Church, for the Old School there was a sigh of relief that the necessary surgery had been performed. Thus James Wood concluded his *Old and New Theology* with these remarks: "The Church purified from error and harmonious in action, may now engage with efficiency and sucess, in her appropriate work of carrying the symbols of her faith to a perishing world."[41]

A fourth cause for the division dealt with the matter of revivalism. This phenomenon was so closely entertwined with doctrinal concerns that at times it is scarcely possible to distinguish one from the other. Theology was the substance; the manner by which revivals were conducted was the form. Under the Plan of Union, whereby the two Churches worked together for the winning of the West, Presbyterians and Congregationalists would sanction only "rational" revivalism in which there was "very little commotional feelings." Such strictures ruled out the camp meeting, which, though born among Presbyterians on the Kentucky frontier, was later forsaken by its Presbyterian parents.[42] Later developments would prove that this abandonment cost Presbyterians dearly in their efforts to convert the frontier.

Charles G. Finney had already made use of the revival in his labors in New York in the 1820s. Far from being an orthodox Presbyterian, he brought into his revivals "new measures"--women participating in prayer meetings, praying for individuals in public, and the "anxious seat." Albert Barnes lent credence to the revival movement in a sermon, "The Way of Salvation," which he preached in 1829, in his Morristown, New Jersey, church. The sermon was largely a reflection of what Nathaniel Taylor had proclaimed earlier in his *Concio ad Clerum*; it sounded more like Yale than Princeton.[43] Finney's basic contribution to the revival movement was his institutionalizing of evangelism. In order to do this, however, he struck at the very roots of the Confession of Faith. The Calvinistic doctrine that man was utterly dependent upon God for the ability to repent was swept under the rug. To Finney the doctrine smacked of passivity. He preached that man was able to initiate repentance--indeed, that he had the duty to repent.[44] Even more, the converted sinner could attain perfection, complete sanctification. His theological system later came to be identified with Oberlin, where he taught theology for many years. That Oberlin Theology became an increasingly disrupting influence among both Presbyterians as well as Congregationalists.[45]

But it was Finney's publication in 1835 of *Lectures on Revivals of Religion* which demarcated his revivalistic techniques from those adhered to by the Old School. In a letter to William Swan Plumer dated 13 September 1837, Archibald Alexander of Princeton complained that "the new Revival Measures, connected with the New Theology, are gaining strength and popularity every day. The stream is deepening and widening, and will shortly pour forth such a torrent as will reach over the whole surface of the land."[46] The interrelatedness of method and content in the New School view of revivalism ushered forth violent objections from the Old School: departure from normal church growth, questionable methods, positive Arminianism substituted for Calvinistic essentials, many spurious conversions, and silence on great doctrines, such as God's electing grace, the spiritual deadness of sinners, and the role of the Holy Spirit in salvation.

Finney also preached that a converted sinner must labor to bring forth a converted society. By 1835 the results of a decade of such preaching was beginning to spill over in the area of social reform. Numerous men, such as Theodore Weld, now turned from evangelism to work fulltime in such programs as the antislavery movement, the prohibition drive, and similar reforms. Thus, Finney revivalism was not an isolated phenomenon per se. It was closely linked to social issues, so that "whether revivalism alone without the antislavery issue would have caused such deep cleavage in the church is problematical."[47]

Closely related, then, to revivalism was a concern on the part of the evangelist for social reform. By far, the most prominent, immediate cause for social change was slavery. It quickly became interpreted as *the* concrete symbol of sin. Hence the support of antislavery causes was a sign of Christian virtue. Participation in the reform often was a supplement or even an alternative to more traditional expressions of religion.[48] Generally speaking, those clergy who rejected or modified orthodox doctrines, espoused New School theology, and favored revivalistic new measures stood in the ranks of the antislavery faction. Their religious views favored social reform. More conservative theologians of the Old School tie tended to resist abolitionism or even actively assumed a proslavery stance. They were not emotionally prepared for anything as radical as abolitionism.[49]

The basic position of the Old School on the slave is revealed in a letter that Archibald Alexander wrote to William Swan Plumer--both Virginians--in June 1830:

> And if you wish for my opinion as to how you may best promote the welfare of those whom Providence has committed to your care, and for whom you must give account, I would say, that you can best promote their happiness by keeping them in your possession and instructing them in the Christian religion.[50]

This brief quotation contains the three distinctive Old School axioms held toward slavery: (1) it is an institution founded in the providence of God; (2) the slaveholder must render a proper stewardship because of his position; and (3) a major part of that responsiblility is orally instructing the slaves one has. There is not one word that even hints that the welfare of the slave could be improved by his freedom. At the Old School convention which preceded the 1837 Assembly, Joshua Wilson of Cincinnati was queried about bringing up the issue of slavery on the Assembly floor. After some hesitation he replied, "I believe that I shall let the Southern brethren manage their own concerns in best."⁵¹ This laissez-faire posture characterized the Old School for the next quarter century. As the slavery issue entered the abolition stage, however, abolition played a more widespread role in the New School. Led by Theodore Weld, the antislavery impulse was rapidly being forged within its ranks.

The fifth major cause for the division of 1837, then, was slavery. The role that this institution played in the schism has been and will continue to be debated by those who study the causes of the division. Clifton E. Olmstead, for instance, termed it "a minor cause of tension."⁵² George M. Marsden placed it as but one among several causative factors in the division.⁵³ Other students either fail to discern its role as a factor, or are certain that it was a major cause for the disruption.

The Old School majority in 1837 refused to let the issue of slavery come on the floor of the Assembly. This was due, largely in part, to the pre-Assembly Convention, which had been called for the purpose of establishing strategy and policy for the Assembly. There appears to have been a tacit understanding among the Old School leaders that the subject would not reach the floor of the Assembly. The rationale behind the strategy was that in the North the Old and New Schools were about evenly divided, but in the South there was little New School sentiment.⁵⁴ Thus, if the Old School party were to succeed in its effort to cut off the four New School-dominated synods, it would need the southern Old School support. Even the Old School abolitionists--and they were few in number in 1837-- were willing to align themselves with the southern proslavery faction in order to purge the Church of the New School heretics. The process of handling the issue was merely one of parliamentary procedure. All the papers relating to the matter were retained in the hands of the appropriate committee until a late period in the sessions. They were then brought to the floor without report. The committee chairman then moved to lay the entire report on the table. The motion passed.⁵⁵ Had the slavery issue been inserted in the Assembly's agenda, E. H. Gillette suggested that it would "have rent the convention in sunder, and not improbably have led to the organization of a Southern Assembly." With the South holding the decisive vote in its hand, "it was clearly understood that the slavery question was no longer to be allowed to disturb the Assembly. Although the members from the South should ever after be in the minority, they had already shaped the policy of the Church."⁵⁶ Technically, the southerners remained aloof from the debate as a group. In uniting with their northern brethren, however, they were able to stave off the abolitionists who were identified with the New School wing. They saw in the conservative theory of history a view compatible with their need to maintain extant institutions against the raging sin of mankind.⁵⁷

Not all are agreed, however, that the slavery question was a major issue in the division. William O. Brackett, Jr., for instance, urged that if the antislavery posture had been the distinctive feature of the New School, the 1836 Assembly, which was controlled by that element, would have taken action on it, as the men of the New School did on other issues about which they were concerned.⁵⁸ Ernest Trice Thompson suggested that "there is no certainty that it was the decisive issue" because the theological conservatism would have aligned the South naturally with the Old School.⁵⁹ The presence, however, of a southern New School element is evidence that not all theological conservatives were in the Old School fold.

More recently, Kenneth J. Foreman, Jr., has set forth three reasons why slavery was not a major factor in the disruption: (1) both parties contained a strong proslavery element, which, if alienated, would cost that side the necessary votes to prevail; (2) there were strong proslavery men in each school; and (3) after the division, antislavery men in both Churches were incapable for more than a score of years to muster a majority in their respective Churches to take a more forthright stand than the Church had taken in 1818, both schools being "a mixed bag of slavery." Foreman thus concluded that "although slavery was a pervasive issue touching everything in America in the 1830s, it was not one of the issues on which the 1837-1838 Old School Presbyterians divided from the New."⁶⁰

Victor B. Howard suggested that the antislavery feeling in central and western New York was oversold in the South, but was much stronger in the Middle West. Had slavery been the chief reason for the exscinding acts, he concluded, the Synod of Michigan, which went entirely New School, should have been removed instead of the Synod of Western Reserve.⁶¹

Prior to the Division, the Presbytery of Mississippi urged that it was "the new opinions, the questions incessantly agitated, that were the "real cause of the divisions and distractions" disturbing the Church.⁶²

The connection of slavery as a factor in the division appears frequently to be interpreted as guilt by association. Since there were numerous abolitionists and abolition societies operating among New School leaders and institutions, it has been difficult to extricate one from the other. Marsden submitted two reasons why slavery was not a primary cause for the 1837 schism: (1) the New School itself was by no means united in support of immediatism, and (2) Old School leaders in the North felt only a "slight concern" over the antislavery position among New School adherents.[63] The New School historian, Edward Morris, interpreted the slavery issue as "more incidental than direct." He noted that the antislavery hostility "was most openly manifest in those regions where the most liberal interpretations of the Symbols prevailed, where revivals were most abundant, and where church government assumed its freest style."[64]

That slavery was an important issue in the schism is seen in some resolutions that were adopted in September 1838 by a group of clergymen and elders in Farmville, Virginia, just a year after the division. They placed the issue of slavery, "which is entirely a civil and political matter, cognizable only by the civil authorities of the states in which slavery exists," outside the jurisdiction of the Church. They even went so far as to renounce the unanimous action of the General Assembly of 1818, whereby the Church had called for an end to the institution: "The act of 1818 upon the subject of slavery was an unwarranted assumption of power, for they had no authority from the word of God, or the constitution of our church . . . ." They further resolved that

> any attempt of the judicatories of the church to carry into effect the aforesaid Act of 1818, or to exercise jurisdiction in any form over the relations of slavery, would be eminently disastrous to the interests of our church in the southern country . . . .[65]

Thus, the urging of Edward Burgett Welsh, that the facts will not sustain the claim that disruption was "largely caused by the controversy over slavery," will not stand up.[66] Rather, the conclusion of Elwyn A. Smith, that the slavery controversy was more important an issue than had previously been held and may have been the factor which tipped the balance in favor of the Old School's efforts to oust the New School element, must be seriously considered.⁶⁷ J. Earl Thompson, Jr., concluded that had the Church followed up its 1818 legislation by demanding immediacy as the only manner by which the slavery issue could be successfully handled, there would have been a division sooner. Failure to implement that decision, however, ultimately caused division anyway.⁶⁸ C. Bruce Staiger has pointed out that the opposition to abolitionism was the one factor that united the ultraorthodox Old School leaders with the more moderate Princetonians. Both stood together in their opposition to the New School premise that slavery was a sin.⁶⁹

A monistic approach to historical causality leads one into a maze of quandaries. The same position obtains in regard to making slavery--or any of the other factors--*the* major reason for the division. On the other hand, to erase it from the list of significant causes in the disruption simply closes one's mind to the exigencies of that period. By itself, slavery was not sufficient cause to divide the Church. Nor can it be isolated from other factors, for the numerous and various causes were so interwoven that it is impossible to extricate one strand from the cloth of causes.

Thus, the unity of the Presbyterian Church--a unity that was buffeted over a lengthy period of time by several factors--came to an ignominious end in 1837. One cause contained the seed for another; one factor only complemented another. By the end of the General Assembly of 1838 any efforts to smooth over the schism were abandoned. Two Churches went their separate ways. In many communities, presbyteries and synods, two separate organizations, often claiming the same name--much to the confused dismay of historians!--existed side by side. In some instances, two congregations even continued worshiping in the same structure. But never together.

NOTES

1. An account of the disruption of 1837 may be found in any history of American Presbyterianism. Of particular value are Edward D. Morris, *The Presbyterian Church New School 1837-1869: An Historical Review* (Columbus, Ohio: Champlin Press, 1905), pp. 43-72; Ernest Trice Thompson, *Presbyterians in the South*, 3 vols. (Richmond, Virginia: John Knox Press, 1963-1973) 1:350-361; and Jacob Harris Patton, *A Popular History of the Presbyterian Church in the United States of America* (New York: R. S. Mighill, 1900), pp. 416-455. For more succinct accounts, see

Sydney E. Ahlstrom, *A Religious History of the American People* (New Haven and London: Yale University Press, 1972), pp. 466-468; and Robert T. Handy, *A History of the Churches in the United States and Canada*, Oxford History of the Christian Church (New York: Oxford University Press, 1977), pp. 192-194.

2. Zebulon Crocker, *The Catastrophe of the Presbyterian Church in 1837, Including a Full View of the Recent Theological Controversies in New England* (New Haven: B. & W. Noyes, 1838), pp. 52-53; Leonard J. Trinterud, *The Forming of an American Tradition: A Re-examination of Colonial Presbyterianism* (Philadelphia: Westminster Press, 1949), pp. 261-264; L. C. Rudolph, *Hoosier Zion: The Presbyterians in Early Indiana* (New Haven and London: Yale University Press, 1963, pp. 119-120.

3. Patton, *Popular History of the Presbyterian Church*, p. 418.

4. Robert Davidson, *History of the Presbyterian Church in the State of Kentucky; with a Preliminary Sketch of the Churches in the Valley of Virginia* (New York: Robert Carter, 1847), p. 344. See also Crocker, *Catastrophe of the Presbyterian Church*, p. 114.

5. Mary Elizabeth Kinner Bratton, *Our Goodly Heritage: A History of the First Presbyterian Church of Lynchburg, Virginia, 1815-1940* (Lynchburg: L. P. Bell, n.d.).

6. Samuel F. Baird, *A History of the New School and of the Questions Involved in the Disruption of the Presbyterian Church in 1838* (Philadelphia: Claxton, Remsen & Haffelfinger, 1868), p. xi.

7. Abel Ross Wentz, "Permanent Deposits of Sectionalism in American Christianity," *Lutheran Church Quarterly* 9 (1936): 27.

8. For representative interpretations, see Robert T. Handy, *A Christian America: Protestant Hopes and Historical Realities* (New York: Oxford University Press, 1971), p. 63; Clifford Merrill Drury, *Presbyterian Panorama: One Hundred and Fifty Years of National Missions History* (Philadelphia: Board of Christian Education, Presbyterian Church in the United States of America, 1952), p. 44; William Warren Sweet, *Religion on the American Frontier*, vol. 2, *The Presbyterians: A Collection of Source Materials* (New York: Harper & Brothers, 1936), p. 100; William S. Kennedy, *The Plan of Union: Or a History of the Presbyterian and Congregational Churches of the Western Reserve; with Biographical Sketches of the Early Missionaries* (Hudson, Ohio: Pentagon Steam Press, 1856), pp. 222-226; P[hilemon] H. Fowler, *Historical Sketch of Presbyterianism*

within the Bounds of the Synod of Central New York (Utica: Curtiss & Childs, 1877), p. 70; Thompson, Presbyterians in the South, 1:350-351; H[enry] Woods, The History of the Presbyterian Controversy, with Early Sketches of Presbyterianism (Louisville: N. H. White, 1843), pp. 55-57; Crocker, Catastrophe of the Presbyterian Church, pp. 55-120; Morris, Presbyterian Church New School, 46-47; J. Aspinwall Hodge, What Is Presbyterian Law as Defined by the Church Courts? 3rd ed. (Philadelphia: Presbyterian Board of Publication, 1884), p. 287; William Henry Foote, Sketches of Virginia, Historical and Biographical, 2nd ser., 2nd ed., rev. (Philadelphia: J. B. Lippincott, 1856), pp. 486-506; Daniel Dorchester, Christianity in the United States: From the First Settlement to the Present Time (New York: Phillips & Hunt; Cincinnati: Cranston & Stowe, 1888), 488-489; Kenneth Joseph Foreman, Jr., "The Debate on the Administration of Missions Led by James Henley Thornwell in the Presbyterian Church 1839-1861" (Ph. D. diss., Princeton Theological Seminary, 1977), p. 27.

9. Andrew E. Murray, Presbyterians and the Negro--A History (Philadelphia: Presbyterian Historical Society, 1966), p. 104.

10. William O. Brackett, Jr., "The Rise and Development of the New School in the Presbyterian Church in the U. S. A. to the Reunion of 1869," JPHS 13 (1928): 119, 124; James H. Rodabaugh, "Miami University, Calvinism, and the Anti-slavery Movement," Ohio State Archaeological and Historical Quarterly 48 (1939): 67; Hubert Vance Taylor, "Slavery and the Deliberations of the Presbyterian General Assembly, 1833-1838" (Ph. D. diss., Northwestern University, 1964), p. 58.

11. C. W. Grafton, "History of the Mississippi Synod Presbyterian Church" (unpublished microfilm of the typed MS dated 1927, Mississippi State Archives, Jackson, Mississippi). Similar views were expressed by Drury, Presbyterian Panorama, pp. 14-15, and John F. Lyons, "The Attitude of Presbyterians in Ohio, Indiana and Illinois toward Slavery," JPHS 11 (1921): 69.

12. The text of the Plan of Union is found in Maurice W. Armstrong, Lefferts A. Loetscher, and Charles A. Anderson, eds., The Presbyterian Enterprise: Sources of American Presbyterian History (Philadelphia: Westminster Press, 1956), pp. 102-104.

13. Baird, New School, pp. 256-272; George D. Armstrong, A Centennial Discourse Delivered before the Presbytery of Lexington, Synod of Virginia, at

Timber-Ridge Church, September 25th, 1886 (Staunton, Virginia: Valley Virginian Power Press, 1887), p. 14.

14. James Wood, *Old and New Theology: or, The Doctrinal Differences which Have Agitated and Divided the Presbyterian Church*, new and enlarged ed. (Philadelphia: Presbyterian Board of Publication, 1855), p. 7.

15. Baird, *New School*, p. 1. See also Colin Brummitt Goodykoontz, *Home Missions on the American Frontier: With Particular Reference to the American Home Missionary Society* (Caldwell, Idaho: Caxton Printers, 1939), p. 241; William Warren Sweet, *The Story of Religion in America* (New York and London, 1939), p. 375.

16. Brackett, "Rise and Development of the NS," p. 165; Kennedy, *The Plan of Union*, p. 225.

17. See the Congregationalist historian, Albert E. Dunning, *Congregationalists in America: A Popular History of Their Origin, Belief, Polity, Growth and Work* (New York: J. A. Hill & Co., 1894), p. 327; Robert Ellis Thompson, *A History of the Presbyterian Churches in the United States*, 2nd ed., The American Church History Series (New York: Charles Scribner's Sons, 1900), p. 72.

18. Kennedy, *Plan of Union*, p. 225.

19. Thompson, *Presbyterians in the South*, 1:290, 299; Earl R. MacCormac, "Missions and the Presbyterian Schism of 1837," *CH* 32 (1963): 43.

20. Drury, *Presbyterian Panorama*, p. 85.

21. Clifford M. Drury, "Missionary Expansion at Home," in *They Seek a Country: The American Presbyterians. Some Aspects*. ed. Gaius Jackson Slosser (New York: Macmillan, 1955), p. 175.

22. Foreman, "Debate on Mission," p. 29; Earl R. MacCormac, "The Development of Presbyterian Missionary Organizations: 1790-1870," *JPH* 32 (1965): 153.

23. "The American Home Missionary Society was an inevitable point of contention," so Louis Filler, *The Crusade Against Slavery, 1830-1860*, New American Nation Series (New York: Harper & Row, 1960; reprinted as a Harper Torchbook, 1963), p. 126.

24. William Henry Roberts, *A Concise History of the Presbyterian Church in the United States of America with an Address on the 200th Anniversary of the General Synod* (Philadelphia: Presbyterian Board of Publication and Sabbath School Work, 1922), p. 56. Roberts's conclusions have been substantiated by Richard C. Wolfe in "The Middle Period, 1800-1870," *Religion in Life* 22 (Winter, 1952-1953): 72-84; Wolfe claimed that the doctrinal differences in the

Presbyterian Church stem from too broad a doctrinal basis brought about by reunion.

25. GAPCUSA [OS], *Minutes* 1837), p. 419; see also MacCormac, "Missions and Schism," p. 32.

26. Cited in Samuel Miller, *Report of the Presbyterian Church Case: The Commonwealth of Pennsylvania, At the Suggestion of James Todd and Others, vs. Ashbel Green and Others* (Philadelphia: William S. Martein, 1839), p. 136; Brackett, "Rise and Development of the NS," p. 162.

27. William Warren Sweet, *Religion in the Development of American Culture, 1765-1840* (New York: Charles Scribner's Sons, 1952), p. 104. See pp. 234-235 for Sweet's succinct but excellent introduction to the various philosophical systems contributing to the new theologies developing in the first four decades of the nineteenth century.

28. Filler, *Crusade against Slavery*, p. 125; [James Gillespie Birney], *The American Churches, The Bulwarks of American Slavery*, 2nd American ed. (Newburyport, Massachusetts: Charles Whipple, 1842), p. 33; Irving Stoddard Hull, in "Presbyterian Attitudes Toward Slavery," CH 7 (1938): 107, suggested that the "basic cause for the division was doctrine, although the abolitionism of the New School men no doubt hastened the breach. . . ."

29. Thompson, *Presbyterian Churches in the U. S.*, p. 124.

30. George P. Hays, *Presbyterians: A Popular Narrative of Their Origin, Progress, Doctrines, and Achievements* (New York: J. A. Hill & Co., 1892), pp. 200-201.

31. [Absalom Peters], *A Plea for Voluntary Societies, and a Defence of the Decisions of the General Assembly of 1836, Against the Strictures of the Princeton Reviewers and Others* (New York: John S. Taylor, 1837), p. 183.

32. Baird, *New School*, p. 1.

33. Wood, *Old and New Theology*, pp. 17-18.

34. Samuel Miller, *Letters to Presbyterians, on the Present Crisis in the Presbyterian Church in the United States* (Philadelphia: Anthony Findley, 1833), p. 111.

35. Elwyn A. Smith, "The Doctrine of Imputation and the Presbyterian Schism of 1837-1838," *JPHS* 38 (1960): 129-151; George M. Marsden, *The Evangelical Mind and the New School Presbyterian Experience* (New Haven and London: Yale University Press, 1970), p. 66; and Sweet, Story of Religion in America, p. 378.

36. For the text of the sermon, see Nathaniel W..Taylor, *Concio ad Clerum: A Sermon . . . Sept. 10, 1828* (New Haven: Hezekiah Howe, 1828). Baird

(*New School*, pp. 191-200) gives a precis and critique of the sermon from the OS stance.

37. Earl E. Pope, "The Rise of New Haven Theology," *JPH* 44 (1966): 121; Wood, *Old and New Theology*, p. 6.

38. Patton, *Popular History of the Presbyterian Church*, pp. 384-385.

39. Elective affinity is a practice whereby a presbytery is erected on the basis of ministers in one geographical area who differ from other ministers in the same area in their theology.

40. Adapted from Morris, *Presbyterian Church NS*, p. 51. See also Thompson, *Presbyterians in the South*, 1:362-363, for another succinct list of differences. The "formal" NS doctrinal statement is the Auburn Affirmation: *Minutes of the Auburn Convention Held August 17, 1837, to Deliberate Upon the Doings of the Last General Assembly in Relation to the Synods of Western Reserve, Utica, Geneva and Genessee and the Third Presbytery of Philadelphia* (Auburn: Oliphant and Skinner, 1837).

41. Wood, *Old and New Theology*, pp. 233-234.

42. Charles A. Johnson, *The Frontier Camp Meeting: Religion's Harvest Time* (Dallas: Southern Methodist University Press, 1955), p. 70.

43. Marsden, *Evangelical Mind and the NS Experience*, p. 52. For excerpts from the sermon, see Armstrong, Loetscher, and Anderson, *Presbyterian Enterprise*, pp. 146-148.

44. Bernard A. Weisberger, *They Gathered at the River: The Story of the Great Revivalists and Their Impact on Religion in America* (Boston and Toronto: Little, Brown & Co., 1958), p. 95. Pp. 91-93 contain a spendid, trenchant account of Finney's dramatic conversion.

45. Sweet, *Religion in the Development of American Culture*, p. 229.

46. Cited in James W. Alexander, *The Life of Archibald Alexander* (New York: Charles Scribner, 1845), p. 477.

47. Weisberger, *They Gathered at the River*, p. 129. The best interpretation on the connection between revivalism and its social impact is Timothy L. Smith, *Revivalism and Social Reform* (New York and Nashville: Abingdon Press, 1957). See also Marion L. Bell, *Crusade in the City: Revivalism in Nineteenth-Century Philadelphia* (Lewisburg, Pennsylvania: Bucknell University Press; London: Associate University Press, 1977), p. 70, and Donald W. Dayton, *Discovering an Evangelical Heritage* (New York: Harper and Row, 1976), pp. 15-24.

48. David Brion Davis, "The Emergence of Immediatism in British and American Antislavery Thought," *MVHR* 49 (September 1962): 229.
49. Charles C. Cole, Jr., *The Social Ideas of the Northern Evangelists 1826-1860*, Columbia Studies in the Social Sciences (New York: Columbia University Press, 1956), p. 217. The slavery issue was not brought to the floor of the General Assembly until 1835, and the Church was not yet clearly divided on religious lines at that time.
50. Quoted in Alexander, *Life of Alexander*, pp. 522-523.
51. Foote, *Sketches of Virginia*, p. 520.
52. Clifton E. Olmstead, *Religion in America Past and Present* (Englewood Cliffs, New Jersey: Prentice-Hall, 1961), p. 79.
53. Marsden, *Evangelical Mind and the NS Experience*, chapters 3 and 4.
54. Crocker, *Catastrophe of the Presbyterian Church*, p. 68.
55. Described in ibid.
56. E. H. Gillette, *History of the Presbyterian Church in the United States of America*, 2 vols. (Philadelphia: Presbyterian Publication Committee, 1864), 2:527. See also Sweet, *Presbyterians*, p. 123; and C. Bruce Staiger, "Abolitionism and the Presbyterian Schism of 1837-1838," *MVHR* 36 (December 1949): 391-414. An excellent interpretation of the relationship of the southern and northern Old School elements in the division is Elwyn A. Smith, "The Role of the South in the Presbyterian Schism of 1837-38," *CH* 29 (1960): 44-68.
57. Donald G. Matthews, *Religion in the Old South* (Chicago and London: University of Chicago Press, 1977), p. 164.
58. Brackett, "Rise and Development of the NS," p. 167; Thompson, *Presbyterians in the United States*, p. 123.
59. Thompson, *Presbyterians in the South*, 1:411-412.
60. Foreman, "Debate on Missions," p. 40.
61. Victor B. Howard, "The Anti-Slavery Movement in the Presbyterian Church, 1835-1861" (Ph. D. diss., Ohio State University, 1961), pp. 86-87.
62. James Smylie, *A Reply of a Letter from the Presbytery of Chillicothe, to the Presbytery of Mississippi, on the Subject of Slavery* (Woodville, Mississippi: Wm. A. Norris and Co., 1836), p. 83.
63. Marsden, *Evangelical Mind and the NS Experience*, p. 93.
64. Morris, *Presbyterian Church NS*, pp. 60-61.

65. *The Proceedings of the Meeting for Prayer and Consultation* (Richmond: Wm. MacFarlane, 1838, p. 36. Just three years later similar thoughts were expressed by the NS element in Missouri: *Declaration and Sentiments Made by the Synod of Missouri [NS] Formed by a Convention of Presbyterian Ministers and Elders Held at Hannibal October 7th, 1841* (Saint Louis: Gazette, 1841), p. 5.

66. Edward Burgett Welsh, "Wrestling with Human Values: The Slavery Year," in *They Seek a Country*, p. 223. E. Douglas Branch, in *Sentimental Years 1830-1860* (New York: Hill and Wang, 1965), p. 328, claimed that "this was the only schism in a major denomination during the generation in which the slavery issue was not the point of cleavage."

67. Smith, "The South in the Presbyterian Schism," pp. 44-63. See also Sweet, *Presbyterians*, pp. 111-125.

68. J. Earl Thompson, Jr., "Slavery and Presbyterianism in the Revolutionary Era," *JPH* 54 (1976): 138.

69. Staiger, "Abolitionism and the Presbyterian Schism," p. 398.

2
The Years of Decision in the South

In numerous instances, the results of the division were lamentable. New and feeble organizations were formed by seceders from old churches. Organizations once strong and flourishing were rent asunder. Lawsuits were instituted to determine the title to church property. Old friendships were broken up, and bitter and lasting alienations were produced. The strength that should have been concentrated for aggressive efforts was frittered away in mutual strife and exasperation. In some instances the animosity was such as could scarcely fail to be transmitted to another generation.[1]

So E. H. Gillete described the condition of the Churches, both Old and New School, after the Assemblies of 1838. Four synods, a presbytery, 500 ministers, and 60,000 communicants "against whom no charge of heresy or immorality had been substantiated" were cast out of the Presbyterian Church.[2] A new age in American Presbyterianism had dawned. An old era had passed away.

Most histories of the New School neglect its southern wing. Yet for a score of years it remained faithful to its northern kin, not out of doctrinal affinity or because of agreement in regard to slavery, but because the men in the South had withdrawn from the Old School after the 1838 Assembly in sympathy with those in the North who had been exscinded without trial. Few in the South who entered the New School ever advocated the distinctive New School doctrines. They had gone into the New School largely because of friendship for the New Schoolmen, because of the "peculiar ecclesiastical moves of the Old School men, 1837-1838 and because of the extremes and unjustifiable representations made of the New School party...."[3] About 10,000 withdrew in sympathy in the year that followed and all told about four-ninths of the Presbyterians gathered around the New School banner.

By far the majority of southern Presbyterians remained Old School. With a few minor exceptions, the southern New School was unable to garner any of the important pulpits in the South.[4] Its congregations were smaller, on the average, than the ones belonging to the Old School. Its presbyteries were not as well organized, and the institutions were never as well developed. And although the New School North was dominated by an abolition element, such a condition did not deter the southerners from aligning themselves with their comrades in the North, who, they felt, had been greatly wronged in being exscinded without trial. The unifying factors that cohered to make the New School were its aversion to Old School ecclesiasticism, its sympathy with those who had been denied their rights by the Exscision Acts, and its ability to tolerate minor differences of beliefs.[5]

In most respects, however, the southern New School had far more in common with the southern Old School than with the northern New School. In 1836 the New School-dominated General Assembly reversed several acts of the previous Assembly. But the greatest threat to the South, which came out of the 1836 Assembly, arose from the issue of slavery--brought to the floor for the first time since 1818. A correspondent of the *Southern Religious Telegraph* (24 June 1836) opined:

> I hope that such another Assembly will never meet but once again; and then only with full and delegated powers amicably to separate, in order that each party may prosecute its own way. . . . And now it becomes a grave and serious question, whether the Southern section of our Church will any more, or again, expose its representatives to the scoffs and taunts, and jeers and misrepresentations, and excommunications and maledictions of the abolitionists, both male and female.

As early as 1832, Virginia-born Archibald Alexander, Professor of Theology at Princeton

Seminary, had recognized the differences between the Old and New School views on theology and slavery. He proposed dissolving the present synods and erecting six new ones, each synod having the supervisory and judicial power of an Assembly, three to be in the North, three in the South. "...By the proposed plan of arrangement, all the churches in the slaveholding states, will be separated from those of the non-slave-holding states, and there will be no opportunity of their coming into collision in the ecclesiastical judicatories."[6]

William Henry Foote claimed that both the New School scion, William Hill, and the Old School leader, George A. Baxter, thought in terms of a southern Presbyterian Church. Hill desired one that would embrace the entire South; Baxter desired three Assemblies--two northern for the Old and New Schools and a southern one. The latter, of course, would be completely Old School. Foote commented that the expectation of a southern Assembly was not abandoned until after the 1838 Assembly, when it became obvious there would be two Churches, each embracing elements in the North and the South.[7]

The only other effort to establish a southern Presbyterian Church in this period was the ill-fated Cassville Convention of 1840. On 2 March 1839, Thomas Magruder, in the first issue of the *Southern Christian Sentinel*, published in Charleston, South Carolina, gave his position in respect to a southern Church:

> With respect to ecclesiastical relations, the Sentinel will advocate a SOUTHERN ORGANIZATION, based on the principles of the plan proposed by Rev. Dr. Alexander, in 1832. This arrangement, it is believed, is entirely practicable and highly expedient. It is now regarded by great numbers at the South, as the most effectual method of restoring peace to our agitated and afflicted Church; and as the only plan which can permanently free the Southern Churches from *Abolitionist* aggression, and from *foreign interference* of every description. Whilst this plan comes in collision with none of the essential features of Presbyterianism, it offers security against many evils inseparable from our present system of ecclesiastical polity, and promises, more certainly than any other plan which has yet been proposed, to effect the *pacification* of the Church.

At the 1837 General Assembly, Elipha White of the Charleston Union Presbytery (South Carolina) voted against the Exscinding Acts on the grounds that they were unconstitutional, unjust, and oppressive. In making his report to Presbytery, he recommended forming an independent Southern Presbyterian Synod or Assembly. Presbytery adopted the paper, but not without protest.[8] Thus, Magruder's plea for a southern Church had not emerged suddenly; there had been considerable agitation for it previously.

Since all southern ministers were viewed as orthodox, it was deemed far more important that they be affiliated with each other in one body than that they be connected with another body some distance removed. A manifestation of this position was the call issued in the spring of 1840 for a meeting to be held in Cassville, Georgia, to consider the matter of a regional Presbyterian Church, erected on New School principles. The call for the meeting was signed by fifty-five ministers and twenty-three elders from a dozen presbyteries. Only sixteen ministers and a dozen laymen met, however. The enthusiasm was high, but the present number was too small to effect a permanent Church. Although the meeting adjourned to meet the next year, that meeting never convened.[9]

In the meantime, the various judicatories on the presbytery and synod level in the South had been meeting and reacting in diverse ways to the actions of the 1837 and 1838 General Assemblies. In most instances the Old School was so strongly entrenched that, apart from a few dissidents, the southern judicatories supported the Exscinding Acts. Nevertheless, there were some instances where New School sympathizers were of sufficient strength to take over courts or, comprising a strong minority, to erect their own presbyteries and synods.

THE SYNOD OF TENNESSEE

The first of these church courts, the Synod of Tennessee New School, was concentrated in the mountains of East Tennessee,--with some congregations in western North Carolina and northern Georgia. It was not the topography of hills and vales that alone set East Tennessee apart from the other two major divisions of the state. The people themselves were a hardy breed. All along the Appalachian frontier the Scotch-Irish, who arrived somewhat belatedly in the colonies after the

English, followed the southwestern drift of the valleys. They differed greatly from the southern planters or the New England merchants and seamen. This "contentious, self-reliant, hardy stock, with its rude and vigorous forest life," brought with them a view of man quite at variance with many colonists.[10] Their preachers proclaimed not only Calvinism, but also the gospel of individual freedom. From the social matrix they created emerged such stalwarts as Patrick Henry, Andrew Jackson, John C. Calhoun, and Abraham Lincoln.

Unlike other frontiersmen, who roamed, the East Tennessee settlers were artisans, farmers, teachers--earnest, serious, devout, brave folk for whom life had stern meaning.[11] Since most of them were Scotch-Irish, they gave the great Tennessee Valley and the adjacent ridges and rills a unity lacking in other parts of the early frontier. Their homogeneity was also observed in their religion. They were Presbyterians to the core, theologically and psychologically--in their instinct for constitutional freedom and their willingness to establish the school, the college, and the church in the midst of the wilderness.[12]

Their religious proclivities were acknowledged by others. Levi Morrison studied theology under the direction of Amzi Bradshaw. Morrison confessed that his real schooling came, however, when he became pastor of the church at Athens, Tennessee:

> I found myself surrounded with brethren of superior advantages, many of them with large, active minds and noble hearts. Besides, Athens happened to be the residence of quite a number of professional men of the first order of talents, few of whom were connected with the church personally, but all of them through their families.[13]

The Rev. Dr. James Gallaher--physician as well as minister--spent a good part of his life in East Tennessee. He commented on the peoples' attachment to the Bible: "Bible history, Bible doctrines, and Bible religion were °the joy of their heart and the boast of their tongue.'"

The Bible was their meat and drink, their source of consolation on earth, and their foundation of hope for immortality.

> The learned theologian, who chanced to pass that way, was delighted and surprised to find, in a new and comparatively rough country, among

a plain, unostentatious people, views of divine truth clearer than the crystal stream that flowed among their towering hills, and sweeter than the salubrious breezes that fanned their mountain country.[14]

An interesting minute is found in the records of Union Presbytery, which underscores the intellectual want of the people. In 1828 the Presbytery heard a report from an agent of the American Sunday School Union. Presbytery then adopted a resolution whereby it approved the objects of the union and recommended its agents and representatives to the benevolent regard of its churches and members. Then Presbytery resolved,

> That while we approve . . . we fully recognize the urgent necessity of a separate organization of our own, for the purpose of placing in our church, sabbath schools and private libraries, *books* prepared with the express view of inculcating the distinctive doctrines of our own church, and thereby placing, in the hands of our S. S. teachers, *helps* that we deem indispensable, and in which we are now deficient.[15]

Only the lack of funds prevented Presbytery from satisfying what it felt was a very great need.

In addition to the people, the topography of East Tennessee also played an important role in shaping the thinking of the inhabitants. East Tennessee was marked by rugged mountain slopes and undulating plains. These features greatly influenced the attitude of the inhabitants toward slavery.[16] In contrast to Middle and West Tennessee, East Tennessee was far removed from markets, so there was no necessity to produce more than could be consumed at home.[17] The family farm was thus the economic base. Fertile valleys and gentle slopes provided a variety of crops. Very little cotton was raised in East Tennessee. The people largely performed their own labor, so that slavery was almost unknown.[18] There developed "an independent and industrious people quite different, in the main, from the aristocracy of the coast."[19]

The personal freedom which these people enjoyed, coupled with a topography more conducive to the family farm than to the plantation, created a matrix quite unfavorable to the institution of domestic slavery. The Rev. John Rankin, who was born in East Tennessee, remarked that in his early boyhood the majority of the people of that area were abolitionists.[20] Further, when the Scotch-Irish settled the area, there were still Indians in the region. Slave labor did not thrive in such a home. This condition stood in stark contrast to that of West Tennessee, which was settled after the subjection of the Indian and by men of considerable means from seaboard. They brought their slaves with them and engaged in the cultivation of cotton on a rather extensive scale.[21]

In the Tennessee Constitutional Convention of 1834, about one-fifth of the delegates favored some action looking toward the distant and gradual emancipation of slaves. None was from West Tennessee. Among the yeoman farmers of East Tennessee, as many as 93 percent in some counties were non-slaveholders, while among the cotton planters of West Tennessee this figure dropped as low as 3 percent.[22] At a time when Illinois was passing a law whereby any free black who stayed in the State 10 days, was fined $50, and could be sold to anyone who would pay the fine if he could not; at a time when citizens of the City of Brotherly Love were burning black Presbyterian churches; at a time when New York blacks were being terrorized and killed by a vengeful mob--at such a time liberty-loving East Tennessee Presbyterians were striving for the freedom of slaves.[23]

They thus emerged early as a breed unto themselves, these East Tennesseans.[24] One of the Early missionaries and leaders in the region was Hezekiah Balch, President of Greeneville College. In 1795 he visited New England on a tour to raise funds for the college. There he encountered Samuel Hopkins and became imbued with his theology. In the troubles Balch encountered embracing Hopkinsianism, he was haled before presbytery sixteen times, before synod four times, and once before the General Assembly. In this last instance he conceded his theological aberration. He returned to East Tennessee, however, where he resumed his preaching, which was greatly colored by Hopkins's views.[25] Balch's figure cast a long shadow over the later religious thought among East Tennessee Presbyterians. For two score years he preached pretty much the same doctrines that Hopkins and Nathaniel Emmons taught. Some argue that the actual number who fell into Balch's train in East Tennessee was not large.[26] Nevertheless, his influence undoubtedly went a long way in making the Synod of Tennessee the only southern synod that had a true New School majority in 1837.[27]

In addition to the New Divinity, which Balch preached and taught, East Tennessee was very

32   The United Synod of the South

dependent on the AHMS and the AES, both of which were viewed as arms of the New School. The churches supported these societies rather than the corresponding boards of the Assembly. Further, the democratic Hopkinsian doctrines fitted the rugged frontier of East Tennessee more adequately than did the more severe forms of Old School Calvinism.[28]

The influence emanating from the Hopkinsian controversy had its effect on the Church's polity. In 1797 the difficulties arising from the debate over this theological aberration led the Synod of the Carolinas to make a division in the Presbytery of Abingdon. From this division came the Presbytery of Union. This action followed an earlier partition in Abingdon Presbytery, which had developed when Balch was examined by the Presbytery on his views. At that time, several of the ministers withdrew and for a season formed an independent Presbytery of Abingdon. These were later won back to the fold. On petition, the original presbytery, however, divided along a line which almost completely separated the two parties, Balch and his followers comprising Union Presbytery.[29]

This division was largely on the basis of elective affinity. In 1810 Union Presbytery was transferred from the Synod of the Carolinas to the Synod of Kentucky because it was "dissatisfied with the theology of the Carolinas in those days."[30] When in 1818 the First Presbyterian Church of Knoxville experienced division, those members who formed the Second Presbyterian Church were largely influenced by the New Divinity which permeated the area. The population of Knoxville at that time was about 400,--yet there were two Presbyterian congregations.

As time passed, other Hopkinsian leaders came into East Tennessee. Three in particular stand out. Charles Coffin of Newburyport, Massachusetts, came to Greeneville College in 1804 to work with Balch. In 1810 he became president of the school; he later became president of East Tennessee College in Knoxville. A second Hopkinsian was Gideon Blackburn, a pupil of Robert Henderson, Balch's son-in-law. Blackburn was especially attracted to Hopkins's doctrine of "disinterested benevolence," particularly as it was concretized in the voluntary agencies. In his later years he was firmly opposed to Church boards.

The third and most influential of all the advocates of modified Calvinism as represented by Hopkinsianism, was Isaac Anderson. In 1819 Union Presbytery sent him to the General Assembly in

Philadelphia. After the sessions, he visited Princeton with a view of enticing seminarians to consider the West as the place to invest their ministry. His efforts were in vain. He returned to the East Tennessee vales, convinced that if that region were to have ministers, it must raise its own. He then organized the Southern and Western Theological Seminary, the forerunner of Maryville College. Thus for over six decades, many of the minds of the East Tennessee clergy were indoctrinated in Hopkinsianism, setting the stage for New Schoolism in that area.[31]

Of more than marginal interest was the founding in 1827 of the *Calvinistic Magazine* by Frederick A. Ross, "a free-lance defender of Calvinism.[32] The journal had two purposes--to wage war upon the Methodists and to uphold the principles of Calvinism. The men associated with Ross in this undertaking were New School in their views, as was Ross. For a quarter of a century Ross led East Tennessee Presbyterians in company with a committed, fraternal, homogeneous group--men who had been born, raised, and educated there.

They held revivals with and for one another, and most of them spent their entire ministry within the bounds of the Synod of Tennessee. It was upon these men that the actions of the "Reforming Assemblies" fell so heavily. They did not relish what they felt.

By 1826 the Presbytery of Abingdon had grown so large that the southern portion was cut off, thus forming the Presbytery of Holston. A dozen years later the Presbytery withdrew from the General Assembly in protest to the Exscinding Acts. Ross presented a paper expressing the reasons for Presbytery's protest and subsequent action of withdrawal, which was adopted.

1. The two Assemblies of 1837 and 1838 arrogated to themselves the power to act in judgment upon the acts of all preceding Assemblies; "& however solemnly their acts may have been done, however obligatory in honor, in justice, in good faith, however beneficial in their effects, however often acted on & recognized by the whole Church, to declare them to be unconstitutional, null, void & of no effect."
2. The protest asserts the power to cut off synods, presbyteries, churches and

ministers "without citations, without charges, without proofs, without a hearing, without Trial; and this though no imputation rests upon the character of the parties thus cut off. . . ."
3. By dissolving the presbyteries without connecting the churches or ministers with any other Presbytery, it thus turns them out of the Church.
4. It asserts the power to delegate to a minority of any church judicatory the power to declare themselves the official judicatory.
5. It asserts the power to enjoin upon presbyteries punishment of its delegates to the Assembly upon pain of exclusion from the Presbyterian Church unless they are obedient.
6. It asserts the power to prescribe to candidates which seminaries they shall attend or the persons with whom they shall study.
7. It asserts the power to control the ministry in its labors by restricting them from preaching to any group not acceptable to the Assembly.
8. It asserts the power to prescribe any conditions it deems proper for either the dissolution or the admission of Presbyteries in the Church.
9. It asserts the power to state which presbyteries shall be represented at the Assembly and upon what terms the delegates shall take their seats.

By a vote of 12-9 Presbytery recognized the New School Assembly, promising to "render all proper respect to it . . . in accordance with the Constitution."[33]

This litany of complaints against the General Assembly is evidence that doctrinal differences were not a major factor in the decision to forsake the Old School. It was rather the unprecedented power which the Assembly had assumed which Ross's paper castigated. The acrimony with which the actions of the Assembly were received by many in the South is best revealed by Isaac Anderson.

> If all the world go with the exscinding party, there is one man who will not. I will go alone rather than in company with any ecclesiastical body whose proceedings I cannot countenance or

indorse, than I can indorse or countenance the Roman Catholic Inquisition.

Ross further added that the "measures of the last Assembly have not been surpassed in any Protestant church, since the Reformation, for injustice, oppression, and tyranny."[34]

Such sentiments were repeated over and over again across the South. None of the southern courts had been exscinded. Nevertheless New School congregations, presbyteries, and synods emerged,--not because of doctrinal affinity with their brothers in the North, but in protest to what they considered were unusual and oppressive methods in settling the New School difficulty. The action of Holston Presbytery--and its rationale for the action--consequently serves as a model for similar actions taken by other judicatories.[35]

By a decisive vote (32-8), the Synod of Tennessee at its annual meeting in the fall of 1838 resolved to adhere to the New School Assembly. It objected to the "unconstitutional and unrighteous acts" in abrogating the Plan of Union and in exscinding the synods. On a more positive note, the Synod expressed its sympathy and support for the AHMS and the AES.[36]

The Synod of Tennessee was the most typical of all the New School synods erected in the South. Theologically, its propensities for Hopkinsianism placed it under the large, heterogeneous umbrella of New School theology. In spite of the efforts of those who have sought to point out that few in the synod actually embraced Hopkinsianism, the facts do not substantiate their position. Further, the theological views taught and held tended to separate Tennessee from the other southern New School synods.[37]

Touching slavery, the position of the ministers and churches in East Tennessee was far more in line with most northern New School leaders than with their colleagues in the South. The seminary at Maryville exemplified the marriage of Hopkinsian theology and an abolition stance, which could be equated with that of any northern institution. Maryville itself was a seedbed of abolition. Isaac Anderson, who not only served as president and professor of theology at the seminary, was also pastor of Maryville's New Providence Presbyterian Church. He was antislavery, if not of the abolition stripe. Frederick Ross manumitted his slaves at a personal cost of $40,000. None of the other synods or constituent presbyteries in the southern New

School was as opposed to slavery as were the East Tennessee judicatories. Further, the Synod of Tennessee remained loyal to the volunteer agencies. The Synod thus was the model synod for the southern New School. No other southern court possessed the homogeneity which marked its constituency.

A portion of the Synod of Tennessee embraced churches in western North Carolina. The division of the Church in North Carolina upset Presbyterian strategy for the western portion of the state for many years. A proposed Western Synod of the Carolinas never got off the ground. The retreat of Presbyterian work in western North Carolina prevented the Old School from enjoying the success it experienced in the rest of the state.[38]

THE SYNOD OF VIRGINIA

The next synod in size and importance of the southern New School judicatories was the Synod of Virginia. In Virginia after the 1838 General Assembly,

> every sort of discussion was carried on during the summer--the calm and fiery, the cool and the passionate, the dignified and the commonplace, the argumentative and the declamatory; with every grade of Christian deportment, from the pure, and elevated, and gentlemanly, and kind, down to the coarse and vulgar, and hard; and in every form of communication, verbal, and by the press; in assemblies large and small; and by pamphlets and newspapers, and monthly and quarterly periodicals.[39]

It was Virginia's George Addison Baxter, Professor of Theology at Union Seminary, who was largely responsible for the plans whereby the reforms were brought to the 1837 Assembly. Upon returning from that meeting, he was not greeted with cordial unanimity. The response of the faculty was not supportive. Even the students demanded that he give a lecture to defend his position. Gradually some of his old friends rallied to his support, but not William Hill. With a vigor that denied his age, Hill took to the pen agaist the actions of the Assembly, and slowly emerged as the leader of those who opposed the proceedings of 1837.[40]

On the last day of the summer of 1837, Dr. William Swan Plumer began publishing the *Watchman of the South* in Richmond, a paper supportive of the Old

School position. In the meantime, the New England-born Amasa Converse removed his paper, the *Southern Religious Telegraph*, to Philadelphia. He so opposed the actions of 1837 that he believed he would have a broader sounding-board there than in Richmond. Nevertheless, as late as the opening of the 1838 Assembly, there was no thought of division in Virginia. The majority Old School expected the minority to coalesce, and the minority New School expected the majority to relax somewhat, anticipating that the 1838 Assembly would step down from the severity of the 1837 Exscinding Acts.

In April 1838, the Board of Directors of Union Seminary met. It received a resolution from the Synod of North Carolina in which the Synod expressed its opinion that the seminary professors should support the action of the Assembly. If they could not, however, the synod would not urge their dismissal so long as they would not use their position to influence the students. The board approved the resolutions of the synod as expressing its own sentiments. The faculty was in the board's presence. Two of the professors indicated that they could not hold back their feelings, but would of necessity desseminate them. The board then resolved that the two men resign, which they did. This action of the board was to have considerable influence in the direction the seminary would take in the future.

Both Hill and Baxter attended the 1838 Assembly. The evening before the Assembly was to convene, there was a meeting of those in sympathy with the exscinded brothers, for some had come to the Assembly from their respective presbyteries in the confidence that they would be received. The olive branch was extended to the men who favored the actions of 1837. Baxter, however, was a member of the committee which refused the plea for pacification. Hill and Baxter never met again. When the clerk called the roll the next day, he refused to recognize any commissioners from the exscinded presbyteries. The New School left the floor of the Seventh Presbyterian Church in Philadelphia and went to Albert Barnes's First Presbyterian Church. There the exscinded constituted themselves a General Assembly. William Hill was in their company.

The Presbytery of District of Columbia was dominated by the New School party. Its delegates withdrew from the 1838 General assembly to join the formation of the New School Assembly. The Presbytery of Abingdon on 7 July 1838 approved the action of its commissioner remaining in the Assembly. The New School members remained until the close of presbytery. Then they respectfully informed their colleagues that they never expected to meet with them again, and they withdrew. Seven churches went Old School, nine New School, and two divided. The New School organized the Presbytery of New River, which was attached to the Synod of Tennessee. A gradual attrition continued from the Old School, so that in the end it was necessary to dissolve the Old School Presbytery of Abingdon and transfer its churches to Montgomery Presbytery.[41]

Winchester Presbytery met in April 1839. It voted not to adopt a resolution introduced by John Loder, which acknowledged the New School Assembly. Shortly therafter the New School party left in a body to go to the nearby court house to conduct its business. There were three ministers--later increased to five--and eight elders. They carried six churches and parts of two others. This left the Old School with ten ministers and twenty-four churches.[42] A portent of things to come arose in a resolution which the New School Presbytery of Winchester passed that year: "Ecclesiastical bodies have no jurisdiction over the civil insitiution. Our commissioners are instructed to withdraw if the General Assembly should legislate on this subject."[43]

The Presbytery of East Hanover included Richmond. William Swan Plumer was pastor of First Church. As Moderator of the 1837 Assembly and a member of the convention, which had met before the Assembly to devise the strategy used to cut off the synods organized under the Plan of Union, Plumer had "passed through a fire as vehement as his previous course in the Assembly has been conspicuous." The New School minority was able to pass a resolution respecting the acts of the two Assemblies. Presbytery, however, interpreted its action only as an expression of presbyters exercising their constitutional right, at the same time by no means "forfeiting their standing or amenability to the Presbytery." Whereupon the New School party then asked to be dismissed. Presbytery adopted a paper, expressing its regrets. The resolution stated that the "character and standing" of their dissident brothers stood unimpeached.[44]

In West Hanover Presbytery the New School members "withdrew as opportunity and convenience prompted, and connected themselves with other Presbyteries, without formal withdrawal or announcement which took place in other Presbyteries."[45] These men united with the New School men of East

Hanover Presbytery to form the New School Presbytery of Hanover.

In 1839 the New School Synod of Virginia was organized. It contained three constituent Presbyteries: Winchester, District of Columbia, and Hanover; New River had been attached to the Synod of Tennessee. By the time the dust had settled in 1840, the New School Synod of Virginia included forty-seven churches, twenty-eight ministers, and about 2,000 communicants. The Old School reported 131 churches, 90 ministers, and 9,350 communicants. For the most part the separation among the ministers was amicable. Unfortunately the wrangling between the two groups led many members to transfer their affiliation to other denominations.[46]

The action of the New School group in Virginia in forming their own judicatories was not a sudden decision. In 1837 "A Presbyterian of Virginia" issued a pamphlet, *Remarks on the Act of the General Assembly of 1837...Submitted for the Consideration of Southern Presbyterians.*[47] The forty-page paper was a rational presentation of what the writer believed was an error in exscinding the four synods. He castigated the pre-Assembly convention whereby the Old School commissioners laid plans to cut off the synods. "Division, nothing *less* than division was the original design in calling the convention . . . a division by fair means if it can be made, but a *division* by *any* means that will effect it" (p. 4). He pointed out that in 1821, when the Constitution had been revised, it was sent down to the presbyteries for ratification. At that time no objection had been raised to the Plan of Union being inconsistent with the Constitution. Would the presbyteries have considered the Plan of Union unconstitutuional, and then voted for the adoption of an instrument which they knew "might afterwards be wielded for *their own ecclesiastical* DECAPITATION!"

> Were not these presbyteries *parties* in the adoption of the constitution? Yes. Whoever heard then of a case either in civil or ecclesiastical governments, where one of the parties to the adoption of a State or church constitution turned around afterwards, and under the authority of that very constituion so adopted, DECLARED *the other party not to be an integral portion of the State or the Church?* (pp. 8-9.)

The pamphlet argued that simply passing a rule whereby no more churches would be organized on the basis of the Plan of Union would have been quite acceptable--but not exscision. The fact that for years the General Assembly reviewed and approved the records of the synods, which in turn approved the organization of their constituent presbyteries, was proof sufficient that the judicatories were constitutional (p. 15).

Then the author engaged in the question of those ministers who had been ordained in "regular" presbyteries, but who had been cut off from the Church because they were serving in unconstitutional presbyteries, exscinded without regular process, evidence, or trial (p. 24). He concluded by pointing out that the acts of the Assembly have *"the appearance* of an ALARMING ASSUMPTION OF POWER! (p. 33).

The significance of the pamphlet is that it states the basic complaint of the New School party in the South: they opposed the manner by which the synods that had been formed on the basis of the Plan of Union had been exscinded from the Church. This is all the more interesting because not a single southern church or judicatory had been formed or was in any way affected by the Plan.

In September 1838, after the failure to heal the breach had completed the exscision, a meeting was held at Farmville, Virginia, attended by representatives from the Presbyteries of District of Columbia, Lexington, East Hanover, and West Hanover, in addition to observers from the local church and from such distant places as Charleston, South Carolina, and Mobile.[48] The roll included almost every New School minister in Virginia. At that time only the Presbytery of Abingdon had been formally affected by the 1838 General Assembly. This meeting for "prayer and consulation" was probably the origin of the movements which caused the Virginia New School ministers and their churches to withdraw from their respective presbyteries.

It is not necessary to examine the report which was drawn up for the purpose of ascertaining "the influence of those measures upon the constitution and character of the Presbyterian church" (pp. 4-5). Rather, attention is directed to the resolutions adopted concerning the action of the General Assembly of 1818 on the subject of the abolition of slavery, an action the Assembly passed unanimously. The preamble stated that the General Assembly "did assume to legislate upon the subject of slavery, which is entirely a civil and political matter, cognizable only by the civil authorities of the states in which slavery exists."

The first resolution affirmed the position that since slavery "in all its relations to the community" is "entirely a civil and political institution," the Church has no right to interfere with the subject. The second claimed that the legislation of 1818 on slavery was an "unwarranted assumption of power," since there was no authorization for such activity from either the Bible or the Church's constitution. The third relegated the entire issue of slavery "under the exclusive control of the governments of the several states in which it exists. . . ." The fourth resolution claimed that the attempt of the Church judicatories to carry into effect the act of the 1818 assembly, "or to exercise jurisdiction in any form over the relations of slavery," would be "eminently disastrous to the interests of our church in the southern country . . ." (p. 36).

The entire problem which the Farmville convention discussed--the issue of slavery is political, not ecclesiastical--must be understood as part of an emerging philosophy of southern Presbyterians: the apolitical nature of the Church. Planted in Farmville, this position was fertilized at the Cassville Convention by a similar resolution. From year to year it would be cultivated by the southern brethren. To the thrust of Hopkinsianism which the Synod of Tennessee accepted, the Synod of Virginia spoke its voice on the issue of slavery as a matter for civil courts only.

SYNOD OF WEST TENNESSEE

The loss of the former Synod of Tennessee to the New School was so formidable that the Old School Assembly changed the name of the Synod of West Tennessee to the Synod of Tennessee, and enlarged its bounds to include all the former area embraced by the former Synod of Tennessee. The only presbytery remaining in East Tennessee was Holston. It was enlarged to include the former Presbyteries of Union and French Broad.[49]

Prior to 1838 there had been no division in the presbyteries that comprised the Synod of Tennessee (OS). However, so upset was T. F. Scott, pastor of the First Church, Columbia, at the acerbity expressed in the General Assembly, that he concluded his report as commissioner to Presbytery, "I do not recognize the body to which this presbytery has declared its adherence as the General Assembly of the Presbyterian Church in the United States of

America, and . . . I disclaim its proposing any authority as such."[50]

Scott's report came after the Presbytery of West Tennessee had voted (11-8, 2 abstentions) to remain in the Old School. There was a qualification, however: "This act being understood so as not to give up the right of private judgment in regard to the wisdom, constitutionality, or expediency of the acts of this or any assembly."[51] Later, in the same session, the presbytery voted not to send any commissioners to the 1839 Assembly,[52] hence acknowledging Scott"s recommendation that the presbytery hold aloof as an independent presbytery until differences could be adjusted. Scott stated that he would make a similar recommendation to synod.[53] The closeness of the voting indicates that the body was fairly well divided between the two parties. In fact, so even was the vote that the action of any particular session of the presbytery was frequently determined by individual elders who happened to represent the churches at the time of a vote.

In 1839 the Old School Assembly called on all synods and presbyteries to show their true colors and expel all ministers and churches that rejected the authority of the Assembly. The Presbytery of West Tennessee endeavored to ignore the act. The Synod of Tennessee, however, took up the cause. Five members of the Presbytery of West Tennessee in attendance at the meeting of Synod refused to acknowledge the authority of the Assembly, and were dropped from Synod's roll. When Presbytery met in 1840, an effort was undertaken to prevent any action on Synod's order. But late in the session an elder insisted that a vote be taken. By a vote of 10-5 the ministers were expelled.[54] The New School ministers and churches then formed the Presbytery of West Tennessee (NS).

The Presbytery of Shiloh went almost unanimously into the New School. The issue which prompted this mass exodus was prompted also by the 1839 action of the Synod of Western Tennessee (OS) when it approved the earlier action of the Assembly which assigned all the Old School congregations to the Synod. The Rev. George Newton voted against Synod's action. Then he and other members of Shiloh Presbytery withdrew. Since most of them comprised the Presbytery, Synod dissolved it and placed what few remaining ministers and churches left to the Presbytery of Nashville.[55]

The Presbytery of North Alabama experienced division over the case of the Rev. Henry Herrick. Although his unusually lengthy examinations in experimental piety, theology, literature, ecclesiastical history, and church government had been sustained when he sought admittance to presbytery from the New School Presbytery of Union, presbytery refused to receive him. The position of presbytery was that he had refused to promise adherence to the Old School Assembly. "Thus was introduced a new test by which to decide the right of membership, unknown to our Form of Government and Book of Discipline."[56] Synod sustained the action of presbytery--in this case the presbytery of West Tennessee. This in turn reverberated and caused division in the Presbytery of North Alabama, an event which "all but ruined Presbyterianism in the Tennessee Valley. . . ."[57]

The schism suffered in the Synod of Tennessee was not over doctrine, but polity: ministers must be loyal to the assembly at all costs. Not imbued with the Hopkinsian theology that tainted East Tennessee Presbyterians, nor standing where the Synod of Virginia did in regard to slavery, the Synod of West Tennessee was composed of men who stood in polity where others wavered.

SYNOD OF MISSISSIPPI

The Synod of Mississippi experienced a division. The New School Presbytery emerged first, the Synod of Mississippi at a later date-- "a division which came about in a strict parliamentary way."[58] The Synod of Mississippi met about five months after the 1837 Assembly. At the time the synod consisted of four presbyteries-- two in Mississippi (Clinton and Mississippi) and two in Louisiana (Amite and Louisiana). The issue of division arose when synod reviewed the minutes of Clinton Presbytery. James Smylie, from the Committee of the Records, which reviewed the minutes of Clinton Presbytery, reported on the examination of that presbytery's records. the Presbytery had set aside the actions of the Assembly, a minute which Smylie did not permit to go unchallenged: ". . . no Presbytery can constitutionally pass a solemn resolve to disobey or set at naught the decisions of the higher courts."[59] Smylie also noted that "a resolution appears on . . . these records which seems to imply that the Clinton Presbytery have separated themselves from our Synod in missionary operation."[60]

On the day before, the Synod had passed an eleven-point resolution which sustained the action of the Assembly in cutting off the four synods.[61] The vote, however, was by a 22-14 margin. Upon the adoption of the paper, several indicated their intent to file a protest against the action of synod.

Point by point the protest traced the errors of the Assembly. It contains the best southern New School apology for withdrawing from the Old School.⁶² Nowhere does the statement contain any reference to the slavery question, further evidence that some men in the South did not understand slavery to be a factor in the 1837 schism.

By the time synod convened in 1838, Clinton Presbytery had divided. Both Old and New School groups claimed to be the true body. However, the synod, after examining the presbytery's minutes, declared the Old School minority to be "the only true Presby. within the abounds of this Synod; and that the majority . . . be regarded as seceders from the Presbyterian church in the United States."⁶³

The synod adopted a lengthy paper in which it declared its "adhesion to what it believes to be the only true and lawful General Assembly," whereby it sanctioned the course pursued by the minority in Clinton Presbytery. It noted that the secession of the majority in the Presbytery was "mainly based" on what the group felt was "the unconstitutionality of the acts of the Assembly of 1837 . . . ."⁶⁴ The basis for synod's support of the legislation of the Assembly was the Plan of Union.

In its closing paragraph of the State of the Church paper, however, the Synod

> would avert to another consideration which should have great weight in determining the course of the Southern churches. The Synod has good reason for believing that an overwhelming majority of the seceding body, and of those at the North who adhere to it, are hostile to one, at least, of the domestic institutions of the south. And we believe that any connection with that body by our churches will be a fruitful source of disaffection and wide-spread evil . . . . In some churches, abolition sentiments have already been made the test of membership, and where this course will end the future alone must determine. We feel bound, therefore, to warn our churches against all attempts to change their ecclesiastical relations, and to place them under the control of a new unconstitutional and revolutionary body.⁶⁵

SYNOD OF MISSOURI

The Synod of Missouri was erected in 1832. Quite feeble, it consisted of three Prebyteries--St. Louis, St. Charles, and Missouri. There was also a Harmony Presbytery, started among the Osage Indians the day before Missouri became a state in 1821. As the Indians left the state, the missionaries remained to labor among the whites who were moving into the area. The synod had only twenty-three congregations and eighteen ministers in 1832, and most of these were supported by the AHMS.[66] No Missouri commissioners attended the 1837 Assembly, and only the Presbytery of St. Charles was represented in 1838.

The next year the General Assmebly directed the Synod of Missouri to meet in St. Charles, since it had not met for some time. Should there be no quorum, the Assembly instructed those present to organize a convention. After drawing up a full statement of events, the convention would forward it to the Synod of Illinois, under whose care the Old School elements would be taken. The name of the anticipated judicatory would be changed to the Synod of Illinois and Missouri.[67]

Most of Missouri's ministers were in the Presbytery of St. Charles. Unanimously this presbytery had resolved that the Assembly of 1838-- which should reject no duly appointed commissioner-- would be the true Assembly. Ministers in other presbyteries took a similar stance. For all intents and purposes, the Missouri New School men remained independent from the New School as the result of a convention held in Hannibal in 1841. The Old School elements, in the meantime, continued to function.[68]

The Hannibal Convention was the turning point for the New School in Missouri. It disclaimed any possibility of uniting with the Old School. It further denounced the legislation of that body, whereby "without notice, without citation, without proof or pretended trial" four synods and a presbytery were exscinded. It further renounced the Old School's action on slavery, "a subject over which, we believe, they have no control, and with which they have no right to interfere." These resolutions prevented the Convention's members from returning to the Old School.[69]

The Convention formed a Missouri Home Missionary Society, an auxiliary to the AHMS, and plans were made to organize a synod in connection with the

New School Assembly in April 1842. The three Prebyteries in connection with the New School Synod of Missouri were Harmony (southwest), Lexington (northwest), and St. Louis (eastern part). At that meeting a circular letter was sent out to the churches as a rationale for organizing the new synod.[70]

SYNOD OF KENTUCKY

The organization of the Synod of Kentucky, after a brief attempt to remain independent, was not unlike that of the Synod of Missouri.[71] In the Bluegrass synod every effort was made to retain the unity of the Church. Largely through the editorial policy of Nathan L. Rice and Robert J. Breckinridge, who published the *Protestant and Herald* in Bardstown, a widening rift developed.[72] Under the leadership of three men--Archer C. Dickerson of Bowling Green, Joseph C. Stiles of Versailles, and Thomas Cleland of New Providence Church--the New School Synod of Kentucky was formed. Its three constituent presbyteries were each organized around one of the three fathers of the movement.[73] A convention to form the New School synod was not held until 19 December 1840 in Lexington. The three Presbyteries were Harmony, Green River, and Providence.

The first minister to break away from the Old School was Dickerson. He was quickly followed by Stiles, after the latter was removed from the ministry by the Presbytery of West Lexington. For these two the Old School in Kentucky had nothing but contempt. Such was not their feeling, however, toward Cleland, whom they dearly loved, and who was also pastor of the largest Presbyterian congregation in Kentucky.[74]

THE NEW SCHOOL IN GEORGIA AND SOUTH CAROLINA

In Georgia and South Carolina there were, technically, no New School judicatories organized above the level of the session. In Georgia, the nearest court allied with the New School was the Presbytery of Etowah.[75] This presbytery was organized in 1839 by former ministers in Hopewell Presbytery, who were dissatisfied by the actions of the Assemblies of 1837 and 1838. The minutes for the Hopewell Presbytery, 10 April 1840, noted that three of its members, Chas. W. Howard, Jas. H. George, and

H. C. Carter, had united to form a "separate and independent presbytery, and have published their declaration of independence to the world . . . ." Their names were erased from Presbytery's roll.[76]

Etowah Presbytery never entered the new School. It remained an independent presbytery.[77] The *Christian Observer* envisioned it as a court around which those "who in their hearts *thoroughly* disapprove the unconstitutional, unjust, and oppressive measures of a small majority in the Assembly of '37" to unite in a "solid phalanx" around Etowah Presbytery.[78]

Etowah Presbytery finally expired in 1842. At that time it had five ministers and five small congregations, all in northwestern Georgia. Later the Presbytery of Chattahoochee was organized. It was attached to the Synod of Tennessee. Its life was also short, and it passed away after a brief existence. What few, scattered churches that did exist in Georgia were usually under the care of Kingston Presbytery, Synod of Tennessee.

Although some have cited the Charleston Union Presbytery in South Carolina as being under the care of the new School Assembly,[79] such was never the case. It was listed in the New School statistical tables for 1839 and 1840, but it never sent commissioners to the Assembly. Charleston Union Presbytery was the majority of Charleston Presbytery. Its members rejected the "basis of 1838 and 1839." The minority of the Presbytery of Charleston was recognized by the Synod of South Carolina and Georgia.[80] Several members of Charleston Union Presbytery did attend the Cassville convention in 1840, but that was the closest they ever came to being even distantly connected with the New School.

A considerable portion of the southern Old School was "disturbed" by the "Reform" Assemblies of 1837 and 1838. By 1840 the southern areas which were safely in the New School camp began in the Valley of Virginia, continuing in a southwesterly direction through the Tennessee Valley to the Huntsville vale. "Pockets" were found in Mississippi, Missouri, and Kentucky. Sympathetic groups were in the Charleston area, the northwest corner of Georgia, and western North Carolina. Only a few congregations in Arkansas ever aligned with the New School. In Texas there were no congregations until after the mid-century, and then only four or five. Florida and Louisiana had none. In 1852 Charleston Union Presbytery returned to the Old School fold. Some foundations for the southern New School had been laid, however, and we turn to the structure that was erected upon them.

NOTES

1. E. H. Gillette, *History of the Presbyterian Church in the United States*, 2 vols. (Philadelphia: Presbyterian Publication Committee, 1864), 2:552.

2. Russel Blain Nye claimed that the New School "seceded" from the General Assembly to form a separate body. See *The Cultural Life of the New Nation, 1776-1830*, The New American Nation Series (New York: Harper & Bros., 1960), p. 228.

3. Thomas C. Johnson, *The Life and Letters of Robert Lewis Dabney* (Richmond: Presbyterian Committee of Publication, 1903), p. 285; R. C. Reed, "Presbyterians: Presbyterian Church in the United States (Southern Presbyterian Church)," *New Schaff-Herzog Encyclopedia of Religious Knowledge*, 9:229-230; Jacob Harris Patton, *A Popular History of the Presbyterian Church in the United States of America* (New York: R. S. Mighill and Co., 1900), p. 464.

4. Harold M. Parker, Jr., "The Urban Failure of the Southern New School Presbyterian Church," *Social Science Journal* 14 (1977): 139-148; reprinted in idem, *SSPH* (Gunnison, Colorado: B. & B. Printers, 1979), pp. 180-189.

5. William O. Brackett, Jr., "The Rise and Development of the New School in the Presbyterian Church in the U. S. A. to the Reunion of 1869,"*JPHS* 13 (1928): 169-170. See also William Warren Sweet, *The Story of Religion in America* (New York and London: Harper and Bros., 1939), p. 379.

6. Archibald Alexander, "The Present Conditions and Prospects of the Presbyterian Church," *Biblical Repertory and Theological Review* 4 (1832): 62-63.

7. William Henry Foote, *Sketches of Virginia, Historical and Biographical*, 2nd series, 2nd ed., rev. (Philadelphia: J. B. Lippincott, 1856), pp. 543-544.

8. George Howe, *History of the Presbyterian Church in South Carolina*, 2 vols. (Columbia: Duffie and Chapman, 1870; Walker, Evans and Cogswell, 1883), 2:569.

9. For a thorough treatment of this meeting, see Harold M. Parker, Jr., "The Cassville Convention: Aborted Birth of a Southern Presbyterian Church," *Historian* 42 (1980): 612-630. For the records of the meeting, see *Minutes of the Southern and South-Western Presbyterian Convention, Held at*

Cassville, Ga., October, 1840 (Charleston: B. B. Hussey, 1840).

10. Frederick Jackson Turner, "Western State-Making in the Revolutionary Era, I," *AHR* 1 (October 1895): 72-73.

11. W. Russell Briscoe and Katherine Boies Buehler, *Her Walls Before Thee Stand (History of the Second Presbyterian Church Knoxville 1818-1968)* (n.p.: n.p., 1968), pp. 7-8.

12. J. E. Alexander, *A Brief History of the Synod of Tennessee, From 1817 to 1887* (Philadelphia: MacCalla and Company, 1890), p. 10.

13. Cited in E. E. Stringfield, *Presbyterianism in the Ozarks: A History of the Work of the Various Branches of the Presbyterian Church in Southwest Missouri* (n.p.: n.p., 1909), p. 193.

14. James Gallaher, *The Western Sketch-book* (Boston: Crocker and Brewster; New York: W. M. Dodd; Philadelphia: William L. Martien, 1850), p. 194.

15. Union Presbytery, MS "Records" (14 September 1828), 4:330, typed copy in the McClung Collection, Lawson McGhee Library, Knoxville, Tennessee.

16. Asa Earl Martin, "The Anti-Slavery Societies of Tennessee," *Tennessee Historical Magazine* 1 (1915): 279.

17. Blanche Henry Clark, *The Tennessee Yeomen 1840-1860* (Nashville: Vanderbilt University Press, 1942), p. 8.

18. James Barnett, "Against the Stream," *Bulletin of the Historical and Philosophical Society of Ohio* 17(1959): 206.

19. Charles Embury Hedrick, *Social and Economic Aspects of Slavery in the Transmontane Prior to 1850*, George Peabody College for Teachers Contribution to Education, no. 46 (Nashville: George Peabody College for Teachers, 1927), p. 13.

20. Cited in Caleb Perry Patterson, *The Negro in Tennessee, 1790-1865*, University of Texas Bulletin No. 2205 (Austin: University of Texas, 1922), p. 181.

21. Martin, "Anti-Slavery Societies," p. 279.

22. Samuel Cole Williams, *Beginnings of West Tennessee: In the Land of the Chickasaws 1541-1841* (Johnson City, Tennessee: Wautauga Press, 1930), p. 212; Clark, *Tennessee Yeomen*, p. 9. Frederick Jackson Turner, in *The United States 1830-1850: The Nation and Its Sections* (New York: W. W. Norton, 1935), p. 216, noted that at the Convention the non-slaveholding mountaineers of East Tennessee were reported as proposing separate statehood.

23. C. W. Heiskell, "Pioneer Presbyterianism in Tennessee," in *Pioneer Presbyterianism in Tennessee:*

Addresses Delivered at the Tennessee Exposition on Presbyterian Day, October 28, 1897 (Richmond: Presbyterian Committee of Publication, 1898), pp. 33-34.

24. A succinct account of the early history of Presbyterianism in East Tennessee is found in Alfred Nevin, ed., *Encyclopaedia of the Presbyterian Church in the United States of America* (Philadelphia: Presbyterian Encyclopaedia Publishing Co., 1884), pp. 652-655.

25. George M. Marsden, *The Evangelical Mind and the New School Presbyterian Experience: A Case Study of Thought and Theology in Nineteenth-Century America* (New Haven and London: Yale University Press, 1970), pp. 40-41.

26. See Walter Brownlow Posey, *The Presbyterian Church in the Old Southwest 1778-1838* (Richmond: John Knox Press, 1952), p. 119; Alexander, *Synod of Tennessee*, pp. 32-33.

27. Ernest Trice Thompson, *Presbyterians in the South*, 3 vols. (Richmond: John Knox Press, 1963-1973), 1:352-354; Elwyn A. Smith, "The Doctrine of Imputation and the Presbyterian Schism of 1837-1838," *JPHS* 38 (1960): 144-147.

28. For trenchant accounts of Hopkinsianism, see Edwards F. Park and F. H. Foster, "Hopkinsianism," *The New Schaff-Herzog Encyclopedia of Religious Knowledge*, 5:364; and Sydney E. Ahlstrom, *A Religious History of the American People* (New Haven and London: Yale University Press, 1972), pp. 407-409.

29. Thompson, *Presbyterians in the South*, 1:353; Alexander, *Synod of Tennessee*, p. 2.

30. Ralph Waldo Lloyd, "Some History of the Three Synods of Tennessee, Alabama, and Mississippi," *JPHS* 23 (1945): 144.

31. Thompson, *Presbyterians in the South*, 1:354-355. For a major response to the charge that Anderson was Hopkinsian, see John J. Robinson, *Memoir of Rev. Isaac Anderson, DD., Late President of Maryville College, and Professor of Didactic Theology* (Knoxville: J. Addison Rayl, 1860), pp. 194-261. For a history of the seminary, see Harold M. Parker, Jr., "A School of the Prophets at Maryville," *Tennessee Historical Quarterly* 34 (1975): 72-90; reprinted in Parker *SSPH* (Gunnison, Colorado: B. & B. Printers, 1979), pp. 110-128.

32. William Warren Sweet, *Religion in the Development of American Culture 1767-1840* (New York: Charles Scribner's Sons, 1952), p. 227. For the purpose of the *Calvinistic Magazine*, see the first issue, published in January 1827, p. 1. For a brief

description of the journal, see T. H. Spence, Jr., "Southern Presbyterian Reviews," *Union Seminary Review* 56 (1945): 96-98; and Alexander, *Synod of Tennessee*, pp. 62-63. E. Brooks Holifield, in *The Gentlemen Theologians: American Theology in Southern Culture 1795-1860* (Durham, North Carolina: Duke University Press, 1978), p. 198, argued that "the journal bore the imprint of the New Haven doctrine, much to the dismay of the conservatives."

33. Holston Presbytery [OS], MS "Minutes" (4 October 1838), pp. 97-100, manuscript copy in the McClung Collection, Lawson McGhee Library, Knoxville, Tennessee.

34. Robinson, *Memoir of Anderson*, pp. 135, 137.

35. For a congregation's action, see Harry Sharp Hassall, "Concord Presbyterian Church--A Study in History and Sociological Survey" (Th. M. Thesis, Louisville Presbyterian Theological Seminary, 1964), p. 23.

36. Posey, *Presbyterian Church in the Old Southwest*, p. 122; Alexander, *Synod of Tennessee*, p. 32.

37. I have suggested that one of the reasons for the refusal of Kentucky Presbyterians to send their candidates to Maryville--which resulted in the establishment of their own ill-fated seminary at Macedonia Church--was due to the Hopkinsianism that Anderson taught at Maryville; Parker, "A New School Presbyterian Seminary in Woodford County," *Register of the Kentucky Historical Society* 74 (1976): 99-111; reprinted in Parker, *SSPH*, pp. 167-169. The unique theological views of the Anderson-dominated Synod of Tennessee were not in accord with the more conservative southern New School element. As early as 1834, W. L. Breckinridge had denominated Tennessee as a region of apostasy (Holifield, *Gentlemen Theologians*, p. 198). Hence the isolation the Synod of Tennessee experienced.

38. For a more detailed presentation of the New School division in North Carolina, see Harold M. Parker, Jr., "The New School Presbyterian Disruption in North Carolina," *Iliff Review* 32 (1975): 51-63; reprinted in idem, *SSPH*, 97-109.

39. William Henry Foote, *Sketches of Virginia*, pp. 538-539. His work contains a splendid eyewitness account of the background whereby the Synod of Virginia and her constituent presbyteries divided, pp. 538-552. For a more concise account, see Thompson, *Presbyterians in the South*, 1:403-407.

40. Foote, *Sketches of Virginia*, p. 544.

41. Goodridge A. Wilson, Jr., *Diamond Jubilee Address on the History of Abingdon Presbytery*

(Pulaski, Virginia: B. D. Smith & Brothers, [1936]), p. 12.

42. The figures are from Foote, *Sketches of Virginia*.

43. Robert Bell Woodworth, *A History of the Presbyterian Church in Winchester, Virginia, 1780-1949, Based on Official Documents* (Winchester: Piper Printing Co., 1950), p. 77.

44. Foote, *Sketches in Virginia*, pp. 546-547. The division of the churches in Richmond between the Old and New School was unique in the South. Richmond was the only southern city with three or more New School congregations--more in the New School than in the Old.

45. Foote, *Sketches of Virginia*, p. 547.

46. Ibid.; Thompson, *Presbyterians in the South*, 1:407.

47. I conjecture that the author was William Hill.

48. *The Proceedings of the Meeting for Prayer and Consultation Held at Farmville, Va., September 5th, 6th, 7th, and 8th, 1838* (Richmond: Wm. McFarlane, 1838).

49. GAPCUS [OS], *Minutes*(1839), p. 170.

50. Presbytery of West Tennessee [OS], MS "Minutes" (9 October 1838), 2:129-130, PHF, Montreat, North Carolina. The name of this presbytery was later changed to Maury.

51. Ibid., 2:128-129.

52. D. D. Little, *History of the Presbytery of Columbia Tennessee* (Columbia, Tennessee: Maury Democrat, 1928), pp. 12-13; West Tennessee Presbytery [OS], "Minutes" (23 June 1838), 2:77-94.

53. Little, *Columbia Presbytery*, p. 12. Actually, Scott's suggestion was voted down, 11-8. However, both parties had an "understanding" in regard to the General Assembly.

54. Little, *Columbia Presbytery*, p. 14; Presbytery of West Tennessee [OS], "Minutes" (3 April 1840), 2:166-167.

55. Robert E. Cogswell, *Written on Many Hearts: The History of the First Presbyterian Church Shelbyville, Bedford County, Tennessee 1815-1965* (Nashville: Parthenon Press, n.d.), pp. 7-29, 36-37, 50, 141-142.

56. West Tennessee Presbytery [NS], MS "Minutes," p. 13, PHF; *CO*, 25 June 1840; Little, *Columbia Presbytery*, pp. 15, 16.

57. James William Marshall, *The Presbyterian Church in Alabama*, ed. Robert Strong (Montgomery: Presbyterian Historical Society of Alabama, 1977), p. 60.

58. C. W. Grafton, "History of the Mississippi Synod Presbyterian Church" (microfilm copy of the typed MS, 1927), p. 186, Department of Archives and History, Jackson, Mississippi.
59. Synod of Mississippi, *Minutes* (1837), p. 34.
60. Ibid., p. 35.
61. For the content of the resolutions of Synod, see ibid., pp. 27-29.
62. For the content of the Appeal, see ibid., pp. 37-43.
63. Synod of Mississippi, MS "Minutes" (1838), pp. 149-150, Department of Archives and History, Jackson, Mississippi.
64. *State of the Church, Being a Minute Adopted by the Synod of Mississippi at its Session in Vicksburg, October 24, 1838, in Relation to the Late Secession from the Presbyterian Body* (New Orleans: Observer Office, 1838), p. 1.
65. Ibid., p. 14.
66. J. B. Hill, "Missouri's Presbyterian Centennial," in Synod of Missouri [PCUSA], *Minutes* (1932), p. 34.
67. GAPCUS [OS], *Minutes* (1839), p. 171.
68. Hill, "Missouri's Presbyterian Centennial," p. 34.
69. *Declaration of Sentiments, Made by the Synod of Missouri, Formed by a Convention of Presbyterian Ministers and Elders, Held at Hannibal, October 7th, 1841* (St. Louis: Gazette Office, 1841), p. 5. The MS "Minutes" of the Convention are prefixed to the MS "Minutes" of the Synod of Missouri [NS], Library, Missouri Valley College, Marshall, Missouri.
70. *A Circular Letter to the Churches under the Care of the Synod of Missouri, Written in Obedience to a Resolution of Synod, Passed at its Meeting in April, 1842* (St. Louis: The Bulletin, 1842). The authors of the *Letter* were John Blatchford, F. C. Gray, and J. T. Tucker. See also John B. Hill, *Presbyterianism in Missouri* (n.p., n.d.), pp. 8-9.
71. For a thorough study of the New School Synod of Kentucky, see Harold M. Parker, Jr., "The New School Synod of Kentucky," *Filson Club History Quarterly* 50 (1976): 52-89, reprinted in idem, *SSPH*, 129-166. See also Gillette, *History of the Presbyterian Church*, 2:537-541.
72. Robert Stuart Sanders, *Presbyterianism in Versailles and Woodford County, Kentucky* (Louisville: Dunne, 1963), pp. 11, 133-134.
73. Prior to the Convention, Dickerson had formed an independent presbytery in Bowling Green, 4

December 1840, consisting of three ministers. The presbytery adjourned to meet at the Lexington Convention on the 9th. Six other ministers united with them to form the Synod of Kentucky [NS]. *CO* 15 January 1841.

74. The organization of the Synod is described in Parker, "NS Synod of Kentucky," pp. 55-65. For a thorough statement of the views of Dickerson for withdrawing from the Old School, see "Expression of Views of B[owling] G[reen] P[resbyterian] Congregation on Division of P[resbyterian] Church--Nov. 19, 1839," Kentucky Library and Museum, Bowling Green; see also *CO* 14 February 1840.

75. The records of Etowah Presbytery have been lost. Most of the material for this movement is found in James Stacey, *A History of the Presbyterian Church in Georgia* (Elberton, Georgia: Star Press, [1912]).

76. Cited in ibid., pp. 184-188.

77. Russell E. Hall, "An Outline History of the Presbyterian Church in America," *JPHS* 26(1948): 238, 239.

78. *CO*, 2 April 1840.

79. Timothy L. Smith, *Revivalism and Social Reform in Mid-Nineteenth Century America* (Nashville and New York: Abingdon Press, 1957), p. 26.

80. For description of the division in Charleston Presbytery, see *Minutes of the Southern and South-Western Presbyterian Convention*, pp. 31-35.

3
Southern New School Ecclesiastical Development

In the years between 1840 and 1857, the ecclesiastical structure of the southern New School underwent considerable change. The courts of the New School South were related, of course, to the fortunes of the New School Presbyterian Church. During those years, their relationship with the southern Old School judicatories, ministers, and churches worsened.

The New School Synod of Virignia typified the attempts of the southern New School courts to function through a structured ecclesiastical system. At its 1845 meeting, a report acknowledged the inability of the synod to secure a general agent for domestic missions. Synod then recommended to each of its presbyteries to make "strong efforts" to obtain for the ensuing year "a competent missionary agent" for their respective bounds.[1] The following spring the *Christian Observer* reported that the Domestic Society of Richmond had worked out an "amicable arrangement" with the AHMS. Each society would pay one half of a "reasonable compensation" for the missionaries which the AHMS would select. Five missionaries were appointed, financial assistance was given to five feeble churches, as well as toward the erection of four new edifices, and repair of three others.[2] Later, the relationship with the AHMS became strained. Finally the New School withdrew completely from the AHMS in 1852. The Synod of Virginia then formed its own Domestic Missionary Society of Virginia in conjunction with the Southern Aid Society.[3]

As early as 1843 the Presbytery of Hanover established a Committee on Education. Its purpose was to underwrite the cost of ministerial education to supply "the waste places within our bounds. We have need, great need for more laborers in this portion of our vineyard, and there are many reasons why these laborers should be brought forth from among yourselves." A committee was appointed to receive funds.[4]

These two instances of organizing programs demonstrate a structural ecclesiasticism which the New School South seldom contemplated, much less implemented. They also point out the loose connectionalism that characterized the entire New School in its early efforts to work out its mission through judicatories. The Old School had developed boards and agencies on the Assembly level. The New School, however, was operating on a quasi-Congregational approach. Little emphasis was placed on the Church qua Church operating its own mission program. Thus, realizing that each judicatory must fend for itself, rather than relying on the denomination, the basic strength of southern New Schoolism gradually gravitated to the level of the presbytery.

The synod of Virginia at its 1845 meeting adopted Delaware College and resolved to raise $10,000 within its bounds in the ensuing year to build up the college's endowment. With both New School Synods of Virginia and Pennsylvania supporting it, the *Christian Observer* enthusiastically predicted that *"Delaware College is sure to rise, and that rapidly,"* taking its place alongside Carlisle and Brown, and becoming a real Constitutional Presbyterian institution.[5]

A major concern of the southern New School was the large black element in the Church's ranks. Two incidents in the history of the Synod of Virginia illustrate the endeavors of the Church in dealing with its black constituency. At the 1851 Fall Meeting of the Presbytery of Winchester, William D. Roby, a black, was introduced to Presbytery "as a person wishing to enter the ministry with a view of preaching the gospel in Liberia . . . ." He was received under the care of Presbytery as a candidate for the ministry.[6] In receiving Roby, the Presbytery treated him as it would any white person who desired to begin his preparation for the ministry, by coming under presbytery's care.

By far the greatest concern the Church had for the black was evidenced in the religious instruction of slaves in the households of church members.[7] Time and again presbyteries exhorted their constituents

Ecclesiastical Development 57

to be faithful in this responsibility. Hanover Presbytery in 1856 passed this resolution:

> Your committee...would earnestly recommend to Pastors, Stated Supplies, and Missionaries within our bounds, the just importance of assembling the colored people at their respective places of worship as often as practicable on the afternoon of the Sabbath day, in order that they may have the Gospel preached to them, and, with the consent of their owners, such other oral religious instruction as they may deem best. Your committee would also recommend to the heads of families, the importance of assembling their servants on Sabbath day, for prayer and oral religious instruction.[8]

Nevertheless, the problem of slavery, brought up at every meeting of the new School Assembly, vexed the southern ministers considerably. At the same meeting of Hanover Presbytery in which the Presbytery urged religious instruction for the slaves in the households of its constituency, it passed a resolution expressing its "decided disapprobation" of the Assembly's "continued agitation" on the subject.[9]

Through this score of years, there was little interest on the part of New School Virginians to entertain any suggestion of reunion with their Old School counterparts. The New School in Virginia contained men of noble hearts and great minds, every bit the equal of the Old School clergy and elders.

Evidence of growth in Winchester Presbytery was noted at the 1855 Fall Meeting. The Stated Clerk pointed out that in the year past, Presbytery had licensed four men, all preachers, had six candidates under its care, "but [was] not able to supply the openings which are constantly presenting themselves within our bounds."[10] Andrew Hunter Holmes Boyd, one of the most brilliant minds in Virginia New Schoolism, was an avid pastor. He led in the organization of mission work west of Winchester. He believed that there was sufficient room for two Presbyterian congregations in a community, providing that their influence and membership extended to outpost work. Although dedicated to the New School cause, he maintained good relationships with the Old School pastor in Winchester.[11]

The strength of East Tennessee was its theological posture. The institutional base for that theology came from the seminary at Maryville. The candidates for the ministry who studied there came almost wholly from East Tennessee, and to East Tennessee they returned. From the classroom to the pulpit the seminary's graduates maintained a cohesiveness--both sociologically as well as theologically--seldom equalled in the annals of American Presbyterianism. If there was any weakness in the ranks of the Synod of Tennessee clergy and churches, it was the want of new thinking.

The 1849 meeting of the Synod took action " to attempt something for the extension of Presbyterian influence." It engaged Levi R. Morrison to visit the congregations and receive offerings for home missions for the purpose of raising salaries from the low level which forced ministers to engage in secular work. In less than a year he had raised $660, nearly a fourth again as much as the whole amount of ministerial support which those churches had paid. Synod hoped that with the continued assistance of the AHMS, most of the "waste places" could be supplied.[12]

At the same time synod realized that its reliance on the AHMS was leaning on a bruised reed. It thus urged its presbyteries to be prepared to respond to any state of conditions that might open up a wider field of home missions than they already possessed with the AHMS. Nothing should be done, however, to disturb the cooperation which the AHMS had provided.[13] This action reflected the tenuous relationship that had developed between the AHMS and the churches in the South.

The Synod of West Tennessee embraced the Presbyteries of West Tennessee, Shiloh, and North Alabama. The topography which this synod covered was not as severe as its sister synod to the east. There were more plantations, a denser and larger population of slaves, and a considerably higher percapita income. The Assembly's statistical tables do not record the three presbyteries until 1843. This reflected the uncertain mind of the synod and its presbyteries in uniting themselves with the New School. Unlike the situation in East Tennessee, where almost all the congregations went New School, and with them the presbyteries, in the Synod of West Tennessee each New School presbytery represented a minority of the former Old School presbytery whence it came. And where some of the churches entered the New School with a large majority, in other instances the New School element represented but a small fraction of the membership.

The newly-organized New School Presbytery of West Tennessee in 1840 expressed its confidence in the AHMS, the ABCFM, and the AES--the three voluntary societies which the Old School had excoriated in 1837. Presbytery further recommended that the churches within its bounds "make special efforts to aid in these times of embarrassment the funds of said societies."[14] Three years later the synod established a Committee on Domestic Missions, charged with the duty "of employing missionaries, determining the amount of compensation each shall receive, and the field of labor each shall occupy." It also directed the committee to use its discretion in applying to the AHMS for aid, either in men or funds.[15]

The synod thus did undertake an aggressive program of church expansion. It was quite apparent that in its early years there was more vitality in the New School presbyteries than in the Old School, not only in numbers, but also in the "younger and more aggressive element" they had attracted.[16] The wealth of the area permitted a great investment in new church development. When the Synod made an appeal across the denomination for funds to place a congregation in Nashville, the *Christian Observer* encouraged the plea:

> They have nobly entered the open field in the growing city of Nashville, and raised four or five thousand dollars to plan a Church, and they now look to their brethren in our Churches to aid them in the work.[17]

The Nashville congregation was organized in January 1857.

Just how loyal the Presbytery of Shiloh was to the New School is debatable. Its relationship to the Synod of West Tennessee is questionable. During the 1840s and 1850s there is no record of the presbytery being in any kind of formal relationship to any higher judicatory. There is little evidence to indicate that the presbytery was ever active in the New School movement. It has been conjectured that "it would seem that the Presbytery of Shiloh and its churches virtually operated independently of either of the major parties."[18] Even though the pastor of the Shelbyville church, Alfred Henry Dashiell, was an avid New Schoolman, he apparently was incapable of infusing his views into the church.[19]

West Tennessee did not harbor the acrimonious feelings toward the Old School that characterized East Tennessee. In the latter there was never any consideration given to the possiblility of reunion of the two Churches. In the Synod of West

Tennessee, however, such a possibility surfaced in 1848. Upon hearing "credible evidence" that there "existed a desire for a re-union of the two divisions of the Presbyterian Church in this country," the Presbytery of Western Tennessee unanimously resolved to "rejoice in any prospects of such a re-union."[20] At the next meeting, however, the reality of the terms of reunion were spelled out: any reunion would permit New School ministers, elders, and members to return only through "examination in detail." Presbytery then resolved that it could not "for a moment entertain the proposition of the brethren of the other division of the Presbyterian Church," and voted that "the farther consideration of this subject be indefinitely postponed."[21]

A similar action was voted by the Presbytery of Shiloh. Its members would never assent to the unqualified assumption of the old School that all New School members were essentially guilty of departing from the Confession of Faith, and would thus have to be examined before restoration to the true Church.[22]

The growth of the Synod of West Tennessee was steady. In 1845 it reported a total of thirty-four churches, twenty-five ministers, and 1,795 members. In 1857 it reported thirty-eight churches, nineteen ministers, and a little over 2,200 members. The decline in the ministerial ranks can be attributed to the stand of the AHMS. The Society gradually withdrew its support from the missionaries who labored in churches with slaveholders in the membership. This policy had two effects. First, fewer men from the North went South to labor. But more telling was that financial aid was gradually withdrawn from the missionaries who were laboring in such congregations.

There was no Synod of Mississippi until 1845. Shortly after the Presbytery of Clinton separated from the Old School, it began to grow in numbers. The presbytery reported just 244 members in 1843. Two years later the presbytery organized itself into the Synod of Mississippi, referring to the "revolutionary measures" taken by the Assembly of 1837.[23] The erection of a synod from a presbytery resulted in a wave of protest that swept over the New School Assembly when it met in its triennial session in 1846. An entire synod had been formed without the prior knowledge or consent of the Assembly. The committee on elections, however, recommended that the commissioners from the three Mississippi presbyteries be seated, giving the synod six votes instead of two. This added strength to the pro-slavery bloc in the Church. The formal action whereby the Synod of Mississippi was recognized due to the "peculiar circumstances" of the case was met by a formal protest signed by eighteen commissioners. They insisted that the action of a presbytery organizing itself into a synod was unconstitutional. Further, the Assembly's action in receiving the synod was interpreted as "encouraging disorder in the Church." The issue of slavery was also injected into the reception of the three presbyteries:

> We solemnly protest against the reception of these presbyteries on the ground, that ministers and church-members connected with said presbyteries are slave-holders, and their commissioners claim and advocate, that the Bible sanctions the institution of slavery, thus increasing and strengthening the slave-holding influence in the Church.[24]

Interestingly enough, of the eighteen commissioners who signed the protest, eight were from presbyteries that had themselves been established on the basis of the Plan of Union, an action that the Old School had deemed sufficient to exscind because they had been irregularly formed.

Three Presbyteries made up the Synod of Mississippi: Clinton, Lexington (South), and Newton. The Synod had a total of nineteen churches, thirteen ministers, and 857 communicants. The scant numbers caused some of the commissioners at the Assembly to raise their eyebrows, but the numbers in every instance were about equal to those of the Synod of Kentucky. To the minds of many, it was the slavery issue that loomed important. It has been charged that the admission of the Synod of Mississippi "extended the area of slavery in the church."[25] Such a judgment is hardly true, since the Presbytery of Clinton, whence the synod was formed, had been in the denomination for several years. Still the synod's relationship to the Assembly was "very slight" at best. It was the only synod without representation at the 1850 Assembly.[26]

The Synod formed its own missionary society in 1851. Two factors contributed to this action. One was due to the failure of the AHMS to grant financial assistance, an increasing position of the Society in regard to churches that had slaveholders in their membership. The other factor was the other side of the coin, the refusal of churches to bend to the demands of the AHMS.[27]

The Synod in 1852 appointed a corresponding secretary and general agent for its new missionary society. Within a year, he reported that he had travelled 3,298 miles on horseback, had raised $2,438.07 for home missions, had written 131 letters, and had preached 163 times. Further, he had visited each congregation in the synod twice, in addition to going to some of the promising places where new churches were being established. In each church a sacramental meeting was held, varying in length from two to eleven days. He remarked that he did not have to "beg" for funds, for everywhere the cause of home missions was received favorably. The churches viewed their gifts as an "investment" through which they could assist weak churches within Synod's bounds.[28]

When the Southern Aid Society was formed in 1853, its major mission was to support southern ministers and churches in light of the refusal of the AHMS to support religious institutions in the South which were connected with slavery. The supplemental aid which the SAS contributed placed the synod's home mission program in a very strong position. The real weakness in the Synod of Mississippi, however, was not the lack of funds; it was the shortage of ministers, a condition which increasingly hounded almost all of the southern New School presbyteries and synods. As the years passed, fewer of the northern-educated ministers would entertain any interest in taking southern churches because of the odium of slavery. Further, the southern churches were not sending forth sufficient numbers of their sons to man the pulpits. In 1844 the *Christian Observer* pleaded the cause of Mississippi:

> There is, perhaps, no section of the country, in which a greater or more blessed harvest could be gathered, as the fruit of evangelical labors. If that field is to be supplied with the ministry needed--an able ministry, adapted to the circumstances of the country--there must be the *united efforts* of many Churches to furnish the supply.[29]

The appeal fell on deaf ears.

A decade later, Alexander Newton of Mississippi addressed the SAS. He pointed out that in the North there were 657 persons for each church, but 524 in the South. Virginia had 2,383 congregations of all denominations, but only 1,087 ministers. In Newton's Mississippi there were only 471 ministers for 1,016 churches. At the same time New York State had 4,134 churches and 4,290 ministers.[30] Alexander Newton was one of the true statesmen in the synod. The idea of the home missionary agent was his brainchild. The success of the Presbytery of Lexington, South, could well be traced to his leadership.[31]

The New School philosophy of loose ecclesiasticism dominated the thinking of Mississippi's judicatories. As the New School increasingly forsook its position of supporting voluntary, interdenominational agencies, and began erecting its own, the response in Mississippi was to cling to the former plan. At its 1854 Fall meeting, Newton Presbytery resolved that

> in relation to the great objects of Church extension, Church erection, Education for the ministry &c, while we regard them as closely identified with the interests of our church, we would recommend that it be left by our Presbytery, to our churches to take such action, in the way of co-operation, as they may think wisest and best.[32]

The bounds of the Synod included not only Mississippi, but spilled over into lower Alabama, particularly along the railroad that extended from Decatur, Mississippi, to Mobile, Alabama. The Alabama city was only the second one in which the southern New School successfully established a congregation.[33] The most significant work outside the Magnolia State occurred, however, in Texas, which had been attached to the Synod of Mississippi.

The *Christian Observer* (2 August 1851) noted that there were three "Constitutional Presbyterian" ministers in Texas. The editor expressed the hope that they would organize a presbytery, and that others would join them in laying the foundations of twenty or more churches on the borders of Mexico. The first New School congregation was organized 22 August 1853 at Garden Valley by William M. King.[34] The Synod of Mississippi laid plans to establish a presbytery in Texas. It requested that all New School ministers living there have their letters of dismission sent to the Stated Clerk of Clinton Presbytery. When three such letters have been received, a meeting of Presbytery would be called. When duly constituted, the new presbytery would report its actions to the 1854 meeting of synod.[35]

The Presbytery of Texas was organized 20 December 1854 at Crocket, with three ministers, four churches, and one candidate.[36] It immediately asked to be received under the care of the Synod of Mississippi. It was centered around the present Dallas-Fort Worth area. Although the prospects for the new presbytery seemed very good at the time of its organization, the work never realized its full potential. Again, the plea for ministers to come to the new area fell on unresponsive ears. "There are many points in the State at which we could have flourishing churches, if we had the men to occupy them," commented William M. King. He then pointed out that financial support was also needed, since the AHMS had withdrawn from the South and he was not certain that the SAS would be in a position to assist. He also asked for men who could teach, for there was a dearth of teachers.[37] W. C. Dunlap observed that there were more new School Presbyterians within the bounds of the new presbytery than those of any other Presbyterian persuasion. People from Indiana, Illinois, Missouri, Kentucky, and Tennessee "have filled up this section," since the economy was largely grain-growing and stock-raising.[38]

The New School simply arrived in Texas too late with too little. The early history of Texas Presbyterianism was largely dominated by the Cumberland and the Old School Presbyterians.[39]

In most areas the New School division was not sufficient to upset the total Presbyterian posture, but such did not obtain for Missouri. Confusion best describes the condition there. Even when the two rival Old School and New School synods were organized, ministers hardly knew where to align themselves. For many year following the division in Missouri, there was a continuing shifting process which frequently put churches into the opposite party from which they had begun.[40]

At the Hannibal Convention a "Declaration of Sentiment" was adopted. The paper repudiated and utterly disclaimed "the cognomen Old School and New School . . . ." It affirmed,

> We are Presbyterians, *substantial, firm Presbyterians* in our government. We heartily approve of the form of government found in the standards of our church, solemnly resolving that no views of *expediency* shall ever tempt us to swerve from the Constitution . . . .[41]

Although the original intent may have been not to identify itself with either party, at the 1843 meeting the Synod of Missouri opted to send delegates to the next New School Assembly

> with discretionary powers, if the way shall be opened and made plain, then and there to connect with the Constitutional Assembly. But if, in the judgment of the delegates, the way shall not be thus prepared, they shall request to sit as corresponding members of that body.[42]

Inasmuch as the next meeting of the Assembly was 1846, this provided the synod with almost a three-year opportunity to observe the conditions of the New School. Thus, when the presbyteries' commissioners did attend the Assembly, they were received. The statistical tables for 1846 revealed a total of thirty-three ministers, fifty churches, and 1,832 communicants in the four presbyteries.

Since the synod had already organized its own home missions agency, it experienced considerable growth after its organization. Further, it profited in no small measure from the administrative ability of Artemas Bullard, pastor of the First Presbyterian Church, St. Louis. He threw himself into the task of home missions. And in Harmony Presbytery, a band of former Maryville students labored with considerable success.[43] The indomitable labors of Timothy Hill as Synod's Agent for home missions met with a fruitful harvest.

For many years Missouri remained the largest state in the union. The deplorable condition of the New School structures, however, caused the *Christian Observer* to ask, "Will the Eastern Churches aid their brethren in *the erection of houses of worship* in the West? This question . . . has been *practically* answered in the negative."[44] A missionary laboring in St. Joseph reported that the lack of a house for public worship was one of the greatest obstacles a Missouri missionary confronted. "We could, I doubt not, double the number of our churches and communicants in one year, if we had suitable houses in which to worship God."[45] Many of the "most efficient" ministers were forced to preach in log cabin dwellings, where beds were spread in the one-room cabins. "In these circumstances, their congregations cannot be expected to increase in numbers."[46]

The peculiar nature of the Missouri frontier severely hindered the financial support which constituents might otherwise have contributed. J. T.

Tucker of Hannibal gave three reasons for the poverty of the Missouri New School churches: (1) small villages, instead of erecting one good church, often have as many as four or five edifices; (2) the lack of cash, due to a natural economy in many of the areas of the state; and (3) so many people have debts that they are endeavoring to work them off.[47] So critical was the financial condition in the Presbytery of Lexington West that in its Pastoral Letter of spring 1846 it listed four conditions which it deemed "of sufficient importance": (1) ministers were too frequently engaged in non-ministerial labors; (2) elders do not attend the Presbytery meetings; (3) churches are neglecting to have installed pastors--not a single pastoral relationship in the Presbytery; and (4) adequate support for ministers is lacking.[48]

A decade later the SAS commented that conditions were scarcely altered:

> Many of the churches in Missouri are surprisingly feeble. Of the ten ministers who compose the Presbytery of Northern Missouri, only one is entirely supported by his people. Of the churches that look to us for aid . . . one of them raises only seventy-five dollars towards the pastor's salary, and none of them more than one hundred.[49]

The New School in Kentucky parallelled Missouri's track in affairs ecclesiastical. It attempted an independent status for a couple of years. It united with the New School Assembly in 1843, but only after the delegates from its presbyteries were satisfied with the Assembly's debate on slavery.[50]

The synod's organization had been structured on shaky foundations. The three presbyteries which made up the synod each had the minimal number of ministers--three. Each presbytery also practically embraced a very small area. The presbyteries were so weak as to be unable to function as judicatories at times. On one occasion the Presbytery of Green River, lacking a quorum (three ministers), had not met for some time. At the 1848 meeting of the synod, the synod temporarily transferred two members to the presbytery, and then adjourned. With a quorum present, the presbytery set about to accomplish its business. When its work was accomplished, the presbytery returned to the floor of synod and transferred the two "loaned" members back to their former presbyteries.[51]

The shortage of ministerial leadership which dogged most of the southern New School also afflicted Kentucky. Lane Theological Seminary, a New School institution, was just across the Ohio in Cincinnati. Its antislavery posture, however, discouraged its graduates from considering southern pulpits. The ministerial shortage seriously handicapped the possibility of the synod's growth. In 1844 the Presbytery of Harmony had ten ministers and an equal number of churches. The Stated Clerk complained that there was "room enough for as many more ministers and churches, if we had the men to occupy the ground and the means to support them." He was certain that if "our brethren in the East only knew our destitutions, and could feel our necessities, they would send us the men and the means both."[52] A decade later, Fencilius Gray reported to Harmony Presbytery that "the few ministers here cannot do half that ought to be done."[53] Ill health and old age prevented some ministers from performing their pastoral duties. There was still the constant hope, however, that "with a due caution of ourselves and the blessings of God, we can enlarge our Synod, as to put its existence on safe grounds. This is our immediate aim." So thought Archer C. Dickerson.[54]

Relations between the New and Old School groups in Kentucky were far from harmonious. The Bardstown-published *Protestant and Herald* maintained a constant barrage of acid comments toward those who had forsaken the Old School ranks. Shortly after the New School Synod was organized, the paper editorialized,

> Except in the case of Dr. Cleland, whose course has been much regretted, there has been no wish to retain any of the other New School ministers. So far as we know, there has not been a sigh or a tear over their secession, and never will be.[55]

New School attitudes, however, were more amicable toward their former co-laborers. There were few instances in which they endeavored to establish congregations where Old School churches already existed. In almost every instance where the two Churches had congregations in the same community, the cause for the division could be traced to the pastor. Such was the case of Archer Dickerson in Bowling Green.

New School efforts to establish congregations in Louisville and Lexington failed. In both instances it was believed that there was ample population to support a New School church. Only in Glasgow did the New School attempt to organize a work where the Old School already occupied the community. Thus, while a somewhat positive feeling characterized the New School attitude toward the Old School, the feeling was not reciprocated, as this complaint of Dickerson indicated:

> No means, promising success, have been left unemployed, to stay our progress, to break us down. They have appealed to our POVERTY and INSINUATED offers of money.--They have appealed to our smallness, and offered us the respectability of their LARGE connexion. They have appealed to our family connexions, and sought to draw us to their Church by those delicate considerations. They have confidently predicted our speedy dissolution, and by personal and private appeals, sought to influence individuals and churches, and to detach them from us. They have watched the circumstances of our vacant congregations, and taken advantage of the death, dismissal, or absence of their ministers, to make indelicate overtures of aid in both ministers and support, in case they would change ecclesiastical relations. And we are sorry to say, these things continue to be done.[56]

The institutions of the New School Synod of Kentucky fared about the same way. Its newspaper, *The Presbyterian Sentinel*, had been established with great expectations. It finally ceased publication on 15 June 1844. Its subscription list was turned over to the *Christian Observer*. The single most ambitious institutional undertaking, however, was the seminary which it established at the Macedonia Church in Woodford County.[57]

At the 1848 meeting of synod, a committee reported regarding the possibility of conducting a seminary. The report noted that native sons who went North to study seldom returned. At the same time, northerners were not interested in coming to Kentucky. The committee thus proposed "raising up, within our bounds, a *Native Ministry*." The theological course would be under the direction of "some approved diving." Seminarians would get practical experience on the field:

> They will know how to strike the blunted consciences with the great sledge-hammer of gospel truth. Continuing to mingle with the great mass of people, they will not have

forgotten to sympathise with their habits of thinking. They will know how to wield the sword of the Spirit with great success, *because* they care less for the *polish* of the blade, than the *keenness* of the edge, and force of the blow.[58]

The "approved divine" whom synod selected was William H. King. The seminary was located adjacent to his Macedonia Church, under the umbrella of promise and enthusiasm. King, however, moved to Texas in 1851. With him went the future of the seminary. The large debt which had been encumbered remained to haunt the synod for several years. The brief existence of the school has been succinctly summed up by Robert Stuart Sanders: "It never met with much success."[59]

Two factors characterized the New School Synod of Kentucky that ultimately led to its demise--paucity of pastoral leadership and the inability of the synod as a whole to envision the missionary possibilities in the Blue Grass state. The New School as a whole viewed the South disdainfully. It was dominated ecclesiastically by the AHMS, and after 1852 the Assembly made no efforts to place missionaries in the South, leaving this policy to the AHMS. Kentucky New Schoolism thus stands as the classic instance in which the antislavery policy of the AHMS dictated the missionary activity in the South.

NOTES

1. *CO*, 24 October 1845.
2. Ibid., 8 and 15 May 1846.
3. Victor B. Howard, "The Southern Aid Society and the Slavery Controversy," *CH* 41 (1972): 214. For similar efforts by the Presbyteries of Hanover and Winchester, see *CO* 24 May 1851 and 21 May 1855.
4. *CO*, 19 May 1843.
5. Ibid., 24 and 31 October 1845.
6. Ibid., 8 November 1851.
7. Charles C. Jones is well known for his book on catechetical instruction, *A Catechism of Scripture Doctrine and Practice for Families and Sabbath-Schools Designed Also for the Oral Instruction of Coloured Persons*, 3d ed. (Philadelphia: Presbyterian Board of Publication, 1852). This monumental work was to the slave what McGuffey's *Readers* were to the white. The title indicates that it was to be used by both master and slave.

8. *CO*, 16 October 1856. The last phrase in the quotation is important: slaves could be instructed orally only, for Virginia, like many southern States, forbade teaching slaves how to read.

9. *CO*, 16 October 1856.

10. Ibid., 8 September 1855.

11. Robert Bell Woodworth, *A History of the Presbyterian Church in Winchester, Virginia, 1780-1949, Based on Official Documents* (Winchester: Pifer, 1950), p. 114.

12. *CO*, 3 August 1850.

13. Ibid., 22 October 1854.

14. Presbytery of West Tennessee [NS], MS "minutes" (9 April 1840), p. 10, PHF.

15. *CO*, 17 November 1843. By this time relations between the AHMS and the southern judicatories of the New School were quite cool, largely over the issue of slavery. The society increasingly refused to appoint missionaries to the South. At the same time it withdrew funds from the support of missionaries who labored in slave-holding areas. It was the society, not the presbytery, who indicated where a missionary would labor. Thus, some of the nuances in the resolutions passed need to be lifted out for examination.

16. D. D. Little, *History of the Presbytery of Columbia Tennessee* (Columbia: Maury Democrat, 1928), p. 16. In its first nine years the New School group that withdrew from the Old School Presbytery of West Tennessee organized six new churches and approved thirteen candidates for the ministry.

17. *CO*, 28 April 1855. The New School organized only two churches in the southern cities--Nashville and Mobile. As a result, the southern New School languished for lack of strong pulpits and insufficient funds. See Harold M. Parker, Jr., "The Urban Failure of the Southern New School Presbyterian Church," *Social Science Journal* 14 [1977]: 139-148; Parker *SSPH* (Gunnison, Colorado: B. & B. Printers, 1979), pp. 180-189.

18. Robert E. Cogswell, *Written on Many Hearts: The History of the First Presbyterian Church Shelbyville, Bedford County, Tennessee 1815-1965* (Nashville: Parthenon Press, n.d.), p. 143.

19. Ibid., p. 54.

20. Presbytery of West Tennessee [NS], MS "Minutes" (1 April 1848), p. 191.

21. Ibid. (7 October 1848), pp. 199-200.

22. *CO*, 29 July 1848. The Old School consistently held to this position until reunion in the North in 1869.

23. Synod of Mississippi [NS], MS "Minutes" (1845), pp. 1-2, Department of Archives and History, State of Mississippi, Jackson.
24. GAPC [NS], *Minutes* (1846), p. 8.
25. Victor B. Howard, "The Anti-Slavery Movement in the Presbyterian Church" (Ph. D. diss., Ohio State University, 1961), p. 115.
26. Edward D. Norris, *The Presbyterian Church New School 1837-1869: An Historical Review* (Columbus, Ohio: Champlin Press, 1905), p. 115.
27. Howard, "The Southern Aid Society," p. 214.
28. *CO*, 12 March 1853.
29. Ibid., 21 June 1844.
30. Ibid., 11 November 1854.
31. Ibid., 5 February 1853.
32. Presbytery of Newton, MS "Minutes" (29 September 1854), 2:3, PHF.
33. See note 17 above. Nashville was the other city where a new congregation was established.
34. *CO*, 1 October 1853.
35. Ibid., 26 November 1853.
36. Ibid., 10 March 1855.
37. Ibid., 15 September 1855.
38. Ibid., 22 September 1855.
39. George H. Paschal, Jr., and Judith A. Benner, *One Hundred Years of Challenge and Change: a History of the Synod of Texas of the United Presbyterian Church in the U. S. A.* (San Antonio: Trinity University Press, 1969), p. 5.
40. John B. Hill, *Presbyterianism in Missouri* (n.p.: n.p., n.d.), p. 10.
41. *CO*, 21 January 1843.
42. Ibid., 9 June 1843.
43. See Harold M. Parker, Jr., "A School of the Prophets at Maryville," *Tennessee Historical Quarterly* 34 (1975): 81; E. E. Stringfield, *Presbyterianism in the Ozarks: A History of the Work of the Various Branches of the Presbyterian Church in Southwest Missouri* (n.p.: n.p., 1909), pp. 188-190.
44. *CO*, 10 May 1844.
45. Ibid., 10 January 1845.
46. Ibid., 20 June 1845.
47. Ibid., 25 July 1845.
48. Ibid., 15 May 1846.
49. SAS, *Fifth Report* (1858), p. 22n. In 1845 Bullard had gone East to secure men and funds. He returned with ten missionaries and about $10,000 for church erection in Missouri.
50. For a history of the NS Synod of Kentucky, see Harold M. Parker, Jr., "The New School Synod of Kentucky," *Filson Club History Quarterly* 50 (1976): 52-89; idem, *SSPH*, pp. 129-166.

51. Synod of Kentucky [NS], typed MS "Minutes" (5 October 1848), p. 43, PHF.
52. *CO*, 15 November 1844; *Protestant and Herald*, 28 November 1844.
53. *CO*, 13 May 1854.
54. Ibid., 2 September 1848.
55. *Protestant and Herald*, 16 June 1842.
56. *CO*, 2 September 1848. Dickerson's immediate cause for lament stemmed from an incident in the Paducah Church, Green River Presbytery. He had fathered the church. It went Old School because it could not get a New School minister. This reflected the reluctance of northern New School clergy to take southern pulpits. See *CO*, 15 April 1848.
57. For the history of this school, see Harold M. Parker, Jr., "A New School Presbyterian Seminary in Woodford County," *Register of the Kentucky Historical Society* 74 (1976): 99-111; idem, *SSPH*, pp. 167-179.
58. *CO*, 16 December 1848.
59. Robert Stuart Sanders, *Presbyterianism in Versailles and Woodford County, Kentucky* (Louisville: Dunne Press, 1963), p. 129.

4

The New School Denomination Emerges, 1840–1857

The New School Presbyterian Church, which was composed of about 85 percent northerners, greatly influenced the southern portion. For two decades, however, the men in the South valiantly endeavored to retain their relationship with the northern majority who, they believed, had been unconstitutionally treated in their exscision from the Church without trial.

In many respects the basic spirit of the New School was more in harmony with the emerging religious attitude developing across the United States. This attitude was increasingly different from that to which the Old School adhered. Revivalism, moral reform, interdenominational cooperation, evangelical piety--these the New School emphasized. These were those characteristics that students of American church history agree were typical of the mainstream of American Protestantism in the latter two-thirds of the nineteenth century.[1] Joseph Belcher in 1856 underscored the fact that the New School brought with it "a liberal spirit, ready to conform to the spirit of the times, and to the more free institutions which were always expected in our happy land . . . ."[2]

In many ways the southern New School bathed in the wash of its northern confreres, adopting for themselves many of the characteristics of the denomination at large. At the same time, however, there was one basic issue on which they separated themselves--their position on domestic slavery.

New School congregations were frequently in bad array. Many had been only recently established. Many were still beneficiaries of the AHMS. Congregations that had remained in the Old School, on the other hand, were fairly well-to-do. Nor had the New School retained many of the institutions, for the courts awarded them to the Old School.³ Hence, the New School as a new and separate denomination was greatly sobered by those factors which had driven it out of the Old School. It was apprehensive lest the world view it as un-Presbyterian and un-Calvinistic. It quickly ceased talking about replacing the Westminster Confession of Faith with a shorter creed destitute of Calvinism.⁴ In many areas of Presbyterianism the differences between the two Churches gradually diminished. And while there was no singular attitude prevailing between the Old and New School across the country as a whole, at the same time, particularly in the North, a more irenic spirit gradually emerged. Normally, when two congregations of the respective Churches existed in the same community, the major mark of identification would be the mode of evangelism. The New School leaned more to the revivalistic technique, the Old School to its essential "one-on-one" approach.⁵

About four-ninths of the Presbyterian Church went New School. The exact figures are very difficult to arrive at for the first years, because both Churches frequently claimed not only the same congregations, but even the same presbytery! Table 4.1 shows the New School presbyteries in the slave-holding states in 1840.

Of course, not all these presbyteries were *officially* connected with the New School at that time.⁶ The three Missouri presbyteries did not enter until 1843; Charleston Union was never in the New School; and the 1840 *Minutes* are the only ones which contain any reference to a presbytery in Arkansas. The southern presbyteries were quite small in comparison to the northern ones. Union Presbytery was an exception, ranking twelfth in the nation in number of members, and sixteenth in number of ministers and churches.

As a whole, the southerners did not share the feeling of the denomination respecting slavery. Every effort was made, however, to retain the southern judicatories in the New School. The leader in this movement was Samuel A. Cox of Brooklyn. He did this for two reasons. First, he associated all abolitionism with religious infidelity. As late as 1854 he asserted that abolitionism had done more to "dechristianize" the New England pulpits than any other single factor. He also feared that the loss of the southern New School constituency would harm the national Union. He was a strong patriot who interpreted the Protestant Churches as couplings holding the Union together. In 1849 he exhorted the New School commissioners not to "weaken the bonds of Union, by following the example of our Baptist and Methodist brethren in their sectional division, North and South."[7]

TABLE 4.1   Statistics of Southern Presbyteries, 1840

Presbytery	Ministers	Churches	Members
Missouri	7	NA	NA
St. Louis	7	13	736
St. Charles	13	20	823
Winchester	7	NA	NA
Dist. of Col.	7	6	757
Hanover	8	8	292
Abingdon	7	14	574
Union	22	23	2,020
French Broad	8	16	1,292
Holston	10	13	1,109
Kingston	11	11	472
New River	5	7	337
Clinton	10	14	681
Charleston Union	21	8	788
Arkansas	8	6	239
	151	158	12,120

If homogeneity was the hallmark of the Old School, heterogeneity marked the New School. In addition to its various theological patterns, internal factors also contributed to New School heterogeneity--differences in temperament, training, and religious associations, all of which operated strongly against the development of unity, of mutual affection, of absorbing devotion to a common cause. The constant agitation against slavery in the General Assembly over the years tended to alienate the southern elements from the main course of New Schoolism. It placed the southern men in a questionable position in the region where, by that time, the issue of domestic slavery had been settled and in most areas the South had become accommodated to its existence.

One of the ways New School heterogeneity manifested itself was through abbreviated creeds. The 1855 Assembly passed a series of resolutions touching these creeds, recommending to "all the

Presbyteries to take special pains to have the book containing the Confession of Faith and form of Government of the Presbyterian Church in the United States of America, more generally circulated among the churches under their care."[8] That the Assembly appointed a committee to look into the matter of abbreviated creeds suggests a lack of harmony with respect to doctrinal views. In addition to the Hopkinsiansim taught at Maryville, there were also other minor theological aberrations in East Tennessee. Frederick A. Ross was one whose orthodoxy was frequently questioned or found questionable. When he was licensed in 1825, both he and David Nelson protested the doctrine of reprobation in the Confession of Faith. But since the Presbytery of Holston had already made up its mind that both men were to be Presbyterian preachers, this matter was simply glossed over. Although Ross regarded himself a Calvinist, there was considerable Arminianism in his theology.[9]

Nor did all New School ministers embrace New School doctrines. There were thus essentially four categories by which men were related to New School theology: Those who thoroughly accepted them, such as would be found in much of the North and in East Tennessee; those who accepted most of the new theology in some modified form; those who adopted some of the "new divinity" in part; and those in the South who rejected the system.[10]

The New School, in spite of the wide range of theological scope, did not fulfill any of the dire prognostications of its inimical critics. It failed to run headlong through the descending path of Taylorism, Arminianism, and Socinianism. Nor did it retract any of the positions laid down in the Auburn Declaration of 1837. It held fast to the assertion that Christ died for all, elect and non-elect alike. It refused to make the Cocceian "federal headship of Adam" a test for orthodoxy. It did trace the common human depravity to Adam's fall, but declined to call this sin unless it resulted in sinful acts. It asserted the natural ability of the sinner to do what God's law required of him, seeing in him only the moral inability, which consists of volutary inclination to evil.[12]

The New School trend toward a more orthodox position, in the long run, however, was not a quirk. It followed rather a basic pattern which often develops upon a division between conservatives and less conservatives. The latter group, after a schism, becomes obsessed with the desire to demonstrate its orthodoxy, even to the point of proving it, with a resulting convergence rather than divergence of philosophy and program. From 1837 onward, the New School became increasingly insistent upon proving that the Old School aspersions upon the orthodoxy of its Presbyterianism were unfounded. Further, within the New School denomination there was a growing emphasis upon Presbyterian polity and forms.[13]

Polity itself was another evidence of New School heterogeneity. It is quite clear that one of the factors which retarded New School progress as a denomination was its inharmonious posture. Its members, seeing the effects which resulted from the exscision acts, became more and more inclined to act independently in missions as a denomination. They gradually withdrew from cooperating in the AHMS and the AES. Such a turnaround, however, took several years to emerge. For the present, immediately following the exscision, the 1840 Assembly recommended the following societies as worthy of the support of New School judicatories and members: the ABCFM, AHMS, AES, ABS, ATS, and ASSU. All were denominated as affording "safe" and "convenient" channels through which the contributions of congregations could reach the purposes represented by the societies.[14]

For several years following the division, the New School demonstrated very little of that vitality and strength that had so characterized the party prior to 1837. The shock of exscision still shook the Church. Further, it undertook a drastic alteration in the function of the General Assembly: beginning in 1840 it experimented for nine years with holding the General Assembly only every third year.

Three reasons have been given for the experiment of the triennial Assemblies. For one thing, the New School party had received setbacks in the 1830s by too frequent meetings of the Assembly. The annual meetings simply did not permit agitations to die down. Further, the Congregational elements in the Church did not accept the idea of a supreme court over the entire Church. Finally, the cost of the annual meeting was greater than the results which issued from it.[15] The altered structure gave the synods, rather than the Assembly, the final appellate jurisdiction in the denomination. This left the latter with little other function than that of an advisory association.[16] Between Assemblies, a comittee ad interim of five ministers, five elders, and the three Assembly Clerks was appointed to do certain house-keeping chores.

During this period of triennial Assemblies, the New School began meeting outside of Philadelphia. In 1846 it convened in Cincinnati--the first time the General Assembly had ever met outside Pennsylvania. In 1847 there was an Adjourned Meeting of the General Assembly--the first and only such meeting in the history of American Presbyterianism. The Presbytery of West Tennessee protested this meeting, and cried for a return to the annual meeting of the Assembly and restoration of its original appellate power.[17] Yet this 1847 meeting became, in the minds of later historians, a turning-point in New School development. It was not so much for what it accomplished as to what it contributed to the process of accomplishment. It was indicative of the "new spirit which was beginning to arise in the body and prophetic of its future advancement."[18]

The period of the triennial Assemblies found the Church off center. It has been pronounced "an inconsiderate and sad mistake," which produced considerable dissatisfaction. Further, the experiment lent itself to Old School assertions that the New School was not composed of sound Presbyterians.[19] Another critic in later years disclaimed it,

> The effect especially at so critical a period, may be easily supposed. It left the body at best a very weak and inadequate bond of union, and at a time when the most constant vigilance, concert, and co-operation were essential to safety, with no provision . . . for the slightest common consultation upon its interests and dangers.[20]

It was during the years of triennialism that the New School began to stir into a denomination. Such awareness began to develop as the New School became increasingly conscious that the AHMS was not sufficient to meet the needs of the rapidly expanding Presbyterian Church on the frontier. In 1847, the General Assembly resolved: "Let every pastor, and *session* and *church*, feel that they are a missionary body, established in the midst of the most important field in the world, and the object of their vocation is to lead all around them to Christ."[21] Such expression was very close to that of the Old School, which had declared that every member of the Church is involved in the total mission of the Church. The Western Missionary Society had been organized by the Presbytery of Pittsburgh in 1802. It pointed out that missions were no longer an option to the Church, but was the main business of the Church in which every member was involved.

Edward D. Morris attributed the denominational awakening to the sense of unity which had developed among the New School men and courts: "The preliminary questions respecting its doctrinal foundations, its ecclesiastical principles and policy, its right to exist, its providential sphere and mission, had for the most part been answered."[22] The number of members and wealth and general ability of the Assembly permitted it to conduct missions at home and abroad, independently of sister denominations.

Sidney E. Mead has pointed out that the denomination is essentially purposive, "voluntary association of like-minded individuals, who are united on the basis of common beliefs for the purpose of accomplishing tangible and defined objectives."[23] The New School had a psychological matrix which fit the denominational model. It was another five years, however, before the functional aspects of denominationalism swept across the New School. the 1852 Spring Meeting of Holston Presbytery's "Narrative of the State of Religion" contained the following statement:

> There is a growth of denominational spirit in our Presbytery, and a hope that the General Assembly will cherish and encourage this growth by organizing a Doctrinal Tract Society, and a Board of Publication. Our love for the American Tract Society and the American Home Missionary Society is strengthening, rather than diminishing, but we wish an appendix to them both.[24]

As early as 1844, "Adelphos" had written a letter in which he commented on the needs of western churches and how eastern congregations might do something for them. At the same time he pointed to the efforts being made by the Old School, and how similar agencies might be erected in the New School. He stated,

> In this section of the church, a plan will, no doubt, be adopted to promote the object--and I earnestly hope that the churches connected with the Constitutional Assembly will not be behind their brethren in their liberality and effort in planting Christian sanctuaries among the destitute in every portion of our country.[25]

The suggestion was a new concept for the New School to ponder. Up to that time the idea of

Church-dominated agencies or boards as tools to carry the mission of the Church had been avoided. It would be some time before a "plan" would be adopted.

Two movements were taking place concurrently in the New School: the growth of a spirit of denominationalism and a declining interest in voluntary agencies that lay outside the control of ecclesiastical bodies. The division of 1837 fostered both movements. The refusal of the Old School to support voluntary agencies financially meant a proscription of them. Many lesser societies, no longer able to claim interdenominational sanction for their operations, speedily collapsed. By 1839 some of the larger ones were experiencing serious financial difficulties.[26] These voluntary agencies had been erected upon the cooperative support of several religious traditions. They became increasingly apprehensive of the growth of denominational self-consciousness.[27] Although they had ignored the emerging rise of denominational boards, they now were entering the fray to slow down or halt the process. They insisted on their own neutrality while at the same time discouraging their missionaries from any activity that would intensify sectarianism. Their attempts to prevent the growth of denominationalism were ineffective. Some of them became unofficial agencies of the Congregational Church.[28] The precipitating factor, however, that worked against the voluntary societies was the Old School-New School controversy.[29]

Within less than a decade after the 1837 Division, the New School, long an advocate of "cooperation" as the cornerstone for missionary operations, began to experience friction in cooperating with the Congregationalists. The reason was quite simple: the Congregationalists were themselves beginning to experience denominational self-consciousness. They were less anxious to cooperate with other developments. This new feeling led in 1852 to their repudiation of the Plan of Union of 1802.

The New School Assembly of 1852 officially ended the New School's involvement in cooperative ventures on the highest levels. It witnessed the establishment of some of its own instruments for carrying out the mission of the Church. In the debate over forming a Committee on Church Extension, Philemon H. Fowler of Utica, New York, cogently argued for the establishment of a Church-controlled agency to administer the home mission program:

> We mean, by church extension, the spreading of Constitutional Presbyterianism, in contradis-

The New School Denomination Emerges

tinction to all other church organizations. The circumstances that called for the co-operative agency no longer exist . . . . We do not want a sectarian spirit among us, but we do need more of a purely Constitutional Presbyterian feeling and action.[30]

The difficulty that confronted the New School was its lack of experience or philosophy in conducting missions within an ecclesiastical framework. It was a functional necessity, rather than any theology of missions, that forced the Church to form its own ecclesiastically-supported missionary work. Further, as the Congregationalists began to develop their own denomination, while at the same time utilizing the cooperative voluntary missionary associations to further their own denominational aims, the New School had developed enough denominational awareness to respond to such actions. Thus, as Earl A. MacCormac concluded, "Their desire to further their own denomination led the New School Presbyterians to repudiate their earlier missionary theory."[31] The New School was finally forced by practical needs to accept the same principles of denominational control over missionary operations that the Old School had been practicing.

One of the first Church-controlled agencies to be established was the Permanent Committee on Education for the Ministry. Its purpose was to serve as the general instrumentality for promoting the cause of ministerial education.[32] Each presbytery was urged to appoint a standing committee on the subject. The theological seminaries, notwithstanding their independent mode of operation, were endorsed and encouraged to make full reports of their students and their general condition to the Assembly.

A second committee organized by the 1852 Assembly was the Publication Committee, purpose of which was to "promote the diffusion of those truths which distinguish us as a Church . . . ." Its duty was to "superintend the publication of a series of tracts explanatory of the doctrines, government, and missionary policy of the Presbyterian Church . . . ."[33] Five years later property was secured and a bookstore was opened in Philadelphia.

Without question, however, the most significant permanent agency established in 1852 was the Committee on Church Extension.[34] As early as 1844 the difficult condition in Missouri had been discussed by Amasa Converse in the columns of the *Christian Observer*:

> The difficulties of infant churches in that region, are probably not appreciated. We need a Church-extension fund--to be applied in such cases, to aid those who are making efforts in the spirit of an enlarged liberality, to rear places of worship in the new settlements of the West.[35]

In 1847, the Assembly established a Standing Committee on Home Missions. In 1850, the retiring moderator, Philip Courtland Hay, used home missions as the theme of his sermon. As one result, the Assembly adopted a series of strong resolutions. They suggested that in the future organization of churches and supplying missionaries to destitute regions, the presbyteries could act by themselves as well as through the AHMS.[36]

The Assembly recommended that each presbytery appoint an itinerant missionary within its bounds. Each synod was urged to appoint such a missionary, also. He would serve as a traveling evangelist, explore destitute fields, prepare the way for the formation of new churches by presbyteries, seek ministers to take charge of them, assist and direct the erection of houses of worship, "and in all other suitable ways . . . promote the works of Church Extension."[37]

The immediate problem that confronted the Church in making this momentous step was how it would affect the relations with the AHMS, which by now was essentially a joint New School-Congregational organization. The Assembly had set up its Committee on Church Extension to provide for those exceptional cases which could not be met under the general rules of the Society. At the same time it was saying, "We have no wish to divert funds from the Home Missionary Society." It requested the AHMS to "arrange its system of appropriations so that applications made by any Presbytery or its churches should not require the official sanction of any of the Society's agents."[38] A few months later, however, the Congregationalists revoked the Plan of Union. In 1861 the New School severed all connections with the AHMS, because the claims of the Church Extension Committee presented to the churches were met with "annually growing sympathy."[39]

So drastic was the change that had come into New School thinking by the establishment of the Standing Committees that Amasa Converse felt it necessary to defend the Assembly's legislation: "These are not new measures. They do not contemplate the erection of a great central power to control the church."⁴⁰

The role of the AHMS was unquestionably a definite factor in the New School's decision to launch its own Church Extension Committee. The Old School apologete, Samuel J. Baird, deemed the AHMS "the most formidable machine for the subversion of Presbyterianism, that was ever invented . . . ."⁴¹ Although the Society was not a Church, its ecclesiasticism was revealed in its managerial operations. The Society, for instance, made the final decision concerning which requests for aid would be granted. The Secretary and agents wielded immense power. Irrespective of how the Society might urge proper relations to local church bodies, such as the presbytery, missionaries were still funded by the Society, reported by the Society, and gave their first loyalty to the Society.⁴² The AHMS even counseled young missionaries to consider the West and to receive Presbyterian ordination.⁴³

The AHMS, however, counselled none of its missionaries to go South. In 1857 it cut off funds to churches that had slaveholders in their membership. The only source for financial support for the New School churches was the Church Extension Committee. The number of missionaries in the South supported by the AHMS had declined each year. In 1841 eight Directors and the Vice President of the Society came from the South. In 1842, six; in 1845, three; in 1846, two--Bullard from Missouri and Eliphat Gilbert from Delaware. In 1845--a typical year--the AHMS supported a total of 943 missionaries. Of these there were only thirty-six assigned to the South, and a score of them were in Missouri. None labored in the Carolinas, Georgia, or Mississippi. In that same year, New York had 211 missionaries and Illinois ninety-eight.

The AHMS argued that it was very difficult to persuade missionaries to consider the South, since most of the men came from the North or the Northeast. But this reasoning failed to satisfy William F. King of Kentucky, who protested, "If Paul had declined to go into any provence [sic] of the Roman Empire until slavery was abolished . . . he would probably have had half as many stars in that crown . . . ."⁴⁴ The missionaries probably did have apprehensions about being received in the slave region. Thus, when offered a choice between going to Arkansas (where only a total of nine labored in the period 1838-1852) or Michigan, they would choose the latter. The officers of the AHMS claimed that it cost more to operate in the South. Further, they stated that the results were more negligible than to undertake the same effort in the free states of the West. The more compact settlements of the Northwest, with its numerous towns and villages, provided better opportunity for the creation of churches that gave promise of attaining self-sufficiency.[45]

There was also a sociological factor: the missionaries had a preference for work among people of like experience rather than among those who had been reared in a different social or religious climate.[46] Table 4.2 reflects the attitude of the AHMS toward the South, as well as the alleged preferences of the missionaries. In 1855, of the total of thirty-nine missionaries in the states of Delaware, Virginia, Tennessee, Kentucky, Georgia, and Missouri, only twenty-one were New School, and of these eleven were in Missouri.[47]

TABLE 4.2 Missionaries of the AHMS Geographically Distributed

Area	1849-50	1850-51	1851-52	1852-53
New England	301	311	305	313
Middle States	228	224	213	215
Southern States	15	15	14	12
Western States	488	515	533	547
	1,032	1,065	1,065	1,087

The Society's evolution toward an antislavery stance took a decade and a half. In 1838, the Corresponding Secretary wrote that there was nothing in the Society's rules of operation or in its principles that touched on abolitionism. In 1844, the Presbyterian layman, Arthur Tappan, raised several questions about the relation of the Society to the institution of slavery. In reply, Milton Badger responded that the Society had never denied assistance to a church on the grounds that its members held slaves, nor had any church been denied aid because its members opposed slavery.[48] The Society claimed it had no jurisdiction over church members.[49]

In 1850 the society insisted that southern missionaries--all fifteen of them--should be allowed to preach against slavery if they felt it their duty. Three years later it withheld commissions from slaveholders, refusing to deny, at the same time, Christian status to them. However, in December 1856 the Executive Committee adopted a rule that denied the Executive Committee adopted a rule that denied aid to churches that contained slaveholding members, unless it could be proved that the relationship was maintained for the benefit of the slave.[50] In the North, even the numerous resolutions passed by presbyteries, synods, and other religious associations had been urged upon the memberships by appointees of the AHMS.[51]

In 1853 the Society sent questionnaires to its southern missionaries. They were designed to furnish information to the Executive Committee relative to difficulties encountered on the field. The replies indicated that the missionaries in the South were becoming increasingly embarrassed by the presence of slaveholding church members in their fields. They further commented that their usefulness was being impaired by the preaching of antislavery sermons.[52]

The survey had an immediate effect on the New School, and in that year it altered its policy toward slavery. Inasmuch as so many of the New School ministers in the North were dependent on the AHMS for financial support, this condition was a powerful incentive for the New School to adopt antislavery attitudes. Hence the action of the Executive Committee in December 1856 was simply the conclusion to a lengthy turn around in the Society's position touching Christian slaveholding. The recommendation of the Executive Committee was approved in 1857. So far as the southern wing of the New School was concerned, only Missouri was vitally affected by the resolution, because the Society for several years had not been sending any missionaries South.[53]

There can be no question but that many of the Society's contributors in the North simply refused to subsidize churches that had slaveholders in their membership. The Synod of the Free Presbyterian Church, organized in 1847 from Old and New School elements in Ohio and adjacent areas, was formed because its founding fathers were concerned that the New School was dragging its feet on the issue of excluding slaveholders from the Church. At its annual meeting in 1858, the Free Presbyterian Church passed a resolution addressed to the New School Assembly urging that body to make slaveholding a term of exclusion. It further proposed ecclesiastical union in case the Assembly should do so.[54] Another factor that contributed to the Society's action was the growing tendency in the South to defend slavery on principle and justify it by Scripture.[55]

The legislation of the New School in 1850 and 1853 advanced the Church's position toward an antislavery stance, which finally led to the withdrawal of the southern judicatories in 1857.[56] In 1846 a group of New School concerned persons and Congregationalists organized the American Missionary Association on principles both evangelical and abolitionist. From its inception, the AMA cut deeply into the income of the AHMS. By 1855 its income reached the $50,000 plateau.[57]

A greater financial threat to the AHMS, however, came from the Southern Aid Society. This organization was formed in 1853 for the avowed purpose of assisting missionaries in the South, the area from which the AHMS had all but practically abandoned. In its Constitution and first Address to the Christian Public, the Society stated its purpose and rationale:

> We concede that the New School Presbyterian and Congregational Churches at the South, are far less numerous than at the North. If, however, this is a valid reason in the judgment of others for withholding aid from the South, it is not so ours. We would "send the Gospel to the *destitute* within the United States," as well as "assist congregations that are unable to support the Gospel ministry."[58]

Thus, the AHMS, which had experienced almost continuous financial growth during the years 1837 to 1853, now began to feel the inroads of two other missionary societies, plus a growing tension in the New School. The years 1854 to 1856 saw a decline in the AHMS's receipts. The decision, then, to forsake any support of slaveholding congregations simply extricated the Society from a quagmire of indecision. Nevertheless, in spite of the New School's erecting a Committee on Church Extension, the Assembly endeavored to retain a favorable relation with the AHMS. It did provide, however, that each presbytery should retain the right to solicit applications for assistance independently of the Society's agents. This tenuous relationship continued to be stretched until 1861. In that year the New School completely severed its relationship with the AHMS.

Closely related to the establishment of the Church Extension Committee was the establishment of the Church Erection Fund in 1854.[59] As early as 1845, the Synod of Missouri, under the aegis of Artemas Bullard, laid plans to raise $10,000 to assist weak congregations to erect houses of worship. Bullard promised that

> we as a Synod do hereby pledge ourselves to the churches in the East, that if the sum of $10,000 is now raised for this object, we will never give our assent for further applications to be made for this purpose to the East, by churches in our connexion."60

The funds raised would be loaned to churches for building purposes without interest.

The goal of the Assembly of 1854 was to raise $100,000. The funds were also to be loaned out on a revolving-fund basis for erecting churches in destitute areas. The funds were available to synods on a percentage basis. The southern synods would receive the following percentages: Kentucky, 2.5; Missouri, 2.5; Mississippi, 2.5; Tennessee, 4; Virginia, 3.5; and West Tennessee, 3.61

The emerging New School denominationalism was hailed by many as a step forward. Holston Presbytery noted that "our branch of the Church of Christ has been remiss in denominational efforts," but with the passage of the legislation which established the Church Erection Fund, "we are, in the providence of God [,] called upon to rise and build up our Zion, and go forward in the strength of our Master."62 Even Old School scions were impressed with the New School's emergence from the cocoon of voluntary associations into the flight of a true denominationally-oriented ecclesiasticism.63

Nevertheless, although the denominational emergence was of prime importance, its tardy development had done irreparable harm to the New School Church. For over fifteen years it had failed to adapt its efforts to the changing economic and political conditions of the country in which it labored.64

There was considerable interest in the South over the shift of emphasis in the Church. The southern judicatories had suffered at the hands of the AHMS and similar voluntary agencies which viewed the South as some sort of a pariah. The adoption of a minute by the Presbytery of Harmony in 1857, just after that fateful Assembly from which the southern judicatories withdrew, is indicative of the feelings of perhaps too many southerners, feelings that had been nurtured through a score of years:

> One great cause of the limited contributions of the South to the Church Erection Fund, to the

$30,000 fund, to the Church Extension Committee, and to the American Home Missionary Society, has been the thought that these were all trusted to the hands of those who intended, ere long, to cast us off--that the ultimate end of all these agencies was the benefit of a region of country supposedly to be more highly favored than our own.[65]

During the score of years in which the New School existed prior to the southern withdrawal of 1857, the General Assembly never once met in the South, never once elected a man from the South as Moderator, never once appointed a southerner as chairman of any important committee of the Assembly. If there was mistrust, as the Presbytery of Harmony suggested, one must seek the reasons.

NOTES

1. So George M. Marsden, *The Evangelical Mind and the New School Presbyterian Experience: A Case Study of Thought and Theology in Nineteenth-Century America*, Yale Publications in American Studies, 20 (New Haven and London: Yale University Press, 1970), pp. x-xi. However, in his study Marsden scarcely gives even lip service to the New School in the South.

2. Joseph Belcher, *The Religious Denominations in the United States: Their History, Doctrine, Government and Statistics. With a Preliminary Sketch of Judaism, Paganism and Mohammedanism* (Philadelphia: John E. Potter; Indianapolis: Stearns & Spicer; Memphis: J. G. Clarke, 1856), p. 668.

3. Johnathan F. Stearns, "Historical Review of the Church (New School Branch) Since 1837," in *Presbyterian Reunion: A Memorial Volume, 1837-1871* (New York: DeWitt C. Lent; Chicago: Van Nortwick & Sparks, 1870), p. 58; Clifford M. Drury, *Presbyterian Panorama: One Hundred and Fifty Years of National Missions History* (Philadelphia: Board of Christian Education, Presbyterian Church in the United States of America, 1952), p. 106.

4. Thomas Cary Johnson, "A Brief Sketch of the United Synod of the Presbyterian Church in the United States of America," *Papers of the American Society of Church History*, 1st ser. 8 (1897): 11.

5. Jacob Harris Patton, *A Popular History of the Presbyterian Church in the United States of America* (New York: R. S. Mighill, 1900), p. 417. Although Patton sets forth the claim that the New

School brought in more members through preaching, the comparative growth of the two Churches does not support it.

6. "The figures in the first series are probably excessive, many churches and ministers being counted who never really cast in their lot with the excluded party," Edward D. Morris, *The Presbyterian Church New School 1837-1869: An Historical Review* (Columbus, Ohio: Champlin Press, 1905), p. 112.

7. Quoted in Dwyn Mecklin Mounger, "Samuel Hanson Cox: Anti-Catholic, Anti-Anglican, Anti-Congregational Ecumenist," *JPH* 55 (1977): 357.

8. GAPCUSA [NS], *Minutes* (1838), pp. 655-656.

9. Frederick A. Ross, "Autobiography of the Rev. F. A. Ross, D. D., in Letters to a Lady of Knoxville, East Tennessee including an account of his life in Virginia and Huntsville to the time of his death in 1883," p. 124, copied from the MS in the Huntsville Public Library, Huntsville, Alabama; Johnson, "United Synod," pp. 28-29.

10. James Wood, *Old and New Theology: or, The Doctrinal Differences Which Have Agitated and Divided the Presbyterian Church*, new and enlarged ed. (Philadelphia: Presbyterian Board of Publication, 1855), p. 20; Johnson, "United Synod," p. 10.

11. For the complete text of the Auburn Declaration of 1837, see *Minutes of the Auburn Convention Held August 17, 1837, To Deliberate upon the Doings of the Last General Assembly in Relation to the Synods of Western Reserve, Utica, Geneva and Genesee and the Third Presbytery of Philadelphia* (Auburn: The Convention, 1837).

12. Robert Ellis Thompson, *A History of the Presbyterian Churches in the United States*, 2nd ed., American Church History Series, vol. 6 (New York: Charles Scribner's Sons, 1900), pp. 138-139.

13. L. G. Vander Velde, "The Synod of Michigan and Movements for Social Reform," *CH* 5 (1936): 58; idem, *The Presbyterian Churches and the Federal Union 1860-1869*, Harvard History Series, no. 33 (Cambridge: Harvard University Press; London: Humphrey Milford, 1932), pp. 481-484.

14. GAPCUSA [NS], *Minutes* (1840), p. 21.

15. Geo[rge] P. Hays, *Presbyterians: A Popular Narrative of Their Origin, Progress, Doctrines, and Achievements* (New York: J. A. Hill, 1892), pp. 203-204. Patton (*Popular History of the Presbyterian Church*, p. 477) saw that the real cause lay with the Congregational element in the New School body: "These respective changes can be traced directly to the influence of Congregationalism, that had been

16. Marsden,*The New School Experience*. 118; GAPCUSA [NS], *Minutes* (1840), pp. 16-17.

17. Presbytery of West Tennessee [NS], MS "Minutes" (3 April 1847) pp. 176-177, PHF.

18. Stearns, "Historical Review of the NS Church," p. 65.

19. *Historical Sketch of the Synod of Ohio (N. S.) From 1836 to 1868* (Cincinnati: Elm Street Printing Co., 1870), p. 10.

20. Stearns, "Historical Review of the NS Church," p. 59.

21. GAPCUSA [NS], *Minutes* (1847), p. 151. Marsden (*New School Presbyterian Experience*, pp. 128-141) presented a splendid development of the "Triumph of Denominationalism" in the New School. It is especially valuable for its contribution in the area of New School theology, which permitted the Church to stand up against both the Old School as well as the Congregationalists within the New School.

22. Morris,*Presbyterian Church New School*, p. 114.

23. Sidney E. Mead, "Denominationalism: The Shape of Protestantism in America," *CH* 23 (1954): 291, 295-320; reprinted in idem, *The Lively Experiment: The Shaping of Christianity in America* (New York and Evanston: Harper & Row, 1963), pp. 103-133. He lists six characteristics of a denomination. Elwyn Smith ("The Forming of a Modern American Denomination," *CH* 31 [1962]: 97) pointed out that a sect becomes a denomination that combines "the separative and the unitive spirit of American Christianity."

24. Holston Presbytery [NS], "Minutes" (11 April 1852), p. 264, PHF. In the "Minutes" two years later (17 April 1854, pp. 321-322), Presbytery expressed appreciation for the New School-sponsored *Presbyterian Quarterly Review*, a journal of theology and contemporary developments. It also noted that several of the families in the Presbytery were subscribing to the *Christian Observer*. Although the *Observer* was not supported by the denomination, it was nevertheless very supportive of what the New School was doing.

25. *CO*, 7 June 1844.

26. Gilbert Hobbs Barnes, *The Antislavery Impulse 1830-1844* (1933; reprint, Gloucester, Massachusetts: Peter Smith, 1957), pp. 162-163.

27. The great apologist for voluntary societies was Absalom Peters, *A Plea for Voluntary Societies, and a Defence of the Decisions of the General Assembly of 1836, Against the Strictures of the Princeton Reviewers and Others* (New York: John S. Taylor, 1837). A Presbyterian, Peters also served as secretary of the AHMS. Earlier, the professor of Church history at Princeton, Samuel Miller, had written *Letters to Presbyterians, on the Present Crisis in the Presbyterian Church in the United States* (Philadelphia: Anthony Findley, 1833), in which he had supported the boards of the Church in Old School-fashion.

28 Samuel C. Pearson, Jr., "From Church to Denomination: American Congregationalism in the Nineteenth Century," *CH* 38 (1969): 87.

29. Winthrop Hudson, *American Protestantism*, The Chicago History of American Civilization Series (Chicago and London: University of Chicago Press, 1961), pp. 107-108.

30. CO, 5 June 1852. See also issue of 12 June 1852.

31. Earl R. MacCormac, "The Development of Presbyterian Missionary Organizations: 1790-1870," *JPH* 43 (1965): 169.

32. GAPCUSA [NS], *Minutes* (1852), p. 170; Morris, *Presbyterian Church New School*, pp. 124-125.

33. For the events leading up to the establishment of the Committee, see William E. Moore, *A New Digest of the Acts and Deliverances of the General Assembly of the Presbyterian Church in the United States of America. Compiled by the Order and Authority of the General Assembly* (Philadelphia: Presbyterian Publication Committee; New York: A. D. F. Randolph, 1861), p. 394. For the action of the Assembly, see GAPCUSA [NS], *Minutes* (1852), p. 176. The *Calvinistic Magazine* 1 (November 1846): 292 carried an abstract of the minutes of the 1846 meeting of the Synod of Tennessee. This was the first plea for such a committee.

34. GAPCUSA [NS], *Minutes* (1852), p. 172.

35. CO, 26 July 1844.

36. GAPCUSA [NS], *Minutes*(1850), p. 315. See also Morris, *Presbyterian Church New School*, pp. 116-117.

37. GAPCUSA [NS], *Minutes* (1852), pp. 171-172.

38. Ibid., p. 171; Stearns, "Historical Review of the NS Church," p. 75; Drury, *Presbyterian Panorama*, pp. 125-126.

39. William O. Brackett, Jr., "The Rise and Development of the New School Presbyterian Church in the U. S. A. to the Reunion of 1869," *JPHS* 13

(1928): 170. The increased giving to the four major areas of denominational benevolences is seen in this chart:

Contributions to New School Benevolent Programs, 1853-1858

Year	Domestic Missions	Foreign Missions	Education	Publication
1853	62,058	53,143	28,922	34,535
1854	101,555	57,614	96,435	32,995
1855	76,871	63,693	37,710	48,322
1856	96,052	55,359	48,921	46,033
1857	96,308	65,767	68,747	68,148
1858	88,439	64,536	55,651	60,592

Statistical table taken from Herman C. Weber, *Presbyterian Statistics: Through One Hundred Years 1826-1926* ([Philadelphia]: General Council, Presbyterian Church in the U. S. A., 1927), p. 20.

40 *CO*, 12 June 1852.

41. Samuel J. Baird, *A History of the New School and of the Questions Involved in the Disruption of the Presbyterian Church in 1838* (Philadelphia: Claxton, Remsen, & Haffelfinger, 1868), p. 263.

42. L. C. Rudolph, *Hoosier Zion: The Presbyterians in Early Indiana* (New Haven and London: Yale University Press, 1963), p. 58.

43. Frederick Irving Kuhns, *The American Home Missionary Society in Relation to the Antislavery Controversy in the Old Northwest* (Billings, Montana: n.p., 1959), p. 1.

44. Cited in Colin Brummitt Goodykoontz, *Home Missions on the American Frontier: With Particular Reference to the American Home Missionary Society* (Caldwell, Idaho: Caxton Printers, 1939), p. 229.

45. Ibid., citing Absalom Peters, *Home Missionary* 5 (1833): 198-199.

46. Clifton E. Olmstead, *History of Religion in the United States* (Englewood Cliffs, New Jersey: Prentice-Hall, 1960), p. 268.

47. Based on statistics in AHMS, *Twenty-ninth Annual Report* (1855), pp. 98-102.

48. This was essentially the position of the American Baptist Home Missionary Society in the mid-1840s; John R. Mckivigan, "The American Baptist Free Missionary Society: Abolitionist Reaction to the

1845 Baptist Schism," *Foundations* 21 (1978): 343-345.

49. "When [the New School] failed to provide for the application of discipline to cases involving slave-holding members, the Society did not complain. Rather, the Society threw the entire responsibility for disciplining such cases on the presbyteries and synods concerned," Frederick Kuhns, "Slavery and Missions in the Old Northwest," *JPHS* 24 (1946): 207.

50. Andrew E. Murray, *Presbyterians and the Negro--A History* (Philadelphia: Presbyterian Historical Society, 1966), p. 113. The text of the resolution adopted by the AHMS was: "Resolved, That in disbursement of the funds committed to their trust, the Committee will not grant aid to churches containing slaveholding members, unless evidence be furnished that the relation is such as, in the judgment of the Committee, is justifiable, for the time being, in the peculiar circumstances in which it exists"; AHMS, *Thirty-first Annual Report* (1857), p. 129.

51. Kuhns, *American Home Missionary Society*, pp. 1, 13, 22; idem, "Slavery and Missions," p. 205.

52. Kuhns, "Slavery and Missions," p. 207.

53. Goodykoontz, *Home Missions on the American Frontier*, p. 292.

54. *Presbyterian Historical Almanac and Annual Remembrancer* 1 (1859): 228. For brief accounts of this movement, see Murray, *Presbyterians and the Negro*, pp. 118-126; and John F. Lyons, "The Attitude of Presbyterians in Ohio, Indiana and Illinois, toward Slavery, 1825-1861," *JPHS* 11 (1921): 70-71, 81-82.

55. The first effort to defend the institution of southern slavery on scriptural grounds was James Smylie, *A Reply of a Letter from the Presbytery of Chillicothe, to the Presbytery of Mississippi, on the Subject of Slavery* (Woodville, Mississippi: Wm. A. Norris and Co., 1836). Among the most radical books published on the subject was that of Frederick A. Ross, *Slavery Ordained of God* (Philadelphia: J. B. Lippincott, 1859). The best review of the southern defense of slavery is William Sumner Jenkins, *Pro-Slavery Thought in the Old South* (1935; reprinted Gloucester, Massachusetts: Peter Smith, 1960). For a collection of representative documents on the proslavery position, see Drew Gilpin Faust, ed., *The Ideology of Slavery: Proslavery Thought in the Antebellum South, 1830-1860*, Library of Southern Civilization (Baton Rouge: Louisiana State University, 1981).

56. Clifford S. Griffin, "The Abolitionists and the Benevolent Societies, 1831-1861," *Journal of Negro History* 44 (1959): 201-202; Victor B. Howard, "The Anti-Slavery Movement in the Presbyterian Church, 1835-1861" (Ph.D. diss., Ohio State University, 1961), p. 237.

57. Griffin, "Abolitionists and Benevolent Societies," p. 204.

58. *Southern Aid Society: And Its Constitution, and Address to the Christian Public, Together with Some Notice of the Convention which Resulted in its Formation, and Extracts from its Correspondence* (New York: Day Book Female Typesetting, 1854), p. 11. The cited quotation is from the AHMS constitution.

59. GAPCUSA [NS], *Minutes* (1855), pp. 493-498; Moore, *Digest*, pp. 375-393.

60. *CO*, 13 June 1845.

61. Just how "destitute" a region could be was not determined from the percentages given each synod. The goal of $100,000 was quickly reached.

62. Holston Presbytery [NS], MS "Minutes" (25 September 1855), p. 362.

63. Wood, *Old and New Theology*, pp. 248-249. See also Thompson, *Presbyterian Churches*, p. 138.

64. Brackett, "Rise and Development of the New School," p. 170.

65. Quoted in *CO*, 13 August 1857.

5
The Southern New School Develops

At its 1839 Assembly, the New School received several overtures relating to the issue of slavery. It simply referred the issue to the synods and presbyteries, "leaving it to them to take such order thereon as in their judgment will be most judicious, and adapted to remove the evil." The Assembly recognized that it was composed "of members from different portions of our extended country, who honestly differ in opinion, as well as in regard to the propriety of the nature of the ecclesiastical action desired in the case . . . ."[1] The following year the Assembly postponed any action on slavery indefinitely.[2] With this assurance thus far that any discussion on domestic slavery would never reach the floor of the General Assembly, the southern wing of the New School rested in the confidence that the fate of the issue was in their hands.

After the 1840 meeting of the General Assembly, the New School went to the triennial meetings. Coupled with this ecclesiastical action were the efforts of such men as Brooklyn's Samuel H. Cox, who made every effort possible to retain the southern judicatories in the New School. Their efforts were made in spite of the spate of resolutions sent up to the Assembly that treated the institution of slavery. The Cassville Convention of 1840 had convincingly expressed the southern axiom regarding the Church and slavery: the issue belonged not in courts ecclesiastical, but political. Thus was affirmed the doctrine of the spirituality of the Church, a position that both the southern New and Old Schools held to most tenaciously.

It was not only slavery which the South treated apolitically. The entire gamut of social issues was similarly viewed: "Shall we end with abolitionism, or go like many others to 'war,' 'woman's rights,' 'chartism,' &c? Some have swept the whole circle. Where will those who sneer at conservatism permit us to *stop* dividing the Church?"[3] On a more pragamtic note, an 1855 appeal for missionaries in Missouri and Kansas pointed out the required qualifications for those who would labor on the frontier:

> We want men, of no political or party stripe . . . men who will let these exciting topics *entirely alone* --who will neither speculate in land or politics, or slavery--who will occupy neutral gound upon this last question--only as they may use the sentiments of Paul on giving instructions to both master and slave, husband and wife, parents and children.[4]

The issue of slavery loomed most important, for the institution thoroughly dominated the South's entire life and thought. It was largely responsible for the migrations that occurred in the South, as land, worn out from farming, forced cotton-growers to seek the unspoiled black soil of Alabama and Mississippi,[5] spilling over in the following years into Texas. The migrant plantation-seekers not only brought along with them the commodity of cotton-growing, but their philosophical concepts as well.[6]

Among those caught in the problem of migration were the southeastern Indians who were forced to leave their lands and move to Arkansas and Oklahoma. Missionaries to the Indians were under the support and supervision of the ABCFM, the "foreign missions" arm of the voluntary societies. Many of the same thoughts that obtained for the AHMS obtained for the ABCFM.

The Indians, particularly the Cherokees and Choctaws, held slaves.[7] From the beginning, the stand of the ABCFM was opposition to slavery. It was unable, however, to declare itself against slavery any more than against any other evil.[8] Such a position could hardly be maintained as the decade of the 1840s progressed, for two factions splintered over the issue. On the one hand, the abolitionists were becoming increasingly strident, more uncompromising with the passage of the year. They sought to make the ABCFM their advocate. On the other hand were the missionaries and their converts, who were loyal church members. The former pleaded that the Board, in allowing itself to become a court of appeal, was disrupting itself, endeavoring to answer questions which lay outside its province. The missionaries were intent on bringing the heathen into the Christian realm. But bringing up the slavery issue, they contended, handicapped them in their efforts. After all, the Indians had learned slavery from their white Christian neighbors. In addition, numerous whites had intermarried with the Indians, bringing their slaves with them into the Indian community.

With Old School support withdrawn, the first memorial touching slavery was presented in 1840 to the Annual Meeting of the ABCFM. New York clergy remonstrated against solicitation of gifts from slaveholders or from persons residing in slaveholding states. The next year a similar resolution was presented by New Hampshire ministers. The purpose of these resolutions was to challenge the board to clarify its ambiguous position toward slavery, for accepting funds derived from slave labor was viewed as tantamount to supporting the institution itself.[9]

By 1842 there arose threats of the formation of another missionary society, which would be based on an antislavery platform. In 1846 the AMA, laboring in both home as well as in foreign missions, was founded. It was designed to be an effective protest against what its New England organizers, rabid abolitionists, deplored as a timid and compromising attitude on the part of both the AHMS and the ABCFM. The organization of the AMA came after two years had been spent by the ABCFM in grappling with the question: Is slavery a sin?

In 1845, the board's committee which had been appointed to study the problem made its report. The report was adopted and contained the following salient points:

1. In preaching and administering discipline, we must be governed by the instruction of Christ and the Apostles.
2. The primary purpose of our labors is to bring men to the knowledge of the Saviour, and to this the efforts of all connected with the Board should be constantly directed.
3. The ordinances of Baptism and the Lord's Supper are to be administered to all who give evidence of a change of heart, and of repentance towards God and faith in Christ.
4. The *missionaries* are the rightful and exclusive judges of what constitutes a claim to church membership.

> 5. The missionaries should give such instruction as is best adapted to develope the Christian virtues and prohibit the indulgence of any known sin.[10]

Here was a report with which any Old School ecclesiastic could agree.

But on 22 June 1848 Selah B. Treat, writing on behalf of the Prudential Committee, reversed the board's position. Although he conceded the right of *congregations* to control their own churches, he asserted that missionaries must preach against the sin of slavery. He justified his position on the grounds that an attack on the institution of slavery was implicit in the New Testament. He further made it clear that one's position on slavery was crucial to his admission into the Church.[11]

Treat's interpretation placed the missionaries of the ABCFM in a vise. In response, Cyrus Kingsbury, who had been a missionary under the Board since 1816, and who had urged patience and forbearance in the matter of Indians holding slaves, wrote that the missionaries were condemned in the North for proslavery sentiment while they were castigated in the South for having abolitionist sympathies. He noted that the southern charges were not unfounded, for the younger missionaries to the Indians had found the presence of slavery among them "highly dissappointing and at times unpalatable."[12]

The quiet that prevailed on the mission field was further fragmented in 1855 when a group of Choctaws forced the passage of a new set of black codes which prohibited the education of the black. When informed of this action, the Prudential Committee decided to withdraw its financial support from the mission boarding schools. It further warned the missionaries that any measures restricting the teaching of the Gospel would force the ABCFM to close its missions.[13] This decision led to a gradual closing of the work among the Choctaws, which terminated in 1859.

The formation of the SAS in 1853 elicited a favorable response from New School men and judicatories in the South. The Murfreesboro Convention of 1853 had convened a few weeks before the SAS was formally organized. The convention scored the refusal of the AHMS to support home missions in the South. Wind of the organization of the SAS was carried to the Convention, and the knowledge that something was being done to form such a society was received favorably--if not with joy. When the SAS was organized, Joseph C. Stiles, one of the triumvirate who had formed the New School Synod of

Kentucky, was the secretary. He was the most important single individual responsible for bringing the society into existence.[14] A strong, representative group of clergy and laymen from both North and South had met to form the SAS, and several southern New School leaders were on the Board of Directors: Frederick A. Ross, Archer C. Dickerson, James G. Hamner, Charles H. Read, and Edward H. Cumpston.

In the first six years of its organization the Southern Aid Society distributed over $55,000 to southern churches, including New School congregations. These funds enabled southern judicatories to become independent of the AHMS. In additon, they permitted the southern New School to move forward in its home missions enterprises. The southern New School was long overdue in new developments. The formation of the Church Extension Copmmittee in 1852 and of the SAS the following year answered a very real ecclesiastical hunger. Since the division of 1837 no aid had been granted for new church development in the lower tier of Southern States. The growing alliance of the AHMS with abolitionism would also have hindered the work of the New School South, even if undertaken.[15] Hence the formation of the SAS came at a most propitious hour.

The society also served another purpose. It was a bond between the North and the South at a time when the ties between the two sections were beginning to snap under political and social strains. Joel Parker of New York exclaimed,

> Under God, this Society has already done something to save the Union! When the salvation of the union can be promoted at the same time with the salvation of souls, what intelligent patriot can refuse to help forward a mission thus doubly blessed?[16]

Victor B. Howard discussed this extra feature of a truly national mission at a time of sectional unrest:

> Few if any benevolent Societies could match the Southern Aid Society membership in wealth and economic leadership. Of the twenty-nine Northern laymen who served as officers, at least seventeen could be included among the elite of commerce, banking and industry. many of these had long-standing business ties with the South. Many were active political figures, including three who were ex-governors, and most

of those who had held public office were lawyers by training and usually by practice.[17]

Converse also commented on the fact that the SAS would make "the Northern and Southern Church ONE in Christ, and one in spirit and hallowed efforts to promote the kingdom of Christ, while many are making an effort to sever the bonds of union."[18]

The role of the college and seminary in the southern New School was important, but in a negative sense. There were very few educational institutions. When the division occurred in 1837, the New School Assembly approved certain seminaries for the "sound and competent training of our ministerial candidates." Of the four institutions so approved, only the South-western Theological Seminary in Maryville was located in the South.[19] The other southern Presbyterian seminaries were Old School: Union Theological Seminary (Hampden Sydney, Virginia), and Columbia Theological Seminary (Columbia, South Carolina).

Nor did the southern New School fare well in respect to colleges. The only school of importance was Maryville College. It was not established until 1842, the seminary there preceding it by twenty-three years. The paucity of colleges greatly hampered the southern New School because the early nineteenth-century colleges tended to be local institutions. That the colleges were local did not exclude their religious zeal. Their primary purpose was to keep young people safely in the South lest they be infected by alien ideas.[20] When William E. Dodd comented on the quality of Presbyterian schools and seminaries in the South, and the influence they made on collegiate development,[21] he was not referring to the very few institutions of the New School in the South.

American theological education experienced three stages. The first involved the candidate who, upon completion of his collegiate course, took up residence at the home of some successful pastor--a "learned divine." There he would study theology, methods of preaching, and pastoral services. The second step developed was the appointment of a single professor in an accredited college to instruct theological candidates. The third phase was the establishment of a separate institution devoted solely to theological training--the seminary. The best the southern New School could develop was a school between the second and third steps: The seminary at Maryville.

Throughout the history of American Presbyterianism there was a close relationship between seminary location and ministerial supply.[22] Seminaries seemed to attract students from their immediate locale, and graduates tended to serve churches in close proximity to the schools where they had studied. This condition largely accounts for the plethora of seminaries conducted by Presbyterians in the middle of the nineteenth century.

Not all students, however, would--or could--receive full seminary training. Many would attend a seminary for a year, then continue their training under an "approved divine." Others found the cost of going to seminary prohibitive. The assistance offered by the AES hardly paid the bills. Presbyteries licensed and ordained men who had attended seminary without consulting the faculty regarding their classroom performance. Nor was formal seminary training required. Many a candidate entered the ministry without the schooling that college and seminary provided. An "educated" minister pragmatically meant anyone which any given presbytery could be induced to accept in a specific case.[23]

The seminary at Maryville, Tennessee, although largely neglected by church historians,[24] nevertheless played a dynamic role in the southern New School in general, in East Tennessee in particular.[25] A total of 159 ministers were trained by Isaac Anderson, who for many years was the only faculty member. Almost to a man, the students came from East Tennessee. They largely returned to the hills and vales whence they had come. They came from that hardy Scotch-Irish stock which made two valuable contributions to the spiritual life of the South: Introducing Presbyterianism to the region and providing an impulse to the education of their youth.[26]

The location of the Maryville seminary, however, never appealed to many outside the immediate area, particularly Easterners. In a letter which Anderson wrote to a friend after the 1838 Assembly, he commented that "this Seminary is almost the only instrument in the South and West, which Constitutional Presbyterians have to maintain the cause of truth."[27] If the purpose of the letter was to gain support, it failed. the Old School also viewed the region with contemptuous disdain: "It has been said on the floor of the Reformed Assembly, that 'East Tennessee was the most polluted place on the earth, and Synod ought to be put down as a common nuisance.'"[28]

The seminary was also handicapped by Anderson's Hopkinsian views. The lack of support from the Board of Education of the undivided Church can be largely attributed to the fact that Hopkinsian doctrines were being taught there. It was probably for this reason that the Cassville Convention turned down Anderson's offer to consider Maryville for its proposed seminary and literary institutions. East Tennessee was honeycombed with the doctrine because the students at Maryville came out of churches where Hopkinsianism had been preached since the days of Hezekiah Balch. They then sat under Anderson whose theology was based on it. After graduation, they returned to the churches prepared to continue Hopkinsianism's spread.[29]

In vain did the Constitution of the Seminary set forth the claim that "we as Presbyterians have adopted the Confession of of Faith which we honestly believe contains the system of truth and grace taught in the Bible."[30] The Old School position in regard to the Confession of Faith was not what was subscribed, but how the indidvidual understood the Confession to which he subscribed. Hence, Anderson's connection with the seminary hobbled its progress.

The size of the student body compared favorably with the enrollment at other schools. In 1828, both Princeton and Andover each reported a hundred students. That same year Maryville reported forty-five. That was twice as many as any other seminary in the United States. That there were black students at the college prior to the Civil War has been "authentically established." Prior to the establishment of the college in 1842, however, Anderson was instructing black students in the seminary--a practice that was quite in accord with his known convictions, attitudes, and habits.[31]

The quality of training the students received at the seminary was a tribute to Anderson.[32] In his report to the 1857 General Assembly, Gideon White commented, "Taking into consideration the outlays and all the attending circumstances, favorable and adverse, no institution has, by the blessing of God, done more to extend and sustain the Redeemer's kingdom, than this child of poverty and prayer."[33]

The second theological school in the southern New School was connected with Macedonia Church, Woodford County, Kentucky.[34] The seminary was established because of the inability of the Synod of Kentucky to obtain sufficient clergy from other New School seminaries to fill her pulpits. Although the core area of the synod was only 200 miles from the seminary at Maryville, the Kentucky New School leaders probably found it more expedient to invest their efforts in establishing their own school than to send their candidates to the Hopkinsian-stained Southern and Western Theological Seminary at Maryville. There is no record of the Macedonia institution ever graduating a student. The "approved divine," William M. King, left Kentucky in 1851 for Texas. His departure spelled the end of the school.

The attempt on the part of the Kentucky New School to conduct such a seminary, however, stands as a symbol of the disarray which plagued the southern New School endeavors. For the most part, the various elements in the New School South were not capable of working together. True, there was a movement of ministers across the South. But there was lacking that coherence which is necessary for any denomination's ultimate success. The erection of the Macedonia seminary further reflects the sectional disdain with which the New School North viewed the Church in the South. The antislavery position of Lane Seminary in Cincinnati prevented most of its graduates from considering Kentucky as a place for ministry. Macedonia also underscores the determination of the Kentucky men to remain in the New School. They could have sent their candidates to the Old School seminary at Danville. This they refused to do. Finally, there was no apparent effort on the part of New School presbyteries in Missouri, Mississippi, or West Tennessee to send their candidates to Macedonia, if those synods even knew of the school's existence.

For the most part, the pens of the southern New School leaders were dry. There was one notable exception, the East Tennessee publication, *The Calvinistic Magazine*. It was the first religious magazine in the Old Southwest. This monthly periodical was published to exhibit and defend the Calvinistic point of view from the attacks it suffered at the hands of Arminian controversialists in the area. The first series began in 1825. It lasted for five years. Its editors were that strong East Tennessee triumvirate of Frederick A. Ross, James Gallaher, and David Nelson. The second series was published also for five years, beginning in 1846. Its editors were Isaac Anderson, Frederick A. Ross, James King, and James McChain. In addition to its assaults on Methodist order and theology, the magazine carried numerous lesser items and articles on the New School churches and ministers in East Tennessee. Its final demise deprived the region of a frequent and lively publication.[35]

For a couple of years the New School in Kentucky published the *Presbyterian Sentinel*. This was a heavy responsibility for a synod of just 900 members. The *Presbyterian Witness* was published in East Tennessee from 1851 to 1860. It was by far the most bellicose New School weekly in the South. It fell into debt, however, and its mailing list was acquired by the *Christian Observer*. Fortunately, for the southern New School as a whole, this latter weekly was a tremendous asset for the movement. It not only carried news in each issue of items which kept the entire New School informed about developments in the South, but its editor, Amasa Converse, was most sympathetic to the southern cause. He remained the major advocate of the southern New School from its origin following the 1837 division until all elements had united with the Presbyterian Church in the Confederate States of America in 1864. Although published in Philadelphia, the *Christian Observer* usually carried news of an event only two weeks after it happened.

The leadership of the southern New School lay primarily in its ministerial ranks. The ranks were thin, however. At the first meeting of the SAS Alexander Newton of Clinton Presbytery noted that "the destitution of the South is a destitution of ministers."[36] Salaries were quite low, and many ministers found it necessary to supplement their meager income by teaching, farming, or engaging in plantation operations. Such work diverted their efforts from their basic calling. This diminished their ability as well as usefulness as ministers.

Although the quality of the New School clergy in the South was good, on one occasion Converse complained that

> men of the first rank, and comparatively few of any rank, have sought admission to the holy office. Hence men of taste and high standing have been disposed to regard the ministry with indifference, and from the ministry have transferred their feelings . . . to the subject with which the office is connected.[37]

Population sparsity in the South frequently prevented the settlement of a pastor over one congregation. This condition necessitated itineration between two or more churches, frequently some distance apart. In turn, this created a lack of regular instruction and pastoral leadership. That preaching stations in the South tended to be farther apart than in the North made the multiple-church pastorate a somewhat discouraging one. Many men preferred to remain in the North, where congregations were larger and where communities were closer together.

The Southern frontier was indeed a mission field. A good "job description" for the potential young missionary was given by Archer C. Dickerson in a letter to Robert Adair, pastor of the First Presbyterian Church, Southwark, Philadelphia, in 1845:

> Passing piety and mental acquirements--our missionary should preach *extemporaneously* altogether--should be fluent in speech, and social in manners; and able and willing to preach at *anytime*--any place--and at a minute's warning--and not over-nice . . . as to his food, beds, and entertainment in general. To sum up all, let him be a man of *common sense*, as well as piety.[38]

Piety alone would not suffice. There was also the need to be "mentally alert" on the field. William H. Smith of Osage Presbytery pointed out the difficulties sectarian doctrines engendered: "The gospel has to contend against Antinomianism, Two-seedism, Campbellism, &C. And a serious hindrance to the progress of pure and undefiled religion is an uneducated ministry."[39]

Normally, the greatest source for ministers is the congregations of the denomination. It was here that the southern New School failed to deliver. Thus J. J. R. [James J. Robinson] observed in 1847:

> The Southern Church has been looking, for this supply, to the wrong quarter. --She has been spending too much on the North and East for a very large portion of her ministers, overlooking, the meanwhile, to a great extent, her own resources in this respect. Instead of educating her own sons for the work, she has been content to supply her pulpits with brethren from the North, who, whatever their zeal, their piety, their ministerial qualifications, can never, from the very nature of the case, labor as successfully at the South as Southern men could do . . . . It is becoming more apparent every day, that if the Southern Church would enjoy the labors of an efficient ministry, *she must educate her own sons for the work*. And I believe her need of more laborers will never be supplied until this is done.[40]

In the meeting of the SAS following its first complete year of operation, Joseph C. Stiles addressed the body. He raised the question, "What are those foundations which should give the Southern Aid Society the cheerful countenance of the Church of God, the active co-operation of every true friend of the country?" In his comments to the question which followed, he stated that more moneys were being spent in the North than in the South--an obvious fact. However, he failed to offer any suggestion beyond the implied recommendation that more money must be spent in the slaveholding states if the Gospel were to make any progress.[41] The solution offered by "J. J. R."--that the South must raise up her own ministers--was far more honest and of greater ameliorative value than that of Stiles'.

NOTES

1. GAPCUSA [NS] *Minutes* (1839), p. 22.
2. Ibid. (1840), pp. 18-19.
3. *CO*, 15 April 1854.
4. Ibid., 14 April 1855. For one of the most logical statements on the doctrine of the apolitical nature of the Church, see the remarks by Andrew H. H. Boyd in Southern Aid Society, *Third Annual Report* (1856), pp. 33-41. A precis is found in *CO*, 20 November 1856.
5. James D. Foust, in *The Yeoman Farmer and Westward Expansion of U. S. Cotton Production* (New York: Arno Press, 1975), pp. 202-203, hypothesized, however, that southern demands for increased slave territory was made for political or long-range expansion purposes, rather than to provide for the immediate expansion of plantation agriculture.
6. Frederick Jackson Turner, in *The United States 1830-1850: The Nation and its Sections* (New York: W. W. Norton, 1935), p. 215, demonstrated how migrating South Carolinians also carried with them the doctrine of nullification into the regions where they moved, at a time when formative influences were strong.
7. Britt Willis, an Irishman, had a Choctaw wife. They and their 300 slaves were forced to move from Mississippi to what is now southeastern Oklahoma; Frances Imon, *Smoke Signals from Indian Territory* (Wolfe City, Texas: Henington Publishing Co., 1976), p. 15.
8. William E. Strong, *The Story of the American Board: An Account of the First Hundred*

Years of the American Board of Commissioners for Foreign Missions (Boston, New York, and Chicago: Pilgrim Press, 1910), p. 52.

9. Robert T. Lewitt, "Indian Missions and Antislavery Sentiment: A Conflict of Evangelical and Humanitarian Ideals," *MVHR* 50 (June, 1963): 41; Strong, *Story of the American Board*, p. 52.

10. American Board of Commissioners for Foreign Missions, *Thirty-Sixth Annual Report* (1845), p. 56; *CO*, 19 September 1845; Robert Meredith, "A Conservative Abolitionist at Alton: Edward Beecher's Narrative," *JPHS* 42 (1964): 97-99.

11. For the gist of the letter, see Lewitt, "Indian Missions and Antislavery Sentiment," pp. 48-49. The decision of the Prudential Committee that the Board could exert no control over the missionaries or the mission churches (*Thirty-ninth Annual Report* [1848], pp. 62-80) conformed to Congregational polity. Lewitt's comment is helpful: "To take away the missionaries' autonomy was to enter into direct conflict with the accepted version of independent worship" ("Indian Missions and Antislavery Sentiment," p. 43).

12. Cited in Lewitt, "Indian Missions and Antislavery Sentiment," p. 51.

13. Clifford Merrill Drury, *Presbyterian Panorama: One Hundred and Fifty Years of National Missions History* (Philadelphia: Board of Christian Education, Presbyterian Church in the United States of America, 1952), pp. 108-109; Lewitt, "Indian Slavery and Antislavery Sentiment," pp. 51-52.

14. For a brief treatment of the philosophy and structure of this organization, see Colin Brummitt Goodykoontz, *Home Missions on the American Frontier: With Particular Reference to the American Home Missionary Society* (Caldwell, Idaho: Caxton Printers, 1939), pp. 292-294; and Clifford S. Griffin, "The Abolitionists and the Benevolent Societies, 1831-1861," *Journal of Negro History* 44 (1959): 195-216. For a discussion of the slavery issue and the suggestions for home mission support, see Victor B. Howard, "The Southern Aid Society and the Slavery Controversy," *CH* 41 (1972): 211-212.

15. Howard, "The Southern Aid Society," 214; Walter L. Fleming, *Civil War and Reconstruction in Alabama* (New York: Columbia University Press, 1905), p. 23.

16. Cited in Howard, "Southern Aid Society," p. 220.

17. Ibid., p. 221.

18. *CO*, 4 November 1854.

19. GAPCUSA [NS], *Minutes* (1839), p. 26.

20. David B. Potts, "American Colleges in the Nineteenth Century: From Localism to Denominationalism," *History of Education Quarterly* 11 (1971): 372; Frank Bell Lewis, "Times of Crisis," in *The Days of Our Years 1812-1962: The Historical Convocation Held April 24-27, 1962 as a Feature of the Celebrations of the Sesquicentennial of Union Theological Seminary in Virginia* (Richmond: n.p., 1962), p. 34.

21. William B. Dodd, *The Days of the Cotton Kingdom* Part One: *The Cotton Kingdom: A Chronicle of the Old South*, The Chronicles of America Series (New Haven: Yale University Press, 1919), p. 110.

22. Elwyn Allen Smith, *The Presbyterian Ministry in American Culture: A Study in Changing Concepts, 1700-1900* (Philadelphia: Westminster Press, 1962), p. 167.

23. Leonard J. Trinterud, "1829-1954: Theological Education--Then and Now," *McCormick Speaking* 8 (6, 1955): 12-13; L. C. Rudolph, *Hoosier Zion: The Presbyterians in Early Indiana* (New Haven and London: Yale University Press, 1963), p. 65.

24. Elwyn Smith (*The Presbyterian Ministry in American Culture*, p. 168) gave the seminary less than a paragraph in his study. Jonathan F. Stearns, in "Historical Review of the Church (New School Branch) Since 1837," in *Presbyterian Reunion: A Memorial Volume 1837-1871* (New York: De Witt C. Lent & Co.; Chicago: Vannortwick & Sparks, 1870), pp. 50-102, does not mention the seminary, although it was the oldest of the New School seminaries. Robert Nuckols Watkin, in "The Forming of the Southern Presbyterian Minister: From Calvin to the American Civil War" (Ph.D. diss., Vanderbilt University, 1969), pp. 279-298, stated that Union Seminary in Virginia and Columbia Seminary were founded "in this period," but referred to Maryville only in passing. In 1838 or 1839 the Presbyterian Education Society, supported largely by Old School funds, withdrew its financial support of Maryville students on the grounds that "the institution was not equipped for its complex work of education"; J. E. Alexander, *A Brief History of the Synod of Tennessee, From 1817 to 1887* (Philadelphia: MacCalla and Co., 1890, p. 20.

25. For a study of the seminary, see Samuel Tyndale Wilson, *A Century of Maryville College, 1819-1919: A Story of Altruism* (Maryville: Directors of Maryville College, 1916), pp. 31-55. See also Harold M. Parker, Jr., "A School of the Prophets at Maryville," *Tennessee Historical Quarterly* 34

(1975): 72-90; reprinted in Parker, *SSPH*, pp. 110-128.

26. East Tennessee Presbyterians founded not only Maryville College, but also Tusculum College, Washington College, and Blount College. The last later became the University of Tennessee.

27. Quoted in John J. Robinson, *Memoir of Rev. Isaac Anderson, DD., Late President of Maryville College, and Professor of Didactic Theology* (Knoxville: Addison Rayl, 1860), p. 141.

28. Cited in ibid., p. 139.

29. For the role of Hopkinsianism in the Division of 1837, see Elwyn A. Smith, "The Doctrine of Imputation and the Presbyterian Schism of 1837-1838," *JPHS* 38 (1960: 129-151. Anderson's Hopkinsianism was a tender subject to those who knew him. See Robinson, *Memoir of Anderson*, who devoted a total of sixty-seven pages to explain the nature of Hopkinsianism and to respond to the question, "Was Dr. Anderson a Hopkinsian?"

30. From the Constitution of the Southern and Western Theological Seminary, Article 32, in Samuel Tyndale Wilson, *Isaac Anderson: Founder and First President of Maryville College: A Memorial Sketch* (Maryville: n.p., 1932), p. 158.

31. Ralph Waldo Lloyd, *Maryville College: A History of 150 Years, 1819-1969* (Maryville: Maryville College Press, 1969), p. 202.

32. In addition to his professorial demands, he was also pastor of Maryville's New Providence Church. A list of the courses taught in the three-year course of study is found in Wilson, *Anderson Memorial*, p. 159.

33. *CO*, 4 June 1857.

34. Harold M. Parker, Jr., "A New School Presbyterian Seminary in Woodford County," *Register of the Kentucky Historical Society* 74 (1976): 99-111; reprinted in idem, *SSPH*, 167-179. See also Louis B. Weeks, *Kentucky Presbyterians* (Atlanta: John Knox Press, 1983), p. 77.

35. For references regarding the *Calvinistic Magazine*, see Charles C. Ross, ed. and comp., *The Story of Rotherwood from the Autobiography of Rev. Frederick A. Ross, D. D.* (Knoxville: Bean, Warters, & Co., 1923), pp. 34-35; Henry Smith Stroupe, *The Religious Press in the South Atlantic States, 1802-1865: An Annotated Bibliography with Historical Introduction and Notes* (Durham: Duke University Press), pp. 49-50; Ernest Trice Thompson, *Presbyterians in the South*, 3 vols. (Richmond: John Knox Press, 1963-1973), 1:456; Alexander, *Synod of Tennessee*, pp. 62-63; and T. H. Spence, "Southern

Presbyterian Reviews," *Union Seminary Review* 56 (February, 1945): 93-109.

    36. Southern Aid Society, *First Report* (1854), p. 31.

    37. *CO*, 30 July 1841.

    38. Cited in *CO*, 30 May 1845.

    39. Cited in E. E. Stringfield, *Presbyterianism in the Ozarks: A History of the Work of the Various Branches of the Presbyterian Church in Southwest Missouri* (n.p., n.p., 1909), p. 189.

    40. *CO*, 12 February 1847. A similar comment from the Synod of Kentucky was in the 16 December 1848 issue.

    41. Reported in the *CO*, 25 November 1854.

6
The New School Deals With Slavery

For a number of years the New School General Assembly labored to retain the small percentage of southerners in its membership.[1] The effort would ultimately be in vain. But no Protestant Church made as great an effort to maintain its essential unity by endeavors of such magnitude. The effort of the New School's legislation over the score of years is evidence that the slavery issue was not a major factor in the schism of 1837.

Nevertheless, there is no doubt concerning the importance of the issue in subsequent General Assemblies. At every meeting of the Assembly, memorials and overtures were sent up from the lower courts on the subject of domestic slavery. They resulted in actions that failed to satisfy the more zealous antislavery factions in the North, and at the same time increasingly excited dissatisfaction and irritation in the South. In fact, so much time and energy were expended on the issue that in the minds of some students of the period there is the belief that the constant embroilment over the issue retarded considerably the growth of the New School.[2]

The history of the New School itself reflects any lack of substantive action that the Church might have taken on the slavery problem. Following the division of 1837, the New School took the position that the Assembly had no authority to exclude judicatories of the Church. Through the subsequent years, this decision resulted in a barrier to its own efforts to discipline the southern proslavery element. If the Church took too strong a stand against slavery, it ran the risk of alienating its southern element; if it failed to take a stand, it stood the risk of losing its more liberal ministers and congregations to the Congregationalists. Thus, it basically followed the policy of condemning slavery in general, while at the same time it left to the lower judicatories the task of taking any substantive effective action. As long as this formula was adhered to, the peace and unity of the Church were preserved; when it was abandoned, the precarious balance was tipped, and the Church experienced division.

The men in the North failed to understand the burden they laid on the southern members at each meeting of the Assembly. "This exciting subject was mingled with the other causes of irritation, from year to year, till it became exasperating," according to William Henry Foote.[3] For its part, the Old School was quite content to abide with the action of the 1818 General Assembly touching slavery. In contrast, at each meeting of the New School it attempted to enlarge on that deliverance.

The action of 1818 on the slavery issue represented the culmination of nearly half a century of reflection upon and experience with gradual emancipation. According to Ernest Trice Thompson, the 1818 declaration can be properly understood and appreciated only in the historical context of antislavery developments in Presbyterianism in the Revolutionary period. Its passage was the quintessential expression of the tradition of gradualism linked with the rejection of immediatism, which had been championed by Virginia's George Bourne.[4]

There were numerous reasons the slavery issue was brought up at the New School Assemblies when hardly a ripple disturbed the Old School's slavery surface. For one thing, many of the New School men had been imbued with the New School concept of evangelism--that the total life of man must be converted, and sin in its every manifestation eliminated. Such had been Finney's preaching that had at first brought the claims of the Gospel to all life's relations.[5] To the evangelicals, slavery was a cancer which required surgery to remove it from the body of the Church. Another factor was the paucity of southern members in the New School. The Old School contained a large southern constituency. That group had played an important role in the Old School's domination of the 1837 Assembly, being largely responsible for expunging the New School synods from the Assembly.[6] With a large percentage of its membership in the North, the middle judicatories--presbyteries and synods--of the New School were merely reflecting the sentiments of their members in forwarding memorials and overtures to the Assembly regarding slavery.

A third factor was the heady influence of former Congregationalists who had entered the New School ranks. Few of these were in the South. By the time the slavery controversy heated up, they had been largely absorbed into the Presbyterian Church--politically, theologically, socially. In the North, however, large numbers of Congregational churches and ministers had come into the New School through the Plan of Union. They brought with them considerable opposition to the institution of domestic slavery.

The amazing characteristic about the slavery debates and the concomitant resolutions adopted at each Assembly was that it took almost a score of years before the southern judicatories had their fill and withdrew. Yet their long adherence to the New School was due in no small part to the determined efforts of New School leaders through those years to maintain the unity of the Church.[7] There was an inordinate pride in the fact that the New School had retained and could retain its unity at a time when the Baptists and Methodists had lost theirs over the slavery issue. In the New School South, despite the waves of antislavery petitions which were presented at each New School Assembly, there was an overriding principle that kept it in the Church: the southern courts had withdrawn in protest to the high-handed manner by which the New School had been unconstitutionally treated in 1837 and 1838. This dedication to principle surmounted all other factors that might have rent the South from the North in the New School.

This study now turns to the meetings of the New School General Assembly. Each meeting is examined as that meeting confronted the most perplexing problem which the New School faced in the first twenty years of its existence: the issue of domestic slavery.[8]

The first New School General Assembly to confront the slavery question took place in 1839. The action of this Assembly is quite significant for the philosophical precedent it set. Having acknowledged that several memorials had been received, the Assembly adopted the following resolution: "That this Assembly does most solemnly refer to the lower judicatories the subject of slavery, leaving to them to take such order thereon as in their judgment will be most judicious, and adapted to remove the evil."[9]

Innocuous though the resolution may appear, it was pregnant with meaning for the fledgling Church.

The New School did not possess at that time the high ecclesiology that characterized the Old School, partly because of the large number of ministers and churches that had a Congregational background. The strength of Congregationalism lay not in the authority of the denomination, but in the Associations. These latter were essentially for fellowship and for conducting certain kinds of religious activity, which could not be carried out on the level of the congregation where true authority and autonomy resided.

In facing the first major confrontation involving the Church, it was thus almost natural that the decision to refer the subject to the lower judicatories would be the logical solution. The Assembly gave particular authority to the synods. They became courts of ultimate appeal and judicial jurisdiction. They replaced the General Assembly on the grounds that this would bar the latter from any appeals of discipline or non-discipline of slaveholders.[10]

Albert Barnes concluded his discussion of the 1839 Assembly by commenting that "there is no suggestion that the institution [of slavery] is designed to be permanent; no intimation that it is a 'patriarchal' institution, or that it is an intimation that it in any way was sanctioned and sustained by the Bible. . . ."[11] By the same token, nothing was said denying the permanency of the institution, or that it was not a "patriarchal" institution, or that it was not sanctioned in the Bible. It was only ambiguously referred to as "the evil."

At the 1840 General Assembly more memorials came to the floor. Following the pattern which had been set the year before, however, the whole subject was postponed indefinitely.[12] More significant than the legislation which dealt with slavery was the Assembly's action in adopting the suggestion of Samuel Hanson Cox that the Assembly meet triennially rather than annually. Such would limit to every three years the possibility of the slavery issue rising to the level of the Assembly. This would prevent any schism-tending clashes from developing between northern abolitionists and southern slaveholders.[13]

The discussion on slavery occupied the Assembly for four days, however, which, according to Barnes, "shows that it was [a subject] which excited deep interest in the church, and was one which the Assembly was not disposed to exclude from solemn and anxious consideration."[14] The South's concern, nevertheless, was seen in the adopted proposal:

> Whereas slavery, as it exists in these United States, is a subject over which the General Assembly of the Presbyterian Church has no control or power to legislate; and which was, after a thorough discussion by the last Assembly, referred to, and declared to belong to the inferior judicatories of the church, whose local and relative business it is to inspect the moral and religious character and conduct of their own members; therefore resolved, That all memorials and petitions on the subject be considered as inappropriate to the functions and relations of the General Assembly.[15]

The Assembly also took exception to the practice of the churches that excluded slaveholders from their pulpits and communion because such action disenfranchises "without a regular trial and conviction" and is "a repetition of the exscinding acts of the new basis Assembly, against which we have taken our stand as friends of the Constitution. . . ."[16]

Reactions to the noncommittal posture of the Assembly varied. The delegates who assembled in Cassville in October expressed their desire that at its next neeting the Constitutional Assembly would take "such order upon this subject as will remove a serious obastacle to an entire union of Constitutional Presbyterians through this land."[17] But James G. Birney, leader in the Abolitionist movement and candidate for President of the United States in 1840 and 1844, had a different view:

> The New School Assembly is more solicitous to have the favor of the few slave-holders who are members, than to have the blessings of the poor who are perishing in their grasp--more earnest to equal the Old School in numbers than to outstrip it in righteousness.[18]

Thus, while the New School concluded its first three Assemblies by taking no action on the question that would hound it for years to come, still the issue would not leave. But, for the most part, the southern elements appeared satisfied, though apprehensive.

The General Assembly of 1843 was unique in American Presbyterian history. It was the first Assembly to meet three years after the preceding one. But the design of Cox that such less-frequent meetings might represent a cooling off period over the slavery controversy failed to materialize. Three the slavery controversy failed to materialize. Three days were spent debating the issue. Finally, by a 66-33 vote, the Assembly passed this resolution: "*Resolved*, That the Assembly do not think it for the edification of the Church for this body to take any action on the subject."[19]

The Assembly's attempt to straddle the issue prompted immediate reaction. The Old School-Kentucky-published *Protestant and Herald* noted that some of the New School members were filled with "disgust and indignation" when news of the Assembly's action reached them. Their response, at first, was to bolt the Church, but upon second reflection they formed different conclusions.[20] John Rankin proposed to form a Free Presbyterian Church, based on the principle that no slaveholder could preach or hold membership in it. Amasa Converse took Rankin's proposal more seriously than did others. He counselled moderation before breaking with the Church:

> . . . When a movement is made to introduce *new* rules or principles into the organization of a church, it is important to know if they correspond with the principles of the holy Scriptures . . . . We would inculcate what the Bible teaches, on this and every subject on which it speaks . . . . In reforms of every kind we would go as far as the Bible goes, and no farther.[21]

In spite of Converse's appeal, five years later the Free Presbyterian Church was organized.

Not pleased with the action of the Assembly, the Synod of Indiana addressed the southern synods connected with the New School. In a very gentle, but firm statement of the inhumanity and sin of slavery, it admonished the South that "the school of liberty" can never come from "the house of bondage," and that emancipation is "*the best preparation for liberty*," inasmuch as "*slavery can never be a remedy for slavery.*"[22]

The General Assembly of 1846 stands as the watershed of the New School slavery agitation. It was also the most unique General Assembly in American Presbyterian history, for it dealt with just one issue: slavery. The Synod of Kentucky at its 1845 meeting had expressed its apprehension about the next Assembly. It also requested its constituent presbyteries to "instruct their Commissioners to the next assembly" relative to its views, for the Synod was quite satisfied with the actions of the two previous Assemblies.²³

Four synods and twenty-nine presbyteries sent memorials to the Assembly on the slavery problem. The Assembly must act. It began with the roll call. Alternately, from top to bottom, every commissioner was given an opportunity to express his views on slavery. This "inordinate discussion respecting slavery" consumed two weeks' time.²⁴ Albert Barnes commented that "there has been no ecclesiastical meeting in our country where the subject of slavery has received so full a discussion, or where so large a portion of its time has been occupied in considering this subject." He described the proceedings as "earnest" and "not an angry discussion."²⁵

By a 92-29 vote, with two abstentions, the Assembly adopted a six-point declaration.

1. The system of slavery was condemned as "intrinsically an unrighteous and oppressive system, opposed to the prescription of the law of God, to the spirit and precepts of the Gospel, and to the best interests of humanity."
2. The Assembly did not recede from the Testimony of the General Assembly from 1787 to 1818, which condemned slavery.
3. The Assembly could not withhold "the expression of our deep regret that slavery should be continued and countenanced by any member of our churches; and we do earnestly exhort both them and the churches among whom it exists to use all means in their power to put it away from them" The perpetuation of slavery in the Church was regarded by many as sanctioning the system.
4. At the same time, the Assembly refused to undertake the degree of moral turpitude on the part of individuals involved in it, "nor would it eclude frodm the Lord's table those who are involved in it . . . ."
5. Those "divisive and schismatical measures" which would divide the Church were condemned.
6. The Assembly again confirmed its position that it possessed no legislative or judiciary power. The matter of Christian character and church membership was left with Sessions, Presbyteries, and Synods, "to act in the administration of discipline as they may judge it to be their duty, constitutionally subject to the General

Assembly only in the way of general review and control."²⁶

During the course of the presentations, two protests were entered. The first stated that the actions of the 1840 and 1843 Assemblies had referred the matter back to the lower courts. Hence, it was considered "injurious to take the welfare of both the Church and the country for this Assembly to take any action upon a subject so interwoven with the political institutions of the States." Nor should the North ask the South "to make any sacrifice of our [South's] usefulness" by being influenced by the noisy "strife of abolitionism." The second protest claimed that it was inexpedient for the Assembly to take any action on slavery, for the protestors did not consider that slavery, "as existing in the southern States, is forbidden by the laws of God and the principles of the Gospel of Jesus Christ, as revealed in Holy Word." Both protests bore the names of southern commissioners.²⁷

For the first time the southern commissioners had spoken back to the North. The latter delegates were somewhat surprised to hear, for the first time, the issue from the other side. The accommodating Amasa Converse thus "counselled" the southerners that there were some things they might do as their "duty" to the North:

1. The South should not withdraw.
2. The southern ministry owes the northern "to give them more information respecting the spiritual condition, discipline, usages, efforts, and progress of the churches of the southern country."
3. "Cannot southern brethren give the northern some just view of the wide extent of the country around them, in which a regular minister was never settled?"
4. "There is a great want of information relative to the condition of slaves in Christian families."
5. If it is true that the declarations and remonstrances on slavery in the North has hurt the cause of the South, then give facts to support the testimony.²⁸

Most of the southern commissioners returned to their presbyteries satisfied that they had been heard. Isaac Anderson, in a letter to an unnamed relative, commented on the work of the Assembly and its affinity to his own philosophy of southern New School ecclesiasticism:

> The church is not commissioned to interfere with the relation of king and subject, or of master and slave, but to instruct in their mutual duties and enforce obedience by the tremendous motives of the Gospel, and discipline master or slave who may be members, but do not perform the mutual duties required by the Gospel.[29]

Typical of the New School moderates was the action taken by the Synod of Missouri in its paper, "Resolutions on the Reciprocal Duties of Masters and Slaves," at its 1846 meeting, held in the fall after the Assembly. The paper declared that "we are not unwilling that this subject should be fully and fairly discussed on all suitable occasions," and stated that the "full and temperate" discussion at the Assembly "has done good, by softening the prejudices equally of the North and South." In addition to underscoring the mutual slave-master responsibilities, the paper pleaded for understanding:

> Living as we do in a slave state, we are yet free to declare to the North and the South, that we desire and pray for the entire removal of slavery from among us, so soon as it can be done with safety and manifest advantage, not so much to the masters, as to the servants themselves.[30]

To Missourians, caution was the watchword.

The Synod of Virginia deprecated the Assembly's action because the resolutions adopted were based on the premise that slavery is a sin per se. At its 1846 meeting it excoriated abolition, and deplored the Assembly's action on slavery so vehemently that the Old School Synod of Virginia invited their former brothers to return to their former connection.[31] Before the next Assembly could convene, the New School Synod of Ohio adopted a memorial requesting that body either to "unsay" all that it had stated on the sinfulness of slavery or else to carry out its declarations to their legitimate results.[32]

The 1846 Assembly had placed the matter of slavery before the Church. Both sides were heard. There was no rush to get to other business. The procedure of the Assembly further revealed how the slavery debate had bogged down the Church. Little else was being discussed; the Church was dangerously bordering on becoming a sect. Having formed no ecclesiastical instruments of and for itself, the New School was becoming gradually dependent on the various missionary agencies, which had increasingly settled views on slavery. The South was being neglected as a mission field. Hence, after this Assembly there developed considerably more tension in the Church than had before existed.

The Assembly of 1849 was the last of the triennial meetings. The experiment, foreign to Presbyterianism, had failed. It had been necessary to hold an Adjourned Meeting of the Assembly in 1847 to consider the business which had been neglected in 1846. Emerging from that experience--the only Adjourned Meeting of a General Assembly in American Presbyterian history--the Assembly in 1847 sent down to the presbyteries for their consideration the proposal that the Assembly return to annual meetings. The proposal passed by a 63-26 vote of the presbyteries.[33]

The most lengthy statement yet adopted by the New School on slavery was the fruit of the 1849 Assembly. Nineteen memorials on the subject were sent up to the Assembly. The wordy paper the Assembly adopted was essentially a graphic review of all prior actions of previous Assemblies. It presented guiding principles for the Church:

1. Civil liberty is the lot of every man.
2. Slavery is an unrighteous and oppressive system, injurious to all concerned.
3. It is the duty of Christians as speedily as possible "to efface this blot on our holy religion" and to obtain the complete abolition of slavery.
4. Where slavery cannot be immediately removed, direct religious instruction and practical knowledge of life should be imparted to prepare slaves for their emancipation.
5. Traffic in slaves and undue severity and breaking up of families should be corrected by church discipline.[34]

It was obvious that this Assembly would be the last meeting to hold the line. Emphasis was placed on slavery as evil, and that the contemplated solution was abolition.

The decade of the 1840s has been termed the "quiet years."[35] The basic attitudes that had ushered in the decade remained, only more solidi-

The New School Deals With Slavery   121

fied, buttressed by increasingly stronger pro- and antislavery apologetics. The 1850 Assembly met in Detroit. So numerous were the overtures and memorials coming to the Assembly over slavery that a committee of seven--five from the North, two from the South--was appointed to consider them. Both majority and minority reports of the committee were published and circulated. Debate on the report lasted a week, and finally the minority report was accepted.

The report contained a preamble and four resolutions. The latter spelled out in no uncertain terms not only the Assembly's position in slavery, but also a procedure whereby the matter could be treated in the Church. The report became known as the "Detroit Resolutions," and the articles are as follows:

> Resolved, 1. That we exceedingly deplore the working of a whole system of Slavery as it exists in our country and is interwoven with the political institutions of the slaveholding States, as fraught with many and great evils to the civil, political and moral interests of those regions where it exists.
>
> Resolved, 2. That the holding of our fellow-men in the condition of slavery, except in those cases where it is unavoidable, by the laws of the State, the obligations of guardianship, or the demands of humanity, is an offence in the proper import of that term, as used in the Book of Discipline, Chap. i, Sec. 3, and should be regarded and treated in the same manner as other offences.
>
> Resolved, 3. That the Sessions and Presbyteries are, by the Constitution of our Church, the courts of primary jurisdiction for the trial of offences.
>
> Resolved, 4. That after this declaration of sentiment, the whole subject of Slavery, as it exists in the Church, be referred to the Sessions and Presbyteries, to take such action thereon as in their judgment the laws of Christianity require.[36]

The report was adopted by an 87-16 vote. All the southern commissioners except one voted against it. The handful of southern delegates in attendance was typical. The Synod of Mississippi had none, and only two of the fifteen southern commissioners were laymen. Only two votes from the North joined the men from the South in opposing the resolutions.

Two points in particular stand out in regard to the Detroit Resolutions. By designating the specific courts where review should take place, the Assembly made the Sessions responsible for discipline, instead of the Synods, as it had done in 1849. More important, however, was the relating of slavery to the Book of Discipline as a disciplinary offence. Until this time, slavery had been considered outside the judicial realm of the Church. Now it was an admitted cause for Church discipline.

The fact that the minority report was adopted was also significant. The debate over slavery consumed five of the twelve days the Assembly met: "a sad precursor of the larger conflict and estrangement that were to follow."[37] Perhaps the most significant result to come from the 1850 Assembly was the formation of a religious weekly originating in the South for the New School. There is a strong possibility that the previous lack of such a paper was "at least responsible" for the southerners not withdrawing at this time, inasmuch as little united action was possible among the scattered groups of the southern New School. But by the same token, it is quite possible that the threat of further slavery legislation was responsible for the beginning of the *Presbyterian Witness* in East Tennessee the following year.[38]

The 1851 General Assembly received but four memorials. This occasioned the Assembly to give thanks that it could "devote . . . time to other subjects which demand attention. . . ."[39] The Fugitive Slave Law had only recently been passed. But after some debate, the Assembly placed the issue on the table as inopportune. This action brought forth a positive editorial observation by the New York *Journal of Commerce*. It viewed the Assembly's action as "creditable to their good sense and wisdom" for not allowing itself to be "caught in the snare which was set for them." Noting that the law was essentially "a matter of civil government," it commended the "conservative course pursued by this Assembly" as "an encouraging sign of the times. . . ."[40]

The General Assembly met in Washington in 1852. Four memorials were presented. Again, the Assembly held its ground. An overture from the Presbytery of Franklin (Ohio) stated that the six southern synods "are charged by 'common fame' with holding sentiments and countenancing practices" regarding the

The New School Deals With Slavery   123

subject of slavery "in direct opposition to the repeated declarations of the General Assembly" and suggested that the synods be cited to appear before the next Assembly to answer the charges according to the Book of Discipline. The Committee on Bills and Overtures responded to the charge contained in the overture, pointing out that prosecution on grounds of "common fame" should be undertaken only with "great caution. Much more, when the character of a Synod is concerned, or, as in the present case, of several Synods; and when the matter in question is one of peculiar delicacy and difficulty."[41]

The book, *Slavery and Anti-Slavery*, appeared in 1852. It pointed to the complete frustration abounding in both Presbyterian bodies that year, for the book had been written by William Goodell in the midst of the slavery agitation, and there was no end in sight. Although Goodell traced the history of the slavery controversy in all the major American denomintations, he was unusually severe with the Presbyterians:

> The discriminating reader will now judge for himself respecting the moral difference between the Old School and the New, in their relation to slavery. The one has more slaveholders under its jurisdiction than the other, but both tolerate the practice. The one does this to retain many members; the other to retain a few. The one does it believing slavery to be a Bible institution; the other, believing it to be 'unrighteous' and 'oppressive.' The one makes no pretense of any intention to discipline any sort of slaveholders; the other holds the rod over the class of them that 'it has no information' of being found within its enclosures, but fears to go out of its boundaries to clasp them to its bosom.[42]

The most crucial meeting yet of the Assembly convened in Buffalo in 1853. Prior to this meeting, the New School had left slavery in the hands of the lower judicatories. But 1853 witnessed a change. This was the year that the AHMS began to put pressure on its missionaries to renounce slavery. In reaction, the New School began to alter its policy as well. The crucial response was the adoption of the following preamble and resolutions:

> . . . it is recommended earnestly to request the presbyteries in each of the slave-holding States to take such measures as may seem to

them most expedient and proper, for laying before the next Assembly . . . distinct and full statements touching the following points:

> 1. The number of slave-holders in connection with the churches under their jurisdiction, and the number of slaves held by them.
> 2. The extent to which slaves are held by an unavoidable necessity °imposed by the laws of the States, the obligations of guardianship, and the demands of humanity.'
> 3. Whether a practical regard, such as the word of God requires, is evidenced by the Southern churches for the sacredness of the conjugal and parental relations as they exist among slaves; whether baptism is duly administered to the children of slaves professing Christianity; whether slaves are admitted to equal privileges and powers in the church courts; and, in general, to what extent and in what manner provision is made for the religious well-being of the slave.[43]

The report was adopted by an 84-39 vote. There were enough abstentions, however, that the adoption was by a plurality, not a majority. Two vigorous protests were lodged.

Frederick A. Ross authored one protest. The action, he maintained, runs counter to the Constitution. The Assembly cannot initiate such a process as the resolution provided. Hence, the southern judicatories should not treat the inquiries with respect. Ross also claimed that the eighty-four votes cast did not constitute a majority, so that the report was not constitutionally adopted.[44]

The second protest came from the ranks of the northern conservatives, headed by Samuel H. Cox of Brooklyn, New York. It charged the action passed as "unconstitutional," an "innovation" whose proper use was "questionable." Rather than reform, the protest insisted that the action would only irritate relations between the two wings of the Church.[45]

In his commentary on the Assembly, Albert Barnes pointed out that ". . . there was no obligation, expressed or implied, to return any answer whatsoever. It was as clearly constitutional and proper not to answer them, unless the ministers and members of the southern churches should suppose that it was proper. . . ."[46] Subsequent events would point out Barnes's error in understanding the import of the Assembly's action.

Nor did it take long before the southern judicatories made official responses to the Assembly's legislation--and in extremely negative terms. A few examples suffice. The Presbytery of Newton (Mississippi) adopted a three-point paper in which it (1) regarded the proceedings of the Assembly as "a novelty," which could "ultimate only in the schism of the church; (2) gave notice that it would not comply with the requests of the Assembly because they were both "uncalled for" and "clearly unconstitutional"; and (3) demanded "a cessation of all agitation in the General Assembly upon the subject of slavery."[47]

The legislation of the 1853 General Assembly was largely responsible for calling the Murfreesboro Convention by ministers in the Synods of Tennessee, West Tennessee, and Mississippi.[48] The meeting was held in Murfreesboro, Tennessee, 1-4 July 1853. Division was in the air. Several delegates predicted that such division would emerge forom the meeting, but again the moderating counsel of Converse placed little substance in the circulating rumors: "If there were any truth or efficacy in these apocryphal predictions of our brethren in the new Basis [Old School] Assembly--our Church would have divided a dozen times, or annihilated, during the last fifteen years, and never have held a meeting in Buffalo." He then pointed out how the New School had been growing in numbers through the years. He concluded his remarks by conjecturing that "we are not disposed to listen to predictions of *division* or *separation*, because a minority of the last assembly adopted a mistaken measure, which we trust will be made harmless."[49]

The convention appointed a committee to make recommendations relative to the legislation of the 1853 assembly, which only recently had adjourned. The committee recommended that the southern presbyteries "should in a united, firm and dignified appeal to the next Assembly, distinctly take their ground, and earnestly insist in the issues being met then and definitely settled. This endless agitation is eating out our vitals, and destroying us piecemeal. The process is as unkind as it is unlawful." The legislation at Detroit, confirmed at the next assembly, and now the action at Buffalo "constitute an important advance beyond that of all preceding Assemblies towards the point of the *separation of slaveholding church members by disciplinary force*." Nevertheless, there was no suggestion of withdrawing from the Assembly, rather there was an affirmation that "we love our brethren, North and West," and will remain with them while they remain on the constitution. When they leave *that*, they leave us!"⁵⁰

In conclusion, the Detroit Resolutions were denounced; appeal was made to the conservative wings of the Northern and Western portions of the Church at the next Assembly; and the Southern presbyteries were urged to send a full representation of both elders and ministers to the next Assembly. The Presbytery of Holston adopted the report of the Convention on the subject of slavery as "embodying the sentiments of this Presbytery respecting that subject."⁵¹

Never before had the southern judicatories reacted with such vigor to the Assembly's actions as they did following the 1853 General Assembly. Together, the minutes of the judicatories and the holding of the Murfreesboro Convention indicated that the union within the Church was weakening. The patience of the southern churches had been stretched as far as could be expected, without snapping. The antislavery stance of the northern-dominated Church was becoming an increasingly heavy burden for the southern churches to bear. The Presbytery of Winchester, meeting in the fall of 1853, noted that the agitation in the Assembly has, "in no single instance, done our churches at the South . . . the slightest good, but has, on the contrary, resulted in a vast amount of evil." Still the Presbytery sought accommodation with its northern brothers.⁵² The Presbytery of Lexington, South (Mississippi) declared that it is of "vital interest to the peace and prosperity of our church, to cease agitating this question in its highest judicatory."⁵³

The South had spoken. The line unifying the Church segments was so taut that any further efforts to test it would destroy the unity of the Church.

But still the overtures from the North came. Eighteen in all reached the 1854 Assembly. One even went so far as to ask for a division of the Church, to which Converse responded that it was "asuicidal act" for which there was no constitutional provision. Another overture asked for a separation from churches in which Christian masters were members--just as reprehensible in Converse's mind as it was unlawful. Others continued to call for further action on the slavery issue. And to these Converse responded most patiently and didactically:

> These Presbyteries seem not to be aware that the General Assembly, more than thirty years ago (1818) exhausted *all its power* in the

testimony it then bore against slavery--and that it has since received no accessions to its power over the subject. They seem not to know that a resolution declaring something an offence, which the constitution does not make an offence, is of no authority whatsoever; and that an Assembly can not erect an inquisition or tribunal of any kind to sit in judgment on the motives of brethren for holding servants, or lands, or any thing else . . . . These brethren ought to be advised that the Assembly must discard or change its constitution . . . before it can take another step on this subject. And such a change can only be effected by the separate action of a majority of the Presbyteries on an overture sent down to them, and the ratification of a subsequent Assembly.[54]

Few of the southern presbyteries responded to the questions of the 1853 Assembly; and those that did, did so through presenting newspaper accounts of their actions, "alike complaining of the action of the Assembly and refusing to give any information on the subject."[55] It was obvious that the Assembly should press the issue no further. The Committee on Bills and Overtures, to whom the numerous memorials were referred, reported that "the consideration of the subject" at present "is undesirable and inexpedient" and moved that "this Assembly take no action on the subject."[56] The report was adopted. Protests to the Assembly's decision argued that the failure of the Assembly to take action virtually abrogated the legislation of the previous Assembly, placing the present Assembly in a position of not approving what had been done only a year earlier.[57]

The most damning indictment of the Assembly's action came from the *New Englander*. That journal castigated all Churches--the New School not excepted--for their refusal to act positively on the antislavery position: "These religious bodies, as represented by their various organs, and by their leading men, have sold themselves into a bondage from which nothing less than the power and grace of God can redeem them."[58]

The Presbytery of Champlain (New York) was equally "aggrieved at the inaction" of the Assembly on the subject, finding it difficult to reconcile it "with our duty to the slave, the master, to the world, or to ourselves." Noting that in the last seventeen years "we have not advanced one step toward clearing ourselves of this wrong," Presbytery in a circular letter to other presbyteries queried, "Is not the set time come? or will we debate and procrastinate and apologize for doing nothing, and find fault with each other, and leave American slavery unrebuked in our fellowship a century longer?" The letter concluded with a call for unity on the part of the northern judicatories:

> If they will hold slaves, our duty is to say, that they cannot do it in our fellowship. And this we propose to say through a solemn vote of the General Assembly, so soon as that can be readily obtained . . . . If you agree with us, will you pledge us your aid on the floor of the Assembly, and we will pledge you ours. [59]

But in the South, the small Presbytery of Harmony (Kentucky) reflected that region's mind when it resolved: "This Presbytery are satisfied with the disposition made of the subject of slavery by the last General Assembly, and . . . they earnestly desire that future Assemblies may dispose of it in like manner."[60]

By now only the most naive could have failed to see the clouds hovering over the Church. The picture was ominous: political parties had been organized, had died, and had been resurrected under new names over the slavery issue; two of the major denominations had suffered schism over it; new missionary societies had formed for assisting only those churches that had no slaveholders, or assisting those that did; only the strong southern element prevented the Old School from passing stronger resolutions against the institution than it had; and increasing pressure from the vast majority of the New School incessantly demanded that more effective ways be taken to remove the odious blot from the Church. Under such meteoric and trying conditions did the New School General Assembly meet in St. Louis for its 1855 sessions--one of the very few times it convened in slave territory.

Two synods, a dozen presbyteries, and a Congregational church memorialized the 1855 Assembly on the slavery issue. The general complaint was that the directives of 1853 had not been implemented. Yet the Presbytery of Philadelphia, Third, of which Albert Barnes was a member, overtured the Assembly, deprecating any action on the part of that judicatory that would disregard the "peace, unity and prosperity of the Church."

With one elder from the South on it, the Committee on Bills and Overtures made its report, a unanimous report. It recommended that the Assembly send out a Pastoral Letter to all churches under its care in which it would reaffirm the testimony of past Assemblies regarding the sinfulness of the system of slavery. The Letter would also express the deep regret at the "intemperateness of word and action" that has been too often the spirit "of those who have conscientiously aimed" at slavery's overthrow on the one hand, and would urge, at the same time, "earnest efforts" on the part of the churches "to remove the evil from the midst of us." It then recommended that a Committee be appointed to report to the next Assembly "on the constitutional power of the Assembly over the subject of slaveholding in our churches" with a view that "this evil be removed from our Church, as soon as it can be done in a Christian and constitutional manner."[61]

In Barnes's comments on the Assembly's adoption of the Committee's report, he noted that the system of slavery was never contemplated in the Presbyterian Church as one to be perpetuated, or that it stood on the same level as the relation of parent to child, or of guardian to ward. "It is an *evil*; it is a *sinful* system; it is a system that is to be wholly '*removed*' as soon as it can be done." Such was his position.[62]

Although the idea of "removing the evil" was in the resolutions adopted by the Assembly, the southern courts found solace in the legislation. The South still held out the hope that such an eventuality might be avoided. It must be remembered that the men in the South understood the Constitution of the Church as providing no possible way whereby the Assembly could do what it had been commissioned to do. The Synod of Mississippi sounded out the other five synods on the possibility of establishing a distinctive southern Church, but the general feeling was that at that time no steps should be taken to precipitate a division. Always in the southern breasts lingered the hope that the brothers with whom they had sympathetically cast their lot in 1838 would never pass the legislation that would drive them from their house.

The Assembly appointed a committee of five to report to the 1856 Assembly "on the constitutional power of the Assembly over the subject of slaveholding in our churches." Included in the committee were Albert Barnes of Philadelphia and Andrew H. H. Boyd of Winchester, Virginia.

The strength of the New School in the South lay in its conviction that the Constitution contained nothing that would permit the Church from taking any substantive action on the slavery issue. They had forgotten, however, that whereas the Old School clung to the letter of the Constitution, the New School held to the spirit.

Throughout the argument in the New School over the slavery question, many memorials had been sent up from the lower judicatories; but there was never one that petitioned the Assembly to alter the Book of Discipline by adding appropriate sections to the Constitution whereby those engaged in the system of slavery--buying and selling, owning, managing, or any other activity--would be subject to the discipline of the Church. Such a procedure would have been very simple: approval at a meeting of the General Assembly, referral to the presbyteries, which required only a majority for approval, and then subsequent approval by the next Assembly. In each of the three steps the antislavery presbyteries would have been more than sufficient to make slavery a condition for discipline. Yet the initial step of the overture was never taken--indeed, one of the salient mysteries in American Presbyterian polity.

The Assembly met in New York in 1856. By far the most important item on the agenda was the report of the "Committee on the Constitutional Power of the General Assembly over the Subject of Slaveholding in our Churches." Four of the members signed the report. Andrew H. H. Boyd submitted a minority report.[63] The majority report acknowledged that the Assembly itself could not commence a process of discipline with an individual offender. Such authority resided solely in a session or presbytery. There was, however, the mediate way by which the Assembly could reach a session:

> In the way of "general review and control," it can reach *directly* only the judicatory next below--that is, the Synod .... Indirectly, indeed, the doings of other bodies may be involved. A Session may grossly neglect discipline, for example, and the recorded indication, or the common fame thereof may not properly be heeded by the Presbytery. The fruit of this heedlessness, or the evidence of it in the Presbyterial records, may call forth no appropriate action on the part of the Synod; and this may be brought by the Synodical records or by general rumor to the knowledge of the Assembly. On the ground either of the record or the rumor, the Assembly may cite the Synod before them. Thus *mediately* may even a Session be reached, but not directly.

This according to Barnes' interpretation, meant that the slaveholder is not prima facie in good standing in the Presbyterian Church. He commented further, "For one, I glory in this position, and deem it an honour to belong to a church where these sentiments have been uttered; these positions taken; and these ends avowed."[65]

Boyd's protest to the Majority Report contained six points. The first stated that because of the Assembly's advisory power, it can bear testimony against anything it may regard as sin in the sight of God, but such testimony has no authoritative or binding effect upon the lower judicatories. He then underscored the fact that the Assembly can regard as heresy or offence nothing that is not distinctly stated to be such in the Church's standards. Since slaveholding is not so alluded to in the Confession of Faith either directly or indirectly, "the relation itself of master and servant cannot in any case be a cause of discipline before any judicatory." Cruelties practiced by those who sustain this relationship, since such are directly prohibited in the Confession, may be a cause of discipline. But in any case, "the General Assembly cannot interpret the Constitution of the Church in regard to offences, unless a case is brought before it from a lower Court by reference, complaint or appeal; or unless the Assembly acts as a Court of Review." Finally, Boyd pointed out that even when a synod is cited to the bar of the Assembly and is required to take up the subject and consider it, the matter is left with the synod to require the presbytery to take further action or to stay all further proceedings as circumstances may require.[66]

Boyd was one of the most intelligent and respected members in the New School South. He was the rational epitome of that point of view. His entire argument was based on the literal interpretation of the Constitution, and in his sight the Constitution gave the Assembly no jurisdiction over individuals.[67] Still his report remained the minority report. The weakness of the southern position was its defense of slavery, even to averring that it was ordained of God and, as existing in this country, was both right and scriptural. Such a position was not only untenable, but at variance with the whole spirit of the Gospel, and increasingly abhorrent to the Christian world.

In the fall of 1856 Archer C. Dickerson of Bowling Green, Kentucky, one of the original pioneers in the Southern New School movement, commented,

> We do profoundly admire and honestly love the American Presbyterian Church. We love her order; we adopt her interpretation of the Bible; we love her catholic spirit; we find her equal no where; and yet, when we would scheme to do her good, or essay to parade her excellencies before others, or gather up the energies of our churches for expansive and aggressive movements, here rises up this hydra monster, the "slavery agitation," and mars all our peace, and cripples all our efforts, and saddens all our hearts, and is constantly pushing into our face the miserable thought of "separation!" We have been patient--will be so; but the "end" must be somewhere. Hopes of peace, so long deferred, do indeed make our hearts sick! This agitation, whatever Dr. Ross or any other Dr. may think, is killing the Southern churches! For one, I devoutly hope the next Assembly will do something decisive, one way or the other. If we are ever to have peace, say so, openly and honestly . . . .[68]

If it was "decisive" action Archer desired, he was not disappointed when the 1857 Assembly met in Cleveland. The 1856 Assembly would be the last one to adjourn with all the New School united when the Apostolic Benediction, dismissing the Assembly, was pronounced. A year later, the Church would experience division and thus join the ranks of the Baptists and Methodists, who had divided over the issue of the role of the Church as it confronted the institution of domestic slavery in America.

NOTES

1. George M. Marsden, in *The Evangelical Mind and the New School Presbyterian Experience: A Case Study of Thought and Theology in Nineteenth-Century America* (New Haven and London: Yale University Press, 1970), p. 101, claimed that the presence of the southerners in the New School "was sufficient to stifle any decisive denominational action against slavery for twenty years." He overestimated considerably the numerical strength of the southern New School and underestimated other factors that worked to keep the Church united.

2. William C. Brackett, Jr., "The Rise and Development of the New School in the Presbyterian Church in the U. S. A. to the Reunion of 1869," *JPHS* 13 (1928): 171.

3. William Henry Foote, *Sketches of Virginia, Historical and Biographical,* 2nd series, 2nd ed., rev. (Philadelphia: J. B. Lippincott & Co., 1856), p. 505.

4. Ernest Trice Thompson, *Presbyterians in the South,* 3 vols. (Richmond: John Knox Press, 1963-1973), 1:136-137. The essential weakness of the report was its failure to provide disciplinary action against the church members who violated its principles. For a recent introduction, as well as text, of Bourne's work, see John W. Christie and Dwight L. Dumond, *George Bourne and The Book and Slavery Irreconcilable* (Wilmington, Delaware: The Historical Society of Delaware; Philadelphia: Presbyterian Historical Society, 1969).

5. For a succinct summary of Finney's contribution to revivalism, see Bernard A. Weisberger, *They Gathered at the River: The Story of the Great Revivalists and Their Impact upon Religion in America* (Boston and Toronto: Little, Brown and Company, 1958), pp. 146-148.

6. For a full discussion of this issue, see Elwyn A. Smith, "The Role of the South in the Presbyterian Schism of 1837-38," *CH* 29 (1960): 44-63.

7. A good example of this is the efforts of Samuel H. Cox. See Dwyn Mecklin Mounger, "Samuel Hanson Cox: Anti-Catholic, Anti-Anglican, Anti-Congregationalist Ecumenist," *JPH* 55 (1977): 347-361.

8. The main sources for much of this chapter are *Minutes* of GAPCUSA [NS]; William E. Moore, *A New Digest of the Acts and Deliverances of the General Assembly of the Presbyterian Church in the United States of America* [New School]. *Compiled by the Order and Authority of the General Assembly* (Philadelphia: Presbyterian Publication Committee; New York: A. D. F. Randolph, 1861), pp. 275-295; and Albert Barnes, *The Church and Slavery,* 2nd ed. (Philadelphia: Parry & McMillan, 1857), pp. 67-121.

9. GAPCUSA [NS], *Minutes* (1839), p. 22; Moore, *Digest,* p. 275.

10. According to Mounger ("Samuel Hanson Cox," p. 356), this concept came from Cox.

11. Barnes, *Church and Slavery,* pp. 72-74.

12. GAPCUSA [NS], *Minutes* (1840), pp. 18-19; Moore, *Digest,* p. 275. In 1839 three overtures were sent down to the presbyteries concerning the matter

of triennial Assemblies, since such would change the Form of Government of the Church. All three overtures were favorably voted on.

13. Mounger, "Samuel Hanson Cox," p. 356.

14. Barnes, *Church and Slavery,* pp. 74-75. See also Edward D. Morris, *The Presbyterian Church New School 1837-1869: An Historical Review* (Columbus, Ohio: Champlin Press, 1905), pp. 99-100.

15. GAPCUSA [NS], *Minutes* (1840), p. 12.

16. Ibid., p. 24.

17. *Minutes of the southern and South-Western Presbyterian Convention,* Held at Cassville, Ga. October, 1840 (Charleston: B. B. Hussey, 1840), p. 6.

18. [James Gillespie Birney], *The American Churches, The Bulwarks of American Slavery,* 2nd. American ed. (Newburyport, Massachusetts: Charles Whipple, 1842), p. 33.

19. GAPCUSA [NS], *Minutes* (1843), p. 19; Moore, *Digest,* pp. 275-276; Barnes, *Church and Slavery,* pp. 75-76.

20. *Protestant and Herald,* 6 July 1843.

21. *CO,* 21 July 1843.

22. Synod of Indiana [NS], typed "Minutes" (21 October 1843), pp. 311-320, PHF.

23. Synod of Kentucky [NS], typed "Minutes" (11 October 1845), pp. 33-34, PHF.

24. Morris, *Presbyterian Church New School,* pp. 156-157.

25. Barnes, *Church and Slavery,* pp. 78-79. *CO* in seven consecutive issues (5, 12, 19, and 26 June and 3, 10, and 17 July 1846) carried extensive remarks of the commissioners, which contain the gist of the arguments. The paper tended to give more space to the remarks of the southern commissioners than the northern.

26. GAPCUSA [NS], *(1846), pp. 28-30;* Moore, *Digest,* pp. 276-277; Barnes, *Church and Slavery,* pp. 76-82.

27. GAPCUSA [NS], *Minutes* (1846), pp. 30-31.

28. Converse's counsel was typical of his desire that the North know more about the South. Since the lines of communication between the two regions were closing for the most part, he besought the southerners to inform the North regarding slavery in their region. This was no tongue-in-cheek advice, but rather a very earnest suggestion on his part, *CO* 3 July 1846.

29. John J. Robinson, *Memoir of Rev. Isaac Anderson, DD., Late President of Maryville College, and Professor of Didactic Theology* (Knoxville: J. Addison Rayl, 1860), pp. 142-143.

30. Timothy Hill, "History of the New School Synod of Missouri," in Synod of Missouri [PCUSA], *Minutes* (1882), p. 58.

31. *CO*, 20 November 1846; Thompson, *Presbyterians in the South*, 1:541.

32. *Historical Sketch of the Synod of Ohio (N. S.) From 1838 to 1868* (Cincinnati: Elm Street Publishing Co., 1870), p. 14.

33. GAPCUSA [NS], *Minutes* (1847), pp. 148-149; ibid. (1849), p. 175.

34. Ibid. (1849), pp. 185-188; Moore, *Digest*, 277-282.

35. John M. Akers, "Slavery and Sectionalism: Some Aspects of Church and Society among Presbyterians in the American South, 1789-1861" (Ph.D. diss., University of Edinburgh, 1973), p. 249.

36. GAPCUSA [NS], *Minutes* (1850), pp. 324-325; Moore, *Digest* p. 283. For the general discussion of the debate, see Barnes, *Church and Slavery*, pp. 84-90. The actions of the 1850 Assembly prompted the publication of the speech that Joseph C. Stiles delivered before the Assembly. His comments centered around two questions: What is the moral character of slavery? and What are the duties of the parties concerned? See Stiles, *Speech on the Slavery Resolutions, Delivered in the General Assembly which Met in Detroit in May Last* (Washington: Jno. T. Towers, 1850).

37. Morris, *Presbyterian Church New School*, p. 116.

38. So Akers, "Slavery and Sectionalism," p. 332, n. 2.

39. GAPCUSA [NS], *Minutes* (1851), p. 13; Moore, *Digest*, p. 283.

40. Quoted in the *CO*, 14 June 1851; See Morris, *Presbyterian Church New School*, p. 120.

41. GAPCUSA [NS], *Minutes* (1852), p. 162.

42. William Goodell, *Slavery and Anti-Slavery: a History of the Great Struggle in Both Hemispheres; with a View of the Slavery Question in the United States* (New York: William Harned, 1852), pp. 161-162. To Goodell, the telling event was the New School's failure to take any action in 1851. He pointed out that this refusal brought great satisfaction to President Millard Fillmore, who sought peace in this disturbing area.

43. GAPCUSA [NS], *Minutes* (1853), p. 333; Moore, *Digest*, pp. 284-285; Barnes, *Church and Slavery*, pp. 92-93.

44. GAPCUSA [NS], *Minutes* (1853), pp. 333-334. In the debate on the floor, Ross stated,

"We will not permit you to approach us at all. If we are morbidly insensitive, you have made us so. But you are directly and grossly violating the Consitution of the Presbyterian Church. The book forbids *you to begin discipline*; the book forbids your sending this committee to help common fame bear witness against us: the book guards the honour of our humblest member, minister, church, presbytery, against all this impertinently-inquisitorial action"; Frederick A. Ross, *Slavery Ordained of God* (Philadelphia: J. B. Lippincott, 1859), p. 21.

45. GAPCUSA [NS], *Minutes* (1853), pp. 335-336; Victor B. Howard, "The Southern Aid Society and the Slavery Controversy," *Church History* 41 (1972): 216-217; Mounger, "Samuel Hanson Cox," p. 358.

46. Barnes, *Church and Slavery*, pp. 96-97.

47. *CO*, 13 August 1853. For equally vehement responses see the following: Synod of Virginia (*CO*, 8 September 1853); Richland Presbytery, MS "Minutes" (6 October 1853), pp. 123-124, PHF; Winchester Presbytery (*CO*, 8 October 1853); Synod of Tennessee (*CO*, 22 October 1853); Presbytery of Shiloh (*CO*, 24 September 1853); Presbytery of Providence, MS "Minutes" (24 September 1853), LPTS; Harmony Presbytery (*CO*, 15 October 1853); Osage Presbytery (*CO*, 12 November 1853); Hanover Presbytery, (*CO*, 10 December, 1853). Clinton Presbytery in Mississippi viewed the action of the Assembly as so unconstitutional that it waited until the April 1854 meeting to make any reply, because it believed that surely the 1854 General Assembly would rescind its action; *CO*, 13 May 1854.

48. For the full text, see *CO*, 28 May 1853.

49. Ibid., 9 July 1853.

50. Ibid., 23 July 1853.

51. Holston Presbytery [NS], MS "Minutes" (23 September 1853), pp. 308-309, PHF.

52. *CO*, 25 March 1854.

53. Ibid., 29 April 1854.

54. Ibid., 20 May 1854.

55. Barnes, *Church and Slavery*, p. 97.

56. GAPCUSA [NS], *Minutes* (1854), pp. 498-499.

57. Ibid., pp. 504-505.

58. "The Southern Apostasy," *New Englander* 12 (November 1854): 662.

59. *CO*, 16 September 1854.

60. Ibid., 7 October 1854.

61. GAPCUSA [NS], *Minutes* (1855), p. 30; Moore, *Digest*, pp. 285-286.

62. Barnes, *Church and Slavery*, p. 101.

63. For the full text of the Committee's report, see GAPCUSA [NS], *Minutes* (1856), pp. 197-

200; Moore, *Digest*, 286-291. *CO*, 29 May 1856, also contains the report of the minority.

64. *Church and Slavery*, p. 121. Barnes reviewed the entire issue and debate, pp. 110-121.

65. Ibid., p. 120.

66. *CO*, 29 May 1856.

67. Boyd must be seen as the continuance of that position which from the beginning of the New School emphasized the necessity of adhering to the Standards of the Church. Of the three--Old School, New School North, and New School South--the last adhered more closely to the *letter* of the Constitution than did the other two.

68. Cited in *CO*, 18 November 1856. Frederick A. Ross opposed any talk of southern secession in the New School until the last moment. After the Murfreesboro Convention of 1853, he wrote a lengthy letter to the *CO* (15 October 1853), in which he concluded: "I regret that the Murfreeboro' Convention intimated the remotest possibility of our secession. I regret their manifesto did not say:-- 'We have no idea of leaving our noble body. If any choose to slough off--we of the South are in, and will remain in the General Assembly.'"

7
The Division of 1857

Following the adjournment of the 1856 Assembly, the delegates from the South sent a communication addressed "To the Ministers and Members of the Constitutional Presbyterian Churches Residing in the Slave-holding States." The document was drawn up and distributed because the signers were apprehensive that the action of the Assembly be misunderstood. Believing that the resolution passed by the Assembly was "ambiguous," they composed the letter "to call . . . attention to the true import of the resolution." The letter was signed by all the commissioners from the slaveholding synods.

The letter pointed out that slavery or slaveholding was not a sin and thus cannot be the basis for Church discipline. The Detroit Resolutions implied that slavedholding is a sin, and could be made cause for discipline only when it violates the obligations of guardianship and the demands of humanity. But the resolutions were not the law of the Church: they merely expressed the sentiments of the Assembly. No action could be taken on the part of the Assembly unless a case should be brought before it by a lower judicatory, by reference, complaint or appeal. It was the signers' judgment that the action of the Assembly, "viewed as a whole, is favorable to the South--inasmuch as it expresses the Consititutional principles by which anything that may be regarded as an offence is to be brought before the Assembly." The letter concluded with the affirmation that the signers were "unanimous in the opinion that there is no occasion for alienation or separation on the part of our churches."¹

The letter assured the Southern New School that the commissioners who had sat through and participated in the debate on the slavery issue could live with the decision. There was no need to withdraw. This was the first time that such "pastoral" counseling had been felt necessary on the part of southern commissioners.

Talk of southern withdrawal from the New School was not new. It had been in the air for some time. In 1855 a "brother in Mississippi" had written that in that synod an increasing number of the ministers was in favor of withdrawing. The northern agitation was not helping the New School in Mississippi. At the same time, the anonymous writer confessed that he did not think "there is much if any disposition to unite with the Old School. Indeed, save for the agitation, the Old School have assumed ground as hostile to the South as the New School have."

Amasa Converse, continuing his pattern of moderation, cautioned that "the importance of ecclesiasitcal union between the North and the South--it is above all price that can be named in gold. The honor of religion . . . require[s] the preservation of the bond of union."² And at its 1856 Stated Fall Meeting the Presbytery of Richland resolved that it had "unshaken confidence in the Consitution of our church, and in the Christian integrity, conservative prudence and fraternal regard of that Genl. Assembly of which [Presbytery] is a competent member." The action of the Assembly "furnishes no ground on which to predicate any fear of exscision," but rather "affords encouraging evidence of the fraternal disposition of a large majority of our brethren and of their intention to sustain our present connection, so long as we stand on a Constiutional basis."³

It was thus against this background of southern confidence in the denomination that the General Assembly convened in Cleveland in 1857. This was to be the most momentous meeting in the history of the New School. The 1856 meeting of Mississippi Synod had responded to the Assembly's action of that year by passing a series of resolutions. The Synod held "ourselves in readiness to co-operate with our brethren in the southern Synods in any action which may seem to be demanded by our relation to the General Assembly . . . ." It further directed its Stated Clerk to "open a correspondence" with a view of "fraternal interchange of opinion" between the other five sister synods.⁴ The Assembly's Committee on Synod Records in 1857 approved the Synod's minutes, failing to heed the warning found in the resolutions.

The critical issue facing the 1857 Assembly was a memorial from the Synod of Western Reserve. It requested the Assembly to direct the Synod of Mississippi to order the Presbytery of Lexington, South, to try the Rev. William E. Holley for having stated that he held slaves "of choice and from principle."[5] In the meantime, Holley had died. Thus, his co-presbyters, holding the same sentiments which he embraced, had instructed their commissioners to transfer the charge to them, from the dead to the living, and to urge upon the Assembly to direct the Synod of Mississippi to proceed against the Presbytery of Lexington, South, if it believed the presbytery to be guilty of an offence.[6]

Other southern New School presbyteries had taken a decided stand, reaffirming that the relation between master and servant was recognized and sanctioned according to the word of God. But the *New York Evangelist*, perhaps the most influential paper in the northern New School, affirmed at the conclusion of a very lengthy article that "by no word or act, nor even by our silence, will we countenance this modern idea, that God's word sanctions slavery, and that it is to be classed with the parental and conjugal relations, and consequently to be regarded as a permanent Institution."[7] It was thus obvious that the Assembly would either have to step down from its previous course of action and prior legislation, or it would be forced to reiterate its former utterances, only expressed in firmer, stronger, more positive terms.

Albert Barnes had written and published his book, *The Church and Slavery*, before the fateful 1857 Assembly. He optimistically declared, "Not a presbytery, not a church, not a man, as far as is known, North or South, has left the church in consequence of the discussion" that had emerged from the 1856 assembly. In fact, he boasted that there was "no other denomination of Christians in the land, not even the Congregational, where the subject has been so freely examined, or has called forth so much prayer and solicitude as to the course which should be pursued by the church. In this respect . . . the New School Presbyterian church is in advance of all other churches in the land," he admiringly concluded.[8] In that same year, the Old School apologete for the proslavery position, George Armstrong, wrote, "The Church and State each has its own appropriate sphere of operation assigned it of God, and neither can innocently intrude herself into the province of the other."⁹ The Old School body had grown more tolerant of slavery, while the New School had gradually taken a more decided stand. Yet, at least in the New School, there was the optimism of Barnes in spite of the editorial cautions of the *New York Evangelist*.

The basis for optimism in the North was not completely groundless. Over and over again, as the annual groundswell in each Assembly had swept closer to a cataclysmic confrontation, the men in the South had sworn anew their loyalty to the New School, a loyalty based on a principle very dear to their hearts. In 1855 George White had commented that the "uneasiness of the South" was not a "precursor of division." Although some had suggested that the South might secede, White reaffirmed "this the South will never do. They have stood by the consititution too long to be driven off by any action which leaves one stone of it left." Then turning to the North, he affirmed,

> We have stood by you in the days of your trouble, and by the grace of God, we will stick to you still--not in anger, but in love. The fidelity of the South has been maintained at too great cost to be so easily abandoned . . . . No, the South is not going to secede; we do not back up our remonstrances by any such argument in terrorem. The South will stand by the Constitution.[10]

The fanatical, radical loyalty of the South to the New School's understanding of the Church's Standards did not go completely unnoticed by all members in the North. Five months before the decisive 1857 Assembly convened, an anonymous writer, "Noth," made these penetrating comments:

> Who are these brethren? Our Church does not embrace another body of Presbyters, of equal numbers, whose loss would be more deeply felt by those who value ministers, in proportion as they preach Christ, and promote revivals. Whatever views may have been entertained of their relations to slavery, I have never heard it questioned that their labors in the gospel, are abundant and successful . . . . When we are ecclesiastically separated from the South, shall we have peace? Brethren who, against their own judgment, permit the thing to be

done, hope that peace will compensate for our dismemberment. It is strange that human nature cannot be read better.[11]

Robert McLain, a native Tennesseean now preaching in Enterprise, Mississippi, looked back to the people whence he had come, and praised their integrity: "They were constitutional in 1838 . . . . they will be constitutional men in 1857; and if so, they and Mississippi Synod will be found battling side by side for constitutional right and constitutional freedom. . . ."[12]

"In 1857 the New School Church split North and South. Most of us have forgotten that."[13] Other Presbyterian schisms have been remembered--the Old Light-New light, the Cumberland schism, the Old School-New School division, the Old School schism of 1861--but few church historians have given much attention to the New School rift.[14] There can be no doubt that the momentous Dred Scott decision of 6 March 1857 played an influential role in the New School Assembly's action of that year. Clifton E. Olmstead has commented that with the decision "moderate evangelists were convinced that the time for charity and patience was over." Even the opponents of radicalism found themselves in the camp of the advocates of immediate abolitionism. Such "came not to bring peace but a sword with which to amputate the gangrenous member of American Society and purify the nation for its divine mission to the world."[15]

The action of two presbyteries prior to the Assembly provided a preview of what lay ahead for the Assembly of 1857. On 10 April 1857 the Presbytery of Knox (Illinois) passed a scathing denunciation of slavery. It declared that every slaveholder in the Church deserved the Church's discipline. If necessary, in order to provide the "peace, and order, and purity" of the Church, let it be done by separation. The overture to the Assembly pointed out that the Presbytery had lost "many of our churches and our church members" because the New School had taken no firm stand on slavery. "Much gound has been lost, and Presbytery cannot consent, always to bear the reproach which this evil casts upon us; and therefore we desire the Assembly to give us assurance of our final separation from it. . . ."[16]

In the South the Presbytery of Shiloh (West Tennessee) deplored the further agitation of the slavery issue because it tended to produce alienation, strife, and mental distrust. The Presbytery unanimously agreed that "no charges of *moral obliquity* can reach the judgment of the conscience of the ministry or the Churches, so as to induce them to abandon the relationship [between master and servant], as sinful. . . ." It charged that on the North rested the responsibility for preventing the "*unavoidable severance* of the South. *If they* WILL, they CAN prevent the forcing *of the ploughshares of division through our branch of the Zion of our God."* If the men of the North purpose to assist their southern brothers, "*who claim to have as sacred a regard for the Word of God and the Consititution of out Church as any other portion of our American Zion,* we would suggest that it is high time that this determination should be made known."[17]

The debate over the slavery question, prompted by the memorial of the Synod of Western Reserve, was lengthy. Two southern commissioners, Frederick A. Ross and Archer C. Dickerson, manned the defenses against the northern onslaught. Ross's defense of the institution spoke with a unique cogency to men of a day which honored and revered the Bible as the infallible Word of God. He was in that beleagured group that took refuge behind the Book and the established traditions of the Protestant faith. He did not agree with Voltaire that the black was a different species. He did, however, disagree with those who placed him in the same category as did the Declaration of Independence which contained the premise that it is a self-evident truth that all men are created equal. Ross thundered, "It is not the truth, in fact that they are created equal. So, then, it is not the truth that God has endowed all men with unalienable right to life, liberty, and pursuit of happiness."[18] In line with orthodox Calvinists--and Ross certainly did not consistently stand in that category--he argued that government is an agent of God. It stands responsible to God for what God Himself would do. Nor can it do more than God would do. It must rule, however, in righteousness; it must not oppress; it must grant life, liberty, and the pursuit of happiness. But it must do so in harmony with the good of the family and the state, just as God Himself would do.[19]

If all men are not thus created equally in attributes of body and mind, Ross contended that " the *inequality* may be *so great* that such men cannot be endowed with right to life, liberty and pursuit of happiness, unalienable save in their *consent*. . . . " Government over men in this class cannot "rightfully rest upon their *consent;* nor can they have right to alter or abolish government in their mere determination."[20]

Albert Barnes's use of the Bible in his attack on slavery had so exasperated Ross that he was prepared to repudiate the Declaration of Independence because it was not Biblical.[21] Ross denied that the doctrine of the equality of man was sanctioned in Holy Writ, but was rather founded on the infidel theories of the Enlightenment. In his view, "all this--every word of it--every jot and tittle, is the liberty claimed by infidelity." Southerners would prefer to take their stand on the Bible, where there are no "false ideas of created equality and unalienable right."[22] Those who charged slavery as a moral evil did so out of a fundamental misconception of the Biblical nature of sin. Pursuing a line of scholastic reasoning in a brilliant fashion, Ross attacked the doctrine of slavery as sin per se. He attempted to demonstrate that slavery, as an institution, was in complete accord with the spoken and written Word of God.[23]

Abolitionists stressed the Golden Rule for their antislavery argument. They over-emphasize the text, according to Ross. He insisted that the Golden Rule did not spell out what man's relations are to his fellowman; it merely told him what he must do when he knew these relationships. The Golden Rule presupposes that he who is required to obey it already understands the relations in which God has placed him and the duties that go with these relationships. God has established the relations of husband-wife, parent-child, master-slave.[24] Ross viewed the abolition agitation a blessing in disguise, for it forced southerners to search for answers to the attack, and in turn they were impelled to discover the Biblical roots of their institution. Finding the answers which they had sought in Holy Writ, they grew in their faith, for the habit of searching the Scriptures brought its inevitable blessings.[25]

But it was not only Ross's views of government and the Scriptures which supported his premises concerning domestic slavery; there were also the conclusions which he drew from history in general, and emancipation in the Caribbean in particular. Both Haiti and Jamaica had abolished slavery, and these two countries loomed as sores on the earth's body. The French Revolution had eliminated slavery throughout the French Empire. But in Haiti, that condition, instead of bringing in the utopian state, had, in Ross's eyes, been followed by a despotism which could very practically furnish a sufficient example to the southerner of the dangerous ends of such speculative systems of thought. Here was an object lesson which recent history itself unfolded before the eyes of the slaveholder that brought the danger close to him. The carnage of Haiti was sufficient to make one shudder with apprehension by realizing the possibility of similar calamities in the South. As William S. Jenkins later noted, "The proponents of slavery continued to use the example of Santo Domingo as the chief objective argument to show the impossibility of emancipation whenever it was proposed within the South by outsiders." Ross's writings are webbed with references to what happened there. He was not unaware of the chaotic conditions which existed in certain parts of the British Empire, where slaves had been freed all at one time--conditions that could also lead the South into chaos.[26]

Unlike many of his southern peers, however, Ross did not consider the institution of domestic slavery as permanent. He could see its end. He favored a system of gradualism in attaining the goal. His fierce denunciations of abolition were directed, not at the slave, but at the northern opponents' attitude toward slavery--visionaries who meddled in a problem about which they had very little practical knowledge.[27]

The speech of Archer C. Dickerson before the 1857 Assembly was published in a small pamphlet, *Anti-Slavery Agitation in the Church not Authorised*.[28] In his remarks, Dickerson complained that the end of the abolitionists is clear, but the means whereby slaveholding is to be separated from the Church is not clear at all. First, there had been free discussion of the issue; then, remonstrance and reproof; then, inquiry concerning disciplinary power; and now, process is directly proposed. He then stated his thesis:

> That the subject of slavery--it being a political institution--lies WITHOUT the province of ecclesiastical supervision:--that the rights and immunities of membership, in the Presbyterian Church, in *no way* and to *no degree*, depend upon the opinions or practicing of individuals, in relation to slaveholding:-- and that all agitation of this subject in our General Assembly is *illegitimate* to their proper functions:--and that this whole subject should, therefore, be totally ignored.[29]

He approached the subject in relation to the Church's Constitution, in reference to the teachings of the Bible, and in the light of the results which the Church had already reached.

Dickerson's address is valuable for its thorough, systematic effort to portray the political, not the ecclesiastical, nature of the slavery issue. The most important portion is the first part, in which he developed the issue as it related to the Constitution of the Church. The rest is merely a rehashing of old themes. He pointed out that there had been no changes in the Church's Standards through all the years of the slavery agitation. He noted that when he became a member of the Presbyterian Church, his holding of slaves did not bar him from communion. Nor did it prevent him from being ordained to the Church's ministry. The Constitution contained the terms for admission as a member and for ordination as a minister.

> Not a word of slave-holding being unlawful was uttered, and none found in the Book! Yet now, after the prime of life spent in her service, and no ordinary share of trials, my fair standing is assailed, in memorials here sent, by entire Synods, and actual disciplinary processes are proposed, looking to my expulsion; and all on ground which existed at the time of my admission, and was known to exist by the Presbytery that ordained me. At the same time, the action of the Presbytery was sustained by the Synod, and its action by the General Assembly.[30]

Dickerson did not deny the Assembly's right to bear testimony against error in doctrine or immorality, but he denied the Assembly's power to ascertain what comprises error or immorality. Such are in the Standards of the Church, and it does not lie within the province of the Assembly--which is the product of the Standards, and which meets only annually--over against the Standards, which have an eternal aura about them, to determine what are errors in doctrine or immorality in practice.

Dickerson then pointed out that the Constitution of American Presbyterianism was written by men who were slaveholders. When it was revised in the early 1820s, it was done by men who were slaveholders. Yet, never was there any mention that slaveholding was or is a sin. And if the Assembly should define what sin is, then we all hold our rights of membership, upon the interpretation of the Bible by the General Assembly, and not upon the Constitution! And as each General Assembly expires with the term of its sittings, no man can know what the tenures of his membership are except as each Assembly may determine![31]

Dickerson concluded his comments noting the dilemma which most southerners face if slaves are immediately emancipated:

> You say, rid yourself of the "foul sin," without regard to consequences! His common sense and honesty both rebel. No. Show him what is to be done with the slave when he is free; where he is to go, and the guarantee of amelioration. All this the slavery agitation of twenty years has failed to do. Cease it, then, and return to the apostolic plan.[32]

The report adopted by the General Assembly (by vote of 169-26) reviewed the actions of the Assemblies of 1787, 1793, 1815, 1818, 1846, 1849, and 1850. Slavery was renounced as

> at will with the whole spirit and tenor of the Gospel of love and good will, as well as abhorrent to the conscience of the Christian world. We can have no sympathy or fellowship with it; and we exhort all our people to eschew it as serious and pernicious error.

This statement was the first intimation in all the Assemblies' slavery legislation that the persons engaged in slaveholding should be barred from the Church.

There then followed the specific reference to the Presbytery of Lexington, South, viz.:

> We are especially pained by the fact that the Presbytery of Lexington, South, have given official notice to us that a number of ministers and ruling elders, as well as many church-members, in their connection, hold slaves "from principle" and "of choice," "believing it to be according to the Bible right," and have, without any qualifying explanation, assumed the responsibility of sustaining such ministers, elders, and church-members in their position. We deem it our duty, in the exercise of our constitutional authority, "to bear testimony against error in

doctrine or immorality in practice in any church, Presbytery, or Synod," to disapprove and earnestly condemn the position which has been assumed by the Presbytery of Lexington, South, as one which is opposed to the established convictions of the Presbyterian Church, and must operate to mar its peace and seriously hinder its prosperity, as well as bring reproach on our holy religion; and we do hereby call on that Presbytery to review and rectify their postion. Such doctrines and practices cannot be permanently tolerated in the Presbyterian Church.[33]

A Protest was immediately presented. First, it stated that the testimony of previous Assemblies had satisfied the South, "as to make it unnecessary to do more than protest against the mere anti-slavery part of such testimony." It then noted that the decision of the Assembly "degrades the whole Southern Church--an assertion without authority from the word of God, of the organic law of the Presbyterian body." It further called attention that the action is, "under present conditions, the virtual exscinding of the South, whatever be the motives of those who vote for the deed." Finally, the indirect exscision was termed "unrighteous, oppressive, uncalled for," an exercise of usurped power, destructive of the unity of the Church, and "adding to the peril of union of these United States."[34] In the reply to the Protests, the respondents claimed that "if the Southern men break with the unity of the Church, the responsibility will be with them, not us."[35]

Although the debates preceding the adoption of the report were "candid and fraternal," division did come, "and the parties separated without bitterness and with sincere mutual respect and love," according to Samuel J. Wilson, who wrote twenty-eight years after the event.[36] There can be no doubt, however, that the men from the South felt themselves as having been judged unworthy of fellowship with their former brothers in the North, because they were not prepared to receive the new interpretation, which they believed usurped the prerogative of the Constitution. Their only recourse lay in withdrawing.[37] They returned to their presbyteries, sustained to a man in their vote for withdrawal, save for Timothy Hill, whose vote to sustain the report made him a marked man in his home Synod of Missouri.[38]

Ecclesiastical schisms are difficult to analyze. Political divisions usually result in civil war, with a view of bringing the dissidents back into a basic national unity whence they had departed. Ethnic divisions manifest themselves in migrations, the cutting of ties. But rifts in the Body of Christ go very deep, indeed threatening the "peace, purity and unity of the Church." How, then, does one interpret or analyze them?[39]

The dilemma of the New School in pressing the issue for so many yars was ponderingly considered by the Church historian, Edward D. Morris, who wrote the first substantive history of the New School:

> It will always be a question whether it was wise for the young Church, with so many practical problems at hand calling for early solution, with so many difficulties besetting it, to carry on for twenty years in every Assembly from the first to last so distracting and divisive a discussion as that which slavery elicited,--whether the successive judgments and measures were all constitutional, equitable, considerate enough in view of all the difficulties developed,--whether the assumption of authority by the later Assemblies did not resemble too closely the course and action of 1837,--whether it would not have been better to refrain at last from a disciplinary proceeding which could have no possible issue but division and separation. There is always room for the antithetic query whether the general sentiment in the Church did not compel such discussion and action.--whether the defense and advocacy of slavery by the separatists was not a flagrant error which could not be condoned,--whether their extrusion was not necessary to the unity and peace of the denomination,--and whether on the other hand it would not have been wiser for them, for the Church, for the country, if they had chosen to abide in a connection and fellowship grievous at one point, but so beneficent in many other ways.[40]

Morris's words were written almost half a century after the 1857 division. The reaction at the time of the schism was mixed, but at the time most of the northern judicatories felt that in the long run it would be a blessing to the Church. The Presbytery of Knox, for instance, acknowledging that the ground the Presbytery had lost could not be regained, nevertheless found solace that no longer would the Congregationalists be pulling churches and members from her already thinned ranks.[41] And the anonymous historian of the New School Synod of Ohio commented in 1870 that ". . . by the withdrawal of the Southern Presbyteries at Cleveland, our branch of the Church was happily rid of this sin and shame."[42] On the other hand, the Trustees of the Second New School Presbyterian Church of Cincinnati protested the division as well as "all agitation of the slavery question in the General Assembly."[43]

Amasa Converse sadly recalled that when George A. Baxter returned from the fateful 1837 Assembly, he justified the casting out of the four New School synods on the ground that "if we had not exscinded them they would have exscinded us for slaveholding." Whereupon Converse commented, "Were Dr. Baxter now living, we would confess to him that we greatly erred in our good opinion of the charity of abolitionism, and that he saw far more clearly than we its nature and tendencies, of which we then had but little conception."[44]

The Old School scion, James Henley Thornwell, acknowledged in a letter to his friend of longstanding, New School M. M. Marshall, that the action of the Assembly was "no more than I have long expected." Reviewing the history of the New School, Thornwell noted that only two alternatives awaited the denomination: "repeated schisms as successive fanaticism became rampant," or "a powerful and gracious revival of true godliness and orthodoxy pervading the whole body." The result of a score of years has been this "most imbecile schism."[45]

On the last night of the 1857 Assembly, a resolution was adopted calling for a Committee of Ten, four from the South. They would be appointed to "meet and confer together in reference to the means which may be safely and properly employed to remove slaveholding from our churches," with a view that the committee would report back to the next Assembly whether any and what means could be effectually employed for this purpose,

> With the concurrence and cooperation of our Southern brethren; and if, in their judgment, no such means can be employed, that the Committee recommend such measures as they deem best calculated to secure the permanent peace and prosperity of our churches.[46]

Seldom has so little been offered so late. In all the debates over the slavery question, save for the Assembly of 1846, there was not a single instance in which the "Southern brethren" were consulted. They were seen as religious, moral, and ecclesiastical pariahs. The purity of the abolition-wing of the Church prevented any normal contact with them. Other men from the North were largely unaware of the difficulties abolition offered. The arguments that the southerners presented in the annual debates were largely ignored.

In the score of years in which there was a southern portion in the New School, not a single southerner was elected Moderator; the Assembly met twice only in slavery territory--in St. Louis and Washington, both on the periphery of slavery; no southerner ever chaired a major Assembly committee; thanks to the action of the AHMS, for most of the two decades the South was bereft of financial assistance in its home missionary undertakings; and the sheer refusal of men who were in the heterogeneous New School to take pastorates in the South smacked of a prejudice that was a far cry from the evangelical position to which many adhered.

Archer C. Dickerson, A. H. H. Boyd, Isaac W. K. Handy, and James G. Hamner were the four southerners appointed to the Committee of Ten. If the Committee ever convened, it left no minutes. Thus those who twenty years earlier voluntarily had cast their lot with the ranks of the exscinded were in turn exscinded.[47] Those who had freely joined with others on the sole basis of their strict adherence to the Constitution of the Presbyterian Church were turned away as they consistently insisted on maintaining their strict adherence to what they believed was Constitutional Presbyterianism.

Small wonder, then, that less than fifteen years later their loss to the New School was described as a "sad result." And the New School "felt itself only the stronger for its diminished numbers."[48] The crushing, concluding blow came in 1859 when the Presbytery of Dakotah sent up an overture to the General Assembly requesting that missionaries be sent to "the Southern States to establish churches, and to instruct the missionaries not to receive slaveholders to the Church until the sin of slaveholding shall have been renounced."[49] Although the overture was referred to the Church Extension Committee, it did nevertheless reveal the sentiment that had finally captured the Assembly: slaveholding is a sin, and it can bar one from membership in the New School Presbyterian Church.

NOTES

1. For the complete text of the Letter, see *CO*, 5 June 1856.
2. Ibid., 8 September 1855.
3. Presbytery of Richland, MS "Minutes" (4 October 1856), pp. 171-172, PHF.
4. Synod of Mississippi [NS], MS "Minutes" (1856), pp. 138-140, Department of Archives and History, State of Mississippi, Jackson, Mississippi.
5. For full text of the minute of the Synod of Western Reserve, see *CO*, 16 October 1856.
6. *CO*, 22 January 1857, carried a letter conveying the information of Holley's demise.
7. Quoted in *Central Presbyterian*, 23 May 1857.
8. Albert Barnes, *The Church and Slavery*, 2nd ed. (Philadelphia: Parry & McMillan, 1857), pp. 70-71.
9. George D. Armstrong, *The Christian Doctrine of Slavery* (New York: Charles Scribner; Norfolk: J. D. Ghiselin, Jr., 1857), pp. 70-71.
10. *CO*, 16 June 1855.
11. Ibid., 8 January 1857.
12. Ibid., 9 April 1857.
13. Edward Burgett Welsh, "Wrestling with Human Values: The Slavery Years," in *They seek a Country: The American Presbyterians. Some Aspects*, ed. Gaius Jackson Slosser (New York: Macmillan, 1955), p. 231.
14. George M. Marsden, in *The Evangelical Mind and the New School Presbyterian Experience: A Case Study of Thought and Theology in Nineteenth-Century America* (New Haven and London: Yale University Press, 1970), p. 129), reduces mention of it to a footnote. Sydney E. Ahlmstrom, in *A Religious History of the American People* (New Haven and London: Yale University Press, 1972), p. 661), refers to it in a sentence. Robert T. Handy, in *A History of the Churches in the United States and Canada*, Oxford History of the Christian Church (New York: Oxford University Press, 1977), p. 194, relegates it to a clause. Among Presbyterian historians, Andrew E. Murray, in *Presbyterians and the Negro--A History* (Philadelphia: Presbyterian Historical Society, 1966), p. 114, dated the division 1858; T. Watson Street, in *The Story of Southern Presbyterians* (Richmond: John Knox Press, 1961), failed to mention it; and Ernest Trice Thompson, in *Presbyterians in the South*, 3 vols. (Richmond: John Knox Press, 1963-1973), 1:544-545, gave two pages to the subject.

15. Clifton E. Olmstead, *History of Religion in the United States* (Englewood Cliffs, New Jersey: Prentice-Hall, 1960).

16. *History of the Presbytery of Peoria* (Peoria, Illinois: H. S. Hill Printing Co., 1888), pp. 57-58.

17. *Presbyterian Witness*, 26 May 1857. In spite of the Presbytery's appeal and protestations, it decided not to send commissioners to the General Assembly.

18. Frederick A. Ross, *Slavery Ordained of God* (Philadelphia: J. B. Lippincott, 1859), p. 139.

19. Ibid., p. 133.

20. Ibid., p. 128.

21. Barnes had been writing a series of commentaries on the New Testament, aimed largely at the intelligent Sunday School teacher and laity at large. His exegesis of particular passages, especially in Romans, had set him at odds with the Old School men in the early 1830s. His interpretation of the particular passages that proslavery apologetes employed, to say nothing of his general approach to the Bible itself, infuriated the latter. Ross's *Slavery* is a collection of materials that he had earlier spoken or written, which were pulled together after the Assembly of 1857. In the small book are four letters which he had written to Barnes in late 1856 and early 1857. In his introduction to the Barnes letters, Ross stated that he had found the latter's views "unscriptural, false, fanatical, and infidel" (p. 93).

22. Frederick A. Ross, *Position of the Southern Church in Relation to Slavery* . . . (New York: Gray, 1857), p. 16. See also Murray, *Presbyterians and the Negro*, p. 70.

23. James Benson Sellers, *Slavery in Alabama* (Birmingham: University of Alabama Press, 1950), pp. 334-335.

24. Ross, *Slavery*, p. 170. Ross had an entire letter to Barnes entitled "The Golden Rule," pp. 160-186. See also Sellers, *Slavery in Alabama*, p. 343.

25. Ross, *Slavery*, p. 36, in the speech which he delivered before the New York Assembly, 1856.

26. William Sumner Jenkins, *Pro-Slavery Thought in the Old South* (Chapel Hill: University of North Carolina Press, 1935; reprint, Gloucester, Massachusetts: Peter Smith, 1960), p. 63; George C. Whatley, III, "The Alabama Presbyterian and His Slave, 1830-1864," *Alabama Review* 13 (1960): 42.

27. Ross, *Slavery*, pp. 76-77; Whatley, "The Alabama Presbyterian," pp. 43-44. Sellers (*Slavery*

in Alabama, p. 334) claimed that Ross's *Slavery* was "the most systematic and comprehensive argument for the institution of slavery ever undertaken in Alabama."

28. Archer C. Dickerson, *Anti-Slavery Agitation in the Church not Authorised* (Philadelphia: King and Baird, 1857).

29. Ibid., p. 5.
30. Ibid., p. 19.
31. Ibid., p. 26.
32. Ibid., p. 53.

33. For the complete text of the Assembly's action on the 1857 slavery legislation, see GAPCUSA [NS], *Minutes* (1857), pp. 401-404; Moore, *Digest*, 291-295; Maurice W. Armstrong, Lefferts A. Loetscher, and Charles A. Anderson, eds., *Presbyterian Enterprise: Sources of American Presbyterian History* (Philadelphia: Westminster Press, 1956), pp. 202-204.

34. The complete text of the Protest is in GAPCUSA [NS], *Minutes* (1857), p. 406.

35. For the text of the Reply to the Protest, see ibid., pp. 408-409. For a very full report of the 1857 New School Assembly, see *CO*, 28 May and 4 and 11 June 1857.

36. Samuel J. Wilson, "The Period From the Adoption of the Presbyterian Form of Government to the Present Time," in *Centennial Discourses, Delivered in the City of Philadelphia, June 1876* (Philadelphia: n.p.: n.p., n.d.), p. 207.

37. In light of the withdrawal of the southern men, twenty-seven in number, one must seriously challenge the premise of those who for years maintained that "the presence of a strong Southern minority group prevented the Assembly from taking a decided antislavery stand"; cf. Clifford Merrill Drury, *Presbyterian Enterprise: One Hundred and Fifty Years of National Missions History* (Philadelphia: Board of Christian Education, Presbyterian Church in the United States of America, 1952), p. 102. There was no time in the score of years that embraced the slavery debate in the Assembly in which the southern element, by numbers or prestige, was sufficiently "strong" to have prevented any legislation the New School would have desired. Two considerations in these years prevented a stronger, firmer, quicker stand on the issue of domestic slavery: first, the ambition of the Church to retain its essential national unity and identity; second, the evolution of the legislation, working along a

continuum which could only conclude in the virtual excision of the southern wing.

38. E. H. Gillett, *History of the Presbyterian Church in the United States of America*, 2 vols. (Philadelphia: Presbyterian Publication Committee, 1864), 2:558; R. C. Reed, "Presbyterians. VIII In the United States and Canada: 2 Presbyterian Church in the United States," *New Schaff-Herzog Encyclopedia of Religious Knowledge*, 9:229-230; R[obert] L. Stanton, *The Church and Rebellion: A Consideration of the Rebellion against the Government of the United States; and the Agency of the Church, North and South, in Relation Thereto* (New York: Derby and Miller, 1894), p. 368; John B. Hill, "Timothy Hill Reports on Slavery," *JPH* 26 (1965): 34.

39 That the schism came in the ranks of the New School was both a relief and a surprise to the northern elements--a relief because the long struggle, which had occupied so much time and energy, was ended; a surprise because so few in the North really expected it. For instance, in 1852 a "Committee of the Synod of New York and New Jersey" wrote a book, *A History of the Division of the Presbyterian Church in the United States of America* (New York: M. W. Dodd, 1852). At the time the book was published, it was quite obvious that there was complete unanimity in the ranks, pp. 214-225. Barnes (*Church and Slavery*) wrote his book in the fall of 1856 after the momentous Assembly of that year. He prided the New School that no person, congregation, or minister had left it. The withdrawal by the southerners, therefore, caught many off guard.

40. Morris, *Presbyterian Church New School*, p. 141.

41. *History of the Presbytery of Peoria*, pp. 59-60.

42. *Historical Sketch of the Synod of Ohio (N. S.) From 1838 to 1868* (Cincinnati: Elm Street Printing Co., 1870).

43. *Central Presbyterian*, 27 June 1857.

44. *CO*, 13 June 1857. Converse had been among those Virginians in 1837 who had disagreed with Baxter's judgment and action. In his Autobiography, he remarked that in censuring the southern element it required ministers, "if they had any regard for their usefulness in their pastoral relations, to withdraw from the fanatical councils of the Northern portions of the Church"; "Autobiography of the Rev. Amasa Converse," *JPH* 43 (1965): 258. William O. Brackett, Jr., in "The Rise and Development of the New School in the Presbyterian Church in the U. S.

A. to the Reunion of 1869" *JPHS* 13 (1928): 171-172, claimed that the division of the Church "was a poor compensation for the loss of the Southern members . . . . And although Isaac Anderson died in January of the year of the division, his biographer conjectured that he would have regretted the action that divided the Church; John J. Robinson, *Memoir of Rev. Isaac Anderson, DD., Late President of Maryville College, and Professor of Didactic Theology* (Knoxville: J. Addison Rayl, 1860), pp. 142-143.

45. Cited in *CO*, 10 September 1857.

46. GAPCUSA [NS], *Minutes* (1857), p. 412.

47. According to William Red, in *A History of the Presbyterian Church in Texas* (Austin: Steck, 1936), p. 113, the deliverance of the Assembly was actually an *in thesi* deliverance, not a judicial deliverance.

48. Jonathan F. Stearns, "Historical Review of the Church (New School Branch) Since 1837," in *Presbyterian Reunion: A Memorial Volume* (New York: De Witt C. Lent & Co.; Chicago: Van Nortwick & Sparks, 1870), pp. 84-85.

49. *Presbyterian Historical Almanac and Annual Remembrancer* 2 (1860): 114.

8
The Richmond Convention

In November 1861 the Constitutional Synod of Virginia, in the throes of the Civil War, reviewed its break with the men at the North in its "Narrative on the State of Religion."

> Four years ago, led by the hand of God to detach themselves from a body now found capable of drawing the sword against us and instigating a war of invasion, we recognize with gratitude the Providence, by which, as a part of the United Synod, we are placed in a position to give us ready access to the hearts of the Southern people, without the damaging consideration of a connection with a body foreign in sentiment to their people. God was, they see, preparing them for the times which are now passing over us, though we knew it not.[1]

If there was any regret that the southern commissioners had withdrawn from the 1857 New School Assembly, there was no recognition of it in this statement. In fact, Frederick A. Ross, who was rapidly assuming the leadership for the southern New School, responded to the conjecture of some northern leaders that the South was not serious in its withdrawal from the General Assembly in 1857 and would probably be back next year:

> As a man killed, and sent to heaven, will not likely come back, to shake hands in society, again, with those who sent him out of this world,--so, neither will the South, released

from Northern wrong, and insult, mingle again with those who have so long outraged the feelings of their brethren.[2]

Just prior to leaving Cleveland, the aged patriarch of Kentucky New Schoolism, Thomas Cleland, read a paper, "Position of the Southern Churches upon the Subject of Slavery," to such as would hear him. So that there would be no misunderstanding on the part of the North where the South stood on the slavery question, Cleland's paper, which he had "prepared with some care," contained perhaps the most lucid, succinct expression of the southern posture available to ecclesiastics, certainly to those in the North who would take the time to read it. The heart of the paper argued:

> But slavery does exist by Divine ordination and recognition, for wise purposes, to be overruled for His glory, in the elevation, civilization, and final redemption of the African race. Sin cannot be predicated of the relation itself, but of the abuse of that relation. It stands in the same category with the family relation in the fact that it is ordained of God. . . . When we say "it is right" for our churches to hold slaves under the present circumstances, we mean to say that they are acting consistently with the spirit and letter of the Gospel in so doing. And were we to assert the contrary- . . . that we hold slaveholding to be wrong, it would place us before the world not only destitute of the spirit of Christianity, but as bereft of every principle of moral honesty.
>
> We believe that the slave is not prepared for freedom; that to give it to him now under all the circumstances would not be best, either for master or slave.[3]

Another paper was also issued by the southern commissioners. Its author was Andrew Hunter Holmes Boyd of the Presbytery of Winchester. This paper called for a convention to be held in Washington on 27 August 1857. The call was extended not only to southern judicatories and ministers; rather it expressed the desire "to have a National Church, a Church made up of all Constitutional Presbyterians . . . who are opposed to the agitation of slavery in the General Assembly." By "holding to the same Confession of Faith, we shall have a common basis as to doctrine and government--and understanding that, however, we may differ in our views respecting Slavery, the subject is never to be introduced into the Assembly either by Northern or Southern men, unless, indeed judicial cases are brought up regularly from the lower courts."[4]

The southern commissioners returned to their presbyteries and churches after the 1857 Assembly as heroes. On 15 June the Second Presbyterian Church of Knoxville, Tennessee, met and took into consideration the "propriety or impropriety" of the action of the commissioners at Cleveland. The pastor, James H. Martin, introduced resolutions justifying the separation, endorsing the action of the southern commissioners in issuing a call for the Washington meeting. In so doing, the resolutions expressed "the desire that Union Presbytery send delegates to said Convention," and suggested Knoxville "as the most suitable place for Union Presbytery to assemble for that purpose." Only one dissenting vote was cast.[5] On 28 June, the church appointed delegates to the meeting of Presbytery.[6]

While a wave of enthusiasm for the convention swept the former southern New School churches, the first obstacle emerged regarding the plans to meet in Washington. There were New School congregations in the capital city, and the District of Columbia was in slave territory. None of the commissioners from the District of Columbia, however, had signed the call for the Washington Convention. From the start, the New School pastors had unanimously opposed holding the convention in the city. Their opposition was on the ground that most of them would be out of Washington in August; more probably, they opposed the calling of the convention in the first place.[7] The location of the convention was thus changed to Richmond.

During the summer months, churches and presbyteries held meetings to act on the call for the Convention. Typical of the actions at these meetings was that of the Session of the First Presbyterian Church, Jonesboro, Tennessee. At a meeting on 5 July 1857, the Session passed a series of resolutions, deprecating the agitation of the slavery issue "in any form as dangerous, not only to the peace and harmony of our beloved Church, but the permanence and stability of the invaluable union of the confederated States of this Republic." It denounced the "rampant sentiments of fanatics and abolitionists." The Session believed that there were many in the North who desired to refrain from any interference in the master-slave relationship. They would be in accord with the basic premise in the call for the Convention--a Church would be erected wherein slavery would not be discussed. The Session concluded its meeting, approving the upcoming meeting of Holston Presbytery. It also elected delegates to the Convention.[8]

The Presbytery of Winchester expressed the hope that many of the northern churches would join the new denomination. Boyd, whose membership was in the Presbytery, had composed the call for the Convention. In that call there was no mention of possible reunion with the Old School Church, for Boyd was adamantly opposed to such a merger. Thus, the Presbytery in its resolutions made the first reference to the rumors which were surfacing regarding such a possible union: "There is no existing Presbyterian denomination with which it would be desirable for us to unite. . . . And besides, we, as constitutional Presbyterians, have a work to do which we dare not forsake before anything less than insuperable obstacles."[9]

Heterogeneity had always been the hallmark of the New School Church. That characteristic now emerged in the South. There were numerous factors that contributed to this condition. For one thing, in many sections of the South the presbyteries were woefully weak. In such cases, churches assumed a polity nearer to Congregationalism than Presbyterianism. Further, the southern presbyteries were seldom represented in the General Assembly. In 1857, the southern presbyteries numbered twenty-one, which meant that if every presbytery were fully represented by the minimal number of ministers and elders, there would have been forty-two in attendance. Yet at that crucial meeting there were fewer than thirty. Presbytery memberships were small. In 1857 sixteen of the twenty-one presbyteries in the South had less than 1,000 communicants. The size of the congregations was small, on the average. Only forty-four congregations had over 100 members in 1857, and four of these were in Washington, D. C. Many presbyteries did not have a single church in the three-figure column.

Even the attitude toward slavery varied. Some believed it was a permanent institution; others believed it was temporary. Some believed that black people were beyond the ability to receive instruction; others labored for their personal intellectual improvement.

Some were violently opposed to any reconciliation with the Old School; others thought that it would be worth investigating. Some had great apprehensions about striking out on an independent course; others favored returning to the New School fold; still others advocated an independent position, letting time take its course. And although there was considerable advocacy that the new Church that was to be formed would be nationwide in scope, surely all but the most naive of the southern Constitutional Presbyterians must have realized that few, if any, of the northern New School would be interested in their cause.

There were two other factors that encouraged ambivalence. One was the feeling of guilt that engulfed many of the New School in the South over the division, which to them moved from the ecclesiastical to the political arena. The Presbyterian Churches had retained their unity in the face of the divisions by the Baptists and the Methodists. Over and over again prior to the 1857 Assembly the appeal had been to the unity of the Church in order to maintain the unity of the country. The New School was a "Church with the soul of a nation." Even when the southern commissioners returned and their withdrawal was applauded, at the same time there was a subliminal feeling among many clergy and laity that it was not only the Church that had suffered division, but the country also. And despite the plea in the call for the Richmond Convention that a Church national in scope was planned, the possibilities for such a reality were very, very slight.

There was also the lack of leadership from two men who might have cleared the air with their counsel. Isaac Anderson died in early 1857, and Thomas Cleland was on his death-bed in the fall of that year. The advice these men might have given was thus denied the southern Church at a crucial time. The vacuum in leadership created had a negative effect when positive direction was being sought.

Thus, there were those who already consigned the Richmond Convention to failure before it ever convened. The Old School was most apprehensive, if not negative, about the prospects of the new denomination. The New School *American Presbyterian*, published in Philadelphia and founded to counteract Converse's *Christian Observer*, excoriated the movement that might result in a new Church. It saw nothing but failure for the proposed venture:

> We regret the policy upon which a portion of them propose to enter, for their sake, as well as for our own and our country's sake; for it promises to result in a present alienation and in a future failure, painful and mortifying to

them, and that without securing any striking advantage to the Church or State, but rather evil to both.[10]

The total statistics of the six southern synods that had been affected by the 1857 withdrawal from the New School revealed a total of twenty-one presbyteries, embracing 284 churches, 169 ministers, and 16,137 communicants.[11] The size of the average southern congregation was 56.82 members--in contrast to 73.24 members in the North.

One of the rumors that began circulating among the southern Constitutional Presbyterians was the possibility of a union with the Old School. This suggestion, however, was meeting with opposition before the Convention was called to order. Matthew M. Marshall, of Fayetteville, Tennessee, expressed the opinion that the way was not "prepared" for such a union. The duty of the Convention was to organize an Assembly--not upon the basis of '37--not upon the Cleveland basis of '57--but upon the basis of the Constitution and the Bible; an Assembly that will forever "ignore" the slavery question, and all questions of a *political and sectional* character, believing that all such tend to corrupt the Church and rend the Union.[12] This was one of the major issues to be debated in the Convention.

The Richmond Convention assembled in the United Presbyterian Church as scheduled on 27 August 1857, at 8:00 p.m. The Hon. Horace Maynard, an Elder in the Second Presbyterian Church of Knoxville, was unanimously elected Temporary Chairman (later Permanent Chairman).[13] The roll revealed seventeen presbyteries present, including the Presbytery of Wilmington, the only judicatory representing a non-slaveholding state.

If the purpose of the much-touted Convention was to attract delegates from all over the nation, the roll indicated that it had failed. It was obvious, also, that the basis for delegate representation was unclear, for the two Virginia Presbyteries of Winchester and Hanover together had about sixty per cent of the total registration. Nor was there an equal representation of clergy and laity. The latter were far more numerous than the former--fourteen ministers from Hanover Presbytery, but forty-eight elders.

The sessions of the Convention were conducted on a very high plane. There were even reports of conversions from the devotional exercises that were held.[14] A Business Committee, composed of one minister and one elder from each synod, was ap-

The Richmond Convention

pointed. The Committee submitted its report, which made up the major portion of the work of the Convention. The Report consisted of a preamble of three parts and five resolutions. The preamble stated that all the previous actions of the New School touching slavery "are a violation of the Constitution of the Presbyterian Church." Slavery does not belong in the courts of the Church as a subject of discussion and inquiry, but rather in the courts of the State. Furthermore, there seems to be no prospect of the cessation of the slavery agitation in the General Assembly so long as there are slaveholders in connection with the Church. The five resolutions were then presented by the Business Committee. They were adopted, having been "elaborately discussed."

1. Presbyteries in connection with the New School were urged to withdraw.
2. Nothing can be made the basis for discipline in the Presbyterian Church which is not specifically referred to in the Constitution as crime or heresy.
3. The Assembly has no right to pronounce any sentence on a lower judicatory or individuals for any cause unless brought before the Assembly as prescribed in the Constitution.
4. All presbyteries which are opposed to the agitation of slavery "in the highest judicatory of the Church," were urged to appoint delegates, in proportion prescribed by our Form of Government for the appointment of commissioners to the Assembly, to meet at Knoxville, Tenn., *on the first Thursday in April, 1858*, for the purpose of organizing a general Synod . . . . The name proposed was "The United Synod of the Presbyterian Church in the United States of America."
5. The Convention delegates resolved to "adhere to and abide by the Confession of Faith of the Presbyterian Church, as containing the system of doctrine taught in the Holy Scripture; and that we adhere to the Form of Government and Book of Discipline of said Church."[15]

In the discussion centering around the fourth resolution, an amendment was proposed adding "South" to the designation of the new denomination. It was withdrawn, however, for very few of the delegates could be found in favor of a strictly sectional Church.[16]

Neither the preamble nor the resolutions contained little that was new. The Report was a distillation of what 98 percent of the southern wing had been saying for years. But there was one additional resolution adopted:

> *Resolved*, That a union between us and our Old School brethren, could it be effected on terms acceptable on both sides, would be conducive to the best interests of the Church of Christ; and this Convention, after a free and full interchange of views and opinions on this subject, do now recommend that the United Synod, when formed and duly organized, shall invite the General Assembly (O. S.) to a fraternal conference with us in reference to such union.[17]

Reunion with the Old School was not a new idea to a good number of the southern New School men. As early as 1848 the subject had been broached in the columns of the *Christian Observer* by James H. C. Leach of Hanover Presbytery. He conditioned union, however, on the grounds that it should be accomplished "upon Constitutional Grounds and Christian Principles" and that it should be accomplished immediately. He then pointed out that in Virginia the overture for union had originated with the Old School men of that State, "who never had any hand in the division" of 1837.[18] At the spring 1848 meeting of Hanover Presbytery, a series of resolutions was adopted, expressing Presbytery's gratification that the Old School Synod of Virginia had "opened the way for a fraternal discussion of the question of reunion," yet Presbytery felt it could take no further steps without the "counsel and co-operation" of the New School Synod of Virginia. It then overtured Synod to appoint a Committee of Conference, to whom this "important business" would be referred.[19]

Although Converse was gracious in carrying the information about reunion feelers (for he himself was opposed to it), he also saw to it that the picture on the other side of the canvas was exhibited. In spite of the rumors, an author who signed himself "Truth" in a response to the overtures from Hanover Presbytery, commented that the chances were very good that a proposition in any Old School presbytery in Virginia, for the purpose of reuniting the whole Church, "would really be discountenanced, if not rebuked. . . . Is it respectful to them," he continued," after knowing all the sacrifices we have made for conscience' sake, to approach us again with *the identical terms* which were proposed before the separation? Is it not a reflection either upon our intelligence or our integrity?" He concluded by observing that only in Kentucky and Virginia of the southern synods was there any feeling towards reunion.[20]

At the 1848 meeting of the Synod of Mississippi a discussion on reunion was held, but Robert McLain reported that "to a man, we are satisfied with our present position," because "the same causes which called us nine years ago, to take a decided stand against unconstitutional proceedings and ecclesiastical usurpation, still exist."[21]

While 1848 saw the matter laid to rest, in 1856, however, the subject came up again. This time it was the Old School Synod of Nashville that resurrected the issue. The Synod understood that "at least a portion" of the New School Presbytery of West Tennessee had indicated a willingness to be reunited with the Synod. The Synod believed that such a reunion could be effected upon the earlier basis of reunion of the Synods of New York and Philadelphia in 1758. The Synod also expressed its "cordial and earnest desire" that such a reunion take place as soon as it can be effected. It further recommended that if any of the Old School and New School presbyteries within its bounds should meet together at the same time and the same place, "they may organize as one Presbytery" upon the same basis as the 1758 reunion.[22]

When the Synod's minutes came up for review in 1857, however, the fire for reunion received a dampening experience.[23]. The General Assembly (Old School) approved the Synod's minutes with one exception--the exception being to the manner by which Synod proposed reunion. It was pointed out that it was imperative on presbyteries "to examine all who make application for admission into their bodies, at least, on experimental religion, Didactic & polemic theology and Church government . . . ."[24] This exception was thoroughly consistent with the Old School position, a position that irritated any kind of relations between the two bodies.

The issue of reunion with the Old School, which was not a part of the Report of the Business Committee, was the one item of business that prompted the greatest debate at the Richmond convention. Boyd of Winchester Presbytery led the opposition. There was no doubt where he stood: with his theological views it would be impossible for him to unite with the Old School. He deprecated a sectional assembly, preferring a general synod that would be national in scope and embrace within its borders ministers, members, and churches North and South. He was firmly opposed to the Old School's stand on subscription--re-examining ministers who transfer into an Old School presbytery. His basic position was to have a meeting in Knoxville, organize, and let whatever union which could be effected occur. But wherever the new Church was to go, he urged that all go together, not "drop off one by one." He opposed the Exscinding Acts, the Old School stand on slavery, and the doctrine of original sin.[25]

Others spoke their minds. Ross urged that the only subject that would give peace to the Church is the proper stand on slavery: that it is ordained of God. James Leach advocated union, but opposed the Old School position on subscription. M. M. Marshall also opposed subscription; but he believed that until the Old School renounced its "nefarious deeds," there could be no union. On the other hand, were such to be the case, there could be a great revival in religion. Charles H. Read, the host pastor of the Convention, declared that he had left the Old School because of principle. He was now in the South, having been called from a New School church in the North. He stood for a permanent Southern Church, thereby creating a foundation from which overtures could originate or be received from the Old School. Archer C. Dickerson deprecated the spirit of the debate. He suggested that it would be wrong to make conditions to which the Old School could never concede.

On the other hand, John Randolph Tucker, one of the most illustrious of the elders attending the Convention, a relative of Boyd, and the Attorney General of the Commonwealth of Virginia, strongly advocated reunion. Using his legal rationalism, he argued that it was idle for the Convention to object to the Exscinding Acts of 1837, when by adopting the first resolution it had virtually exscinded the entire northern branch. At best, as it now stood, all that could be hoped for is a sectional Church, a condition which he deplored as long as the honor and rights of the South did not demand it. His sentiments were echoed by W. H. Matthews, a minister in the same Presbytery of Hanover where Tucker resided. The Pennsylvania delegates were heard. The desire for a nationwide Church, not a sectional one, had brought them to the Convention. Rest from the slavery agitation could not be found by entering the

Old School, but only by pursuing the original call for the convention for a purely national Church.[26]

In sum, the arguments against adopting the proposed resolution approving proposed union with the Old School fell into four categories: (1) objection to the Exscision Acts, which must be repudiated; (2) subscription, the purpose of which was to guarantee doctrinal purity in the Old School; (3) doctrinal differences; and (4) the possibility that the southern Constitutional Presbyterians by joining the Old School would only escape the frying pan of the slavery issue to jump into the fire which the Old School offered. On the other hand, those favoring reunion did so because they believed that the issues which had divided them in 1837 had been dulled by time.

The resolution was carried. Boyd and Marshall refused to vote, and Ross decried the entire procedure as "a sop to Cerberus."[27]

In light of the Convention's expectation, it was a failure. The withdrawing southerners had not rightly read the northern mind. Six weeks prior to the convention, the *Presbyterian Witness* had blithely predicted that since the call was addressed to all, a national Church would emerge to occupy National ground--"ignoring the slavery agitation." That only one northern presbytery was represented, plus only one delegate from the District of Columbia, must have woven a disheartening pall over all the Convention's deliberations. The much-anticipated support from the North simply did not materialize. Certainly, the slavery debates on the floor of the Assemblies in the 1850s had given the South exposure to the minds of northern commissioners. There can be no doubt that some of the commissioners were exposed to a side of the issue that they had never before considered. But there is a vast difference between sympathy and commitment.[28]

The Philadelphia-based *American Presbyterian's* reaction to the Convention's proceedings all too clearly expressed the mind of the North:

> Will our brethren at the South continue their assertion *that the change of opinion and position has been at the North and not at the South?* Do they expect us to forsake the General Assembly, and to create another schism in the Church, that we may get upon the lofty platform of "Slavery ordained of God?" Can they be so credulous as to believe in their convention, that conservative men . . . will be able to introduce discord and strife into churches,

presbyteries, and synods, to get upon the "high ground" which leaves the present position of the Old School in the "fogs" of abolitionism?[29]

The prospects for any possible reunion with the Old School also received a prophetic jolt in a letter James Henley Thornwell wrote to his New School friend, M. M. Marshall. Thornwell emphasized the firm stand of the Old School as he pointed out the only was reunion could be consummated. For congregations, those who wish to unite must make the fact known through their session to the proper presbytery, be received, and enrolled. For ministers, they apply to one of the Old School presbyteries, "precisely as any other minister from any other church." Upon giving the information needed and receiving satisfaction from the presbytery, they are then enrolled as any Old School minister. Thornwell concluded by stating, "Our doctrine, order, discipline and practice are all settled and known. They who approve them will join us, they who want to make disturbance are not wanted."[30] John Randoph Tucker continued to urge his New School associates in the South to "stand firm on the platform of the Convention, break no ranks; so that in our united councils, we may obtain Union without Old School friends if we justly can, or secure the strength of a firmly knit Church, if we cannot."[31]

The response to the Richmond Convention came quickly from the southern judicatories. The Synod of Tennessee formally withdrew from the New School General Assembly in its 1857 meeting, declaring itself "for the time being" independent.[32] The Presbytery of Richland also withdrew from the Assembly and appointed delegates to the up-coming Knoxville meeting.[33] Likewise did the Presbytery of Newton.[34] The Presbytery of District of Columbia debated the possibility of leaving the General Assembly. The elders voted unanimously to do so, and endorsed the action of the Richmond Convention. Three ministers, however, did not vote, and three others voted against the proposal. An observer concluded, "Our Churches are all right, but what we are going to do with our pastors, we do not know."[35]

The Synod of Kentucky was in complete disarray by the time the Convention convened. Only two of its presbyteries were represented in Richmond. The Presbytery of Providence existed on paper only. Its old patriarch, Thomas Cleland, lay on his death bed. For the present, the synod withdrew from the Assembly and voted to stand independent, until God in His Providence shall open up the way for further action; and further, that we will not, as individuals, change our present position, and that we will recommend our churches not to change theirs until this Synod shall have another meeting . . . .³⁶

And although he did not speak formally for the entire synod, Dickerson remarked that the feeling in Kentucky was "universal" for union. He further believed that the cause of Christ would be materially advanced if it could be formed and that the South would be able to withstand the assaults of the North better. There were conditions, however. The Old School must repent of its action touching the exscinding actions of 1837 and 1838. These bar any possibility to union. "Let us make a common basis, and both live hereafter on equal terms," was his recommendation.³⁷

The Old School, Richmond-published *Central Presbyterian*, although very interested in the activities and developments which came out of the Convention, very frankly admitted that the possibilities of union with the Old School were "faint and few." The editors pointed out that there were individuals among the former New School who desired it, but not all in the church. Frederick A. Ross in particular was singled out. Ross was accused of developing a Church with a peculiar type of Calvinism. He wanted more latitude than the Old School could possibly give him. Although not mentioned by name, Andrew H. H. Boyd was placed in the same category, along with others. Although the Convention consented to a *proposal* for conference with the Old School, such action does not necessarily involve union.³⁸

The Philadelphia Old School *Presbyterian* merely noted that "we have examined the reports of the speeches made on the occasion, and from this investigation . . . we feel perfectly satisfied that these Southern seceders from the New School cannot and should not be admitted into our Church as a body." Whereupon the *Presbyterian Witness* fumed, responding that the members in Richmond did not ask for admission as a favor, but simply to meet the Old School men "as brethren," offering "union in the spirit of that divine charity which our Lord and Master teaches."³⁹ The editor was livid with the *ex cathedra* postures the two Old School papers had assumed in delivering their opinions.

Perhaps. But the two papers (1) were both Old School, (2) supervised by men of no mean ability (the *Central Presbyterian* edited by T. V. Moore and Moses Hoge and the *Presbyterian* published by William S. Martien), and, (3) who spoke fairly well for both South and North Old Schoolmen. Editors of religious weeklies in those days wielded tremendous influence. The papers were not denominationally controlled; they were operated for the Church, not by it. Beliefs and where one stood on controversial issues meant much more then than today.[40] Further, there were not only the editorials, but also frequent excurses by leading theologians of the day--in this instance, such men as James H. Thornwell, Robert J. Breckinridge, Charles Hodge, and J. R. Miller. These men bent like an iron rod in a breeze. The papers, thus, did not look into the future to ponder what the Old School might do; they *knew*. Time proved them correct.

In the 3 November 1857 issue of the *Presbyterian Witness*, the editor, Andrew Blackburn, expressed his own distaste for the proposed union. He declared that the up-coming United Synod could hold its own for four reasons: (1) liberal Calvinism is better than Old School Calvinism in combatting the errors of Arminianism; (2) the ministers of the United Synod are "good men"; (3) there exist "wealth, intelligence, high social position, earnest piety" among the people; and (4) the new United Synod will be the only Presbyterian body free from the agitation of slavery.

He then listed five reasons why he opposed union with the Old School: (1) the proposal would grant the Old School the opportunity of dictating the terms; (2) unless the United Synod agreed to such terms, it would be broken; (3) many of the United Synod ministers would be rejected by the Old School on doctrinal grounds--in East Tennessee perhaps as many as one-half would not be able to meet the doctrinal requirements; (4) such a union would bring only strife, not the desired peace; and (5) the New Schoolmen from the South would never feel at home, for they would always be viewed by themselves and others as inferiors. True union comes only when both sides make concessions. He failed to see any concessions being made by the Old School.[41]

When James M. McLean of Mobile wrote, favoring a union of the proposed United Synod with the Old School, the editorial column of the *Presbyterian Witness* replied that two conditions must be met before union could be consummated. First, the New School must be recognized as "orthodox Constitutional Presbyterians," with no presbytery examinations. Second, the reception of the United Synod must be such as to express a disavowal of the Exscision Acts of 1837-1838, and a guarantee that the United Synod would not be thrown out without a trial. "We are justified," Blackburn continued, "in demanding of them a pledge for constitutional and Presbyterian conduct toward us in the future." He doubted, however, that such a guarantee would ever be accorded the United Synod.[42]

Two weeks before the Knoxville meeting, the *Presbyterian Witness* presented a decalogue of "Reasons for Not Joining the Old School." They are summarized as follows:

1. Doctrinal differences still exist, just as they did prior to 1837.
2. There are differences in receiving the Confession of Faith. The Old School insists that everything be received; the New School receives it as a system of doctrines, with the right to reject what is in it which it cannot accept.
3. Differences abound on important principles. The Old School makes the Assembly a legislative body or judicial body at will. The New School looks on presbyteries as the only law-making bodies of the Church. The Assembly is merely a court of appeal.
4. The temper of the two is different: the Old School is rigid, the New School flexible.
5. Reunion with the Old School would be a sin, for the United Synod cannot forgive the Old School since it has never repented.
6. To go to their presbyteries by examination would violate the established laws of the New School.
7. Union would promote peace for no one. Those who know how the Old School and the New School get along in East Tennessee realize there could be no peace.
8. Union would inflict serious injury on the Old School, since most of the United Synod is in the South. At present, the Old School is silent on slavery. But with a sudden influx of Southerners, it might be forced to speak out on the issue to its own harm.
9. It would injure the United Synod. The proposed Church is on its way to peace. Let's not jump out of the boat and get into the waters of abolitionism.

172 The United Synod of the South

    10. The Old School position on slavery is not sound. The action of 1818 on the issue is still its position.[43]

The last word had been spoken. The presbyteries had appointed their delegates to the Knoxville meeting, where a new Presbyterian Church, committed to the proposition that the discussion of slavery does not belong in ecclesiastical halls, was waiting to be born.

NOTES

1. Quoted in *CO*, 28 November 1861.
2. Ibid., 11 June 1857.
3. For the full text of the paper, see *CO*, 4 June 1857. The paper was signed by twenty of the southern commissioners. Some had already left for home.
4. For the full text of the invitation, see *Presbyterian Historical Almanac and Annual Remembrancer* 1 (1858-1859): 135-136; also Appendix A.
5. For the full text of the resolutions of the meeting, see ibid., p. 138; *Knoxville Register*, 18 June 1857.
6. Second Presbyterian Church, Knoxville, Tennessee, MS "Minutes" (28 June 1857) Second Presbyterian Church archives. For similar action, see J. R. Nankivell, typed "Short History of Mars Hill Presbyterian Church, November 1823--November 1923," Lawson McGhee Library, Knoxville; and *CO*, 16 July 1857.
7. Thomas Cary Johnson, "A Brief Sketch of the United Synod of the Presbyterian Church in the United States of America," *Papers of the American Society of Church History* 8 (1897): 15. Johnson asserted that the southerners had selected Washington as the site of the Convention with a view of winning the Presbytery of District of Columbia over to their cause.
8. Cited in Judith Haws Hash, "A History of the First Presbyterian Church of Jonesboro, Tennessee" (M. A. thesis, East Tennessee State University, 1965), p. 160. The idea that slavery would not be discussed in the prospective Church had tremendous appeal to the southerners. They consistently believed in the apolitical nature of the Church--slavery being a political, not a religious issue. The apprehension of the Session that the division of the New School Presbyterian Church would presage the division of the nation was a thought that was

developing among many churchmen of the day. This idea has been recently examined in greater detail by C. C. Goen, *Broken Churches, Broken Nation: Denominational Schisms and the Coming of the American Civil War* (Macon, Georgia: Mercer University Press, 1985).

9. *CO*, 16 July 1857. Boyd's theology and personality dominated the Presbytery of Winchester. For actions taken by other southern New School judicatories, see the following: Synod of Mississippi [NS], MS "Minutes" (1857), pp. 176-182, Department of Archives and History, Jackson, Mississippi; Union Presbytery, MS "Minutes" (15 July 1857), 316-322, PHF; typed copies are in the McClung Room, Lawson McGhee Library, Knoxville; Holston Presbytery [NS], MS "Minutes" (15 July 1857), pp. 407-408, PHF and *Central Presbyterian*, 8 August 1857; Presbytery of West Tennessee [NS], MS "Minutes" (16 July 1857), pp. 257-277, PHF; Presbytery of Lexington, South, *CO*, 20 August 1857; Presbytery of Northern Missouri, MS "Minutes" (11-12 August 1857), pp. 135-137, Murrell Memorial Library, Missouri Valley College; First Presbyterian Church, Huntsville, Alabama, microfilm "Minutes" (5 August 1857), p. 80, History Room, Public Library, Huntsville; Osceola, Missouri, Presbyterian Church, MS "Minutes" (August 1857), p. 24, PHS.

10. Quoted in *Central Presbyterian*, 18 July 1857.

11. GAPCUSA [NS] *Minutes* (1857), Appendix, passim. For a full tabulation of the Synods' and Presbyteries' statistics see the table on page 176.

12. *CO*, 23 July 1857.

13. *CO* (3, 10, and 17 September) carried good coverage of the Convention. For the complete Roll and the major actions of the Convention, see *Presbyterian Historical Almanac* 1 (1858-1859): 137-138. Maynard was one of East Tennessee's most illustrious figures.

14. Johnson, "Brief Sketch of the United Synod," p. 16.

15. *Presbyterian Historical Almanac*, 1 (1858-1859): 138. For the text of the Committee's Report, see ibid.

16. *Presbyterian Witness*, 22 September 1857, quoting the *Richmond Dispatch*.

17. *Presbyterian Historical Almanac* 1 (1858-1859): 138.

18. *CO*, 11 March 1848.

19. Ibid., 22 April 1848. The Presbytery of Winchester passed similar resolutions about the same time; ibid., 10 June 1848.

20. Ibid., 29 April 1848.
21. Ibid., 2 September 1848.
22. Synod of Nashville, MS "Minutes" (13 October 1856), pp. 114-115, PHF.
23. A similar reaction confronted the proposed reunion of the Independent Presbyterian Church and the Presbytery of Bethel in the Synod of South Carolina at this same Assembly. See Harold M. Parker, Jr., "The Independent Presbyterian Church and Reunion in the South, 1813-1863," *JPH* 50 (1972): 100-105; reprinted in Parker, *SSPH*, pp. 68-73.
24. Synod of Nashville, MS "Minutes" (13 October 1856), p. 115.
25. *Central Presbyterian*, 5 September 1857; *CO*, 3 September 1857.
26. *Central Presbyterian*, 5 September 1857, carried a very thorough account of the debate.
27. *Presbyterian Witness*, 7 July 1857.
28. An example will suffice. In Ross's *Slavery Ordained of God* (Philadelphia: J. B. Lippincott, 1859), he reproduced the speech he had delivered to the Assembly in 1853. In parentheses and brackets such comments as "laughter," "true, true," "much good-natured excitement" are found. Ross was very popular in the North, for he spoke in a style the people could understand. Further, his own example of manumitting his slaves was not overlooked. But it is one thing to laugh with one's opponent, quite another to forsake one's bastion in favor of the trenches of the opposition. It was precisely here that the South misunderstood the North. The abolitionists had captured the Northern New School, and the pressure of the Western Congregationalists combined to create a condition the New School could not resist. Nor were the New School Presbyterians singular in experiencing the impact of the abolitionists. For a similar abolition influence among Northern Baptists, see John R. McKivigan, "The American Baptist Free Mission Society: Abolitionist Reaction to the 1845 Baptist Schism," *Foundations* 21 (1978): 340-355. The ABFMS was to the Baptists what the AMA was to the New School: an organization committed absolutely to non-support for proslavery missionaries or churches.
29. *American Presbyterian*, 10 September 1857.
30. Cited in *CO*, 10 September 1857.
31. Ibid., 17 September 1857.
32. *Presbyterian Witness*, 29 September 1857.
33. Richland Presbytery, MS "Minutes" (8 October 1857), p. 183, PHF.
34. Presbytery of Newton, MS "Minutes" (10 October 1857), pp. 48-50, PHF.

35. *CO*, 29 October 1857.
36. Synod of Kentucky, typed "Minutes" (6 November 1857), pp. 83-84, PHF.
37. *CO,* 17 September 1857.
38. *Central Presbyterian*, 12 September 1857.
39. *Presbyterian Witness*, 22 September 1857.
40. It is not by mistake that Lewis G. Vander Velde, in his contributive study, *The Presbyterian Churches and the Federal Union 1860-1869*, Harvard Historical Studies (Cambridge: Harvard University Press; London: Humphrey Milford, 1932), devoted an entire chapter to the subject, "The Voice of the Old School Press" (pp. 132-182).
41. *Presbyterian Witness*, 3 November 1857.
42. Ibid., 9 February 1858.
43. Ibid., 16 March 1858.

STATISTICS OF SOUTHERN NEW SCHOOL SYNODS AND PRESBYTERIES, 1857

	Presbytery			SYNOD		
	Chs	Mins	Membs	Chs	Mins	Membs
MISSOURI				57	39	2290
St. Louis	9	11	611			
North. Mo.	9	6	592			
Lexington	21	11	569			
Osage	18	11	518			
VIRGINIA				48	39	4173
Winchester	18	8	1085			
Dist. Col.	13	13	1496			
Hanover	17	18	1592			
KENTUCKY				21	14	1028
Harmony	9	5	352			
Providence	6	4	499			
Green Riv.	6	5	177			
TENNESSEE				84	38	5286
Union	31	18	1992			
Holston	18	11	1833			
Kingston	21	8	783			
New River	14	9	678			
WEST TENN.				38	19	2209
West Tenn.	7	5	568			
Shiloh	17	4	916			
Richland	14	10	725			
MISSISSIPPI				36	20	1151
Clinton	12	7	358			
Lexington, South	9	3	296			
Newton	10	5	408			
Texas	5	5	89			
Southern New School Totals				284	169	16137
New School Totals				1679	1595	139115
Percentages in South				16.9%	10.6%	11.6%

9

The Knoxville Meeting and Aftermath

On 1 April 1858 the United Synod of the Presbyterian Church in the United States of America was formally organized in Knoxville, Tennessee. Knoxville stood in sharp contrast to Richmond. The latter was the only city in the South where New School congregations outnumbered Old School. The New School Presbytery of Hanover, in which Richmond was located, was somewhat smaller in membership than Union Presbytery, locale of the Knoxville-Maryville axis, but its congregations were stronger and its ministerial leadership was a credit to the Church. In addition, the theology of the Hanover men was never questioned by their Old School counterparts. This could not be said of the Hopkinsian-ridden ministers of Union Presbytery. Further, Richmond was in a real sense an urban center, whereas Knoxville in 1858 was hardly more than a typical southern village.

The commissioners who gathered on that spring evening in Knoxville to launch a new Presbyterian Church knew why they had assembled. Their goal was singular: to form a Presbyterian Church in which the issue of slavery would not be discussed in the judicatories of the new Church. The Rev. J. D. Mitchell of the Presbytery of Piedmont preached the sermon[1] and then presided in the organization of the United Synod.

When the Roll was prepared, it revealed the following commissioners present:[2]

Presbyteries	Ministers	Elders

I. The Synod of Virginia

1. Winchester	A. H. H. Boyd	William Engle
2. Dist. of Col.		
3. Hanover	C. H. Read	W. F. Gaines
4. Piedmont	J. D. Mitchell	T. F. Leftwich

II. The Synod of Tennessee

1. Union	G. S. White	Daniel Meek
2. Holston		Samuel Rhea
3. Kingston	J. N. Bradshaw	A. D. Keyes
4. New River	George Painter	T. P. Clapp

III. The Synod of West Tennessee

1. Shiloh		
2. Richland	G. E. Eagleton	T. J. Kennedy
3. North Alabama	F. A. Ross	C. N. Ordway

IV. The Synod of Mississippi

1. Clinton	C. Parish	J. Montgomery
2. Lexington, South	J. McCampbell	
3. Newton	R. McLain	
4. Texas		

The Synods of Kentucky and Missouri were not represented. The Presbytery of District of Columbia was expected to be present since it was a part of the Synod of Virginia, but the expectation was never realized. The Presbyteries of Shiloh and Texas had no representation, the latter probably due to distance. Among the first actions of the new Church was the formal adoption of the name for the new denomination, "The United Synod of the Presbyterian Church in the United States of America." Then the Church passed the following resolution:

> *Resolved*, That the United Synod do adhere to and abide by the Confession of Faith of the Presbyterian Church, as containing the system of doctrine taught in the Holy Scriptures; and that we adhere to the Form of Government and Book of Discipline of said Church.

Officers were then elected: Moderator, Charles H. Read; Stated Clerk, T. D. Bell; Permanent Clerk, Joseph H. Martin; Temporary Clerk, Robert McLain; Assistant Clerk, J. N. Bradshaw; and Treasurer, David B. Payne. All but the last were clergy. The Synod organized itself around eight Standing Committees. Its sessions lasted through the morning of 8 April, and it adjdourned to meet in the Second Presbyterian Church, Lynchburg, Virginia, in May 1859.

The records of the first meeting indicate that the commissioners came to do their work, and they did. The first meeting of the United Synod was not that of a sect; it was the meeting of rational, organized churchmen, who from the start began as a Church in every respect of the word. On Monday, 5 April, the United Synod adopted a lengthy Declaration of Principles, consisting of a Preamble and nine enumerated paragraphs. The Preamble stated that such a statement was needed "in order to avoid misapprehensions of our position" and to "place upon permanent record, a statement of the principles which have governed us in forming a separate organization . . . ."[3]

Considerable time was given to the paper from the Bills and Overtures Committee, chaired by A. H. H. Boyd. The report dealt with the proposed union with the Old School Presbyterian Church. The document contained eight specifications. The basis for union was the mutual acceptance of the Westminster Standards, plus the Directory of Worship, Form of Government, and Book of Discipline. The United Synod's view of slavery as a political institution was included, plus the assurance that slavery would not be discussed on the floor of the Church's judicatories. It also listed as "indispensable to an honorable union on our part" the condition that "the Presbyteries connected with this Synod shall be united as Presbyteries, and without an examination of their ministers . . . ." Other matters in the Plan of Union dealt with the mechanics of putting it into operation. In the event that no union could be agreed upon, the two-man committee of Charles H. Read and M. M. Marshall was delegated to propose to the Old School Assembly the establishment of mutual correspondence in the future between the two bodies.[4] Since the Old School Assembly would be meeting the next month, it was the hope of the commissioners that information on the proposed Plan of Union would not only be affirmative, but would also be quickly disseminated across the Church.

Inasmuch as some of the congregations had contributed to the Church Erection Fund of the New School before the separation, the Synod directed a committee led by Boyd to see if any of the funds could be returned to the Synod.

The United Synod organized a Board of Domestic and Foreign Missions consisting of two members from each presbytery. It would work with the existing missionary organizations of Hanover and Piedmont Presbyteries. A Permanent Committee on Church Erection was also formed, as were a Permanent Committee on Education and a Board of Trustees.

The Church also claimed four institutions of learning under its jurisdiction. North Alabama College was located in Huntsville, Alabama. It had been founded in the 1850s, but as yet had no physical property. Piedmont Institute was located in Liberty, Virginia. It was under the immediate control of the Presbytery of Hanover. Caldwell College, Rogersville, Tennessee, had been organized in 1856. Of the four, by far the most established, together with a theological seminary, was Maryville College. Several of the men in attendance at that meeting were graduates of the school. Since the Synod was just getting organized, it could not formally receive any of the educational institutions under its care until the next meeting. It did, however, commend them to the support of its members.

The Committee on Church Erection noted the assistance which the SAS had given the Synod's churches in the past, "not to support or direct the Missionary work in this wide field--but to *aid us* in carrying it on." The Committee also expressed its concern for the important task "of *sustaining Missions among our slaves*." Fidelity to Christ's command, "Go, preach the Gospel to every creature . . . obligates us to devise and adopt more effective measures for reaching the thousands of our plantation servants who are not regularly and systematically instructed in the knowledge of the gospel." Each presbytery was urged to establish a Committee on Missions. Without the approval of such a committee, Synod would not approve any missionary to labor within the bounds of the presbytery.

The United Synod inherited two foreign missionaries--Michael Kalopothakes, a missionary in Greece, and S. A. Rhea, a missionary to Persia.

Other "housekeeping" matters were taken care of. Thus, when the United Synod adjourned from its first meeting, it had accomplished a creditable amount of work. There was no looking back to the past, no regret that the ties with the New School had been severed. The commissioners had come from a large geographical area, yet they had been laboring together, physically and psychologically, for a score of years. They were not strangers to one another. A set of principles had been adopted; agencies were established through which the Church would conduct its work; able administrators were appointed; and a proposed Plan of Union had been worked through. The total work of the Church's first meeting was summed up in the words of A. H. H. Boyd on the eve of the coming meeting when he said,

> I think . . . we should go forward, and organize as if we expected to live till the Millenium . . . . Let no hope of union keep us from organizing a permanent body, with all our educational, missionary and other schemes laid with a view of permanence.[5]

His hopes had been realized, and the new Church was well launched.

The statistics for the United Synod were published with its first *Minutes*. The tables revealed a total of 96 ministers, 167 churches, and 10,205 communicants. There were no unsubstantiated claims in the tables. No figures included Missouri or Kentucky Synods, nor were there any figures for the Presbyteries of District of Columbia or Shiloh.

The overture for union with the Old School General Assembly almost died aborning. The 17 April 1858 issue of the Old School *Presbyterian* reported that the United Synod had adopted a paper on union with the Old School. "We presume the paper is in accordance with the discussions of the Richmond Convention, and of course proposes impracticable terms," was the editor's response. Two Old School stalwarts, Robert J. Breckinridge of Kentucky and Benjamin M. Palmer of New Orleans, were in attendance at the General Assembly. The "indispensable" terms for union, which the United Synod had enumerated, were shredded by the attacks of these defenders of the faith. Breckinridge argued that the southern wing of the Old School had no desire to bring up the issue of slavery again. It would be brought out of the closet if union with the United Synod were accomplished. The question of subscription had been settled twenty years earlier at the cost of schism. The issue of ecclesiastical power-- the Old School insisting on the role of the General Assembly, the United Synod casting such authority into the hands of the presbyteries--ushers in a new and foreign question. The very existence of the Old School depends on a strong General Assembly. Finally, Breckinridge argued that the issue of slavery had been settled harmoniously in the Old School, and it was not politic to disturb its repose. "It is my deliberate judgment, in the sight of God, that there is no way for these two bodies to come together, so as to strength each other's hands," he concluded.⁶

Between the meetings of the two Churches, the *Presbyterian*, the journalistic bastion of the Old School, had editorialized that "our readers will find but little difficulty in judging . . . as to whether or not this United Synod will be merged with our General Assembly. We can scarcely conjecture how, in case it had been their distinct purpose to close the door against such a consummation, it could have been done more effectually." The editor excoriated the Plan line on line, precept on precept.⁷

A decade earlier, Lewis Cheeseman, "a scholar, a theologian, and an earnest, eloquent and successful defender of 'the faith once delivered to the saints,'"⁸ wrote a book in which he delineated the differences between the two wings of Presbyterianism. Prophetically, the Old School scion had declared,

> Our infallible rule of faith and practice, is the Bible, our epitome of it, is the confession of faith. In that instrument our views of christianity are fully stated without reserve, and without ambiguity; and if the New School desires a union with us, they ought first to retract their errors, and to make an honest subscription to our standards. We ought to expect no less from them; they ought to expect no less from us.⁹

The position of the United Synod on the issue of doctrine was that the southern New School had never been suspected of irregularity, that for the most part there was no widespread doctrinal unsoundness in the United Synod. True, there were a few men who held distinctive New School doctrines--or at least doctrines hostile to the Old School--but such could be counted on the fingers of one hand.¹⁰ It was just over this that the Old School insisted on examination and subscription.¹¹

The failure of the proposed union came as no real surprise to the United Synod. In fact, its anticipation was probably what had urged the delegates at the natal meeting to proceed with all dispatch to structure their Church. The changes in the Constitution of the Presbyterian Church that were adopted by the United Synod were prepared basically by Boyd, who had foreseen the rejection of the proposed union. That the presbyteries ratified his proposed changes placed the Church in gratitude to him.[12] The supreme judicatory of the United Synod "evidently stood in the relation of a superior judicatory, or provisional General Assembly under the name of a Synod," according to J. E. Alexander.[13] And the structuring of the Board of Domestic and Foreign Missions was a departure from the New School practice of relying upon the extra-ecclesiastical agencies for the prosecution of its benevolent undertakings.[14]

One of the most visionary actions the United Synod took at its first meeting was to anticipate the establishment of a theological seminary. Having formally severed its relationship with the New School, it would have to wait upon candidates from the South for its future clergy. This ministry would also have to be southern-trained. On the occasion of the inauguration of Archibald Alexander at Princeton, Samuel Miller had commented,

> When the church herself provides a seminary for the instruction of her candidates for the ministry, she can at all times inspect and regulate the course of their education; can see that it be sound, thorough, and faithful; can direct and control instruction; can correct such errors; and make such improvements . . . as the counsels of the whole body may discover.[15]

The sage advice of Miller was not wasted on the ecclesiastically-bent minds of the United Synod fathers.

One might ponder why the seminary at Maryville was not immediately contemplated as the United Synod's theological institution. It was located in the geographical heart of the Church; the Synod of Tennessee contained almost half of the communicant membership of the Church. Isaac Anderson was no longer living. His personal influence and theological views would not be felt by the seminarians studying there. Although many of the Tennessee commissioners had studied there, Maryville never entered the discussion. Just as the 1840 Cassville Convention had passed by any consideration toward the school, so also did the United Synod.

Boyd attended the 1858 New School Assembly to seek the funds that the churches in the United Synod had contributed to the Church Erection Fund. The quest was to drag on for two or three years ultimately to end in failure. The 1858 Assembly postponed any immediate action on the request on grounds that (1) suitable time was needed to study all claims; (2) the Assembly needed to know precisely how many presbyteries and synods had defected in order to ascertain what portion of the funds would be claimed; and (3) final adjustment of claims might be made as the result of mutual confidence and prayer, in order to satisfy all parties.[16]

Most of the numerical losses which the United Synod suffered could be attributed to the failure of the Synods of Missouri and Kentucky to enter the Church. Thus the developments in these two courts need to be examined in order to understand why they did not enter the new Church in 1858. For Missouri, the years 1857-1859 represent a period of uncertainty resulting in division; for Kentucky, the uncertainty surrounding the events of 1857 spelled the demise of the Synod.

John Van Horn Barks had attended the Cleveland Assembly as a commissioner from Missouri's Osage Presbytery. Since he did not have time in his return from to his home from Cleveland for a called meeting of Presybtery, he invited some of the ministers and elders to meet in Osceola on 4 August to discuss what the presbytery might do. R. A. Morrison, of the Bentonville, Arkansas, church, reported that his congregation had passed a resolution urging the presbytery to instruct its delegates to the Richmond Convention to pursue a union with the Old School. Levi morrison of Springfield opposed such a union. William H. Smith supported the Assembly's action, noting that it did no more than "the exigency of the case demanded, viz., to condemn the ultra-southern view." Barks stated that he could not return to the New School. He disliked, however, the idea of a southern organization "because I doubt the possibility of securing a number of sufficient strength and respectability to carry on church matters in a strictly pro-slavery organization . . . ." He favored a union with the Old School.[17] This informal "convention" of Missouri ministers reveals the lack of decisive, unanimous thinking on the part of Missouri Presbyterians following the 1857 Assembly.

The Presbytery of Osage thought that, for the present, it "advisable to remain in the same organized capacity as heretofore, in connection with the Synod of Missouri, and recommend our churches to do the same . . . ."[18]

The Presbytery of Lexington (Missouri) also met on 4 August. It asserted that the Assembly's action at Cleveland "has forfeited the claim [of the Assembly] to be regarded as 'the *Constitutional* General Assembly of the Presbyterian Church.'" The Presbytery, however, opposed the idea of a new

Church being erected in the South. It deemed it "better that our several Synods and Presbyteries at the South should remain in an independent condition, until God in His providence shall point out, more clearly than we can now discover, the path of duty for us."[19]

The only southern commissioner at Cleveland to vote with the North on the slavery issue was Timothy Hill from St. Louis. His vote was the only instance in all the long debate in the New School on the slavery issue that came from a southerner. That vote made him a marked man.[20] Serving as Secretary of the Missouri Home Missionary Society, Hill wrote the Synod's Stated Clerk, urging that all ministers be present at the 1857 Synod. In his letter he set forth his own desires for an independent status "rather than open my throat for the Acts of 1837, or the whole system of slavery."[21]

Interestingly enough, Hill was elected Moderator. That meeting of Synod came in the midst of troublous days. The sympathy for the Richmond Convention became evident. At the same time there were those "cultivating the acquaintance of the Old School," while others favored an independent synod.[22] No one favored New School status. It was the division in the Synod, manifested in the ministers leaning either toward the United Synod or a return to the Old School, which prompted Hill's independent status proposal.[23] But the fact that Hill had been elected Moderator, with every member aware of his position on the proposed destination of the synod, was a harbinger of how the synod would vote.

When the committee appointed to study the question of synod alignment reported, it gave both a majority and a minority report. The majority recommended withdrawing from the New School, but did not favor, "for the present," a connection with the proposed United Synod. It recommended that synod "remain in an independent position, until God in his providence shall indicate a different source." The minority report recommended remaining in the Assembly--a course of action suggested for the first time. After considerable debate, the phrase "for the present" in the majority report was deleted. The report of the majority was put to vote and it carried, 17-10. There was, however, an understanding that no member would leave synod to join another body within the year. And a subsequent vote passed, by which synod unanimously declined to have anything to do with the proposed United Synod to be formed in April 1858.[24]

A month before the Synod had met, Benjamin Wallace, Secretary of the Assembly's Church Extension Committee, wrote Timothy Hill:

> We are all very anxious that you should preserve the Synod of Missouri intact for the Assembly. If you can only get three ministers in the Presbytery of Northern Missouri, and can make one of the Presbyteries of Osage and West Lexington, I would do it, even if there are at first only six ministers out of St. Louis Presbytery. It is vastly important that the skeleton at least of the Synod remain . . . .[25]

Thus, Hill's statesmanship in directing the Synod into an independent status ran counter to the Assembly's desires, but it kept the Synod intact.

Hill was simply reading the signs much better than the seaboard ecclesiastics. With the numerous options, which could very badly have divided the Synod, he opted for one that at least preserved its unity for another year. Further, 1857 was a good year for New School Missouri Presbyterians. The Presbytery of Osage, for instance, reached a high water mark that year with nine churches and 304 members.[26] The Presbytery's adamant opposition to the New School surfaced at its meeting on 24 November 1857. It voted not to send commissioners to the Assembly as long as it "adheres to the unconstitutional action on the subject of slavery." At the same time it broke bond with the rest of Synod by voting to send commissioners to the Knoxville meeting,[27] although they did not attend.

Other dissatisfactions with the Synod's independent status began to appear. Barks wrote Timothy Hill that he had no confidence in Synod's present independent state, unless it would lead to union with the Old School. "*The thing to be done is to unite with the Old School*. If we can get all together, well; if not, we go by Presbyteries, either in whole or in part."[28]

Pressure to reconsider also came from the Board of Church Extension. It notified Hill that since the Board was an ecclesiastical committee, it was not able to disburse funds beyond the bounds of the Church. Secretary Wallace advised Hill that even if the Presbytery of St. Louis could remain in the Assembly, "the way could be clear to appoint a General Agent for the Presbytery, who could extend himself ad libitum over the State." He cautioned that men in the synod must consider whether "your present position is the best, all things considered.

We know you are honest and true; but it must be a painful question to you how Missouri is to be evangelized in your present attitude."[29]

The communication from Wallace apparently brought Hill around to reconsider synod's decision to take the independent track. Hill's membership was in the Presbytery of St. Louis. That presbytery had opposed synod's becoming independent in the first place, but had acquiesced in the hope of maintaining the integrity of the synod with a view of keeping it intact for the Assembly.[30]

The Presbytery of St. Louis met on 18 December 1857. In a lengthy statement it reviewed the actions of both the Assembly of 1857 and the subsequent decision of synod. Rather than interpreting the actions of the Assembly as exscinding any portion of the Church, or as establishing "a doctrine of the church that is not so established by the Confession of Faith," the presbytery interpreted the actions simply as

> reiterating the solemn testimony which the Presbyterian Church . . . has constantly and consistently borne from the beginning, against the system of slavery, and to apply that testimony . . . to those who were understood to have avowed and disseminated opposite sentiments in approbation of that system.

Admitting that perhaps the men from the South were misunderstood or their views misrepresented, the presbytery confidently declared that "our brethren will yet show that they do not mean to defend and sanction the system of slavery . . . ." But if those men do wish to be understood as having taken their position in defense and support of the system of slavery, "we cannot regard the reproof and warning of the General Assembly, as giving any just cause to dissolve our connection with the church of which that General Assembly is the bond of union . . . ." Although the presbytery did not deem the action of the synod as the wisest course to pursue, it urged all ministers and churches to continue "in their present relations to the Synod in order to maintain its integrity."[31] Thus, although this influential presbytery sought to retain the unity of the synod, it did so at the cost of its own basic position that the Assembly was quite correct in adopting the legislation that it had.

When the Synod of Missouri convened in September 1858, it spent two days discussing its position. Five sets of opinion were expressed: (1) some desired to go to the United Synod, influenced no doubt by the ecclesiastical manner by which the new denomination had organized itself; (2) some desired to return to the New School, observing that the Assembly had been consistent in its deliverances on slavery since its natal days; (3) some preferred going Old School; (4) some pleaded for the present status quo--independence; and (5) others would dissolve the Synod and let each man and each church seek its own way. A reporter commented that "These various and conflicting opinions and preferences were freely and candidly expressed, but with an evidently fraternal regard for all and each other."[32] In the end, the synod opted for each man to go his own way in the coming year. Hardly had the decision been made when some of the courts began to form new connections, thus fracturing the unity of the past year. Indeed, "this was a time of darkness."[33]

The Presbytery of Osage resolved itself into an independent presbytery until its Stated Spring Meeting in 1859. Its rationale for taking such action was the general belief that some of its members desired to connect themselves with the Old School, while others preferred the United Synod. Presbytery advised all who desired to withdraw to do so by vote at a regular church meeting by March.[34] Upon meeting at the March 1859 session, presbytery voted to connect itself with the United Synod. It was attached to the Synod of Mississippi.[35]

The destinations of the ministers in Osage Presbytery reflect the indecision of the Presbytery to take any substantive action relative to retaining its essential integrity: G. U. Harlan, A. Jones, W. C. Requa, and J. V. Barks went Old School; L. R. Morrison, J. B. Ricketts, A. G. Taylor, and John McMillan took the name of Osage Presbytery into the United Synod; A. W. Morrison made no decision; and William H. Smith returned to the New School.[36] In the meantime, St. Louis Presbytery returned to the Assembly.[37]

When the new School Synod of Missouri convened in 1859, it struck Osage Presbytery from its roll and enlarged the bounds of St. Louis Presbytery to include Osage's former ground. Synod also encouraged any churches which were formerly in connection with that presbytery, and which desired to remain in connection with the Synod, to contact the Stated Clerk of the Presbytery of St. Louis.[38] Synod rescinded the minute of 1857, whereby it had withdrawn from the New School Assembly.[39]

Thus the United Synod was denied the Synod of Missouri, which, after two years of independency, returned to the New School fold, save for the Presbytery of Osage. But the unity that had characterized the synod was splintered. Of those who were members of the synod at the time of the Cleveland Assembly in 1857, eight remained in the New School, seven went Old School, nine were in the United Synod, and four or five still had not made up their minds where their destination would be. The fractured condition led a correspondent to the *Christian Observer* caustically to comment, "A picture this, sufficiently sad,, to satisfy any mind, it would be supposed; but just what might have been anticipated by the enactors of that disastrous deed."[40]

The year 1857 was a devastating year for the Synod of Kentucky. The reaction to the Assembly's legislation left New School Kentuckians with the feeling that there was no longer any place for them in the Assembly. At its 1857 Meeting, synod formally withdrew from any connection with the New School, "to stand independent until God in His Providence shall open the way for further action." like the Synod of Missouri, the Synod of Kentucky urged its ministers and churches not to change their positions "until this Synod shall have another meeting . . . ."[41] When the synod adjourned, it then went as a body to the bedside of its venerable patriarch, Thomas Cleland, where each member bade farewell to his beloved mentor and brother. Cleland died shortly thereafter.

With the death of Cleland, the synod lost its nerve. Even Archer C. Dickerson, who long had held high the flag of New Schoolism in Kentucky, now advocated a return to the Old School. In an early 1858 article, which appeared in the *Christian Observer* comment was made on the splendid cooperation which the Old and New School congregations were enjoying in Bowling Green--an omen of coming events.[42] Synod met in 1858. After adopting a minute relative to Cleland's death, it then approved a series of resolutions which reduced the synod to a presbytery--The United Presbytery of Kentucky-- placing itself precisely where it was before the Lexington Convention.[43] Only seven ministers were present at this synod meeting which was held in Lebanon. Archer C. Dickerson, Thomas H. Cleland the Younger, and Belville Roberts favored union with the Old School; Fencilius Gray preferred the United Synod; S. Y. Garrison, Benjamin Mills and William T. McElroy opted for an independent status. The congregations were also divided. With such indecisiveness, it was not strange that synod took the step it did: recommending that the new presbytery appoint a committee to confer with the Old School Synod of Kentucky with a view of arriving at terms of union in which the entire Presbyterian Church could labor.[44]

The last official meeting of Kentucky Presbytery convened in October, 1858, a few days before the meeting of the Old School Synod of Kentucky. The latter body was adamant that the New Schoolmen must be received through examination and subscription.[45] The feelings between the two bodies, however, had moved from acerbity to a more mutual stance through the years, a condition favorable to the presbytery. The Stated Clerk was directed to write out letters of dismission, turn over the records to the Synod of Kentucky, and the Presbytery adjourned *sine die*.[46]

The demise of the Synod of Kentucky prompted an acrimonious journalistic jibe by the *Presbyterian Witness*:

> We were not surprised at the result.--It was clearly foreseen and calculated from the first. These New School brethren, now received into the lap of the mother church, have practically said that, for twenty years, they have contended for nothing--been schismatics and disturbers of the peace without cause. And, by their present position, they now say that they believe slaveholding to be a "blot upon our holy religion"--a thing to be done away as speedily as possible.[47]

So was the Synod of Kentucky denied to the United Synod. Kentucky experienced its demise only a year after the crucial 1857 Assembly; Missouri suffered splintering division. Only a portion of Missouri entered the new Church; Kentucky offered nothing. In the meantime the United Synod confronted other problems of polity which required its attention.

NOTES

    1. For the text of the sermon, see *Presbyterian Historical Almanac and Annual Remembrancer* 1 (1858-1859): 139-142. He made reference to the Cleveland Assembly and following events only in the closing sentences of the sermon. Slavery was not mentioned in the sermon.

    2. USS, *Minutes* (1858), p. 4; *Presbyterian Historical Almanac* 1 (1858-1859): 142-143. The MS

"Minutes" of the United Synod are in PHF. However, they are not complete, the entries ending in the middle of a resolution in the 1860 session. In addition to the published *Minutes*, a fairly full account of the annual meetings is found in the *Presbyterian Historical Almanac*. CO is also a valuable source for the proceedings of the annual meetings. The USS did not meet in 1862 because of the conditions brought about by the war.

    3. USS, *Minutes* (1858), pp. 7-11; *Presbyterian Historical Almanac* 1 (1858-1859): 143-145. For the text, see Appendix B.

    4. For a complete text of the Plan of Union, see USS, *Minutes* (1858), pp. 14-15; *Presbyterian Historical Almanac* 1 (1858-1859): 146-147; they are reprinted in Appendix C of this volume.

    5. *Knoxville Register* 8 April 1858. Both the *Register* and *Brownlow's Knoxville Whig* of that date carried very extensive accounts of the sessions. For further descriptions of the meeting, see Robert L. Bachman, *Historical Sermon, Preached by the Pastor, Rev. Robert L. Bachman, D. D., in the Second Presbyterian Church, Knoxville, Tennessee, September 23, 1906* (Knoxville: Gaut-Ogden, n.d.); and Thomas Cary Johnson, "A Brief Sketch of the United Synod of the Presbyterian Church in the United States of America," *Papers of the American Society of Church History* 8 (1897): 19-23.

    6. *Presbyterian Witness*, 25 May 1858.

    7. *Presbyterian*, 24 April 1858.

    8. Alfred Nevin, *Encyclopaedia of the Presbyterian Church in the United States of America: Including the Northern and Southern Assemblies* (Philadelphia: Presbyterian Encyclopaedia Publishing Co., 1884), p. 137.

    9. Lewis Cheeseman, *Differences between Old School and New School Presbyterians* (Rochester: Erastus Darrow, 1848), p. 207.

    10. Johnson, "United Synod of the South," pp. 27-28, mentioned four men in the United Synod whose theology would probably not have been acceptable to the Old School: A. H. H. Boyd, Arthur Mitchell, J. D. Mitchell, and Frederick A. Ross.

    11. For the complete text of the Old School response to the United Synod's proposal for union, see GAPCUSA [OS], *Minutes* (1857): 289-290; *Presbyterian Historical Almanac* 1 (1858-1859): 48-49; *Princeton Review* 30 (1858): 558-559. Timothy L. Smith, in *Revivalism and Social Reform in Mid-19th-Century America* (New York and Nashville: Abingdon Press, 1957), p. 198, placed responsibility for the failure of the union on the United Synod: "They

refused to join even the Old School communion, regarding its principles insufficiently clear in defense of slaveholding." Thomas Cary Johnson ("The United Synod of the South," p. 27) attributed the Old School refusal of union to an "unnamed" factor: the Old School was "not only tenacious of reputation for strict construction in theology, she had in the main kept clear of partisan and un-biblical discussion at once by taking into her own communion a body with such a history as the United Synod had."

12. "Autobiography of the Rev. Amasa Converse," *JPH* 43 (1965): 259: "The eminent services rendered to the Church by Dr. Boyd at this crisis in her trials merit a grateful and lasting memorial in her memory."

13. J. E. Alexander, *A Brief History of the Synod of Tennessee, From 1817 to 1887* (Philadelphia: McCalla & Co., 1890), p. 34.

14. Ernest Trice Thompson, *Presbyterians in the South*, 3 vols. (Richmond: John Knox Press, 1963-1973), 1:546.

15. James W. Alexander, *The Life of Archibald Alexander, D. D., First Professor in the Theological Seminary at Princeton, New Jersey* (New York: Charles Scribner, 1854), p. 336.

16. *Presbyterian Historical Almanac* 1 (1858-1859): 110-111.

17. John Van Horn Barks to Timothy Hill, 4 August 1857, cited in John B. Hill, *The Presbytery of Kansas City and its Predecessors, 1821-1901* (Kansas City, Missouri: Burd and Fletcher Printing Co., 1901), p. 119.

18. *CO*, 20 August 1857.

19. Ibid.

20. John B. Hill, "Timothy Hill Reports on Slavery," *JPHS* 29 (1951): 34.

21. Ibid., p. 36.

22. *CO*, 8 October 1857, citing the St. Louis correspondent of the *New York Evangelist*.

23. Hill, "Timothy Hill Reports on Slavery," pp. 35-36.

24. Synod of Missouri [NS], MS "Minutes" (3 October 1857), p. 197, Murrell Memorial Library, Missouri Valley College; Hill, "Timothy Hill Reports on Slavery," p. 37; Synod of Missouri [PCUSA], *Minutes* (1882), p. 59.

25. Wallace to Hill, cited in Hill, "Timothy Hill Reports on Slavery," p. 36.

26. E. E. Stringfield, *Presbyterianism in the Ozarks: A History of the Work of the Various Branches of the Presbyterian Church in Southwest Missouri* (n.p.: n.p., 1909), p. 19.

27. *CO*, 24 December 1857.
28. Barks to Hill, 8 December 1857, cited in Hill, *Presbytery of Kansas City*, p. 121.
29. Wallace to Hill, cited in Hill, "Timothy Hill Reports on Slavery," pp. 38-39.
30. Charles A. Anderson, ed., "Presbyterians Meet the Slavery Problem," *JPHS* 29 (1951): 39n.
31. *CO*, 25 February 1858.
32. Ibid., 14 October 1858.
33. Hill, "Timothy Hill Reports on Slavery," p. 39; Synod of Missouri [PCUSA], *Minutes* (1882), p. 59.
34. Stringfield, *Presbyterianism in the Ozarks*, p. 126. The ambivalence in the Presbytery should come as no surprise. The majority of the ministers had been taught by Isaac Anderson. They were theologically more at home with their co-laborers in the United Synod than they would be anywhere else; see Harold M. Parker, Jr., "A School of the Prophets at Maryville," *Tennessee Historical Quarterly* 34 (1975): 81, reprinted in Parker, *SSPH*, p. 119.
35. For examples of how local churches responded, see Osceola Presbyterian Church, MS "Minutes" (13 November 1858), pp. 36-39, PHS; Stringfield, *Presbyterianism in the Ozarks*, p. 191, for the Springfield church; Presbytery of Northern Missouri, MS "Minutes" (22 October 1858), p. 142, Murrell Memorial Library, Missouri Valley College, for the Palmyra church.
36. Letter of Barks to Timothy Hill, 25 March 1859, cited in Hill, *Presbytery of Kansas City*, p. 121.
37. Ibid.; and Hill, "Timothy Hill Reports on Slavery," p. 35.
38. Synod of Missouri [NS], MS "Minutes" (23 September 1859), p. 207.
39. Ibid., p. 209.
40. *CO*, 27 October 1859.
41. Synod of Kentucky [NS], typewritten "Minutes" (6 November 1857), pp. 83-84, PHF; *Presbyterian Witness*, 22 December 1857.
42. *CO*, 7 January 1858.
43. Synod of Kentucky [NS], "Minutes" (11 June 1858), pp. 87-88; *Presbyterian Witness*, 13 July 1858.
44. Ibid.; *Central Presbyterian*, 26 June 1858.
45. United Presbytery of Kentucky, "Minutes" (22 October 1858), p. 91; Synod of Kentucky [OS], MS "Minutes" (14 October 1858), 7:314-316, LPTS.
46. United Presbytery of Kentucky, "Minutes" (22 October 1858), p. 92. For a more thorough treatment of the decline and demise of the Kentucky New School

Church, see Harold M. Parker, Jr., "The New School Synod of Kentucky," *Filson Club History Quarterly* 50 (1976): 818-85, reprinted in Parker, *SSPH*, pp. 158-162.

    47. *Presbyterian Witness*, 5 November 1858.

10
The United Synod Polity and Leaders

It is not until reading the account of the 1857 Assembly that the average student of the New School movement becomes aware of the fact that there was a southern element in the Church. Then the issue of the slavery controversy is quickly reviewed, followed by rapid sketch of the withdrawal of the southern presbyteries. Those historians who do acknowledge the exscision of the six southern synods usually view the loss with the satisfaction a surgeon would employ after removing a cancer. Typical was the studied response of E. H. Gillette to the southern withdrawal in 1857. The Church "had thrown off an incubus which for years had oppressed it and crippled its energies."[1]

The confusion that caused the splintering of the New School in Missouri and its death in Kentucky was not peculiar to those two synods. The General Assembly removed the Synods of Tennessee and West Tennessee from its roll in 1859. Mississippi and Virginia Synods were retained until the following year, with the hope that they would return to the fold. The Presbytery of District of Columbia was a part of the Synod of Virginia, and the New School was reluctant to cut off the national capital. So the presbytery was transferred to the Synod of Pennsylvania, and then Virginia was struck from the roll.[2]

The Synod of Tennessee almost unanimously left the New School. Only five of its ministers and two of its congregations failed to enter the United Synod. In the fall of 1857, the synod, anticipating the formation of the United Synod, counselled its constituent presbyteries to send delegates to Knoxville. As a judicatory, it adopted a resolution whereby it withdrew from the New School. After remaining in an independent status for a year, it entered the United Synod in a "kind of anomalous connection."[3] It united with the United Synod at its meeting in 1858. It was not a difference in theology that had prompted the Synod to withdraw, but rather what it deemed were "unconstitutional" and "unrighteous" acts on the part of the Assembly in abrogating the Plan of Union and passing resolutions that exscinded the southern synods.[4]

In a Pastoral Letter, which it sent to its churches explaining its position in joining the United Synod, the Synod of Tennessee stated first that in so doing "we do not commit ourselves as a body, or as individuals, to any particular opinions on the subject of slavery or slaveholding." Rather, the Synod was merely taking the "broad ground" which had been posited at the Richmond Convention, which provided that "the discussion and agitation of the subject of slavery, except as regards the moral and religious duties arising out of the relation of master and slave, shall be excluded from our ecclesiastical meetings . . . ." The Synod viewed such a position as "Scriptural, rational and right." It was a stand that "is calculated to keep us free from strife and contention, and to leave us at liberty to prosecute, with harmony, devotedness, and undivided energy, our appropriate work."[5] Only one minister, Thomas Brown, voted against the Letter.

By far the largest presbytery in the United Synod was Union Presbytery, centered around Knoxville and Maryville. The presbytery also had some congregations in western North Carolina. It was characterized by an essential oneness.

The basic unity of Union Presbytery, however, did not quite extend to its sister Presbytery of Holston. Here several of the stronger congregations were lukewarm at best toward the United Synod. At a meeting on 24 March 1858, the Jonesboro church requested presbytery not to send commissioners to the United Synod's organizational session. The congregation also voted to "stand independent of all connexion with the Synod, and also of the Cleveland Genl. Assembly."[6] Six months later, however, by a 24-20 vote the congregation decided to enter the United Synod--a vote that indicated that the church was still somewhat uneasy about its position. Nevertheless, the church then voted to make the decision unanimous.[7] The Timberridge Church suffered a division over the issue of the United Synod,⁸ and the nearby Greeneville Church voted in 1858 to become independent.⁹

By a narrow vote of 5-4, the Presbytery of Holston decided, on the eve of the first meeting of the United Synod, to send commissioners to Knoxville. The minority lodged a protest against presbytery's action. At the August meeting of presbytery, however, the report of the commissioner to the United Synod was unanimously adopted, as was the Declaration and Principles of the United Synod. Then the Presbytery of Holston officially withdrew from the New School and formally attached itself to the United Synod.¹⁰

It was the Synod of West Tennessee, however, that suffered the greatest attrition in the period between the 1857 Assembly and the organization of the United Synod. At the Knoxville meeting the Presbytery of Shiloh was not represented. Nor was the Presbytery of West Tennessee. The latter presbytery had been dissolved by the Synod of West Tennessee and united with the Presbytery of Shiloh on 10 October 1857.¹¹ In April 1859 the Presbytery of North Alabama and Richland merged under the name of North Alabama Presbytery.¹² In the meantime, the recently reorganized Presbytery of Shiloh was too enfeebled to carry on. It was dissolved and the churches taken under the care of the Presbytery of North Alabama.¹³

The thirty congregations that had constituted the Synod of West Tennessee in 1858 were now reduced to twelve, all in the Presbytery of North Alabama. When the Presbytery of Shiloh dissolved, few were the ministers, numerous were the vacant churches, and hope for the future was not apparent. At the last meeting of the presbytery, the Stated Clerk wrote that each minister and congregation was now left to seek its own connection. It was the desire of presbytery that in each congregation the entire church would go with the majority, so that no lingering minorities would be left behind.¹⁴ Most of the churches gravitated toward the Old School. One exception was the Beth Berei congregation of Marshall County, which voted unanimously to join the United Synod. It was attached to the Presbytery of North Alabama.¹⁵

The Synod of West Tennessee had been looted by Old School ministers who took advantage of vacant churches. So bad was the impact on the Synod that the Presbytery of North Alabama demanded that all "O. S. bodies . . . leave us to attend to the spiritual welfare of our own churches."¹⁶ The Synod of West Tennessee simply died of attrition. The remains of what had been a synod were gathered into one presbytery, which was attached to the Synod of Mississippi. The Synod of Mississippi, unlike her two sister Synods of Virginia and Tennessee, which were characterized by geographical compactness, gradually emerged as the ecclesiastical dumping ground of the United Synod. It embraced not only the state of Mississippi, but also southern Alabama, north central Texas, portions of Missouri, and congregations in Arkansas.

Two aspects of the Assembly's actions in 1857 were especially irksome to the Synod of Mississippi: The fact that the slavery issue for years had been singled out from among others, "its evil and abuses harped upon and held up for reproof and rebuke, for year to year, as if they were the only evils under the sun," and the Assembly's condemnation of the Presbytery of Lexington, South for sustaining in its communion those who held slaves, believing it to be right.[17] The synod withdrew from the New School at its 1857 meeting. It remained in an independent status until after the Knoxville meeting. Then, when it had examined the minutes of the sessions and the Declaration of Principles, it approved the latter "as an embodiment [sic] of the faith and principles of our Church as furnishing a basis upon which every Presbyterian should be proud to stand." The Synod then voted to unite with the United Synod,[18] following the lead of its presbyteries, who had already taken similar action.

The Synod of Missouri suffered greatly. The antislavery views of the New School, coupled with the decision of the AHMS to withdraw support from churches that had slaveholders on their rolls, prevented the growth of congregations in rural and village areas. It has been the opinion of not a few historians that the abolitionists' stance only hurt the New School cause in Missouri.[19] Two presbyteries were affected by the confusion spawned by the Cleveland Assembly.

Osage Presbytery voted to unite with the United Synod in March 1859, having found agreement both in polity as well as its philosophy.[20] The Presbytery added 315 members to the ranks of the United Synod-- as well as an appeal for ministerial assistance.

The second Missouri presbytery that sought admittance into the United Synod was the Presbytery of Lexington West. This court embraced the northwest portion of Missouri, north of Osage Presbytery. In 1859 it reported eleven ministers, twenty-one churches, and 569 members. At its meeting on 10

September 1859, Presbytery resolved that it was "not desirable" to maintain its independent and separate status any longer. It deemed it "proper and right here to express and record their approbation of the platform of principles laid down by the United Synod . . . and also our desire and determination to connect themselves with that body."[21] It urged its churches also to connect themselves with the United Synod.[22] At the 1860 meeting of the United Synod, the Committee on Church Polity recommended that the presbytery be received. The United Synod adopted the recommendation and received the minister commissioner.[23]

The reception of the two Missouri presbyteries added little strength to the United Synod; however their defection all but destroyed the New School Synod of Missouri. In 1862 Timothy Hill wrote, "We have now in Missouri only three churches in [St. Louis] Presbytery, and five small churches enfeebled by the recent troubles in Northern Missouri . . . ."[24]

Another distant presbytery attached to the Synod of Mississippi was the Presbytery of Texas. Following the first meeting of the United Synod, in December 1858 the presbytery resolved: "We honestly, sincerely, and *unanimously* stand with you on the platform of the UNITED SYNOD. Our heads, and hearts, and hands are cordially with you in this cause . . . ."[25] In 1859 Samuel A. King attended the United Synod. He addressed the assemblage about the needs for financial assistance in Texas. Cash and pledges in the amount of $508.50 were received for the purpose of planting missionaries there.[26] The unusual request for funds was due to the three successive years of crop failures, which had substantially reduced the ability of the people to support their churches. The lack of sufficient funds had reduced the ministerial numbers to the point where presbytery could hardly meet.[27] It was unable to elect a commissioner to the 1860 United Synod because of a lack of quorum to conduct Presbytery's business.[28]

In the Synod of Virginia, the only real opposition to the United Synod came from the Presbytery of District of Columbia. The Synod's 1857 meeting recorded only three negative votes regarding the Knoxville meeting. Synod divided the Presbytery of Hanover. The western portion formed the Presbytery of Piedmont. The New School Assembly attached the Presbytery of District of Columbia to the Synod of Pennsylvania, leaving the Synod of Virginia with three Presbyteries: Hanover, Piedmont, and Winchester.

The total membership in 1859 for the United Synod was up considerably over 1858. The increase, however, was on paper only. At that time the United Synod still claimed the Presbytery of District of Columbia. The 1,248 members of that presbytery boosted the total membership of the new Church to 12,125. But even subtracting the presbytery's membership, the total for the United Synod was 10,877, still a good increase over the 10,205 reported in 1858. In 1860, the total membership was 10,872.

The leadership of the United Synod contained men of unusual ability. Though never recognized by the New School Assembly, this detracted nothing from their ability or stature. The leadership consisted of men on two levels: those who had originally withdrawn from the Old School to enter the fray with the New School side in the late 1830s, and those who through the score of years following either transferred into the southern presbyteries or were ordained by them. The first group bore the scars of innumerable ecclesiastical battles. They were men who, having weighed the cost, had entered the struggle on principle. Strongly had they resisted any effort or temptation to return to the Old School fold.

Several of these stand head and shoulders above the common cut. One of the most important of this group was Frederick Augustus Ross, pastor of the First Presbyterian Church, Huntsville, Alabama. He had grown up in East Tennessee. And although he lacked the formal education provided by a theological seminary, he possessed a brilliant--if somewhat erratic--mind. His theological sword had been honed in East Tennessee as he confronted not only the Old School, but also the Arminianism of the Methodists. Never one to shun a theological debate, his skirmishes had sharpened his intellectual acumen considerably. He had also gained the respect of many by manumitting his slaves. He was in great demand as an evangelist, and in his earlier days he had travelled with James Gallaher on several evangelistic campaigns. He made quite a name for himself, especially in the joint effort with Gallaher in Cincinnati in the 1820s.

On the cover of the April 1847 issue of the *Calvinistic Magazine* was the notation that the journal was edited by Isaac Anderson, Frederick A. Ross, James King, and James McChain. All were leaders in the southern New School, and all but

Anderson, who died in 1857, entered the United Synod. Among the magazine's agents were George Painter, Nathan Hood, J. S. Craig, Fielding Pope, William Eagleton, and William C. Dunlap. Thus the core for the leadership of the United Synod was being developed in East Tennessee a decade before the new Church came into being. Ross was the nucleus of that leadership.

Ross opposed union with the Old School. He was quite cognizant that his brand of Calvinism did not quite square with that of the Old School. So prominent a role did Ross play in the United Synod that it was commonly referred to as "Dr. Ross's Synod."[29]

The most intellectual of the United Synod men was the pastor of the Presbyterian Church at Winchester, Virginia, Andrew Hunter Holmes Boyd, one of the martyrs of the United Synod. Born into an inheritance of $100,000, he was in a family that also promised him splendid political prospects. These he forsook for the ministry. Such was his sprightliness, acuteness, balance, and vigor of mind that he was regarded as the best equipped debater on theological topics. His knowledge ranged over a wide variety of topics. It was in the field of religion, however--didactic and polemic theology, church history, biblical criticism--,that he held sway over most of his peers.[30] He was tapped to be the professor of ecclesiastical literature in the proposed theological seminary of the United Synod. Only his early death as the result of the most extreme deprivations as a hostage during the Civil War deprived the Church of his dynamic contributions at the age of fifty-one.

Boyd's theological views, like Ross's, would hardly have found acceptance in Old School circles. Throughout his life he held to a theological position that the ultra-Calvinist would hardly acknowledge as orthodox. Yet he insisted on his Calvinism.[31] When the day came for the United Synod to consider union with the Presbyterian Church in the Confederate States of America, Boyd's presence caused many of the latter to urge union with the United Synod in order to deny him the chair in the proposed United Synod seminary, so that he would no longer be able to influence those students who would sit at his feet.

No man was stronger in the defense of the southern position on the slavery issue. From the Cleveland Assembly through the Richmond Convention to the first meeting of the United Synod, Boyd adamantly stood without reservation or hesitation for a Church that need not bow its head to any denomination. It was he who wrote the Declaration of Principles; it was he who had composed the defense of the withdrawing southerners in 1857. As pastor, this man of "indefatigable mental industry" was a leader in home missions work around Winchester. He believed in the "power of persuasion rather than the persuasion of power" and was remembered by those who knew him "as a man of utmost kindliness."[32]

In the natal days of the United Synod, the *Presbyterian Witness* spoke highly of him:

> Dr. Boyd is not capable of intentionally misrepresenting his brethren. He is not the man to act the demagogue. We have never known a more candid and honest debater than he is. Cool, self-possessed, and of a delightful christian temper, he makes his points deliberately, ingenuously, and manifests no disposition to conceal the truth or pervert it.[33]

No biographical study of Boyd has been produced; nor did any book come from his pen--only articles, many of which did not bear his name. Nevertheless, here was a giant among men.[34]

Joseph C. Stiles was a leader in the formation of the New School Kentucky Synod. He left Kentucky just a few years after the synod was organized. In later years he achieved fame as Secretary to the Southern Aid Society prior to the Civil War and as a chaplain in the Confederate Army in the 1860s. He developed his theological views in the Campbellite debates in Kentucky and then in the Old School-New School confrontations at a later period. He was elected to be the professor of systematic and pastoral theology in the United Synod's proposed seminary. His labors in the SAS were responsible for infusing new life into the southern New School congregations after the AHMS withheld funds from churches in the slave states. His pen issued forth a veritable flood of pamphlets and articles, to say nothing of sermons.

Although late in associating himself with the United Synod, yet Amasa Converse in his journalistic endeavors was a major factor in disseminating information and inspiring the young denomination, particularly during the trying days of the Civil War. A native of New Hampshire, Converse had edited the *Visitor & Telegraph* in Richmond, from 1827 to 1839. From there he moved to Philadelphia, where he edited the *Christian Observer*. Thus, during the early days of the United Synod, he lived in the

North. But his earlier years in the South had developed a great sympathy for southern ideals. His journalism attempted to interpret the southern cause and plight to the North. He was quite capable of understanding the problems that vexed the southern New School elements, and through his columns he attempted in a moderating fashion to caution the northern wing in its legislation touching the slavery issue. Upon the outbreak of the Civil War, he was expelled from Philadelphia by Federal authorities, and he returned to Richmond, where he continued the publication of the *Christian Observer* until 1869.

When the Old School-New School controversy began to heat up, Converse endeavored to compose the differences between the two parties. Failing this, he became a New School apologist, not on doctrinal, but on polity grounds. His weekly columns carried voluminous amounts of information about the New School in the South. His coverage of the Assemblies was thorough. And when the United Synod emerged, the columns of the *Christian Observer* carried very delineated accounts of the annual sessions. It is very doubtful if there was anyone in the United Synod who was more genuinely admired across the Church than Amasa Converse--nor one who was more influential.[35]

Following the death of Isaac Anderson, John J. Robinson assumed his mentor's mantle, serving as president of Maryville College from 1857 to 1861. His leadership directed the college and seminary in the early years of the United Synod. He was elected Moderator in 1859. During the Civil War he was pastor of the United Synod congregation in Rogersville, Tennessee.

In 1851 William Montgomery King left his pastorate at the Macedonia Church, Woodford County, Kentucky, where he also headed up a theological seminary.[36] He moved to Texas, taking with him his seventeen-year old son, Samuel Alexander King. Young King studied theology under J. H. Zivley. At the age of twenty-two he was ordained. The two Kings made up a large percentage of the United Synod ministerial force in Texas Presbytery. Their work was characterized by dedicated sacrifice and labor under the most difficult of conditions. After serving in the pastorate for forty years, Samuel King was elected professor of theology in the Austin Presbyterian Theological Seminary in 1902, a position he held for a dozen years. In 1892 he was elected Moderator of the General Assembly of the Presbyterian Church in the United States. He combined the rare talents of keen mental acumen with pastoral missionary zeal.[37]

Joseph M. Martin was pastor of the Second Presbyterian Church, Knoxville, when the first meeting of the United Synod was held. While a student at the institution, which ultimately became the University of Tennessee, he was converted under the preaching of Frederick A. Ross. He then opted for the ministry. He was endowed with phenomenal memory. J. J. Robinson wrote, "I have known him to write his speech for the college rostrum, read it over two or three times, and deliver it *memoriter* without blunder or pause."[38] He served the United Synod in several capacities. However, it was as pastor of the Knoxville Church where he made his most lasting contribution, for that congregation was a symbol of the New School in East Tennessee. With the exception of the New Providence Church in Maryville, Knoxville's Second Presbyterian Church was the most influential New School-United Synod congregation in the Tennessee Valley. Unfortunately, after the Battle of Knoxville in 1863, certain persons were ordered out of Knoxville by Federal authorities. Martin was in that number.[39]

In Missouri, Levi R. Morrison was responsible for bringing at least a portion of the Presbytery of Osage into the United Synod. E. E. Stringfield wrote that he, more than any other person, was responsible for checking "the stampede of the New School churches of this section into the Old School fold . . . ."[40] He also was a victim of the war. In 1861, at the age of fifty-five, he was seized as hostage on grounds of being a southern sympathizer. He was forced to march sixty miles with his hands tied behind him. He never recovered from this experience, and he died six years later from the infirmity this depredation caused. Had he lived, he might have saved the Presbytery of Osage in its entirety for the United Synod.

There were numerous other clergymen in the United Synod who should at least be mentioned: Fielding Pope, I. H. K. Handy, J. D. Mitchell, T. D. Bell, James Leach, George E. Eagleton, Matthew M. Morton, Andrew Newton, William H. McGuffey (of *McGuffey's Readers* fame), Charles H. Read, and James Hood. These and many of their colleagues were far above average as churchmen.[41]

In addition to the ministers mentioned, there were also several laymen who contributed considerably to the leadership of the United Synod. One of the most prominent was Horace Maynard, an elder in the Knoxville Church. A native of Massachusetts, Maynard moved to Tennessee upon graduation from Amherst in 1838. After teaching at the University of Tennessee, from 1839 to 1841, he studied law. In 1857 he was elected to Congress. In the fall of that year he chaired the Richmond Convention. As a Whig, he opposed secession; but when the southern states began to secede, he made numerous addresses in which he called for a sympathetic understanding of the southern people. His position was that the southern disunionists were sincere patriots who had been frightened by northern denunciation, which preached the "irrepressible conflict." When the war broke out, however, he supported the Union. He was of the opinion that slavery had a better chance to exist under the Constitution than under the Confederacy. He was Tennessee's Attorney General from 1863 to 1865. Later he served as Minister to Turkey and Postmaster General.[42]

Another prominent layman was John Randolph Tucker of Virginia. He was a brother-in-law of A. H. H. Boyd and Attorney General of the Old Dominion. He served on numerous committees of the United Synod. Another Virginian, David B. Payne, served the United Synod as Treasurer. And a third Virginian, Peachey R. Grattan, appears time and again in the lists of committee and board members of the Church's agencies.

Like most of the Churches of that time, the United Synod was dominated by clergymen who chaired the most important denominational committees. Thus, the names of many of the laity are obscured. Yet the number of names that have "M. D.," "Hon.," or "Esq." connected with them indicates that the lay leadership of the Church was far from impoverished in training and education. Such men, of course, were always elders in the Church. Many of the more recent developments in Presbyterian polity and practice, whereby laity are "co-opted" to serve on committees or other ecclesiastical groups within the Church, were not in vogue at that time. One may hazard the opinion, nevertheless, that the laity of the United Synod did not lag far behind the laity in other American Presbyterian bodies. Indeed, they were men who could and did work at the same desks as did the clergy.

NOTES

1. E. H. Gillette, *History of the Presbyterian Church in the United States of America*, 2 vols.

(Philadelphia: Presbyterian Publication Committee, 1864), 2:558.

2. Robert Bell Woodworth, *A History of the Presbytery of Winchester (Synod of Virginia): Its Rise and Growth, Ecclesiastical Relations, Institutions and Agencies, Churches and Ministers, 1719-1945, Based on Official Documents* (Staunton, Virginia: McClure Printing Co., 1947), p. 82.

3. This is an expression used by J. E. Alexander to describe the relationship of the Synod of Tennessee to the United Synod, *A Brief History of the Synod of Tennessee, from 1817 to 1887* (Philadelphia: MacCalla & Co., 1890), p. 33. The term was picked up by Ralph Waldo Lloyd, *Maryville College: A History of 150 Years, 1819-1869* (Maryville: Maryville College Press, 1969), p. 103.

4. Alexander, *Synod of Tennessee*, p. 32. The United Synod was a formation of presbyteries, not synods. The latter joined only because their constituent presbyteries had already united.

5. The text of the Pastoral Letter is found in ibid., pp. 33-34 and *CO*, 7 October 1858.

6. Judith Haws Hash, "A History of the First Presbyterian Church of Jonesboro, Tennessee" (M. A. thesis, East Tennessee State University, 1965), p. 164, citing the Minutes of the church for 24 March 1858.

7. Ibid., citing the church Minutes for 12 September 1858.

8. J. E. Alexander, "A Historical Sketch of Timberridge Presbyterian Church." Typed copy in the McClung Room, Lawson McGhee Library, Knoxville, copied from the Greeneville *Democrat*, 26 January 1888, n.p.

9. MS "Extracts from the Presbytery of Abingdon," p. 112, PHF.

10. Holston Presbytery [NS], MS "Minutes" (4 August 1858), p. 424. See the report of the meeting in *Presbyterian Witness*, 17 August 1858.

11. Presbytery of West Tennessee [NS], MS "Minutes" (10 October 1857), n.p., PHF.

12. *Presbyterian Witness*, 5 May 1859.

13. Ibid., 9 June 1859.

14. *CO*, 21 April 1859.

15. *Presbyterian Witness*, 9 June 1859.

16. Presbytery of North Alabama, MS "Minutes" (18 May 1860), pp. 236-237, PHF.

17. *Action of the Synod of Mississippi on the Exposition of Principle and Duty in Relation to Duty, by the Late General Assembly at Cleveland, Ohio, Containing the Report of the Committee and the Series of Resolutions Adopted on that Subject at*

Their Sessions at Shongalo, Miss., July 16-19, 1857 (Jackson: F. M. Gailor, 1857), pp. 5-7.

18. Synod of Mississippi [NS], MS "Minutes" (1858), pp. 210-211, Department of Archives and History, State of Mississippi, Jackson, Mississippi.

19. George Miller stated in *Missouri's Memorable Decade: 1860-1870. An Historical Sketch, Personal--Political--Religious* (Columbia, Missouri: E. W. Stephens, 1898), p. 43: "After a lifelong study of the slavery question, and the steps leading to the dreadful civil war, I feel sure that the harsh and denunciatory methods of the radical abolitionists never advanced the anti-slavery sentiment of the nation." For similar sentiments, see E. E. Stringfield, *Presbyterianism in the Ozarks: A History of the Work of the Various Branches of the Presbyterian Church in Southwest Missouri* (n.p.: n.p., 1909), p. 19.

20. *CO*, 5 May 1859, contains the eight reasons why the Presbytery opted for the United Synod.

21. *Presbyterian Witness*, 5 May 1859.

22. *CO*, 29 September 1859.

23. USS, MS "Minutes" (19 May 1860), pp. 51-52. See also *Presbyterian Historical Almanac and Annual Remembrancer* 3 (1861): 189. The reception of the Presbytery was probably pro forma at best. The ministerial commissioner, Robert Glenn, was received, but there was no statistical report given. Thus, how many churches, ministers, and members were received is not known.

24. Timothy Hill to H. A. Nelson, 7 March 1862, cited in John B. Hill, "Home Mission Changes in Missouri, *JPHS* 29 (1951): 250.

25. *Presbyterian Witness*, 24 December 1858. Only three ministers were present at this meeting. See also William Stuart Red, *A History of the Presbyterian Church in Texas* (Austin: Steck Co., 1936), p. 114.

26. *CO*, 26 May 1859.

27. Ibid., 16 December 1858.

28. Ibid., 24 May 1860.

29. For further information on Ross, see his autobiography, "Letters to a Lady of Knoxville, East Tennessee, including an Account of His Life in Virginia and Huntsville to the Time of His Death in 1883" (MS in the Huntsville, Alabama Public Library); Charles C. Ross, ed. and comp., *The Story of Rotherwood from the Autobiography of Rev. Frederick A. Ross, D. D.* (Knoxville: Bean, Waters & Co., 1923); Tommy W. Rogers, "Dr. Frederick A. Ross and the Presbyterian Defense of Slavery," *JPH* 45 (1967):

112-124; J. E. Alexander, *Synod of Tennessee*, pp. 120-122.

30. Thomas Cary Johnson, "A Brief Sketch of the United Synod of the Presbyterian Church in the United States of America," *Papers of the American Society of Church History* 8 (1897): 19.

31. *Presbyterian Historical Almanac* 9 (1867): 427.

32. Woodworth, *History of Winchester Presbytery*, p. 87.

33. *Presbyterian Witness*, 22 September 1857.

34. One can only regret that nothing even approaching a cursory study has ever been done on Boyd. Nor is there any evidence that his papers are extant. For a succinct biography, see *Presbyterian Historical Almanac* 9 (1867): 425-428.

35. A good account of Converse is "Autobiography of the Rev. Amasa Converse," *JPH* 43 (1965): 197-218, 254-263; the original MS is at PHF. For a popular history of the *CO*, see the issue of 4 September 1963.

36. For a history of this seminary, see Harold M. Parker, Jr., "A New School Presbyterian Seminary in Woodford County," *Register of the Kentucky Historical Society* 74 (1976): 99-111; reprinted in idem, *SSPH*, pp. 167-179.

37. S. M. Tenney, comp. and ed., *Souvenir of the General Assembly of the Presbyterian Church in the U. S.* (n.p.: n.p., 1924), pp. 68-69.

38. J. J. Robinson, *In Memoriam* (n.p.: n.p., n.d.), p. 20.

39. Mary U. Rothrock, ed., *The French Broad-Holston Country: A History of Knox County, Tennessee* (Knoxville: East Tennessee Historical Society, 1946), pp. 141-142. Martin was erringly designated as the pastor of the First Presbyterian Church, which was Old School.

40. Stringfield, *Presbyterianism in the Ozarks*, p. 191.

41. A complete list of all the ministers who served in the United Synod is found in *Presbyterian Historical Almanac* 9 (1867): 465-466. Several who died have obituaries written in the annual issues of this work. Some biographical sketches are in Alfred Nevin, ed., *Encylopaedia of the Presbyterian Church in the United States of America: Including the Northern and Southern Assemblies* (Philadelphia: Presbyterian Encyclopaedia Publishing Co., 1884). Only the barest information on life and service is found in E. C. Scott, comp., *Ministerial Directory of the Presbyterian Church. U. S. 1861-1941* (Austin, Texas: Von Boeckmann-Jones, 1942). A similar work is

that of Edgar Sutton Robinson, *The Ministerial Directory* . . . (Oxford, Ohio: Ministerial Directory Co., 1898). Robinson's work is somewhat limited in that only vitae of living ministers were included, and by 1898 most of the former United Synod men were dead.

42. Fletcher N. Green, *The Role of the Yankee in the Old South* (Athens: University of Georgia Press, 1972), pp. 31-32; Charles F. Bryan, Jr., "A Gathering of Tories: The East Tennessee Convention of 1861," *Tennessee Historical Quarterly* 39 (1980): 27-48.

11
The United Synod at Work Antebellum

The Moderator, Charles H. Read, opened the sessions of the 1859 meeting of the United Synod in the Second Presbyterian Church, Lynchburg, Virginia, on the evening of 19 May. A total of thirty-four commissioners from twelve presbyteries were present. John J. Robinson succeeded as Moderator. The presbyteries were now gathered in three synods instead of four, the Synod of West Tennessee having been dissolved.

Charles H. Read and Matthew M. Marshall reported on their visit to the Old School General Assembly touching union. The Assembly voted down the union. A. H. H. Boyd reported on his visit to the New School Assembly relative to seeking funds which the southern presbyteries had contributed to the Church Erection Fund prior to the division of 1857. The New School had refused to respond to the request of the United Synod. A report of receipts and disbursements revealed that the southern churches had contributed a total of $3,131.05 to the Fund, and a total of $2,700 had been disbursed to the churches. Three Synods--Tennessee, West Tennessee, and Mississippi--had already received back more than they had contributed.[1]

The United Synod commended two papers to its constituents: The *Christian Observer* of Philadelphia and the *Presbyterian Witness* of East Tennessee. The former was especially commended

> . . . for their bold and manly advocacy of principles which form the basis of our organization. In this . . . they have shown a

stronger attachment to truth and principle than to a party organization, and a fixed purpose to be the true expositors and defenders of the constitution formed for us by our fathers, though it has been done at the sacrifice of much personal interest.²

Kind words were also expressed for the *Witness* as "being the peculiar exponent of the doctrines of our Church," and, unlike the *Christian Observer*, which still served the New School, was "depending almost exclusively for support upon the churches who stand in connection with this body . . . ." The United Synod recognized the importance of the Church paper: "That we must have a paper, as a medium through which our members may be informed as to the position we occupy . . . is a settled question."³

By far, the most farsighted action of this meeting was the action that led to the establishment of a theological seminary. The wording of the brief introduction to the ten resolutions which opened the way for the seminary is indicative of the importance of a seminary in the minds of the fathers of the United Synod: ". . . being deeply impressed with the importance of a theological seminary to the permanent interests of our denomination." The substance of the ten resolutions, each of which was adopted seriatim, is as follows:

1. A theological seminary shall be established under the supervision and control of the United Synod, and shall be called "The Theological Seminary of the United Synod of the Presbyterian Church in the United States of America."
2. It shall be located in the vicinity of the University of Virginia.
3. A sum of $100,000 shall be raised to provide for buildings and to endow three professorships of at least $25,000 each.
4. Subscriptions to the fund shall not exceed five years to pay.
5. Provision was made for a Board of Directors of eight ministers and seven elders.
6. There shall be at least three professors. Upon inauguration, each shall be required to adopt the Confession of Faith of the Presbyterian Church in the manner set forth in the Declaration of Principles.
7. A committee was appointed to apply for an act of incorporation from the Virginia legislature.

8. Provision was made for the funds collected.
9. At this meeting the Synod shall elect a Professor of Systematic and Pastoral Theology. When the endowment has reached $50,000, the Board shall elect a Professor of Ecclesiastical History and Biblical Criticism. Elections by the Board are subject to the review and decision of the United Synod in 1860.
10. If the funds raised for two professorships have been met, the seminary would open in October 1859.[4]

The fifteen-member Board of Directors reads like a Who's Who in the United Synod. A seven-member Board of Trustees was also chosen.

Joseph C. Stiles was unanimously elected the first professor. The entire structuring of the seminary package reveals, however, the thoughtful planning and considerable work on the part of the committee, which A. H. H. Boyd chaired. The manner in which the United Synod acted on the committee's recommendations reveals the enthusiasm tempered with logic in the establishment of the school. For not only were the details well developed, but the larger goal of the seminary was also envisioned. From its location adjacent to a university, certain academic advantages would accrue. It remained only to secure the funds and the seminary would be functioning.

In the operation of domestic missions, the synod urged presbyteries to meet their own needs first and then forward remaining funds to the Board of Missions. Presbytery committees of missions were likewise encouraged "to inquire as to the most desirable places within their bounds where missionaries can be properly employed," and to correspond with the Board of Missions respecting the wants of churches and "destitute fields." Presbyteries were urged to request their congregations to take up an offering for domestic missions, and to receive an annual offering for the mission in Greece.

The field of education consumed a large portion of the synod's energies. The synod "earnestly recommend to the churches in its connection" the establishment of schools for the "early scholastic training" of children, such schools to have "convenient buildings and competent teachers."[5] At the same time, the enthusiasm for the new seminary so swept the assembled delegates that they and the guests in attendance pledged $21,300 in subscriptions.[6]

At its first meeting, the synod had determined that as soon as the Synod of Tennessee had decided on one institution of higher learning, the United Synod would receive it under its care. In the year that had passed, the Synod of Tennessee recommended Maryville College to the synod and transferred it "as far as the charter thereof permitted" to the United Synod. The synod received the College under its care with the conditions in the report of the school's trustees. It also pledged "to place Maryville College in such a condition as will make it worthy of our denomination, and as will command the confidence and patronage of the community." It then appointed a committee of seven to examine the physical facilities of the College and to "inquire into the system and course of study pursued there, and report to Synod any such changes or extension thereof, as they may deem necessary to accommodate the institution to the wants of the country and the day."[7]

Regarding education for the ministry, a Committee of Education consisting of nine members was appointed "to superintend all matters pertaining to the education of indigent young men, within our bounds, who are looking forward to the work of the Ministry." Presbyteries were asked to report to the committee the names of those who were in need of financial assistance. Each minister was expected to preach at least one sermon a year on the subject of education, at which time a collection would be received and forwarded to the committee. The treasurer would make an annual report to the United Synod of all funds received and disbursed as well as the names of students who received assistance. The last Thursday of February was set aside

> for a day of prayer for the blessing of God on all candidates for the ministry under the care of our Presbyteries, and that God would raise up many more who shall go forth among our destitution, preaching the Gospel of Jesus Christ.[8]

The 1859 Statistical Report is quite interesting. A column had been added for the number of "Colored Communicants." A total of 423 was listed. There were seventeen candidates for the ministry,[9] and six licentiates. The Presbytery of Osage was added to the Roll, and the Presbytery of District of Columbia was still retained. Receipts for the four major departments of the United Synod were as follows: Domestic Missions, $3,242.92; Foreign

Missions, $1,257.67; Education, $11,519.01; and Publications, $3,133.23. The presbyteries in the Synods of Tennessee and Virginia contributed very well to the denomination's work. Apart from the giving of the Presbytery of North Alabama, however, the contributions from the presbyteries in the Synod of Mississippi were negligible.

In assessing the work of the 1859 Synod, the *Presbyterian Witness* remarked that three things characterized it: harmony in all deliberations, generous hospitality by the folk of Lynchburg, and the Christian kindness and courtesy of other denominations.[10] Far more, however, was accomplished than these generalities admit. It is very doubtful whether any Presbyterian body up to that time had taken such momentous steps in one annual meeting to outline a comprehensive plan of education, which embraced local schools, a collegiate institution, and a theological seminary. Coupled with the actions of 1858, the United Synod at the close of its second meeting had progressed toward its goals, reflecting the dynamic, imaginative leadership it possessed.

The 1860 session was held in the recently-constructed First Presbyterian Church, Huntsville, Alabama. Part of the Synod's agenda was the dedication of the commodious edifice where Frederick A. Ross held forth.[11] Synod convened on the evening of 17 May with the sermon by John J. Robinson. The next day, C. M. Atkinson of Canton, Mississippi, was elected Moderator. Among the thirty-five commissioners at the meeting was S. A. Rhea, missionary to Persia. A new presbytery, the Presbytery of Northern Missouri, was added to the roll. Only two presbyteries were not represented: Texas and Lexington, South.

The presence of the "missionary to the Nestorians" helped to spur interest in foreign missions. Rhea preached to the synod, and both his message and his person were well received. There was also a lengthy communication from the synod's missionary to Greece, Michael Kalopothakes, which was published as part of the 1860 Minutes.

Communications were also received from Mobile, Alabama; Woodford County, Kentucky; and Texas, all seeking financial aid. In spite of the formal dissolution of New School work in Kentucky, three congregations had not rejoined the Old School.

The committee appointed to visit Maryville College reported. More property had been acquired to provide space for growth. Two additional professorships needed to be established. The President, John J. Robinson, was delegated agent for the college and was engaged in raising funds for the school's endowment.

Subscriptions were again taken for the proposed seminary, and the amount pledged was reported at $60,323.05. However, the plans to locate the seminary adjacent to the University of Virginia had been turned down by the university. On the brighter side, Boyd had been chosen by the Board to be the second professor of the seminary, filling the chair of ecclesiastical history and biblical criticism--a very important appointment.

The progress that had marked the first year of the Synod's existence appeared to have slowed down in the second. But if there was any discouragement, it never surfaced. The *Presbyterian Witness* summed up the advancement of the United Synod after two years, by pointing out that

> we have the pure constitution and standards of the Presbyterian Church, established by the fathers long ago, with the excellent Declaration and Platform of Principles, adopted at the organization of the United Synod, reprinted in the minutes of last year, and to be republished this year. Let us gird ourselves anew for the work, and go forward.[12]

The United Synod was now two years old. It had met three times in divergent parts within its bounds: Knoxville, Lynchburg, and Huntsville. By the time it would meet in 1861, the political situation in the nation would have changed drastically. It would have a dramatic impact on the fledgling Church. But Fort Sumter with its blazing cannons and entrapped garrison was eleven months away, and no one in May 1860 knew what the next year would bring.

The Church was organized for service. It had boards to conduct its business in the areas of domestic and foreign missions and ministerial education. Its polity had been reorganized so that its synodical structure was somewhat stronger, although the Synod of Mississippi still represented a congeries of presbyteries scattered over a wide geographical area. Further, the United Synod had also gained institutions.

Maryville College was one of the oldest of the Presbyterian colleges in the American transmontane. The school was greatly encumbered with indebtedness and unfinished buildings in 1858. It was for these reasons that the Committee of Seven had been appointed by the United Synod to visit the campus and see what could be done. The committee returned and recommended that the college with all its property be transferred to the United Synod on condition that the synod make it the denomination's college. All properties and funds should be placed under the control of the United Synod. Should the United Synod ever cease to exist, all would revert to the Synod of Tennessee, a "proviso wisely made in a transaction so hazardous."[13] So the United Synod received the college with these conditions, conditions which would loom in importance in the years ahead.

On the eve of the Civil War, the endowment of Maryville College stood at $16,000. Its property consisted of two one-half acre lots with three buildings, one unfinished. The library contained 6,000 volumes. The indebtedness stood at $1,000, and the enrollment was 100.[14] The condition of the school was judged to be good. So far as the seminary was concerned, it never entered the plans of the United Synod. The minds of the fathers were to establish a theological seminary on a much larger scale at some other place.[15]

Virginians desired to locate the seminary adjacent to the University of Virginia. It was thus quite a shock to the seminary's Board of Directors when it received the negative response of the university's Board of Visitors. Seminarians would not be permitted to attend lectures without charge, nor would they have the use the library.[16] This change in plans led to putting off the seminary's opening until fall 1861, and by that time the war had broken out.

The enthusiasm for the seminary was manifested not only in the selection of Stiles and Boyd as the two professors, but also in the celerity by which funds for the seminary were raised. That almost $70,000 in cash and pledges had been raised in a year prompted the *Christian Observer* to comment that this "is a fact in the history of such institutions without parallel."[17]

The United Synod was formed on the proposition that the issue of domestic slavery did not belong in the halls of the Church's judicatories. It was ostensibly neither a proslavery nor an antislavery posture. The statement by Boyd before the 1860 meeting of the Synod of Virginia contains the most concise, trenchant pronouncement emanating from any of the denomination's lower courts:

> . . . the UNITED SYNOD IS NOT A PRO-SLAVERY BODY; that as *an ecclesiastical* body, it is neither PRO-SLAVERY nor ANTI-SLAVERY. It

maintains that the subject is not appropriate to the functions of ecclesiastical judicatories, except to secure the observance of the relative duties of master and slaves as taught in the New Testament.[18]

And the *Christian Observer* did not hesitate to lend its support that the United Synod was the only ecclesiastical body in the United States "from whose councils this fruitful source of unprofitable controversy is now excluded, and must ever be excluded by the fundamental principles on which she is organized."[19]

At the same time, the United Synod was quite concerned about the personal relation between master and slave. At its first meeting, Dr. W. F. Gaines of the Presbytery of Hanover was asked to describe his plan of religious instruction for the slaves on his plantation. He responded that after breakfast on every Sunday morning he commands his slaves to assemble for religious instruction. While gathering, they sing; but after all are assembled, he then proceeds to catechize them orally, using the "admirable" catechism prepared by Charles C. Jones. He also frequently calls on slaves to lead in prayer, which they often do "with great effect."

The result had been that many of his servants have acquired "a degree of biblical knowledge which is perfectly astonishing." He also encouraged the commissioners to teach their slaves to read. He confessed that there had been a time when he feared to do this, but that time has passed. Then he commented, "They are my friends, not my enemies; I look upon them as my life-guard. After our children, our servants have the next claim on us." He further counseled the commissioners to teach them "thoroughly in the doctrines, precepts and promises of the gospel of Jesus Christ," and to instruct them "in the principles of Presbyterianism."[20]

In the Annual Narrative on the State of Religion for 1859, it was pointed out that "*Our Colored Population* has not been left without the means of grace." Now that the United Synod has been "freed by our present position, from those odious suspicions that once interfered with any effort to evangelize our servants," ministers have free access to them. Slaves were cordially invited to worship in the churches of the United Synod. In fact, the Narrative pointed out that some pastors held special services for them. One reported the conversion of more than thirty in his congregation. The report concluded, "Our success in winning souls to Christ from this class of our population is matter of encouragement to do more for them in the future."[21]

In spite of such glowing reports and optimistic hopes, however, the United Synod--along with most southern Presbyterians--could not get through to the black population in any substantial numbers. It was estimated that in 1858 the black Presbyterian membership in the South was 12,000 in the Old School, 20,000 in the Cumberland Presbyterian Church, only 2,000 in the United Synod.[22] Richard C. Reed placed the total black church membership in the South at 500,000 to 600,000 out of a total black population of 4,000.,000--about one out of eight.[23] If these figures are correct, it would place the total number of slaves in United Synod households at about 16,000 to 18,000.[24]

The grace of liberality had not been fully developed by the southern New School churches. This resulted in poorly paid ministers and constant appeals for funds for all causes. The SAS continued supporting the former New School churches and missionaries in the South.[25] Poor stewardship was coupled with the fact that churches were not giving their sons to the ministry. The United Synod faced a constant shortage of ministers, quite in contrast to the southern Old School. A plan adopted by the Presbytery of North Alabama called for an appeal to be made to the Southern Aid Society for assistance, "the amount to be graduated according to the judgment of the Ch. Extension Committee." The plan allowed for a salary of $500 for a single man, $700 for a married man.[26]

The meager salaries promised--and which were not always paid--frequently forced ministers into other work, such as teaching. This denied congregations their fulltime labors. Many were forced to serve two or more churches in order to eke out an existence. But it was the lack of consistent support on the part of the members and congregations to missionary causes that deprived the agencies of the Church of those funds sufficient to carry on their mission.[27]

So far as the two foreign missionaries were concerned, the United Synod endeavored to support Michael Kalopothakes,[28] but it was embarrassingly in arrears in that support. There is no record of the United Synod having ever given him any financial support.

Statistically, it is very difficult to ascertain much growth in the United Synod. This condition resulted from two factors. The numbers lost by attrition from the time the commissioners walked out of the Cleveland Assembly to the actual formation of the United Synod the following April were considerable. It is really not until 1860 that one sees statistical tables that can be determined as somewhat reliable--184 congregations and membership of 10,872 represent a fairly good base, statistically speaking. But these figures are considerably below those of 1857, when the six southern New School synods reported a total membership of 16,137 in 284 churches. Some of the loss can be attributed to the demise of the Synod of Kentucky and the quagmire of ecclesiastical perplexity in Missouri following the 1857 Assembly. But there was attrition in more established areas such as East Tennessee, and the evaporation of the Synod of West Tennessee was a tragic episode from which the Church never recovered.

The Church, of course, expected to grow. Perhaps it would have, had not the war interrupted its infant years. Even so, the *Presbyterian Witness* could boast in 1859 that the United Synod was the fifth largest Presbyterian body in the United States, and was exceeded by only one in Canada. The editor concluded that the new Church was not as small as one would think. There was no need to be discouraged or feel ashamed of size.[29] The *Christian Observer* echoed those sentiments quite well when it noted, "Our firm conviction is, that the United Synod will continue to grow and expand."[30]

NOTES

1. *Presbyterian Witness*, 9 June 1859.
2. USS, *Minutes* (1859), p. 52.
3. Ibid., p. 53.
4. Ibid., pp. 54-55.
5. Ibid., p. 63. Since most of the congregations of the United Synod were located in villages, rather than the more "urban" areas of the South, this recommendation had considerable merit. There is little evidence, however, that it was ever implemented. Many Presbyterian ministers did operate schools in the nineteenth century, for their collegiate training well qualified them for such work.
6. *Presbyterian Witness*, 2 June 1859.
7. USS, *Minutes* (1859), p. 62.
8. Ibid., pp. 62-63.
9. The official statistics report twenty-seven, but this is a printing error.
10. *Presbyterian Witness*, 2 June 1859.

11. The magnificent edifice, a splendid example of modified Gothic architecture, had only recently been completed. Its dimensions were 89' by 50', with a full basement. It still stands.

12. *Presbyterian Witness*, 31 May 1860.

13. James E. Alexander, *A Brief History of the Synod of Tennessee, From 1817 to 1887* (Philadelphia: MacCalla & Company, 1890), pp. 21, 22, 35.

14. Samuel Tyndale Wilson, *A Century of Maryville College 1819-1919: A Story of Altruism* (Maryville: Directors of Maryville College, 1916), p. 102.

15. *CO*, 7 October 1858.

16. Ibid., 26 May 1859.

17. Ibid., 9 August 1860.

18. Ibid., 1 November 1860.

19. Ibid., 18 October 1860.

20. Ibid., 15 April 1858.

21. USS *Minutes* (1859), p. 66. See also comments of Fencilius Gray of Missouri in *CO*, 29 November 1860.

22. Ernest Trice Thompson, *Presbyterians in the South*, 3 vols. (Richmond: John Knox Press, 1963-1973) 1: 443n, citing *Presbyterian Magazine* 8 (1858): 567.

23. Richard C. Reed, "A Sketch of the Religious History of the Negroes in the South," *Papers of the American Society of Church History*, 2nd. series, 4 (1914): 195.

24. Of course, these figures are far from the small numbers reported annually in the Minutes of the United Synod's "colored communicants." If the 2,000 members are correct for 1858, the ratio of one member for each eight slaves would be about right. There is no question that many congregations simply did not report their slave communicants when compiling their statistics for presbytery.

25. In 1859 the SAS listed the following recipients in the South: The Synod of Mississippi; the Presbyteries of District of Columbia, Piedmont, Hanover, Osage, Northern Missouri, St. Louis, New River, Union, Northern Alabama, and Texas; and the five congregations around Versailles, Kentucky; SAS, *Sixth Annual Report* (1859), pp. 9-21.

26. Presbytery of Northern Alabama, MS "Minutes" (21 May 1860), p. 239, PHF.

27. In 1860, not including the Presbytery of District of Columbia, there were 184 congregations. The Statistical Table reveals that only thirty-nine churches contributed to Domestic Missions, twenty-eight to Foreign Missions, and forty-three to Education. Total receipts to Domestic Missions

amounted to $2,445.55; Foreign Missions, $1,729.12; and Education, $2,528.88. These contributions total $6,703.55, or about 60 cents per member. Even in those days of relative austerity, this was not substantial support. The Presbytery of Lexington, South, did not contribute one cent for any of the three causes. Six of Mississippi's seven presbyteries contributed nothing to Domestic or Foreign Missions.

28. Clyde W. Taylor, "Greek Hostility to Evangelical Witness," *Christianity Today*, 20 January 1958. T. Saloutous, in "American Missionaries to Greece: 1820-1869," *CH* 24 (1955): 152-174, failed to mention either Kalopothakes or the United Synod's mission in Greece.

29. *Presbyterian Witness*, 14 April 1859.

30. *CO*, 18 August 1859.

12
The Years of the War

The Civil War was crucial, vital to the future of the United Synod. When the war began, the Church existed; when the last shots were fired, the Church had been organically assimilated with the former Old School Presbyterian Church in the South, the Presbyterian Church in the Confederate States of America.[1] The war affected the United Synod both positively and negatively.

On the negative side, the young Church simply lacked the resources to withstand the war's effects. The funds it had been receiving from the SAS were no longer forthcoming; its plans to launch a seminary collected dust on the shelf; the heterogeneity that had long characterized its constituency proved to be a factor that would ultimately divide its ranks; the location of the churches in the rural and village areas of the South deprived the Church of that lay leadership which the urban centers provide; and the strength of the Church lay in East Tennessee, a pro-Union region.

On the positive side, however, the Church called forth the meager resources at hand to continue functioning as a Church, not a sect; the Church remained loyal to its concept of the spirituality of the Church; its leadership, though limited as men, left the pew for the battlefield and the pulpit for the camp, and fulfilled its responsibilities in a most heroic fashion. But perhaps the most significant positive factor which emerged from the conflict was the realization that in most respects very little differentiated the United Synod from its Old School cousins, a realization that became concrete in the union of the two bodies in 1864.

When the first wartime meeting of the United Synod convened in May 1861, all the area in which its congregations were located, except Missouri, had withdrawn from the Union. Fort Sumter was now history. There would be no major battles between the two armies that were forming until July. Then the Confederates would rout a Federal force a few miles from Washington. The United Synod met in Richmond, the Confederate capital since Virginia had joined the Confederacy. Richmond had three United Synod congregations.

Only three presbyteries failed to answer the roll call at the 1861 meeting. Even Missouri's Osage Presbytery was represented. A total of twenty-seven commissioners was present. The minutes of this meeting are unique in one way: There is no reference to the organization of the Confederate States of America. Eleven States had withdrawn from the Federal Union. The commissioners were assembled in the capital city of a new nation. Yet there was no mention of political division. The Narrative on the State of Religion paper did recognize political turmoil. The first three paragraphs of that paper refer to "civil commotion, discord and strife, the up-heavings of society, the dissolution of government, and the gatherings of the mighty hosts for deadly conflict." Such expressions, however, appear quite out of place with the actions which the Synod took, actions not unlike those that had been taken at previous meetings. Even the presence of the Osage Presbytery commissioners did not cause a ripple.

One of the most interesting aspects of the 1861 sessions was the "Free Conversation on the State of Religion," which was conducted on Saturday morning, 18 May. The report of this activity was carried by the *Christian Observer*. A dozen presbyteries reported through their commissioners important developments within their bounds. Three topics kept surfacing in the commissioners' remarks: The unsettled conditions of the country, the role and value of the Sabbath School, and the work among the black people.

John W. McMurran of Winchester Presbytery, whose bounds embraced Maryland, the District of Columbia, and northwestern Virginia, commented that the past year had witnessed political excitement so great that preaching did not appear to have the same effects as in other times. James M. McLean of the Presbytery of Newton (east Mississippi and western Alabama) reported that one recent convert had considered preparing for the ministry. He now felt, however, that the providence of God and the duty to his country required him to use his efforts in the defense of his country. But when the war is over, he anticipates returning to the task of preparing for the ministry.

Almost every commissioner reported on the emphasis being given to the Sabbath School work. John M. Caldwell (Union Presbytery) stated that in his congregation which embraced fifteen square miles he had nine Sunday Schools, four operating all year round. Four-fifths of his members had come through the Sunday School, a testimony supported by Frederick A. Ross of Huntsville, Alabama, who further cried, "If there are any churches without pastors, let me urge you--let me beg of you, as you love God, as you love your own souls, keep up the Sunday Schools . . . ." A common theme expressed was "the Sabbath School is the nursery of the Church."

The third area which was greatly discussed was the work among "the people of color." Several commissioners noted that both white and black people attend the morning worship services together, and then the black people would return for "special services for them" in the afternoon. But they were more than just a mission field. Two presbyteries (Kingston and Newton) reported that there were black evangelists working within their bounds, who preached not only to the blacks (probably slaves), but also to white congregations as well. In fact, "Uncle Joe" of Kingston Presbytery (southeastern Tennessee) "received more attention" than any other man at presbytery. He was well-known and highly appreciated as a faithful preacher.

One of the major problems to come before the Synod in 1861 was that of Home Missions. The elimination of support by the SAS placed a burden and challenge on the Church:

> In view of the suspension of the Southern Aid Society at this juncture--what are we to do? Resolutions are easily passed, but what good do they accomplish, except to stir up the members of the Synod, who take part in the debates on them. We ought to establish the rule that if a pastor cannot be sustained in these times by his own church when cut off from outside assistance, an arrangement should be made, if possible, to divide his labors with vacant churches in the neighborhood so as to be supported, if possible, by their united efforts for the time being. We must take such a step as

this in view of the suspension of the Southern Aid Society . . . .

Thus spoke E. H. Cumpston of Winchester Presbytery.³

A major difficulty that continued to manifest itself was the attrition of United Synod congregations by entering the Old School. Ross claimed that in the Presbytery of North Alabama all the wealthy churches had entered the Old School. Only the Huntsville church in that presbytery could be classified as being not poor.

A new work had begun under the leadership of J. M. McLean in Mobile. He complained, however, of the lack of denominational zeal. It was not uncommon for United Synod Presbyterians on coming to Mobile to unite with the stronger, wealthier Old School churches there. His comments had been precluded by James Bradshaw of Kingston Presbytery who pointed out that "it has been the peculiar misfortune of New School Presbyterianism in the South to permit enterprises in which they embark to fail from want of interest and sympathy." He then referred to the efforts to establish a church in Nashville as an example. "We must work for our church with a proper denominational zeal, though not bigoted," he concluded.

The lack of financial support and denominational lukewarmness had not suddenly arisen in the southern New School elements. They had been there for years, a heritage of the New School itself. One must not forget that it was only a matter of a few years prior to the organization of the United Synod that the New School had actually begun the process of organizing its own ecclesiastical agencies. Now that the United Synod was cut off from all outside support, the barrenness of its stewardship suddenly became apparent. This feature was a basic difference between the Old School in the South and the United Synod. The former was well-organized, with boards and agencies abounding within its area; but for the United Synod, although the leadership was present to administer the programs the Church had launched, the laity had not been trained to support them with responsive, responsible stewardship.

The issue of the seminary again came before the Synod. The plan to have a seminary near the University of Virginia having been thwarted, the committee was not examining other possibilities. In the interim, the General Agent was urged to collect the principal that had been pledged toward the seminary. If such were not possible, he should at least get the interest. The Board also suggested that a temporary arrangement might be made to accommodate those students who desired to begin their theological instruction.

For the present, Joseph C. Stiles, the seminary's first professor, was tapped to be the Church's evangelist, preaching wherever opportunity opens. His salary would be $2,000 per year plus travel expenses--a handsome arrangement for that time.

To assist in supporting the causes of the Church, the Synod voted to take up quarterly offerings for the following purposes: commissioners' fund, education, home missions, and foreign missions. The purpose was "not intended as a mere paper resolution, but to receive the attention of the Synod, and urge on every church, and every members of every church, that he and she have something to do in all these subjects."[4]

The United Synod adjourned its 1861 meeting, having accomplished little more than holding the line. Apart from comments on the floor respecting the paper on "State of the Church," no action was taken to indicate that one of the greatest internecine struggles in the history of mankind was about to break forth on the American continent. This "business as usual" approach would be drastically altered, however, and it would be two years before the delegates could meet again, because of war-caused interruption.

Only four years earlier the southern New School presbyteries had withdrawn over the issue of the discussion of slavery in the Church. Secession began with the scepter of slavery hovering over the nation. No one in 1861 could have anticipated what awesome struggle lay ahead. The South had withdrawn from the Union "very much as she would have gone to a frolic." She found it inconceivable that the north would go to war for the sake of the "nigger."[5] The *Christian Observer* in 1860 had carried a Thanksgiving sermon by the respected A. H. H. Boyd, "The Benefits We Enjoy as a Nation," which typified the feelings of many in the South in general, in Virginia in particular.[6]

The statistics for 1861 revealed that the United Synod had 11,581 members (including 1,062 in the Presbytery of District of Columbia), 199 churches, and 121 ministers. The strength of her numbers was in the great Tennessee River watershed, the Synod of Tennessee embracing 5,260 members (about one-half of the total membership of the Church), eighty churches, and forty ministers.

"If Maryland was held in the Union by force, East Tennessee was similarly held in the Confederacy," observed Clement Eaton.[7] East Tennessee was decidedly pro-Union in its sentiments. It contained a yeomanry who held few slaves and disliked aristocrats around Nashville and the cotton-growing region of West Tennessee. Joe Bell among the Whigs and Andrew Johnson among the Democrats were devoted Unionists. That influential editor of East Tennessee's *Knoxville Whig*, "Parson" Brownlow, was such a dedicated Unionist that when Tennessee joined the Confederacy, his paper was suppressed and he was thrown into prison.

The agricultural economy of the region did not depend on slave labor. For the most part, the people were small farmers or merchants. In the 1860 census Knox County reported only one farm of over 1,000 acres. Out of a total of 2,397 farms of all sizes, 957 were from twenty to fifty acres in size. Knox Countians owned 2,370 slaves.[8] In the referendum to secede, although as a state Tennessee voted by more than a 2-1 margin to leave the Union, East Tennessee voted 2-1 to remain, her votes counting for more than 70% of the pro-Union votes cast.

Salem Church, founded about 1807 by Samuel Doak eight miles southwest of Jonesboro, contained several slaveholders. During the Civil War, however, not a single one was a secessionist. Not one member of the congregation joined the Confederate forces, although a number went north during the war and enlisted in the Federal forces. "The slaveholders of this church *all remained firm* union men during the war."[9] There were cooperationists in every southern State--men opposed to immediate secession. They were particularly strong in the southern Piedmont and the mountainous sections of the South where slavery was relatively weak, and where the United Synod was the strongest.

The importance of East Tennessee to the Union is seen in the numerous attempts of Lincoln to create a loyalist government in this geographical heart of the Confederacy by constantly ordering military operations into the region. Yet in spite of its predominantly Unionist population, it was in this portion of the war's western front where the Federal efforts most often bogged down.[10]

There was no area in the South where more acrimonious feelings developed between the two partisan groups than in East Tennessee. This bitterness between those who permitted slavery and those who opposed it gradually permeated the Synod of Tennessee. Numerous United Synod ministers were forced from their pulpits. In 1863, Union Presbytery passed a resolution whereby it would not license, ordain, or receive from another presbytery any minister who was opposed to slavery or who did not sympathize with the Confederacy. Less than eighteen months later, Union Presbytery dissolved its relationship with the United Synod to rejoin the new School Presbyterian Church. In the fall of 1864 a sobering picture of ecclesiastical conditions in East Tennessee was carried in the *Christian Observer*:

> . . . Yankee rulers . . . trample upon their rights, compel every native Tennessean loyal to the State of his birth to leave his home and family and seek refuge among strangers, destroy or take their property, strip them of their worldly possessions, break up their churches, burn their villages and their outhouses, deprive them of all comfort and security. No man's life is safe . . . . Mob law triumphs . . . . With the destruction of civil and political rights the public rights the public exercise of religious worship is rapidly being destroyed. Many of our ministers have been compelled to flee the country--others have abandoned the work of the ministry and devote their attention to the support of their families . . . . Most of the Presbyterian Churches [with]in the lines of the enemy are already closed.[11]

The role of the religious paper as a morale factor in the Civil War has been studied.[12] There was thus great joy in the United Synod when the *Christian Observer*, having been closed in Philadelphia by Federal forces on 22 August 1861, resumed publication in Richmond 19 September.[13] Throughout the war years, Converse "never seemed to lose faith in the notion that God would come to the aid of His chosen people once He had thoroughly tested them."[14] Through the columns of the *Christian Observer* during those years, Converse loomed more as a pastor to the Church-at-large than he did as an editor. At the same time, he frequently failed to comprehend the material that he received, digested, and then published in his paper.

The issue of 10 April 1862 contains two such instances of this. One was the report of the Confederate capture of Fort Craig, New Mexico Territory. This he pronounced as "an important victory for the Confederacy." With this triumph he prophesied that New Mexico would become "the territory of the Confederate States." Actually, the battle was indecisive and could not match in significance the two more decisive victories which Federal forces gained over the Confederates at the same time, victories that forced the latter out of New Mexico.

The second example of Converse's poor comprehension of a battle recorded in the 10 April 1862 issue of the *Christian Observer* was his failure to grasp not only what had happened at Shiloh (or Corinth), but also the import of the battle that baffles the modern mind. His reporting of this very significant encounter reveals either his naivete or a deliberate attempt to turn around the events of history: "The signal victory achieved by the Confederate troops near Corinth, last Saturday, is perhaps the most important event of the war. The Northern papers were anticipating a magnificent triumph at Corinth." Unfortunately for the southern cause, the Confederates lost the battle. More important for the North was the emergence of Ulysses S. Grant as a commander, later to be tapped by Lincoln to bring to conclusion the War in Virginia.

Nor did all the propaganda come from the pen of the editor, as this literary soliloquy from a Tennessean indicates:

> In the mutations of time, I find war declared against my native country, and a set of hired mercenaries already invading my native State (Tennessee). They are still moving forward, like an avalanche, as if they intended to abolish the last vestige of civil and religious liberty. My grandfather served in the old revolution to establish the freedom which we have been enjoying; and is it possible that I could supinely fold my arms and lull myself to sleep upon some cushioned sofa, and see the invader come into my native State, and abolish the last appearance of free government, and desecrate the hallowed soil where sleep the bones of my ancestors, without raising an arm against the ruthless foe? NEVER, NEVER, NEVER![15]

Some articles appeared in the paper's columns, without question, to excite patriotism mixed with religious fervor in the face of the godless enemy. One example suffices. In the spring of 1862 a party of Federal--always referred to as "Yankee"--soldiers intruded the home of Dr. Shumate of Faquier County,

Virginia. The commanding officer attempted to enter the door that led into the chamber of Dr. Shumate's daughter. The physician informed the officer that it was his daughter's private chamber and that if he persisted in forcing the door he would kill him. When the officer turned the bolt on the door, the father shot him. Upon hearing the shot, soldiers ran into the room and quickly dispatched the "gallant father." "Comment is unnecessary" was the concluding statement in the article.[16]

Like all southern clergy, the men in the United Synod never entertained the prospect that the Confederacy would lose. Charles H. Read of Richmond commented that God had never destroyed a nation in which there was an evangelical Church.[17] But as the initial southern victories became fewer, and Federal victories became not only more frequent but of greater significance, a noticeable change began to emerge in the articles--which were also sprinkled with editorial observations. The fall of New Orleans in the spring of 1862 was a crushing blow to the Confederacy. Converse, however, editorialized that the event was not an occasion for despondency, but for "earnest, unceasing prayer, and united and undaunted effort in the defence of our homes and of rights dearer than life." It "is a time to look to God for succor, and not to distrust his Providence, or Grace." He then dipped into his reservoir of journalistic exchanges and printed an article from the *Southern Christian Advocate*:

> We cannot afford to fail. To lose our cause is to lose everything except our souls, and to many this loss would be imminent. It would be to lose all on earth we hold dear. To say nothing of the ignominy of subjugation, a thought no high-minded man can endure. . . . "[18]

God, country, wealth, family--all were interlaced. To lose one is to lose all.

The denominational quarterlies were directed mainly to the clerical and lay leaders. The religious weeklies were far more influential than either the quarterlies or the secular papers, for they were directed toward the average church member and family.

The *Christian Observer* performed more than the service of gathering and transmitting news. Almost every issue carried a column of receipts to the various boards and agencies of the Church which had been sent via the paper. Since it was published in

Richmond and lay outside the immediate touch of the enemy, many readers would send their funds to Converse, who in turn would convey them to the Treasurer of the United Synod. For instance, in the 26 March 1863 issue Converse reported receiving funds for the following purposes: for sending the *Observer* to soldiers; for the distribution of Bibles, tracts, and other literature; for Domestic Missions; for Foreign Missions; and for Fredericksburg sufferers. Thus, not only did the paper's columns sustain the individual, even to the point of directing him to hope where there were really no grounds for hope, but they also ministered to the Church-at-large as the editor received funds and saw to it that they were channeled to the proper destinations.

The sudden advent of the war caught the United Synod in a precarious financial position. Its people had not been disciplined in stewardship and were still depending heavily on northern contributions to undergird its labors. At the 1861 meeting, it was reported that in the previous year seven ministers had been assisted by the Southern Aid Society.[19] The Domestic Missionary Society of Hanover Presbytery contributed $1,780 toward the support of five "feeble" churches, and it also gave $305 to the United Synod's Board of Domestic and Foreign Missions. It was the only presbytery, however, that sent the Synod any statement of its operations. In that year only nine of the presbyteries reported that they had raised any funds for Domestic Missions. This was an indication that the presbyteries themselves were either poorly organized to carry on their work, or that there was a general lethargy toward doing the work. Of the 199 churches listed in the 1861 Minutes, only thirty-four reported that they had contributed to Domestic Missions. The years of dependence on the North had taken their toll.

War's specter spread quickly across the land. Within less than a fortnight following Sumter, the Presbytery of North Alabama, noting the "present disturbed state of the country," stated that it was "prudent" for the Presbytery to decline any obligation for missionary work for the coming year. Congregations were encouraged "to raise what they can" for missionary work, but the actual work of missions within the bounds of the presbytery was for all intents abandoned for the next twelve months.[20]

It was not the meager financial support, however, that was the greatest obstacle to missionary work during the war. Rather, it was the whole mentality of the war conditions, which permeated the entire Confederacy. On the home front there was so much energy spent in the prosecution of the war that spiritual matters frequently lagged. Joseph C. Stiles, the Synod's evangelist, made this interesting commentary on the scene when he wrote,

> The war mind of the country, as you are well aware, constitutes in these days a powerful obstacle to the success of religious means, by confining the thought and heart of the nation to an earthly subject of the very deepest interest and excitement--thereby making it difficult to arrest the mind to those solemn claims of the kingdom, which carnal nature always feels to be so abstract and unwelcome. This it was which early induced me to abandon the cities and towns of Tennessee as theatres of prominent labor, because they were centres of political intelligence, and their population were so constantly discussing the *war news*, that attendance upon the sanctuary and attention to the messages of the gospel, on week days, I found it difficult to secure.[21]

Following a tour of duty as chaplain in the Confederate Army, George E. Eagleton was employed by Union Presbytery's Committee on Missions. In his first seven months, he held seven sacramental meetings, preached seventy-one sermons, made 400 pastoral visits, traveled 2,200 miles, distributed 8,000 pages of tracts, and raised $110 for the American Tract Society, $232.75 for the *Christian Observer*, and $369 for home missions.[22] His labors were probably the exception, however, since this area was occupied by Federal forces in 1863. In fact, after 1863 about the only substantial area of the United Synod not behind Union lines was Virginia. The work of home missions continued there, for at its 1863 Fall Meeting the Presbytery of New River received a congregation at Wytheville, Virginia.[23]

The ministerial ranks of the United Synod suffered greatly during the War. At least four of its ministers were officially Confederate chaplains.[24] In addition, there were others who ministered to army units from their pulpits and through short-term assignments. The position of the Presbyterians in the Confederacy was that the army presented one of the greatest opportunities for evangelism that the Church confronted. Nor did the exemplary devotion and conduct of such generals as Robert E. Lee, Thomas J. "Stonewall" Jackson, and

Leonidas Polk--the last a bishop in the Episcopal Church--damage the cause of religion. Jackson even appointed Robert L. Dabney, a theologian of no small stature, as his chief of staff.

When it became obvious that the United Synod would not be able to meet in 1862 because of Federal troops in the area, and because both the Moderator and the Stated Clerk were behind Federal lines, P. B. Price, Treasurer of the Board of Missions, submitted his report to the *Christian Observer* for publication. One of his resolutions touched the opportunity accorded the Church in ministering to the troops of the Confederacy:

> Resolved, That the Army of the Confederate States presents a most inviting and hopeful field for the successful prosecution of the work of Domestic Missions among our soldiers, and that a prompt and special appeal in its behalf should be made in all the congregations of our denomination who appreciate the noble sacrifices of our soldiers in defence of our common country, and who sympathise in the perils of their exposed condition, and their great need of spiritual counsellors and religious instructors, at once to provide the necessary means to enable the Board to occupy the field to the utmost practicable extent.[25]

That the churches took their opportunity seriously to minister to the Confederate soldiers is seen in the Narrative on the State of Religion of the Synod of Virginia in 1862:

> Much of the time a large part of our ministers has been given to the soldiers, especially the sick and wounded. Some have been officially connected with the hospitals, and others have given to them much incidental labor.[26]

Charles H. Read, pastor of the largest congregation in the United Synod, on one occasion preached seven times to a "large and attentive" congregation of soldiers, and also administered the Lord's Supper. In addition, he preached to the troops in Fredericksburg. These and similar services were usually arranged for local clergy by the chaplains or, in many instances, regimental commanders.[27]

By far the most popular and effective of the United Synod preachers to Confederate troops was Joseph C. Stiles, who "gave himself . . . as an

Evangelist to the army work with an apostolic fervor and zeal . . . ."[28] Born in 1795, he was in his mid-sixties when the war began. In 1864, he preached to the Army of Tennessee in Dalton, Georgia, where he held forth for two weeks, twice a day, in a large church. The comment was made that "almost everyone spoke of a marked improvement in attendance upon religious services and an increased interest" in religious matters as the result of his preaching.[29] Samuel S. Smith, in commenting on Stile's effectiveness, wrote that "the army owes a debt of gratitude for his arduous labors and efforts to save sinners from the wrath to come."[30]

Stiles was more than a voice to the troops, however; he also spoke in a most prophetic voice to the Confederacy. He was especially unsympathetic toward the speculator and those who lived well and accumulated much while brave young men suffered on the battle line.[31] He felt that if the Confederacy were to be converted, however, the conversion must begin with the army.

> If our army is a body of Christians, when the clash of arms and the din of war shall have hushed in our borders, and they be scattered broadcast over the land, they will be to our country as "the salt of the earth," preserving it, and giving us a moral and religious character that will make us a nation that can truly be called the people of God.[32]

The southern clergy suffered greatly at the hands of both the Federal government as well as Union troops; and the ministers of the United Synod were not exempt from such treatment.[33] A good example of such treatment is the experience of Isaac W. K. Handy, pastor of the Portsmouth, Virginia, congregation. On an informal occasion, he made some critical remarks when his church was within Federal lines. He was arrested and confined at Fort Delaware. On several occasions his freedom was offered him, but the Washington-born clergyman refused to take the oath of allegiance, which was conditional for his release. While he was detained, however, he visited the troops in their prison barracks and, in company with two Methodist chaplains, led a revival. Finally, through the offices of the Presbytery of Hanover, his release was secured for him in an exchange.[34]

Andrew H. H. Boyd was not so fortunate. This brilliant man was seized as a hostage for a Federal spy. He was detained in an unheated barn for a considerable time in the cold, damp winter of 1864. So great were his deprivations that shortly after his release from captivity he died, on 16 December 1865, at the age of fifty-one.[35] A third United Synod minister in Virginia to be detained was Charles Nourse, a teacher in Leesburg. Thus, in the early fall of 1864, three members of the Synod of Virginia were under Federal detainment.[36]

It was in East Tennessee, however, that United Synod ministers experienced the greatest shame and deprivation. As Union forces gradually secured the region, minister after minister was forced to leave his pulpit and his home. Most of the East Tennessee ministers in the United Synod were indigenous to the region and had been educated under Isaac Anderson. In many respects, they were the most parochial of all the Synod's clergy, both by birth and by training. At the same time, their close brotherhood made them suspect to Union authorities--guilt by association. The case of Fielding Pope is illustrative of the difficulties which these men faced. His entire ministry had been in East Tennessee. He had succeeded his mentor, Isaac Anderson, as pastor of Maryville's New Providence Church. From the moment he began his ministry to the church, he had maintained the same pastoral diligence that had characterized Anderson's years of service to that congregation. As long as Confederate forces occupied East Tennessee, those of Union persuasion gradually ceased their attendance at worship services. Some even left the region. Others went so far as to conceal themselves in buildings and caves near their homes. When Federal forces arrived in the scene, Union sympathizers returned to their homes and those of Confederate persuasion left the area or underwent the usual harassment by Federal troops or supporters. When the war was over, Pope was deprived of his pulpit and forced to leave the scene of his lifelong ministry. He died a short time later in Georgia.[37]

Maryville College closed its doors shortly after the war began in 1861. By the time the strife was over, the school's president, John J. Robinson, had also been forced to leave East Tennessee. Prior to his enforced exit, he had never supplied a church outside his native region, save for a few years in Kentucky. The crime of Joseph Martin of Knoxville was "patriotism, loyalty to the land of [his] birth, [his] residence and [his] affections." Forced to resign his pastorate, he moved to South Carolina, where he continued his ministry around Yorkville.[38]

Mention has been made of the home missionary work which engaged the labors of George Eagleton in East Tennessee. In September 1864, he was administered a savage beating at the hands of Union soldiers for preaching in New Market. The *Religious Herald* (1 September 1864) called this treatment "the most diabolical and savage act of maliknant [sic] cruelty of which we have record."[39] Threats of scourging and beating and death were levelled constantly against those who would not leave the country. In a short time there were no ministers remaining in East Tennessee who were loyal to the South.

One of the greatest losses the United Synod suffered during the war was the failure of the proposed theological seminary to materialize. With no place found where the school might be located; with only one-tenth of the pledges paid; with the prospects of men being available to comprise a student body almost nonexistent, the plans were simply laid on the shelf. In the fall of 1862, Boyd was directing the studies of two men. Since the area around Winchester where he lived was protected by strong Confederate forces, it was suggested that other young men might go there to study under him.[40]

The perplexity was that there were very few, if any, young men who were even thinking about preparing for the ministry in the wake of the war's excitement. Nor did this condition take long for others to notice. "A Son of the South" queried the *Christian Observer*, "From what source is the Southern Presbyterian Church to obtain her future ministry? Where are our pious youth out of whom God shall call a ministry?" He then noted that the seminaries had given many of their students and professors to the war, and concluded, "I fear camp life will not nourish the spirit of piety or prepare men for efficient ministers of the Gospel." But Converse reassured him:

> Many of them, we trust, are in the school of moral discipline which the Lord has appointed for them,--and if the people pray to the Lord as directed, to send forth laborers--He will find and send them into his field and gather in his harvest.[41]

In addition to appointing Joseph C. Stiles as evangelist for the Church, two other ministers were also appointed to serve in the same calling: George A. Caldwell of Athens, Tennessee, and W. H. Vernor of Lewisburg, Tennessee. The three missionaries scarcely had the opportunity to serve as commissioned. Stiles gravitated toward preaching in the army; Caldwell was a prisoner; and Vernor, though free, was behind Federal lines. The condition of the latter two prompted Converse to comment,

> The suspension of the labors upon which these two brethren had so recently entered is a serious blow to the operations of the Board, and their condition is doubtless such at this time to claim for them the sympathies and prayers of Christians.[42]

One of the major factors in bolstering morale in the Confederacy was the pulpits of the new nation. One proof of the Church in support of the Confederate cause was the efforts of Union generals to take over the appointment of ministers loyal to the Confederacy as well as to superintend religious affairs in the territory they occupied. In most cases, difficulties arose simply because southern churchmen had been actively engaged in promoting and supporting the noble cause, and they continued to voice Confederate sympathies even after their areas and neighborhoods were occupied by Union forces.[43] The removal of Martin from the pulpit of Knoxville's Second Church was accompanied by the closing of the church's doors.[44] Minutes for several years are lacking for the New Prospect Church, a few miles south of Knoxville. This condition caused the historian of that congregation to conclude, "The part played by the church in that conflict is unrecorded. If the absolute break in the records be a true indication, the church ceased functioning for the duration of the struggle."[45]

The higher judicatories suffered also. On 9 September 1864 Holston Presbytery met as per adjournment, but there was no quorum. The next day still brought no quorum. So the Stated Clerk made the following entry in the records: "It is believed that the action in the premises will be in accordance with the spirit, if not the strict letter of the Constitution," and then noted that those who were present proceeded to the ordination of Jonathan W. Bachman. This action was taken because of the exigencies of the War.[46] After all, he was present on that day, and there was no assurance that he or they would be present at another time.

The United Synod's foreign missionary, Michael D. Kalopothakes, M. D., was a native Greek ministering to his people.[47] The war interrupted normal contacts between him and the United Synod. As a result, an embarrassing indebtedness developed. Not all the blame, however, can be placed on the war. For prior to the outbreak of hostilities, the Church had failed to support him fully. He nevertheless continued his work in Athens, largely distributing religious literature. Gradually through the war years, the Board of Missions was able to eliminate its indebtedness to him.[48]

S. A. Rhea, a member of the Presbytery of Holston, was a missionary to Nestorian Persians, but he was not under the formal care of the Synod's Board of Missions. The *Christian Observer* from time to time carried copies of his letters.[49] In spite of a recommendation at the 1860 meeting of the Synod to contribute to his support, little action was taken to implement the fervor of the hour. Again, the churches failed to support the program of the denomination as they should have. This failure, when compounded by war's exigencies, greatly handicapped the work of the Synod.

The conduct of the war dominated every aspect of southern life, the churches being no exception. The war was interpreted by all religious figures and institutions as nothing less than a religious conflict in which the very cause and purpose of God were at stake. In its understanding of the struggle, the United Synod was no exception to the general thought. This resolution of the 1861 Synod of Mississippi clearly underscored its belief very well:

> We regard the cause of our country as the cause of God--a cause which demands the prayers, the contributions, and the personal efforts of the whole Church, from the minister who officiates at the holy altar to the humblest communicant.[50]

So closely allied was their devotion to God and the outcome of the battles that victories were attributed to Him because of the devotion of the people, whereas defeats were attributed to the people because of their lack of pious zeal. In the spring of 1864, Sherman began his "march to the sea." In a letter from Washington, Georgia, George Caldwell underscored this relationship of piety to victory, lack of devotion to defeat:

> A feeling seems now to be pervading the army, that we have deserved the chastisements of the Lord, and that we must repent before the scourge will be removed from us. I think that 9

out of 10, even of the ungodly soldiers, would confess to some such feeling as this. Now is the time for earnest prayer and effort.⁵¹

The victories of 1861 that the Confederacy enjoyed were denied her the next year. In February 1862, Forts Henry and Donelson fell to Union forces. Two months later, the crucial Battle of Corinth (Shiloh) was fought. On the Mississippi, only the area around Vicksburg remained in Confederate hands. Following the fall of Fort Henry, Commodore Phelps proceeded up the Tennessee River and took Florence, Alabama. On 9 April, just a week following the Battle of Corinth, a force headed by General O. M. Mitchel from Nashville took Huntsville by surprise, extending his raid as far south as Russellville, Alabama. He then pulled his forces back to the Tennessee River and continued holding all Alabama north of the river, including Huntsville. Mitchel also captured some 100 miles of the important Charleston to Memphis Railroad, thus interrupting the plans of the United Synod to meet in Chattanooga in 1862. And although Confederate militiamen had defeated Union forces at the Battle of Wilson Creek just south of Springfield, Missouri, in 1861, the following spring at the Battle of Pea Ridge in northwestern Arkansas, the Confederates suffered a crucial, if not staggering, defeat.

The year 1862 was thus a crucial year for both the United Synod as well as the Confederacy. Osage and Texas Presbyteries were now cut off from the main body of the Church. The area of North Alabama Presbytery was in the hands of Federal Forces. The Mississippi presbyteries were now out of geographical contact with the Synods of Tennessee and Virginia. In the East, major battles had been waged in that portion of Virginia where the United Synod was strong. Only East Tennessee had not yet been despoiled by Union raids. Clement Eaton pointed out that "the Confederate Congress was weakened in prestige by the fact that many of its members, as a result of the capture of large regions by Federal troops, represented only °imaginary constituencies.'"⁵² Alter a few proper nouns, and the same description would obtain for the United Synod.

Only three presbyteries with a total of seven commissioners were able to get to Chattanooga in May 1862. Since a quorum was eleven, those present set the next meeting of the United Synod for Knoxville in May 1863.

The Synod of Virginia met in the fall of 1862. That meeting produced a document that was later adopted at the 1863 meeting of the United Synod, *The Position, Relations and Prospects of the United Synod: in Reference to the Moral Issues Involved in the Present War*. Most of the paper is an historical review of the events that brought the United Synod into existence. It affirmed that the position taken on the subject of slavery--that it should not be discussed on the floor of ecclesiastical judicatories--had enabled the Church to enjoy "peace among ourselves and some good measure of prosperity under God's blessing upon our efforts to preach the Gospel and preserve a pure christianity in our churches." The developments which the Church had enjoyed in its four-years' existence have demonstrated that the position "was not taken too soon, or too firmly maintained."

The paper referred to two moral issues involved in the war: the "Higher Law" doctrine, which places issues above written constitutions, and the "coercive policy" by which conscientious and legal rights are invaded and despoiled, making separation and self-government the only possible alternative. To both issues, the United Synod stood opposed. At that time, the Church did not occupy a station of despair. It had the Constitutional principles of the Presbyterian Church, which had been of use "in the cause of religion and the interests of society at large; there are churches to nourish and open fields to occupy the service of Christ; and there is a great work to be prosecuted in the Confederacy by all the evangelical Churches."[53]

Although the United Synod noted that half of its congregations were or had been within the lines of the enemy during some portion of 1862,[54] it was not swamped by despair.

The Battle of Stone's River in middle Tennessee began the year 1863. It was a staggering defeat for the Confederacy. In April the Presbytery of Holston met. In its "Declaration on the State of Our Country," it painted one of the most realistic insights into the mind of a beleaguered people one will ever behold. It noted that

> Church organizations are broken up in many places, and the grey-headed members wander as outcasts in the earth to escape the hands of ruthless soldiery. Magnificent and costly temples, built and dedicated to God amid the prayers and tears of our pious fathers and mothers, have been mutilated or destroyed by the sacrilegious hands of our enemies. Ministers of Christ, who once proclaimed the 'word

of life' to listening ears and tearful eyes and throbbing hearts in those holy temples, have been driven as exiles from their flocks or shut up as a felon from the light of day within the thick walls and prison doors of some gloomy *Bastile* [sic]. The plow stands in the furrow,-- farms lie uncultivated; and famine and sorrow in ghostly form stride through the earth.

The paper continued. "This dreadful state of our Country is not wholly political in its bearing. There is a great under-current, hidden it is true at the first out break, but palpable now, which spreads its moral poison through every minutie [sic] of the desolating flood." The charge then was levelled against church declarations which began in the North and which

> resulted in tearing asunder *three* of the largest and most influential churches in the land. It would even dare to legislate on the subject of slave-holding. Thus the tide of abolitionism has rolled on in its polluting power for 70 years, till finally it culminates in all the horrors of a civil war upon the interests, social, political, and religious, of our beloved country.

The paper concluded with a cry of repentance:

Finally: We are deeply sensible of our own sins. We have been an ungrateful people, and have greatly neglected the many duties we owe to the colored race which God has given us to train for him . . . . In humble submission to the Divine will, we will cry unto God night and day to shield us in this our day of great trial, and guide us and sanctify to us all the tribulations through which we are called in the Providence of God to pass.[55]

With twenty-eight commissioners present, the United Synod convened in Knoxville, 21 May 1863. Only the Presbyteries of North Alabama and Newton came from the Synod of Mississippi to join the other seven Presbyteries from the Synods of Virginia and Tennessee. Fielding Pope was elected Moderator. And although the Synod had not met in two years, it was able to transact its business in just three days.

On the first day, a communication was read from the Presbytery of North Alabama touching the subject of union with the General Assembly of the Presbyterian Church in the Confederate States of America (the southern Old School). The communication was referred to the Committee on Bills and Overtures. A second overture came from Hanover Presbytery. It conveyed information that the General Assembly of the Presbyterian Church in the Confederate States at its recent meeting had adopted a fraternal minute in reference to the reunion of the two Churches. It had appointed a committee of five ministers and two elders to confer with a similar committee, which it requested the United Synod to appoint.[56]

The Committee on Bills and Overtures acknowledged these actions of the Assembly as seeming to be "every way sincere, honorable and satisfactory . . . ." It made three recommendations, which were adopted. First, it proposed that a similar committee of five ministers and two elders be appointed to meet with the corresponding committee of the Assembly. It then commissioned the committee "to arrange such a formal union of the Presbyterian Churches at the South, upon the basis of the Confession of Faith and Form of Government, as in its spirit and terms shall be honorable and acceptable to both parties . . . ." Finally, the committee was directed to report at the next meeting of the United Synod.[57]

The report of the Board of Education, more than any other agency of the Church, reflected the impact of the war upon the Synod: "Our Theological Seminary has been arrested in all its arrangements. Maryville College is closed." And with one exception, every candidate for the ministry was in the army. The Synod, however, did not view that last statement as necessarily a negative development, for "the providential training which our candidates are receiving, in the camp, the hospital, and the battle field, may render them better fitted for the labours and trials of the calling they have in view."[58]

The Confederate army was viewed as "the widest and best field for missionary labor now open to the Church," and Joseph C. Stiles was cited and commended for the work he was doing as an evangelist among the troops.

"The Narrative on the State of Religion within the Bounds of the United Synod" also reflected the impact of the War on the Church. It acknowledged that large portions of the Church were behind Federal lines. At the same time there were many references to the effect that the ordinances and activities of the churches had not been disturbed.[59] Gone, however, was the optimism that had marked the Synod's sessions of 1861. A cursory examination of the 1863 Minutes reveals that the burden and suffering of the War were taking a heavy toll on the life of the Church.

Within two months after the 1863 meeting had adjourned, Vicksburg and Gettysburg were fought. In August the Federal drive for Chattanooga began, and at the same time Burnside's Army of the Ohio began its foray to Knoxville. That city fell in early September. The Confederate attempt to regain Knoxville failed, and from that time, East Tennessee--the heart of the United Synod--was in Federal hands.

Following the Battle of Antietam, President Lincoln had issued a preliminary proclamation, which stated that if the seceded States did not lay down their arms and return to the Union by 1 January 1863, he would declare their slaves to be free forever. When the day of condition arrived, he announced the Emancipation Proclamation. The pronouncement itself had little force, for it freed only those slaves who were in territory still in rebellion, and over which the Union could enforce Lincoln's directive. But it satisfied the abolitionists. It infuriated the South, and it prompted the "Address to Christians Throughout the World, By the Clergy of the Confederate States of America."[60] Of the 154 clergymen who signed it, forty-two were Presbyterians, the largest denominational group by far. And of the forty-two Presbyterians, twelve were United Synod.[61]

The first part of the Address was a presentation of the constitutional argument for the right of a state to secede. The position of John C. Calhoun was recalled. The second part was an extended defense of slavery, a benevolent institution based on the Scriptures.

> We testify in the sight of God, that the relation of master and slave among us . . . is not incompatible with our holy Christianity, and that the presence of the Africans in our land is an occasion of gratitude on their behalf before God . . . . The South has done more than any people on earth for the Christianization of the African race.[62]

The question was then raised, "Can emancipation obtain for them a better portion?" The response was that abolition was regarded as "an interference with the plans of Divine Providence"; and even when slaves are freed, there is no place that offers them "any better things than they have at home, either in respect to their temporal or eternal welfare." Abolition was indicted as the latest attempt to wreck the South: it caused the war and was endeavoring to destroy religious men who were striving to guide slaves along Scriptural grounds.

The British were unimpressed. Henry Hotze, a Swiss commissioned by the Confederate Department of State, arranged for the distribution of the pamphlet in Britain. He secured the aid of an English Presbyterian house to have it stitched under the same cover with the current numbers of every respectable religious publication in Britain, as well as the *Quarterly* and *Edinburgh Review*--a combined circulation of about 250,000. Although this feat gave the Address wide distribution, it incensed British antislavery advocates.[63]

That 1863 was a year of decline for the Confederacy is reflected in the weekly columns of the *Christian Observer*. The more the year progressed, the less the reader learns of United Synod churches and judicatories outside of Virginia. By the end of the year, almost all religious news centered around Virginia, reflecting the continual advancing encroachment of Union lines into the South and the severing of ties with the rest of the South.

The war not only halted the growth of the United Synod; it pealed out its death knell. The only prospect for hope lay in some sort of union with her Southern Old School kin. Although not necessarily more astute as ecclesiastics, the men of the Assembly had a longer heritage and experience as a Church, greater wealth, more numerous institutions. It was most propitious for the United Synod that in the midst of war, the General Assembly of the Presbyterian Church in the Confederate States of America held out its hand in peace.

NOTES

1. The southern presbyteries of the Old School withdrew after the 1861 Old School General Assembly. In December 1861, in Augusta, Georgia, they formed the Presbyterian Church in the Confederate States of America. For a splendid account of the birth of that Church, see Ernest Trice Thompson, *Presbyterians in the South*, 3 vols. (Richmond: John Knox Press, 1963-1973) 1:530-571.

2. *CO*, 30 May 1861. This issue carries a thorough account of the proceedings of the United Synod meeting.

3. Ibid.

4. Ibid.; USS, *Minutes* (1861), p. 148.

5. John F. Hume, *The Abolitionists: Together with Personal Memories of the Struggle for Human Rights 1830-1864* (New York: G. P. Putnam's Sons, 1905), p. 48.

6. *CO*, 28 November 1860.

7. Clement Eaton, *A History of the Southern Confederacy* (New York: Free Press, 1965), p. 93.

8. Mary U. Rothrock, ed., *The French Broad-Holston Country: A History of Knox County, Tennessee* (Knoxville: East Tennessee Historical Society, 1946), p. 127.

9. George Miller, *Missouri's Memorable Decade: 1860-1870. An Historical Sketch, Personal--Political--Religious* (Columbia, Missouri: E. W. Stephens, 1898), p. 25.

10. William L. Barney, *Flawed Victory: A New Perspective on the Civil War*, New Perspectives in American History Series, ed. James P. Shenton (New York and Washington: Praeger, 1975), p. 44.

11. *CO*, 29 September 1864.

12. James W. Silver, *Confederate Morale and Church Propaganda* (New York: W. W. Norton & Co., 1967).

13. North Alabama Presbytery, MS "Minutes" (4 October 1861), p. 265, PHF. For the Synod of Virginia, see *CO*, 21 November 1861. See also Henry Smith Stroupe, *The Religious Press in the South Atlantic States, 1802-1865: an Annotated Bibliography with Historical Introduction and Notes* (Durham, North Carolina: Duke University Press, 1956), pp. 63-64.

14. Silver, *Confederate Morale*.

15. *CO*, 10 April 1862.

16. Ibid., 24 April 1862.

17. Ibid., 6 March 1862.

18. Quoted in ibid., 8 May 1862.

19. USS, *Minutes* (1861), p. 163.

20. Presbytery of North Alabama, "Minutes" (27 April 1861), p. 255.

21. *CO*, 1 May 1862.

22. Ibid., 28 May 1863.

23. Ibid., 19 November 1863.

24. The four were George E. Eagleton, W. A. Crawford, J. D. Mitchell, and J. A. Zivley; Record Group 109, War Department Collection of Confederate Records, Chapter I, vol. 132: Register of Appointed Chaplains; microfilm copy, National Archives and Records Service. The key word here is "appointed," for many clergy served unofficially and temporarily as chaplains throughout the war to units in their immediate area.

25. *CO*, 1 May 1862. For a similar resolution by Piedmont Presbytery [PCCSA], see ibid., 10 September 1863.

26. Ibid., 13 November 1862.

27. Ibid., 7 April 1864.

28. William W. Bennett, *A Narrative of the Great Revival which Prevailed in the Southern Armies during the Late Civil War between the States of the Federal Union* (Philadelphia: Claxton, Remsen & Haffelfinger, 1877), p. 54.

29. *CO*, 18 February 1864.

30. Cited in Bennett, *The Great Revival*, pp. 209-210. In a letter to the *CO* (27 November 1862), Stiles commented that he would preach for two hours at a time and then spend an additional two hours "meeting with inquirers."

31. For Stiles's vituperative, condemnatory preachments against wickedness among Confederate civilians, see Bennett, *The Great Revival*, pp. 270-272.

32. Ibid., p. 402.

33. By far the most notorious case of ministerial harassment was that suffered by the Old School Samuel B. McPheeters of St. Louis. His experience was written by John S. Grasty, *Memoir of Rev. Samuel B. McPheeters, D. D.* (St. Louis: Southwestern Book and Publishing Co.; Louisville: Davidson Brothers & Co., 1871). The introduction was written by Stuart Robinson of Louisville, who also felt the dual wrath of government and military and for several months was exiled to Canada.

34. For Handy's case, see Thompson, *Presbyterians in the South*, 2:81; Bennett, *The Great Revival*, pp. 392-393; *CO*, 29 October 1863.

35. *CO*, 18 February 1864.

36. Ibid., 8 September 1864.

37. Alex[ander] Bartlett, *A History of the New Providence Church, Maryville, Tennessee. A Discourse Delivered October 15th, 1876* (Maryville: College Printing Office, 1877), pp. 8-9; Thompson, *Presbyterians in the South*, 2:126.

38. *CO*, 18 February 1864; Thompson, *Presbyterians in the South*, 2:81-82, 126.

39. Cited in Silver, *Confederate Morale*, p. 89, n. 26.

40. *CO*, 27 November 1862.

41. Ibid., 24 April 1862.

42. Ibid., 21 January 1864.

43. Silver, *Confederate Morale*, p. 99.

44. There are no records of the church between 27 September 1863 and 20 July 1864; see Second Presbyterian Church [Knoxville, Tennessee], MS

"Minutes" book (dated from 2 January 1841 to 13 February 1870) and the "Church Register" from 24 October 1819 to 13 February 1870, in the church archives. W. Russell Briscoe and Katherine Boies Buehler, *Her Walls Before Thee Stand (History of the Second Presbyterian Church, 1818-1968)* (n.p.: n.p., [1968]), p. 16, and *Historical Sermon, Preached by the Pastor, Rev. Robert L. Bachman, D. D., In the Second Presbyterian Church, Knoxville, Tennessee, September 23, 1906* (n.p.: n.p., n.d.), unpaginated.

45. Horace E. Orr, "One Hundred Years of the New Prospect Presbyterian Church, Knox County, Tennessee, 1834-1934," *East Tennessee Historical Society Publications* 7 (1935): 57.

46. Holston Presbytery [USS], MS "Minutes" (10 September 1864), p. 69, PHF. For fifty years after the war, Bachman served as Pastor of the First Presbyterian Church, Chattanooga. In 1910, he was Moderator GAPCUS. Apparently no one through the years ever questioned the validity of his ordination!

47. For a brief biography, see *The New Schaff-Herzog Encyclopedia of Religious Knowledge*, 12:555, s.v. "Kalopothakes, Michael."

48. For a thorough report of his work in the field, see USS *Minutes* (1861), pp. 159-161.

49. See the issue of 30 May 1861 as an instance.

50. Taken from *CO*, 28 November 1861.

51. Quoted in ibid., 7 April 1864. Caldwell's quotation suggests that there had not been sufficient repentance on the part of the ungodly, or prayer on the part of the godly. On 2 September Atlanta fell--not because of Jefferson's ineptness in replacing the incapable Bragg or Johnston, whose defensive tactics were questionable at best, or even because of Sherman's tactics, but because of theological reasons.

52. Eaton, *A History of the Southern Confederacy*, p. 63.

53. After its adoption by the Synod of Virginia, it was printed *in toto* in *CO*, 6 November 1862, and other Richmond papers. When the USS met in 1863, it voted to have the report published, because of its historic value, in a more convenient form. It was printed by Charles H. Wynne of Richmond, on 11 December 1863, as a 12-page pamphlet.

54. *CO*, 13 November 1862.

55. Holston Presbytery [USS], "Minutes" (11 April 1863), pp. 50-52.

56. PCCSA, *Minutes* (1863), p. 137.

57. USS, *Minutes* (1863), pp. 190, 196. The USS committee consisted of Joseph C. Stiles, J. D. Mitchell, Charles H. Read, F. A. Ross, and J. J. Robinson, ministers, and J. Randolph Tucker and James F. Johnson, elders.

58. Ibid., p. 193.

59. Ibid., p. 201.

60. For the text of the document, see Peter G. Mode, *Source Book and Bibliographical Guide for American Church History* (Menasha, Wisconsin: George Bantam Publishing Co., 1921), pp. 611-615; and Edward McPherson, *The Political History of the United States of America during the Great Rebellion*, 3rd ed. (Washington: Solomon and Chapman, 1876), pp. 517-521; and Robert R. Mathisen, ed., *The Role of Religion in American Life: An Interpretive Historical Anthology* (Lanham, Md: University Press of America, 1982), pp. 155-167.

61. United Synod ministers who signed it were Charles H. Read, Amasa Converse, Thomas W. Hooper, P. B. Price (all of Richmond), Jacob B. Mitchell (Lynchburg), Thomas D. Bell (Harrisonburg, Virginia), J. H. C. Leach (Farmville, Virginia), Matthew M. Marshall (Tennessee), Joseph H. Martin (Knoxville), Frederick A. Ross (Huntsville), J. M. McLean (Mobile), and C. M. Atkinson (Canton, Mississippi).

62. From Mathisen, *Role of Religion in American Life*, p. 165.

63. See W. Harrison Daniel, "English Presbyterians, Slavery and the Crisis of the 1860s," *JPH* 58 (1980): 52-53; Donaldson Jordan and Edwin J. Pratt, *Europe and the American Civil War* (New York: Houghton Mifflin, 1931), p. 169. The *English Presbyterian Messenger* (October 1863) carried a reply to the "pro-slavery wail" of the Confederate clergy. Over 150 Scottish clergy alone had signed the protest. The issue also contains information that 750 French Protestant clergy and 4,000 English clergy had agreed in protesting the recognition of "a Confederacy which lays down as the corner-stone of its constitution the system of slavery as it exists in the Southern States." Hence, the "Address" won few, if any, of Britain's church leaders to the Confederate cause. Indeed, it may have resulted in creating a far more negative response.

13
Reunion With the Old School

When the Presbyterian Church in the Confederate States of America--the Southern Old School--was organized in Augusta, Georgia, in December 1861, a spirit of fraternity, amity, and confidence prevailed over its sessions. Forty-seven presbyteries--all within the bounds of the Confederacy, all with a common background of ecclesiastical experience in the Old School Assembly, all of which had voluntarily withdrawn their ecclesiastical relations with that body--were represented. The new Church quickly expressed a desire to consider union with the various elements of Presbyterian and Reformed Churches that were in the Confederacy, thereby forming one strong national Presbyterian Church. At one time, proposals were made to include overtures for unions with the Cumberland Presbyterian Church, the Independent Presbyterian Church, the Associate Reformed Synod of the South, the United Synod, and the German Reformed Synod, all existing within the Confederate States.[1]

In 1863 the union with the Independent Presbyterian Church--actually a union between that Church and the Presbytery of Bethel in the Synod of South Carolina--was approved by the General Assembly. More definite plans were made to solicit union with the United Synod of the South. A very capable committee was appointed, composed of Robert L. Dabney, J. N. Waddell, William Brown, J. B. Ramsey, and E. T. Baird, ministers, and Col. J. T. L. Preston and F. N. Watkins, Esq., elders.

In many respects, however, the union between these two southern Churches had actually begun shortly after the Old School--New School rift of 1837. For within a few months after that division, at least three broad bases for union were laid down. After discussing these bases, attention will than be given to the detailed struggle for the consummation of that union in 1864.

The first basis was the actual occurrence for the formation of the New School: the Exscinding Acts. By this legislation, the Old School majority drummed out of the Church, without trial, four entire synods and a presbytery. The very fact that this action was followed by protests and numerous withdrawals by both ministers and congregations who sympathized with the exscinded is indicative that the Acts were not popular. For "the synods and their whole constituency, ministers and church-members, were swept away by the same unforeseen decree, confounding the innocent with the guilty, and condemning all unheard."[2] Twenty years later the southern synods of the New School, which had left all in 1838 and in the years immediately following, out of sympathy with their maltreated brothers, experienced a similar kind of treatment at the hands of the exscinded.

In 1861 the Old School Church--that victorious majority, which had expunged the New School in 1837--passed the Gardiner Spring Resolutions, which exscinded its southern element.[3] Small reason, then, that the exscinded in both instances would seek comfort with one another.

The United Synod had not been formed out of judicatories that had been charged with heresy, as was the Independent Presbyterian Church. Nor was it a Church that had never been a part of the main stream of American Presbyterianism, as was the Associate Reformed Synod of the South. Rather, the United Synod was a denomination that had been maltreated and humiliated before the world by an overwhelming majority, a Church that had sat at counsel with the forefathers of the Old School Confederate Presbyterians for decades before their withdrawal in 1838. The fellowship of suffering for a like cause thus had much to do with ultimately bringing these two groups together, for the various exscinding actions hastened the day when the two southern Churches would seek, and find, solace in one another.

The second basis for union was the position on slavery. The leading Old School journal in 1837 had gone behind the actions of the Assembly of that year and hinted that the reason for exscinding the New School courts was that they had "dared to oppose slavery."⁴ Although the official records are silent on the issue of slavery as a factor in the division of 1837, there was a strong feeling among the abolitionists that the Exscinding Acts "were a deliberate attempt to weaken the anti-slavery forced in the Church."⁵ As has been noted, the United Synod left the New School over the slavery agitation in 1857, a minority largely dominated by abolition spirit. A common understanding of the slavery question was thus the second ground two churches shared. The only real difference was that in the United Synod the matter of slavery would not be brought to the floor of any judicatory through an act of legislation; in the Old School slavery was not discussed *de facto*.

The third basis for the ultimate union was an event which took place early in the life of the New School Church, the drawing up and signing of the Auburn Declaration. The New Schoolmen resented the doctrinal errors that had been attributed to them by the Old School apologists. In the summer of 1837 a strategy committee, formed of New School advocates, met in Auburn, New York, and drew up a doctrinal paper that gave the position of the New School party on the controversial doctrines.⁶ The document was never signed by any of the southern New School ministers. Thus was preserved their doctrinal purity intact. No taint of theological aberration or error was ever lodged against the United Synod as a whole, only informally against two or three individuals.

It was generally understood--and accepted-- across the South that the only reason there was a southern New School movement was that the southern judicatories had withdrawn from the General Assembly in 1838 in protest to the Exscinding Acts, not because of any doctrinal affinity with the main body of the New School. There was no Beecher, no Barnes, nor any other such person in the New School South that was ever tried for heresy. Rather, one would go some length before finding as militant and sound a group of men who headed up the *Calvinistic Magazine*, which defended East Tennessee Calvinism from the barbs of Methodist Arminianism.

It is significant that the overture for union originated with the Southern Presbyterian Church.⁷ In 1858 the United Synod had sought union with the Old School, only to have the door slammed in its face. Times were greatly altered in 1863. Further, while there was some agitation between the two groups, in Virginia they had long since learned to work out an accommodation. As early as 1855 the Old School Synod of Virginia had sent a communication to the New School Presbytery of Hanover regarding the appointment of an annual day of Thanksgiving in the Old Dominion. The Presbytery's Stated Clerk communicated that the Presbytery "reciprocates the kind and fraternal feelings which prompted the sending of said communication, and signify the hearty concurrence of Presbytery . . . ."[8]

In responding to the suggestion of possible reunion with the Old School in 1857, Robert L. Dabney responded for the Old School in an article. He regarded the desire to increase in numbers without concern for doctrine and organization "as the introduction of an element of weakness and disorganization earnestly to be deplored, and if possible interdicted." He then added that the Old School does believe "that among Southern New School Presbyterians there are thousands who are sound in doctrinal views and steadfast in attachment to the standards of our church, *one with us* in principle, sentiment, and all that constitutes true denominational fellowship and unity." Further, any union would be for the New School "the wisest, safest and happiest solution of the difficulty" that has arisen over their ministers being driven "by the unrighteous action of their late Northern associates."[9]

Dabney then pointed out some reasons why it would be advantageous to the United Synod to unite with the Old School: (1) if the New School South persisted in forming a separate denomination, it would be limited to southern members; (2) the proposed denomination would be numerically small and scattered--a misfortune to any body; and (3) the dependence on the North for ministers would soon come to an end, as would reliance on the SAS. He then scored the sympathy of the southern New School for the exscinded New School North: "Has not this duty of sympathizing testimony for Northern brethren been sufficiently performed?" Dabney queried. "Have they not, with a vengeance, requited you from further obligations of this nature?" he continued.

Further, the matter of abolition in the Old School had been settled by its legislation of 1845, with only thirteen votes opposing it. So satisfactory was that action that all secular papers in the South endorsed it, and all southern Presbyterians in the Old School were satisfied with it.

Dabney then asked how should union be consummated? "We would receive any given church, session and minister, into any given Presbytery, in exactly the same way in which one Old School Presbytery would receive them from another Old School Pres-

Reunion With the Old School   253

bytery." Why should the New School be apprehensive about being examined when received into an Old School Presbytery, when the Old School does precisely the same with its own members? The Old School

> can safely give to our brethren of the other connection these two assurances . . . that on the one hand we will all feel a respectful friendship, a sympathy with the difficulties which injustice has imposed upon them, and a sincere desire for any wholesome and hearty union of our interests; and on the other hand, that no approbation of a reunion is prompted by any self-interest on our part, or will ever be followed by any annoying solicitations.

Thus wrote Dabney in 1857 after the Cleveland Assembly.[10]

In spite of Dabney's insistence on receiving the New School elements precisely as the Old School required, the counsel he gave was not nearly so discouraging as one might first interpret. The southern New School was held up as being basically orthodox--and this from among the most orthodox of southern Old School theologians!

Interestingly enough, in its Stated 1860 Spring Meeting, the Presbytery of Lexington, South, approved a resolution to dissolve that court's relationship with the United Synod and seek union with the Old School Assembly. The Shongalo church protested the resolution, however, urging that with the political shadows lengthening across the land, this was an additional reason "for adhering still closer to an organization which has battled against error and fanaticism . . . ."[11]

Only the shortage of time appears to have prevented the first Assembly of the Southern Presbyterian Church from pursuing the path of reunion with the United Synod. "An Esteemed Pastor," a delegate to that meeting, wrote that, had there been more time,

> more decided action would have been urged in reference to the union of the Old and New School Presbyterians. That I regard as a matter of the very highest moment. It is especially a practical and important question for the eastern and middle division of this State. It is so for my Synod.[12]

And the *Christian Observer* began 1862 by noting that the question of reunion had come *"not from the*

United Synod, but by [the Assembly's] own members."[13]

Whether the matter of reunion would have come up at the 1862 meeting of the United Synod is academic, inasmuch as the Synod failed to meet for want of a quorum. The columns of the *Christian Observer* for the period between January 1862 and May 1863, however, remained silent on the subject. But in 1863 the General Assembly approved the union with the Independent Presbyterian Church and Bethel Presbytery if such could be worked out.[14] This same Assembly opened the doors for further discussion of reunion with the United Synod.

The first formal step toward reunion came from East Hanover Presbytery of the Southern Church. At its 1 May 1863 meeting, it overtured the General Assembly "to take such steps as its wisdom may suggest, at its appropriate meeting in Columbia, to bring about a union between the Old School and New School Presbyterians in the Confederate States."[15] The communication was routinely referred to the Assembly's Committee on Bills and Overtures. When the Committee brought its report to the floor of the Assembly, it noted that West Hanover Presbytery had sent up a similar overture. It further commented that most of the presbyteries in touch with the Synod were favorably impressed with the ministers and members of that Church. Upon the recommendation of the committee, the Assembly appointed a committee of Conference of five clergy and two laity and the United Synod subsequently did the same. The two committees were composed of probably the best men in each Church.

The joint committee met in Lynchburg, Virginia, in July 1863, in the lecture room of J. B. Ramsey's Southern Presbyterian Church. The committee formed itself into an interlocutory committee. Then constrained silence existed for some time. Finally, Robert L. Dabney stood up, shoulders shrugged, hands in his pockets, "trying to look as much like a codhopper as he could," according to William H. McGuffey. He spoke, "Well, brethren, as nobody seems ready, I would like to try to talk a little." According to McGuffey, he then "made the most adroit speech possible, and one of the best I have ever heard." It was apparent that he had not come to the meeting without adequate preparation. His remarks captivated the United Synod delegates. When he concluded his remarks, Joseph C. Stiles remarked, "Dr. Dabney's views are marked by entire fairness, and if the spirit of magnificent equity which breathes through them prevails in this joint committee, the breach between us is healed, and more to the same purpose."[16]

Diligently did the joint committee labor to bring in a report which would satisfy both Churches. By far the greatest hurdle would be theological. Finally a six-article Plan of Union was unanimously adopted by all the delegates except the Assembly's E. T. Baird. It was later noted that

> in a paper he stated that he withheld his signature because, in several places, the language of the articles was liable to misapprehension and might become a matter of trouble thereafter; otherwise he endorsed the Plan and was cordially in favor of union.[17]

The First Article of the Plan of Union contained a declaration touching certain doctrines and practices, which had formerly been grounds for debate. Four doctrines in particular were discussed: (1) concerning the fall of man, original sin, imputation of guilt, the origin of sin, etc.; (2) concerning regeneration; (3) concerning the atonement of Christ; and (4) concerning the believer's justification. There was also a statement concerning revivals and another concerning voluntary societies and the function of the Church. Articles 2 and 3 dealt with the organic incorporation of the Synod's presbyteries into their respective Southern synods. Article 4 treated the union of local churches in the same communities. Article 5 related to the transfer of all funds of the United Synod under the appropriate committees of the Assembly, and Article 6 stated that when the written Plan of Union has been adopted by the General Assembly and the United Synod, it would be in full force.[18]

Debate immediately began to be waged upon release of the plan. The primary article debated was the first with its doctrinal statements. John P. Campbell of Marion, Alabama, recognized that the inclusion of the theological statement would be very difficult for many. He suggested that his colleagues were going to have to let bygones be bygones and look forward to the future under Christ. Men in both Churches

> must consider how many and how great are the doctrines of agreement and harmony between them, also how few and unimportant the points which separate them, and then resolve, in the name of Christ and by the grace of God, they

will make the latter subordinate to the former.[19]

However, his colleagues in the South Alabama Presbytery did not agree with him, and opposed the union.[20]

A second Alabama presbytery, Tuscaloosa, also resolved that the union would not be consummated on the basis of the report of the Joint Committee. It was apprehensive of the doctrinal section. The Presbytery did favor union, however, if both groups "declare that they continue to receive the Confession and the Catechisms of the Presbyterian Church, as containing the system of doctrine taught in the Holy Scriptures," and approve of its governmental discipline.[21]

East Alabama Presbytery favored union, but deemed it inadvisable for the General Assembly to adopt "the doctrinal basis *in extenso.*"[22] Montgomery Presbytery (Synod of Virginia) regarded the proposed union with "great satisfaction" and did "most cordially and unanimously" approve it on the basis of the Plan of Plan Union.[23]

The Southern Assembly convened 5 May 1864 in Charlotte, North Carolina. The delegates did not refrain from engaging in a very lengthy debate on the Plan of Union. Through the nine months from the time the plan had been drawn up until the hour of the Assembly's convening, the opposition had come from South Carolina, led by J. B. Adger, and from New Orleans, mainly by Benjamin M. Palmer. At the spring 1864 meeting of the Presbytery of South Carolina, Adger had presented a paper which was unanimously adopted:

> This Presbytery does not hesitate to declare that it is finally and unalterably opposed to any union with the United Synod except upon a formal and distinct repudiation by them of every one of the New School errors which have been entertained by those with whom they so long continued to maintain the closest fellowship.[24]

The four-day debate at the Assembly commenced when Palmer brought in the report on behalf of the Committee on Ecclesiastical Union with the United Synod.

The Southern Church numbered in its ranks theological and ecclesiastical giants who waged titanic verbal warfare on the Assembly floor. For three hours Dabney spoke, supporting the Plan. Two

Reunion With the Old School 257

of those hours were used in defending Article 1. With lucid patience he pointed out that the Plan did not contain a definitive theological statement.[25] He then dealt with the portion of Article 1 that treated the Atonement. He remarked that "there is among Calvinists, among ourselves, a slight difference in the arrangement of some details concerning the atonement and its application; yet both classes have always recognized each other as holding the essentials of the doctrine of particular redemption."[26] He returned again to the basic purpose of the Joint Committee in coming up with the doctrinal statement which it did: to state those features of the doctrine that distinguished Calvinists from Arminians and the New England School. The gist of the doctrinal minute on the Atonement says, or expressly implies, "that Christ was our substitute; that his sufferings were truly vicarious; that they were properly penal; that they were a true satisfaction to justice; that they were necessary to make pardon possible, consistently with the perfections of God." He then raised the rhetorical question, "Is not this right?"[27]

Dabney continued,

> We did not claim that our phraseology was absolutely the best, but only that *it would do*. We admitted that language is an instrument so flexible that an indefinite improvement may be made in the verbal dress of any thoughts by continued care and criticism.[28]

Dabney has been accused of compromising his position in his defense of the plan. As professor of theology in the Assembly's Union Theological Seminary, he was no novice to theological loci. Frank Bell Lewis has urged that Dabney's attitude in this matter indicated that he advocated union between the two bodies, not because there was complete doctrinal accord, but because he considered union most desirable for the consolidation of Southern Presbyterianism. He was aware of heretics in the United Synod with whom he did not share theological opinions. But he was confident that the New School aberrations could be overcome when the New School element had been absorbed in a larger and sounder body. His basic position was that the entire possibility of reunion was an act of Providence: the two bodies had been growing closer to one another both theologically as well as ecclesiastically, and reunion would give strength and homogeneity.[29]

Adger was not impressed with such logic. Opposed to the plan, he desired to receive the United Synod by having each presbytery declare its desire for union as well as make a hearty adoption of the Confession of Faith. He pointed out that the Independent Church had been received into the Southern Church through a presbytery. This was the only way. He further remarked that the General Assembly did not have the authority to receive an entire body such as the United Synod as a Church. In addition, the Synod represented a body that had remained in the New School and had elected "that man" [A. H. H. Boyd] as professor in its proposed seminary.[30] Every man in the Southern Church would regard him as heretical. The strength of a Church, according to Adger, lies not in numbers, but in testimonies and doctrines. Herein lay the weakness of the United Synod. Moses Hoge, pastor of Richmond's Second Presbyterian Church, spoke for union. The United Synod was fighting and suffering just as were Southern Presbyterians. The Independent Church had been received with minor doctrinal differences, yet there was "union in essentials."[31] Love and good feelings, according to Hoge, have much to do with modifying men's opinions and preparing them for a well-cemented union.

Elder Samuel Barnett of Georgia opposed the Plan. He suggested that it be submitted to the presbyteries for their approval.

Benjamin M. Palmer of New Orleans opposed it—PERIOD.

Dabney came back in rebuttal. The United Synod would educate their ministers in their seminary, with their men, and in their doctrines. There would be an inevitable tendency to magnify the differences. In union, however, all will stay together, and the New England influences, which had been the source of troubles in the Church, would never again return. Dabney would thus destroy his foes by putting them under the same roof with himself.

Adger returned to the fray. Not only did he deny the right of the Assembly to make such a union, but he now doubted that even the presbyteries could. He used the Plan of Union of 1801 as an example to support his case.

Palmer now gave three reasons for his opposition. At the division of the Old and New Schools, the southern New School courts failed to support the efforts of the Old School Assembly to maintain the truth. Instead, they went off with a group "notoriously unsound." Second, the testimony about the United Synod is uncertain. Some say they are sound;

others, with equal opportunities of knowledge and acquaintance, say they are not. Finally, the United Synod never seems to have made a clear, unreserved subscription to the Confession of Faith. Only if the Standards remained intact would he be for union.

D. H. Cummins of Memphis Presbytery declared that Tennessee was ready for union. J. L. Kirkpatrick of Concord Presbytery (North Carolina) said that he prayed that union would come about before his death. William S. White of Lexington Presbytery (Virginia) had held prejudices with the Old School in 1837; now he had entire confidence in the United Synod men in Virginia. James McKee claimed that Alabama wanted union on the basis of the Confession of Faith. Elder John B. Logan of Roanoke Presbytery (Virginia) stated that union was already anticipated and that two New School ministers were already preaching in Old School pulpits in Montgomery Presbytery.[32]

At this point, the debate was arrested. A committee was appointed, consisting of one minister and one elder from each of the Assembly's synods. Both Adger and Dabney were on the committee. In due time the committee returned to the floor and made its report, which contained four resolutions. The first resolution commended the original Joint Committee, particularly the spirit of brotherly love and harmony in which the conference of the committee was held. The second resolution stated that the Assembly believes that the most satisfactory terms of union to be the "cordial adherence" of the two bodies to their existing symbols of faith and order.

The third resolution dealt with particular amendments to the Plan of Union, the major alteration being the deletion of the controversial section on doctrine. The excision of these passages simply left the doctrinal basis for union thus: "The General Assembly and the United Synod declare that they continue to receive and adopt the Confession of Faith and the Catechisms of the Presbyterian Church, as containing the system of doctrine taught in the Holy Scriptures, and approve its government and discipline." The fourth resolution stated, "That the Assembly proposes the omission of the doctrinal propositions of Article I . . . ."[33]

The Assembly then engaged in a debate on the committee's report. The amended Plan of Union was finally adopted by a 53-7 vote. Some who voted for the plan did dissent, however, from the fourth resolution; by the same token, some who voted against the plan did so because of the fourth resolution. Adger cast a negative vote because he regarded the Plan of Union as a "retraction of the Church's Testimony in 1837, and as being calculated to give rise to future troubles in the Church, and as assuming that the Assembly has unlimited powers."[34]

That a compromise had been worked out in the committee is without question. Both Dabney and Palmer had won their points. Palmer had raised sufficient questions about the possibility of looser interpretation of the doctrinal statement, and had objected to adding it as an additional doctrinal standard of the Church. He was thus responsible for its defeat as a part of the basis for reunion. Dabney won his point in having the total revised Plan approved.

In the meantime, the presbyteries of the United Synod had unanimously adopted the doctrinal statement, as had a large majority of the Assembly's presbyteries. Yet the United Synod asked for no changes. "No alteration was [thus] made in the position, the regulations, or the principles of our Church,"commented E. T. Baird of the Assembly, "and what is more important, *none was asked*. The reason was obvious: we are like-minded; and well did the Assembly of 1864 assert that our conferences had shown such unanimity as might 'ground an honourable union.'"[35]

The 1864 meeting of the United Synod was to have been held in Dublin, Virginia, but the presence of Union forces in the area forced a change of its place and date to Lynchburg, 25 August 1864. Amasa Converse was elected Moderator. Just seven presbyteries--Winchester, Hanover, Piedmont, Holston, New River, Kingston, and Union--were represented. Only seventeen delegates were present. Boyd was not in attendance, but he made his position known. Now a very sick man, he was unable to fight against the Plan of Union. He did, however, communicate his thoughts to the Synod. He saw no reason union should not come about. He would, nevertheless, continue to hold to his New School theology, particularly in respect to the extent of the atonement.[36]

The debate over union on the floor of the United Synod was one-sided. Each commissioner offered his reasons for union. Perhaps the most representative comment was that of Randolph Tucker: "We are free from abolitionism and all the isms which then sundered the Church. There was never any difference between the Old School and the New School Presbyterians in the South. Quixotically we took up the cudgel in favor of our New School brethren who twenty years after cudgelled us in return. . . . Why should men who agree in sentiment and are laboring in the same cause refrain from pulling all together?"[37]

Far from beaten, the United Synod men who had hung and clung together for a quarter of a century could enter the union with pride and the satisfaction that they had stood their ground well. The Synod voted unanimously to adopt the Plan of Union, and the United Synod of the Presbyterian Church in the United States of America ceased its separate existence on Saturday, 27 August 1864. It concluded its Narrative on the State of Religion with these remarks:

> And now in closing this last narrative that is ever to be written by our Synod, we would most gratefully acknowledge once more that "goodness and merey [sic] have followed us all the days of our lives." And we can but express the hope that in entering upon our new relations, we may carry with us our former zeal, energy, and activity; that combining with our brethren of the Assembly, we may together promote each others [sic] welfare and happiness--and more than double our efficiency in the salvation of a perishing world.[38]

In the terms of the Plan of Union, it was agreed that the United Synod presbyteries and synods would enter the respective Old School judicatories, thus preserving the succession and guard the property rights and charter rights of the Assembly's courts. Thus various mergers took place. Typical of the manner by which this was done was the action of the Synod of Virginia in connection with the Assembly.

It was in the Old Dominion that the original impetus for reunion had initiated. The presbyteries quickly approved the report, which had been adopted by the joint Committee of the Assembly and the United Synod. The Old School Presbytery of East Hanover at its 26 August 1863 meeting gave its approbation to the Plan of Union and "expressed the hope that it may be carried into full effect at as early a date as may be practicable."[39] This action was quickly followed by that of the United Synod's Presbyteries of Winchester and Hanover, the Synod of Virginia, and the Presbytery of New River.[40] In the fall of 1864, the Old School Synod of Virginia voted to receive the roll of the Presbyteries of the United Synod in Virginia. The Moderator of the United Synod's Synod of Virginia presented the roll.

"After a full and free expression of mutual gratification on the part of the members of both bodies, that this union had now been so happily consummated, the resolutions were unanimously adopted." After prayer by the two Moderators, C. H. Read was unanimously elected Moderator of the Synod of Virginia.[41]

So genuine was the reunion which occurred among Virginia Presbyterians that one of the members in attendance commented, "Sir, I declare that for the last two hours I have actually forgotten that there is a war, though for a long period I have never been able to banish remembrance of it for such a length of time."[42]

And Robert L. Dabney reminded the reunited brothers that one of the important lessons they must learn from their new estate is to "accord to those who differ, or are supposed to differ from us in opinion, the same honor and intention to do right that we claim for ourselves."[43] The Narrative on the State of Religion in the Synod of Virginia for 1864 carried this description of feeling:

> Christian ministers and people long severed are reunited. Differences of opinion and diversities of sentiment are forgotten; everything that hinders cordial and fraternal reconciliation banished; and to-day we think the visible body of Christ more like what the sacramental host of God's elect should be than ever before: for now we see a large and living exemplification of that charity, which is the bond of perfectness.[44]

Because of the intensity of the war on the eastern front, implementation of reunion in Virginia proceeded slowly. For instance, reunion in Winchester Presbytery was not consummated until the muskets were silent. Finally on 31 August 1865 the two presbyteries united. The emerging presbytery contained twenty ministers, thirty-one congregations, and 1,500 members. Yet so impoverished were the churches that not one could support its minister.[45]

Reunion in Texas was accomplished only during the closing days of the conflict. On 4 May 1865 the Synod of Texas received the United Synod's small Presbytery of Texas "according to the articles of union." At that same meeting of Synod, the Presbytery of Texas was dissolved and its four ministers and four churches were placed in the corresponding presbyteries of the Synod of Texas.[46]

In Mississippi, the Presbytery of Central Mississippi was the major beneficiary of the reunion. It received seven ministers and fifteen congregations. The reunion of the Presbyteries of North Alabama and Maury considerably strengthened Presbyterianism in that region. In Missouri, the Presbytery of Osage disappeared, dissipated by war.

Southern Presbyterian purists have long insisted that in every instance of organic union by the Southern Church with another ecclesiastical body, such union "in every case was on the basis of perfect doctrinal affinity . . . ."[47] It is obvious, from this description of the reunion of the United Synod with the Southern Church that this claim cannot be fully substantiated. Not only did the earlier union with the Independent Presbyterian Church come about because of concessions to that Church's doctrinal views, but this was a mark also of the union with the United Synod. The latter's Committee on Union had approved the doctrinal bases for union because they were in accord with the essential beliefs of the denomination, but they were not to the liking of the more orthodox Old Schoolmen. It was for this reason that, in the midst of the debate on the Plan of Union, the Assembly appointed its committee to try to work out some accommodation that would be acceptable to everyone. The committee returned to the floor of the Assembly with the recommendation that Article 1--the doctrinal article--should be eliminated from the Plan of Union, for it would be more politic to do that than to risk the possibility of voting down the plan because of the doctrinal content of that Article, which a number of the leading and influential men at the Assembly could not abide.

Morton Smith indicated that the very fact that the United Synod "united with the Old School Southern Assembly on the latter's terms and without any hesitancy regarding subscription to the Standards in the strictest sense was evidence of the United Synod's orthodoxy."[48] But the very fact that the Article on doctrine was removed from the Plan of Union is pragmatic evidence that doctrine played quite a role in the actual union, although not a formal role. If anything, it points out that there was considerable difficulty among some of the Old School Presbyterians as to how the Standards were to be interpreted. Article 1 revealed a position quite agreeable to the United Synod men, but not to the Assembly's. Further, it must be remembered that in 1858 the Old School Assembly hardly entertained the notion of receiving the United Synod, but many of the men who were present at that Assembly but opposed the union proposed then now favored it in the South in 1864, more for pragmatic reasons that for "perfect doctrinal affinity." Such men as Ross and Boyd in the United Synod could support union because there were no doctrinal conditions--the Old School itself had removed them.

The reunion has now been discussed across the entire South where the two Churches overlapped, except in Tennessee. It is to that region that this study now turns.

NOTES

1. GAPCCSA, *Minutes* (1861), pp. 9, 13.

2. *American Bible Repository*, 2nd ser. 1 (1839): 491.

3. The Spring Resolutions, passed at the 1861 Old School General Assembly, stated that the Presbyterian Church would remain loyal to the Federal Union. The presbyteries in the South by that time were in another nation, and could not be loyal to that government; hence they withdrew to organize their own Assembly. For the legislation regarding the Spring Resolutions, see GAPCUSA [OS], *Minutes* (1861), pp. 303-344, passim. For discussion of the event, see Lewis G. Vander Velde, *The Presbyterian Churches and the Federal Union 1861-1869* (Cambridge, Massachusetts: Harvard University Press, 1932), pp. 48-84; Ernest Trice Thompson, *Presbyterians in the South*, 3 vols. (Richmond: John Knox Press, 1963-1973), 1:564-571; Robert Ellis Thompson, *A History of the Presbyterian Churches in the United States,* American Church History Series (New York: Christian Literature Co., 1895), pp. 152-158; Thomas C. Johnson, *A History of the Southern Presbyterian Church*, American Church History Series (New York: Christian Literature Co., 1894), pp. 317-323.

4. *The Biblical Repertory and Princeton Review* 9 (1837): 478-483; see also Elwyn A. Smith, "The Role of the South in the Presbyterian Schism of 1837-38," *CH* 29 (1960): 44-63.

5. *Presbyterian Enterprise: Sources of American Presbyterian History*, ed. Maurice W. Armstrong, Lefferts A. Loetscher, and Charles A. Anderson (Philadelphia: Westminster Press, 1956), p. 164.

6. For the text of the Auburn Declaration, see *Minutes of the Auburn Convention Held August 17, 1837, to Deliberate Upon The Doings of the Last General Assembly in Relation to the Synods of*

Western Reserve, Utica, Geneva and Genessee and the Third Presbytery of Philadelphia (Auburn: Oliphat & Skinner, 1837). See also Armstrong, Loetscher, and Anderson, eds., *Presbyterian Enterprise*, pp. 166-171.

7. This is the popular name, and shall be employed for all practical purposes to designate the Presbyterian Church in the Confederate States of America (1861-1865) and the Presbyterian Church in the United States (1865-1883).

8. Cited in *CO*, 13 October 1855, from the minutes of 27 September 1855.

9. "Our Position," *Central Presbyterian*, 11 July 1857; reprinted in Robert L. Dabney, *Discussions: Evangelical and Theological*, 2 vols. (London: Banner of Truth, 1891; reprinted, 1967), 2:176-183.

10. Ibid., p. 180.

11. *CO*, 14 June 1860. The presbytery's records have been lost. Thus, one does not know what the reaction was to the original resolution, except that the presbytery did remain within the USS.

12. Quoted in *CO*, 2 January 1862. From the context, I believe the writer was from the Synod of Nashville.

13. Ibid.

14. For a discussion of this union, see W. A. Alexander, *A Digest of the Acts and Proceedings of the General Assembly of the Presbyterian Church in the United States* . . . . (Richmond: Presbyterian Committee of Publication, 1888), sect. 632.

15. GAPCCSA, *Minutes* (1863), p. 137.

16. Cited in Thomas C. Johnson, *The Life and Letters of Robert Lewis Dabney* (Richmond: Presbyterian Publication Committee, 1903), p. 286. McGuffey, who was present during the sessions, was professor of moral philosophy at the University of Virginia and author of the popular *McGuffey's Readers*.

17. Alexander, *Digest*, sect. 627. See also unsigned article in the *Southern Presbyterian Review* 16 (1864): 253-264. Further, see *Presbyterian Historical Almanac and Annual Remembrancer* 7 (1865): 319-320.

18. For the full text of the *original* Plan of Union, see *Presbyterian Historical Almanac and Annual Remembrancer* 7 (1865): 315-322.

19. *CO*, 24 September 1863.

20. South Alabama Presbytery, MS "Minutes" (23 April 1864), pp. 7-10, PHF.

21. *CO*, 5 and 12 May 1864.

22. Ibid., 12 May 1864. This presbytery had some contact with the United Synod since the

Huntsville church lay within its geographical bounds.

23. *CO*, 19 May 1864.

24. Thompson (*Presbyterians in the South*, 2:120), quoting minutes of the Presbytery of South Carolina (May 1864), pp. 483-487.

25. For the portion of his speech that treated the doctrinal articles of the Plan of Union, see Dabney, "Speech on Fusion with the United Synod," in idem, *Discussions*. 2:298-311.

26. Ibid., p. 305.

27. Ibid., p. 307.

28. Ibid., p. 308.

29. Frank Bell Lewis, "Robert Lewis Dabney" (Ph.D. diss., Duke University, 1946), p. 87. See also Morton Howison Smith, *Studies in Southern Presbyterian Theology* (Jackson, Mississippi: Presbyterian Reformation Society and Amsterdam: Drukkerij en Uitgeverij Jacob van Campen, 1962), p. 195.

30. The fact that Joseph C. Stiles was on the Joint Committee from the Synod probably raised some eyebrows among the Assembly's men. But perhaps the wisest thing the Synod did was not placing Boyd on the Committee. He could have served. He was in his prime. But his presence would without doubt have drastically impaired the effectiveness of any report that the Conference Committee could have brought in. Boyd, however, never raised his voice against the Plan.

31. It has been pointed out through the recovery of the journal of Robert Young Russel, that the Independent Presbyterians were permitted to enter the union with Bethel Presbytery, and ultimately with the Southern Church, while still teaching the distinctive peculiarities of their doctrinal tenets. Russel commented, "These peculiarities I have imbibed from what I understand to be the teachings of the Bible, and until convinced of their being errors, can never consent to renounce or abandon them;" Robert Y. Russel, MS "Journal," 5:57-63, PHF. See Harold M. Parker, Jr., "The Independent Presbyterian Church and Reunion in the South, 1813-1863," *JPH* 50 (1972): 108; reprinted in idem, *SSPH*, p. 76.

32. The debate over the issue is well covered in the *CO*, 26 May and 2 June 1864; see also Johnson, *Dabney*, p. 287. Smith (*Studies in Southern Presbyterian Theology*, pp. 196-201) also has a good presentation of the debate.

33. GAPCCSA, *Minutes* (1864), pp. 270-276; Alexander, *Digest*, sect. 627 (pp. 401-403).

34. GAPCCSA, *Minutes* (1864), p. 276; Alexander, *Digest*, sect. 627 (p. 403).
35. *The Distinctive Principles of the Presbyterian Church in the United States, Commonly Called the Southern Presbyterian Church . . . .*, ed. E. Thompson Baird, 3rd ed. (Richmond: Presbyterian Committee on Publication, n.d.), p.x.
36. Johnson, *Dabney*, p. 286.
37. *CO*, 1 and 8 September 1864, carries the discussion of the USS.
38. Ibid., 22 September 1864. The last meeting of the USS authorized the publication of 200 copies of its minutes. No evidence exists, however, that this was ever done. Nor have the original minutes been uncovered. Thus the 1, 8, and 22 September 1864 *CO* issues carry almost the only available account of the last meeting.
39. As reported in *CO*, 10 September 1863. The same issue carried word that Piedmont Presbytery had unanimously adopted the report.
40. Reported in *CO*, 22 and 29 October and 12 and 19 November 1864, respectively.
41. Synod of Virginia [OS], *Minutes* (1864), pp. 348-349.
42. *Central Presbyterian*, 10 November 1864.
43. Ibid.
44. Synod of Virginia [OS], *Minutes* (1864), p. 362. For another description of the Virginia reunion, see *CO* 20 and 27 October 1864.
45. R. B. Woodworth, "The History of Winchester Presbytery (with Particular Reference to Evangelism)," in *Diamond Jubilee Presbyterian Church in the United States* (Pulaski, Virginia: B. D. Smith & Bros., [1936]), pp. 9-10.
46. Synod of Texas, MS "Minutes" (4, 6 May 1865), pp. 115, 122-123, PHF. See also Levi Tenney et al., "History of Central Texas Presbytery, 1854-1938," unpublished typed MS, PHF, and William Red Stuart, *A History of the Presbyterian Church in Texas* ([Austin]: Steck Co., 1936), p. 115.
47. Thomas Cary Johnson, "The Presbyterian Church in the United States," *JPHS* 1 (1901): 76; idem, *Southern Presbyterian Church*, p. 359; William Childs Robinson, *Columbia Theological Seminary and the Southern Presbyterian Church* (n.p.: n.p., [1931]), pp. 54-63; R. C. Reed, "Presbyterians: VIII In the United States and Canada: 2. Presbyterian Church in the United States," *New Schaff-Herzog Encyclopedia of Religious Knowledge*, 9:230; Smith, *Studies in Southern Presbyterian Theology*, p. 359.
48. Smith, *Studies in Southern Presbyterian Theology*, p. 35. For discussion in further depth of

this issue, see Harold M. Parker, Jr., "Southern Presbyterian Ecumenism: Six Successful Unions," *JPH* 56 (1978): 98-101; Parker, *SSPH*, pp. 199-202.

14
Postwar Reactions to the Union

Very shortly after the union took place between the United Synod and the Southern Presbyterian Church, E. Thompson Baird commented that

> a large part of the United Synod never united with the Assembly. There were elements in it that could not, or at all events did not harmonize with us. The Presbyteries of the District of Columbia and of Ozark [sic] (in Missouri) did not unite with us, and a majority of the ministers and churches of East Tennessee did not.[1]

One of the anomalies of the Civil War was the presence of pockets of population loyal to the Federal Government. East Tennessee was the largest area within the Confederacy that maintained an essential sympathy with the North. The acerbity of the conflict there between Confederate sympathizers and the pro-Union groups can hardly be underscored sufficiently. It was from out of the residual loyalist group that the New School regained much of its former ground in East Tennessee--virtually the only area in the South were such a phenomenon occurred.

One of the representative characters of East Tennessee was the Methodist clergyman-editor, William Gannaway Brownlow, more popularly known as the "Fighting Parson" of Knoxville. He was pro-slavery, but also rabidly pro-Union. When Confederate forces first marched into Knoxville, he was arrested, then released and sent to Federal lines.

When Knoxville was regained by Federal troops, he regained his former influence and power. He represented that breed of East Tennesseeans who remained intensely loyal to the government. And the former United Synod congregations in East Tennessee which returned to the New School fold after the war merely followed in his train.[2]

In March 1865, with the war still being waged, but there being no question about the outcome, Abraham Lincoln delivered his Second Inaugural Address. Lincoln pleaded that the citizens of the reunited states would exercise charity toward all, malice toward none. Within a month he would be the victim of the assassin's gun; and in about two months the General Assemblies of the Old and New School Presbyterian Churches in the North would meet. The war was over just a few days before Lincoln's martyrdom. It is most unfortunate for the cause of American Presbyterianism that the charity for which Lincoln cried was not extended to the South. As Ernest Trice Thompson commented, "The real tragedy in the relations of Presbyterians North and South occurred after the war was over."[3]

The Churches for the most part failed to offer themselves as examples to the politicians of how to bind up the wounds of a hurt and bleeding nation. Rather, through their zeal--which frequently exceeded that of the most radical of the reconstructionists--they drove the breach of sectionalism deeper than it had ever existed. The only divided Church which immediately decided to forgive and forget was the Episcopal. When the war was over, the Episcopalians managed to ignore the existence of any secession; and when the alleged *de facto* independence ceased, the seceding bishops and their dioceses returned to their places, leaving no trace of secession on their records. The undivided Cumberland Presbyterians resumed their somewhat interrupted unity with little difficulty.

It is not the actions of men that must be judged; rather, it is their intentions. And it is frequently difficult to work through the maze of deeds to seek out the roots of intent. There is no doubt that in the minds of northern Church leaders the churches and members of the South had become so depraved that only with the assistance of missionaries from north of the Ohio was there any hope of their being purged of their sins and their guilt.[4] But in reaction, the Churches in the South--Presbyterians, Methodist, and Baptists--in their efforts to reach every level of their people so identified themselves with their constituents that those from the North were viewed as meddlers, and the result was that the broken spiritual ties were not united.[5]

In the minds of some, the Reconstruction plans of Thaddeus Stevens and the "Radical Republicans" combined a genuine concern for human equality with a realistic view of the importance of the black vote for the Republican party. On the other hand, Andrew Johnson, a native of East Tennessee, sought a speedy readmission of the rebel States. In the ensuing clash between Stevens and Johnson, Reconstruction emerged as a political issue rather than as a carefully planned program.[6] In the Presbyterian Churches Old and New School, no plan had been conceived to deal effectively in any manner with the South once the war should end; thus, the meeting of the New School Assembly in 1865--as well as that of the Old School the same year--treated the recent war by declaring secession a crime and the withdrawal of the southern Churches a schism.

The difficulties of reconciliation that arose in East Tennessee among the New School Presbyterians were caused by the actions of the Assembly of 1865 and certain loyalist ministers who began returning to the area. With Union armies in control of the area in 1864, Andrew Johnson had taken the position that secession was unconstitutional, that Tennessee was never out of the Union and thus had never ceased to be a state in the Union. It was not difficult, then, for what few loyal ministers there were in Tennessee to refuse to recognize the withdrawal of the southern elements from the New School in 1857,[7] for to them the cords that bound the nation were the same as those that bound the Church.

There had been representatives from the East Tennessee Presbyteries of Holston, Union, and Kingston at the last meeting of the United Synod in August 1864, when reunion with the southern Presbyterian Church was voted unanimously by those who were present. It may thus come as a surprise that when Union and Kingston Presbyteries of the former United Synod met in September 1864, with southern Presbyterian ministers necessarily absent, they voted unanimously to reconnect themselves with the New School Assembly.[8] The Assembly then proceeded to recognize these two presbyteries as part of its body and proceeded to enroll the commissioners as members.

Union Presbytery had met on 1 September 1864 with three ministers, three elders, and a licentiate to be ordained present. It rescinded the action of its last meeting, by which it resolved not to receive or ordain any minister "who does not sympathise with the South in her present struggle for independence, or who holds that slaveholding is sinful and ought to be abolished." Eight ministers and eight elders had voted to support the motion. There had been no negative votes, and two elders had refrained from voting. Now that action had been rescinded, with Presbytery "deeply" regretting and lamenting "that so many of our brethren have been so far forgetful of the imperitive [sic] demands of patriotism and humanity as to range themselves on the side of wrong and injustice, and against their country and freedom . . . ."[9]

But it was at the meeting on 7 April 1865 that saw Union Presbytery formally reorganize itself. Nine of its members who had been absent from the previous two meetings of Presbytery, being southern sympathizers, were advised to be present at the next meeting to give an account of themselves. Then Presbytery passed a series of lengthy resolutions regarding the war, which was viewed not only as "a crime against civil government: it is a crime against God, for it is rebellion against his authority."[10]

At its Stated 1865 Fall Meeting, Presbytery approved the following resolutions:

> . . . we are of the opinion that all those who profess christianity and have aided or abetted in the late rebellion should confess their wrong before the proper church Judicatory . . . . We are . . . of the opinion that the mere fact that a man has taken the amnesty oath is not sufficient to reinstate him in the church. He owes it to the church to make a full and frank confession of his wrong and abide by and acquiesce in the decisions of its Judicatories. If a man has taken the amnesty oath and is unwilling to confess before a church Judicatory that there is wrong in rebellion it would be hard to escape the conclusion that he is insincere.

On those grounds, the Presbytery proceeded to strip officially from its roll the names of Fielding Pope, J. J. Robinson, J. M. Caldwell, C. C. Newman, J. H. Alexander, J. Hood, and Jas. H. Martin "till they give evidence of repentance for complicity in rebellion."[11] At that same meeting, W. H. Smith, who at one time was identified with the late rebellion, confessed "that events have convinced him that rebellion was wrong, and that so far he has sympathized with it he has been in the wrong," and he was recognized as a continuing member of the presbytery.

In the meantime the New School Assembly of 1865 had received Elder John J. Dixon of the Mars Hill Church in Kingston Presbytery as a commissioner. With his reception, the Assembly then passed four resolutions treating the reconstruction of the New School in the South. With two presbyteries recognized (Union and Kingston), the Assembly proceeded to reconstruct Holston Presbytery, using as a nucleus two pastors and a teacher who was working in the area. Two congregations, Greeneville and Timber Ridge, were put under the care of the presbytery. With three presbyteries, there was now a sufficient number to erect a synod; hence, the restructuring of the Synod of Tennessee, thereby giving the presbyteries a synodical relationship. The synod was directed to meet at New Market, on 12 October 1865. Conditions were also established for the erection of the Presbytery of New River, should such be possible. If not, the bounds of Holston Presbytery would be enlarged to embrace those of New River. But in no case were the presbyteries "to recognize or admit, as a member of their respective bodies, any minister known to be disloyal to the Government of the United States."[12]

The Assembly was not surprised that the Presbyteries of Union and Kingston sought admittance to that body. As early as 1864, the Permanent Committee on Home Missions had advised that the time was not too far distant when missionaries could be sent to the South and Southwest. It felt that the South would welcome them. Furthermore, the federal government had extended the Assembly an invitation to enter upon this work without delay.[13] Thus the attendance of Lamar (Union Presbytery) and Dixon (Kingston Presbytery) spurred the Assembly's hopes for re-entering the South.

The Home Missions Committee was instructed to send ten pastors to spend three months each in the South.[14] In fact, the New School had already attempted to undertake work in the old Osage Presbytery, but a raid by the Confederate Price toward Kansas City had disrupted this effort. Tennessee and Missouri, however, were specifically targeted as the areas for the Assembly to labor in.[15]

The reconstruction of Holston Presbytery serves as an example of the manner by which the New School reestablished itself. The "loyal element" of the presbytery expressed a desire to reestablish its relationship with the General Assembly. Thus, the Assembly declared the ministers who would compose the Holston Presbytery: Rufus P. Wells and Nathan Bachman, who were pastors in the presbytery, and Samuel Sawyer of the Presbytery of Ft. Wayne. Sawyer had labored in East Tennessee in the years 1848 to 1857. In 1864 he responded to a request of the Committee on Home Missions to return to reorganize churches there. He was well-known in the area.[16]

At the direction of the Assembly, Wells convened the Presbytery on 4 August 1865. A circular letter had been sent to the former New School churches and ministers in the area, inviting them to come to Presbytery's reorganization. In the letter was a word of caution advising some deep soul-searching:

> We believe that Ministers of the Gospel have encouraged, aided, and sanctioned the plans and efforts of seeking the overthrow of the best government that, under God, was ever devised by man, have committed a real wrong which should not only be confessed, but heartily forsaken, and that such Ministers should be required to refrain from the functions of their office so long as their brethren might think necessary for the honor of religion.
>
> We are well aware that we sever ourselves from brethren with whom we have taken sweet counsel, and shared the delightful labors in former years; but if they can see no wrong in giving encouragement to, and praying for the success of men that for four long years have striven by wicked and barbarous means, to break down the institutions of this land, the final experiment of the world in free government, we say let the separation take place.[17]

Rufus P. Wells, J. W. Elliott, and Samuel Sawyer were present. Samuel A. Rhea, missionary to Persia, and Bachman were listed as being absent. In addition to the Greeneville and Timber Ridge congregations, Jonesboro and New Bethel were also represented. F. A. McCorkle of the Old School Holston Presbytery was admitted to Presbytery "on the grounds that his convictions and feelings were with the Union men."[18]

The 1865 Assembly directed the Synod of Tennessee to meet in New Market, 12 October 1865.[19] The Report of the Committee of Home Missions for 1865 contained a vivid description of the work of ecclesiastical reconstruction which awaited the Church in East Tennessee:

> In Eastern Tennessee, in connection with the labors of our missionaries, the two Presbyteries of Union and Kingston, once in our connection, but separated from us the last seven years, have resolved to return to us. But the churches are greatly weakened. At the first, the loyal ministers and loyal people were either compelled to flee from the State, or, if they remained there, they did so at the peril of their lives. Subsequently, disloyal ministers and people in great numbers, following the fortunes of the rebellion, have been driven from the State. Church edifices have been used for hospitals, stripped for the service of the soldiers, or left to decay. Many of the people are impoverished.
>
> . . .
>
> The work in Missouri and Eastern Tennessee we think may be considered a fair type of what must be done in fourteen of the Southern States. Both the labor and the expense will be very great. Prejudices will yield very slowly. It will be difficult to repair or build anew church edifices, and the requisite number of ministers of Christ to supply the wants of so wide a field, it may be impossible to find. But however slow, difficult, or costly the work, we must hold ourselves in readiness to aid all that need assistance.[20]

So spoke the New School's Committee on Home Missions.

The *Christian Observer* (28 December 1865) carried a different story:

> The condition of the Church is . . . more deplorable than that of any other State. Every Presbyterian minister between the Wautauga and Hiwasse, who was engaged in the pastoral work, with perhaps two or three exceptions, has been driven away. Their places have been supplied by importations from the North and elsewhere. The ministers, severed from the congregations to which they are bound by the friendships of long years' duration, must find new homes among strangers, and thousands who have no confidence in the piety of the men engaged in the holy work of stealing their churches, are deprived of the usual means of grace. The Rev. Samuel

Sawyer, the Secretary of War of the New School Assembly, North, makes it his boast that he has driven away the ministers, and wrested from the congregations forty out of the fifty-two churches in East Tennessee. His mode of procedure is to visit the members of the congregation and session, advising them that there is a very general dissatisfaction with their minister. If he can draw from any of them an acquiescence in his opinion he has the material for establishing his charge, which is duly exaggerated and diligently repeated, until the desired strife is kindled in the congregation, and the pastor driven away. The opportunity is given him to preach until he can import a suitable man to minister to their wants.--If, on the other hand, the people vindicate the character of a beloved pastor, it is an evidence that they themselves are rebels and traitors, and they become liable to vexatious persecutions for treason, and to the more terrible retributions of mob law.

To help fill the vacancies created by such forced action, numerous men from outside the South were brought in. John Bunyan Reeve visited East Tennessee in the Interest of the Home Missions Committee in the summer of 1865. Described as "one of the best types of the grand possibilities of the Afro-American,"[21] he organized a black congregation in Knoxville. In 1867 David Morrison Wilson came to Athens' Mars Hill church from Congregational churches he had been serving in Ohio.[22] Other ministers (with their judicatory of dismission in parentheses) who came to the Synod of Tennessee within a few years after the war were Henry Cherry (Congregational Church, 1864), James A. Griffes (Presbytery of Saginaw), P. J. H. Myers (Presbytery of Brooklyn, 1866), Isaac Emory (Congregational Church, 1867), D. R. Shoop (Presbytery of Cayuga, 1867), G. W. Levere (Presbytery of Brooklyn, 1866), Calvin Waterbury (Presbytery of Dubuque, 1866), S. V. McCorkle (Belvidere Presbytery, 1866), James G. Mason (Presbytery of Nassau, 1867), and William B. Rankin (Old School, 1866).[23]

Two men from East Tennessee played a very prominent part in reorganizing the synod. Thomas J. Lamar, who found the records of the synod, led in reconstruction of the synod at New Market in 1865. "The ecclesiastical machinery was salvaged from the dump heap and set to going again."[24] The other leader was Thomas Brown. In 1858 the Synod of

Tennessee had voted almost unanimously to withdraw from the New School and connect itself to the United Synod. Only Brown's vote prevented the vote from being unanimous. His dissent was honored when, in 1865, he was called to be Moderator of the reconstructed synod. He wisely guided the new synod, which reassumed its allegiance to the New School Assembly.

The New Market meeting was attended by a dozen ministers. Among its first actions was to withdraw officially from the United Synod on the basis that the Synod of Tennessee had united with the Southern Presbyterian Church without synod's consent. In reality, the Synod of Tennessee had not met since 1862 because of the war. When the United Synod united with the Southern Church in 1864, it did so by presbyteries, not by synods. Thus, the 1865 New Market meeting was actually a reorganization of a Church court necessary in order to define anew the synod's ecclesiastical character and relations. Having disavowed the merger of the United Synod and the Southern Church, the synod expressed its desire to unite with the New School General Assembly since it had no formal relationship to a superior Church judicatory.[25]

Thus, in a matter of a decade, the Synod of Tennessee had run the ecclesiastical gamut. In 1856, it was a member of the New School General Assembly. Two years later, it became a member of the United Synod of the South, and in 1864 its constituent presbyteries had voted to unite with the Southern Presbyterian Church. In 1865, it reunited with the New School. The effects of this ecclesiastical musical chairs were evident in the synod's statistics. In 1857 the synod reported forty-two ministers, eighty-three churches, and 5,286 communicants--one of the largest synods in the New School. In 1866 it reported twenty-three ministers, forty-six churches, and 1,323 communicants (although that last figure was 2,858 the next year, reflecting a possible correction in reporting statistics).

But the damage had been done. Nor did all the losses go into the Southern Church, for in 1867 the statistics of the Presbyterian Church in the United States reported a total of thirty-two churches, thirteen ministers, and 1,639 communicants in East Tennessee. Years later, in an unsigned historical article appearing in the *Knoxville Sentinel* (16 January 1909), the author commented, "Unfortunately this division, in many cases, split churches, even in small towns. The result has been to weaken

Presbyterianism in the entire section and to diminish its influence for good."

One significant development emerged out of the reorganization of the Synod of Tennessee. In 1858 the Synod of Tennessee had transferred the control of Maryville College to the United Synod with a conditional clause, which stated that if the United Synod should ever cease to exist, the college would revert to the Synod of Tennessee--both "the control of the College and its property." In 1860 an amendment to the College's charter legalized the transfer agreement. Just eight days after the surrender of Ft. Sumter, President J. J. Robinson closed the college with a chapel service. Professors John S. Craig and Thomas Lamar supported the Union; Robinson and a tutor, the Confederacy. When the war was over, it was essentially Lamar who returned to Maryville and began the tedious process of binding up the scars which the war had inflicted on the college.[26] Friends of the school were found in the North, and a sum of $65,000 was gathered, saving the institution from extinction. A new campus site was purchased; the first of the present-day buildings was erected; and a new era began for the college.[27]

With the union of the United Synod and the Southern Presbyterian Church in 1864, the former no longer existed. Thus, the control of the college was assumed by the Synod of Tennessee. In 1872 a belated attempt was made by Robinson to gain control of the school, but in 1880 he withdrew it from the courts. The Southern Presbyterians, however, scathingly denounced the conditions whereby they lost the school, pointing out that not one of the trustees "had ever been a trustee of the college, or belonged to the old Synod of Tennessee."[28]

The inherent value of the college to the Synod of Tennessee is inestimable. Addressing the New School Assembly in 1866, Thomas Brown accorded considerable credit to this singular institution for keeping the Synod of Tennessee in the General Assembly: "The ministers educated at that institution had generally been loyal men, and had exerted an influence for good during this rebellion."[29] Forgotten in his remarks, of course, was any reference to the purge which drove many Maryville men from their pulpits and the region in the ecclesiastical reconstruction which had taken place.

The only other area in the South that the New School attempted to recover after the war was the Presbytery of Osage, largely because the Synod of Missouri had remained on the Assembly's roll throughout the war. The region the presbytery occupied was greatly devastated by the conflict. Many of the places of worship were destroyed and congregations scattered. Two ministers of the Presbytery, John McMillan and L. R. Morrison, "were murdered in cold blood by Federal soldiers." The new Missouri constitution which went into effect in September 1865 forbade all who ever had said or done anything in favor of the late Confederate government to preach or teach. When enforced, it would deprive of their pulpits what few ministers of the antebellum presbytery were left, "for all were sympathizers."[30]

L. R. Morrison was taken prisoner by Federal forces and suffered considerable maltreatment. He was

> attacked with rheumatism in so severe a form that he was a cripple for life, and could not walk or stand erect; so that when he preached, which he continued to do as long as he lived, he was seated in a chair. Thus fearless and faithful, he toiled on, meekly enduring the trials and afflictions allotted to him, until the end came, and on December 29th, 1867, in the 63rd [year] of his age being released from his labors and sufferings by death, he was called to his reward.[31]

When the war was concluded, the Presbytery of Osage was reorganized with its former boundaries, but with entirely new ministers--not unlike the situation in East Tennessee--and with new churches, also recently reorganized, composed of new members.[32] For all intents, the old presbytery had become extinct in 1861.[33] Three churches made up the new Presbytery. And, parallel to the condition in East Tennessee, ministers were imported to organize the court. At its first meeting, the reorganized presbytery directed its commissioners to the General Assembly to request that body's approval of its reorganization and to attach it to the Synod of Missouri.[34]

The New School also entered East Tennessee with a view of seeking out the black population. This effort was quite in contrast to the general thrust of the abolitionists, who still dominated New School thinking. Andrew Murray lucidly and trenchantly explained this seeming inconsistency of the abolitionist:

> The abolitionist's concept of slavery as a moral evil made him impatient with any tem-

porizing about immediate and unconditional emancipation. He felt that freedom was an end in itself, and that the slave, once freed, could solve his own problems. For this reason, the abolitionists made few plans for dealing with the complicated social and political problems which followed emancipation.[35]

The New School sent George W. LeFevre, an ordained black minister, to labor among the blacks in Knoxville. He organized the Shiloh Church, the third Presbyterian church in the city. He later began work at New Market and Maryville, thus laying the foundations for what later became the Synod of Blue Ridge.[36] Of the eleven churches organized in the score of years following the War in Union Presbytery, five were black congregations. Holston Presbytery had six black churches, Kingston Presbytery three.[37] Prior to the post-bellum period, however, churches had been integrated, with blacks enrolled as communicant members with whites.[38]

For the most part, however, the New School did little to assist freed slaves in their plight except to issue eloquent pronouncements on their behalf. Not until 1864 did the Assembly direct the Home Missions Committee to "adopt some specific arrangements, whereby the institutions of the Gospel may be given to the large and increasing number of Freedmen, who have been emancipated during the present civil war."[39] The next year, however, the Committee confessed that "the difficulties of the undertaking, and especially the lack of the right men for it, have rendered our efforts fruitless."[40] The greatest obstacle to working in the postwar South was the demand for missionary activity in the West and Northwest, where the New School found itself in competition with the Old School and Congreggationalism, leaving "little to spare for the needs of the newly-freed slaves," according to Andrew Murray.[41]

But not only was the New School incapable of supporting the work among blacks in East Tennessee; it was equally difficult to support work among the white congregations. At the 1866 Fall Meeting of the Union Presbytery, a request was sent from the Presbytery of Kingston to Union Presbytery "to suffer Rev. E. N. Sawtell, a member of [Kingston] Presbytery to remain their [sic] for the present, without a dismission from us, as our Presbytery is small."[42] At that same meeting of Presbytery, the Committee on Education reported that it had twenty-six churches, but only ten ministers, including two whose membership was in other presbyteries. The Committee then commented:

> Our appeals to our Northern brethren have not brought the needed help. The Macedonian cry, if heard, has not been heeded. Brethren, who have come into our midst, in whom our churches have trusted, & whom they would have sustained to their utmost ability, have turned from us to return to the apparently more inviting fields of the North West.[43]

The solution the Committee proposed to Presbytery was the familiar solution to raise up "a ministry at home, by the education and consecration of suitable young men of our own churches"--a procedure that had characterized Union Presbytery prior to the war.

The New School united with the Old School in the North in 1869. The last New School statistics are for that year. In 1857, the New School claimed 16,137 members in six border and southern synods; in 1869 it had 6,220 members in two synods. Of this number, 2,707 were in the Synod of Tennessee, which now embraced not only the Presbyteries of Holston, Union, and Kingston, but also those of Nashville, New Orleans, and Austin. At least, the invasion of the South after the war was partial redemption.

NOTES

1. *The Distinctive Principles of the Presbyterian Church in the United States, Commonly Called the Southern Presbyterian Church, As Set Forth in the Formal Declarations and Illustrated by Extracts from Proceedings of the Assembly, from 1861 to 1870; and Explanatory Remarks*, 3rd ed., ed. E. Thompson Baird (Richmond: Committee of Publication, 1870), p.x.

2. For a study in invective hatred, and anticipated vindictiveness, see William Brownlow, *Sketches of the Rise, Progress, and Decline of Secession, with a Narrative of Personal Adventures among the Rebels* (Philadelphia, 1862).

3. Ernest Trice Thompson, "Presbyterians North and South--Efforts Toward Reunion," *JPH* 43 (1965): 1.

4. Clifton E. Olmstead, *History of Religion in the United States* (Englewood Cliffs, New Jersey: Prentice-Hall, 1960), p. 102.

5. Robert T. Handy, *The Protestant Quest for a*

Christian America 1830-1890, Facet Books: Historical Series (Philadelphia: Fortress Press, 1967), p. 12.

6. Andrew E. Murray, *Presbyterians and the Negro--A History* (Philadelphia: Presbyterian Historical Society, 1966), p. 132.

7. Ernest Trice Thompson, *Presbyterians in the South*, 3 vols. (Richmond: John Knox Press, 1963-1973), 2:123-124.

8. One must raise the question: Did the three Tennessee presbyteries actually enter into union with the PCCSA? Technically, a negative answer must be given. For one thing, there are no minutes of any of the three presbyteries from 1863 until *after* the union was voted in August 1864. Did the commissioners at that meeting of the USS have formal commissions from their respective presbyteries, much less directions to vote for union? Or did they attend on their own appointment? Since the presbyteries had no recorded meetings from early 1863 to the Lynchburg Synod, at which time union was voted, the only conclusion which one can draw is that the Tennessee delegates were not commissioned, and had neither the right to be admitted to the Roll or to vote on the Plan of Union.

9. Presbytery of Union, typed "Minutes" (September 1864), 6:8, McClung Room, Lawson McGhee Library, Knoxville, Tennessee.

10. Ibid., (April 1865), 6:11.

11. Ibid. (Fall 1865), 6:15-16.

12. GAPCUSA [NS], *Minutes* (1865), pp. 12, 15-16.

13. Ibid. (1864), pp. 489-490.

14. Ibid. (1865), pp. 12, 14-15, 21.

15. Ibid., pp. 25, 76.

16. *Encyclopaedia of the Presbyterian Church in the United States of America: Including the Northern and Southern Assemblies*, ed.f Alfred Nevin (Philadelphia: Presbyterian Encyclopaedia Publishing Co., 1884), p. 807.

17. Holston Presbytery [NS], MS "Minutes," (18 August 1865), 2:1, Tusculum College Library, Tusculum, Tennessee.

18. The assertion that Rhea remained in the New School is one of those marginal perplexities that helps to obscure exactitude in the study of Presbyterianism at this time. He is claimed as having been received by the PCCSA with the USS in 1864, E. C. Scott, comp., *Ministerial Directory of the Presbyterian Church in the United States 1861-1941; Revised and Supplemented 1942-1950* (Atlanta: Hubbard Printing Co., 1950), p. 575. Inasmuch as Rhea died 2 September 1865, his reputed decision to return to

Postwar Reactions to the Union 283

the former New School Presbytery of Holston or remain in the one connected with the Southern Assembly is largely academic; his is, however, just one of numerous examples of the difficulties one has in endeavoring to be precise in arriving at statistics. For a description of the reorganization of Holston Presbytery, see *CO*, 28 September 1865. For a vivid description of the deplorable conditions existing within the bounds of the presbytery, see Thompson, *Presbyterians in the South*, 2:127-133.

19. GAPCUSA [NS], *Minutes* (1865), p. 15. There is some question whether the Presbytery of Kingston ever united with the Southern Presbyterian Church. The Presbytery had not met since April 1862. J. R. Nankivell (typed "Short History of Mars Hill Presbyterian Church, November 1823-November 1923," copy in the McClung Room, Lawson McGhee Library, Knoxville) claimed that "no record appears of any expressed intention or attempt on the part of Kingston Presbytery, or its constituent churches, to unite" with the GAPCCSA (p. 6). He then proposed that "Kingston Presbytery, or those *assuming voice for it as a body*, failed or refused to ratify this action of the United Synod . . . ." (p. 7, italics mine). A further instance of the confused condition in Kingston Presbytery is seen in the attendance of Elder John J. Dixon at the 1865 New School Assembly. His comment as to his reason for being there is most enlightening:

> We were without any lawful officers except myself . . . and the inducement was to take the shortest ways I could to re-construct our church, to reunite us, and to procure a minister to preach Christ and him crucified. I was not governed by the book of discipline nor the advice of the church, but acted as I thought best for the interests of the church.

The "church" was his Mars Hill congregation, not the Presbytery of Kingston! See Reba B. Boyer and Budd L. Duncan, *A History of Mars Hill Presbyterian Church* (n.p.:n.p., [1973], pp. 8-9. This footnote on Kingston Presbytery provides an interesting insight into the confused ecclesiastical conditions in East Tennessee following the war.

20. GAPCUSA [NS], *Minutes* (1865), pp. 76-77.
21. *Presbyterian Encylopaedia*, pp. 747-748.
22. Ibid., p. 1015.
23. J. E. Alexander, *A Brief History of the Synod of Tennessee, From 1817 to 1887* (Philadelphia: MacCalla & Co., 1890), pp. 143-148.

24. Samuel Tyndale Wilson, *Thomas Jefferson Lamar: A Memorial Sketch* (Maryville, Tennessee: n.p., 1920), pp. 34-35.

25. Alexander, *History of the Synod of Tennessee,*, pp. 35-36; John M. Scott, "A Brief Outline of Presbyterian History," in *The New Bethel Sesquicentennial, 1782-1932, Comprising an Account of the New Bethel Presbyterian Church, Sullivan County, Tennessee, and Various Other Matters Pertaining Thereto* (Bristol, Tennessee: n.p., 1932), p. 19.

26. Ralph Waldo Lloyd, *Maryville College: A History of 150 Years, 1819-1969* (Maryville: Maryville College Press, 1969), pp. 10-11.

27. *Maryville College Bulletin* (1946), p. 19.

28. *Central Presbyterian*, 24 July 1872, cited in Thompson, *Presbyterians in the South*, 2:127.

29. *Proceedings of the General Assemblies Old and New School Presbyterian Churches, Convened at St. Louis, May 17, 1866* (ST. Louis: n.p., 1866), p. 31. The *Maryville College Bulletin* (1903), pp. 1-32, contained an address by President S. T. Wilson, "The Debt that Presbyterians Owe to East Tennessee," which conveyed the same thought.

30. *CO*, 3 August 1865.

31. E. E. Stringfield, *Presbyterianism in the Ozarks: A History of the Work of the Various Branches of the Presbyterian Church in Southwest Missouri* (n.p.:n.p., 1909), p. 192, quoting Hill, *History of Kansas City Presbytery*.

32. John B. Hill, Presbyterianism in Missouri (n.p.:n.p., n.d.), p. 9.

33. Stringfield, *Presbyterianism in the Ozarks*, p. 189n.

34. Presbytery of Osage, MS "Minutes" (22 April 1866), pp. 1-7, Murrell Memorial Library, Missouri Valley College, Marshall, Missouri.

35. Murray, *Presbyterians and the Negro*, p. 131.

36. Clifford Merrill Drury, *Presbyterian Panorama: One Hundred and Fifty Years of National Missions History* (Philadelphia: Board of Christian Education, Presbyterian Church in the United States of America, 1952), pp. 135, 361.

37. Alexander, *History of the Synod of Tennessee*, pp. 151-155.

38. For instance, the Session of the Second Presbyterian Church, Knoxville, on 24 September 1865 dismissed eight of its "colored" members to join the First Colored Presbyterian Church of Knoxville, Second Presbyterian Church, MS "Minutes" (24 September 1865), p. 153, Archives, Second Pres-

byterian Church. This was the first record of any dismissals of blacks in the Session's minutes.

39. GAPCUSA [NS], *Minutes* (1864), p. 467.
40. Ibid. (1865), pp. 76-81.
41. Murray, *Presbyterians and the Negro*, pp. 117-118; Lewis G. Vander Velde, *The Presbyterian Churches and the Federal Union 1861-1869* (Cambridge: Harvard University Press, 1932), pp. 446-453.
42. Presbytery of Union, typed "Minutes" (Fall, 1866), 6:45.
43. Ibid.

15
Results of the Union

In spite of the forsaking of the union of the United Synod of the South with the Presbyterian Church in the Confederate States of America by some churches, presbyteries, and ministers following the war, thereby making a wedge in the total effect of the act, some significant contributions emerged from the union.

The Southern Presbyterian Church was strengthened numerically. The denomination began in 1861 with approximately 70,000 members. In the first statistics released after the war in 1866, 66,528 members were recorded and several presbyteries did not report. In spite of the almost 10,000 members the United Synod added through union, the statistics reveal a slight decrease. The war had reduced the numbers of Southern Presbyterians considerably. The loss was so considerable that even the additions which the United Synod brought did not completely compensate for it. Thus, if there was a contribution to the Southern Church in the area of statistics, one is forced to seek other categories than membership to find a more positive result.

From a statistical stance, the real strength of the union lay in the number of churches and ministers which the United Synod brought to the Southern Church. Again, in both cases of ministers and congregations, it is virtually impossible to ascertain precisely how many entered the union from the United Synod. In regard to congregations, the safest estimate would be that 190 entered the union in 1864. Subtracting the fifty-five churches in Tennessee and Osage Presbytery--not all of which were in existence in 1864--would net about 145 congregations.¹ A similar confusion exists over the precise number of ministers who entered the Southern Church through the union.² Statistics reveal that there was an average of about 120 ministers in the United Synod each year. But some of these were never formally connected with the synod, and of that number there also were those who withdrew from the Southern Church after the war. Perhaps about ninety remained in the reunited Church long enough to be effective.

Although the actual figures may be too hazy to make precise statistics, these ministers and churches, nevertheless, added new blood to the Church, and in the two decades immediately following the union they were major factors for the rapid growth of the Southern Church in that period. Many of these congregations still exist and in turn have mothered other churches. In this respect, one may conclude that the former United Synod congregations more than added an immediate contribution through the union.

The union contributed to the Southern Church some prominent ministers and families whose influence extended for many years. Some of the ministers, such as George Eagleton and Samuel A. King, served into the twentieth century. Two future Moderators of the Southern Assembly came from the ranks of the United Synod: Samuel A. King and Jonathan Waverly Bachman. For many years, Michael D. Kalopothakes was a missionary to Greece. Former United Synod ministers and elders served subsequent meetings of the Assembly as members and chairmen of important committees. But the real strength was in the pulpits which the ministers occupied so faithfully for years. As pastors, they brought large numbers to the Church as they also labored in the work of presbyteries and synods.

A second contribution to the union was the consolidation of Presbyterianism in the South. After this union, only two Presbyterian groups of any size were left in that region: the Cumberland Presbyterian Church and the Associate Reformed Presbyterian Church. In many areas, particularly in Virginia, Tennessee, and Mississippi, overlapping work was eliminated as former congregations of the United Synod and the Assembly were united. And had the New School not successfully wooed the Tennessee presbyteries back to her fold after the war, it is very doubtful whether the northern Churches would have ever acquired a toehold in the South.

A third contribution was the spirit which pervaded the union. This was a union between two Churches that had lived in separate houses for over a quarter of a century. The union, however, was consummated in the midst of the greatest conflict this continent had ever experienced. It would take their Northern counterparts five more years--and years of military peace--before they could reunite. It may be charged that it was the war that brought the two Southern groups together; if true, it was nevertheless an event that failed to unite the same Churches in the North.

A fourth contribution was the slight bending of the Southern Church in its theological position. In each of the six unions which the Southern Church experienced, with the exceptions of those with the Synods of Kentucky (1869) and Missouri (1874), the Southern Church made some concessions. The very fact that the first draft of the Plan of Union contained a doctrinal section, which was quickly dropped when opposition developed, reveals a condescending posture respecting the Southern Old School Church. These doctrinal articles, which were actually interpretations of the Confession of Faith, could have been a stumblingblock to the Southern Church in later years, had they stood. The Assembly revealed its wisdom, although not its unanimity, in cutting out this section from the Plan of Union. It permitted the Southern Church to receive those who adhere to the spirit of the Constitution, if not the letter. At the same time, it did not necessitate the Confession to be rewritten, nor was there any need of a "popular" explanation of the Confession of Faith, which would interpret any of the doctrines.

The New School South was never marred with the doctrinal looseness with which the Old School charged the wing of the Church north of the Ohio. The men in the South had withdrawn in sympathy for New School judicatories that had been exscinded without trial, not because of doctrinal affinity. A score of years later they withdrew from the New School because of slavery agitation and the legislation connected with it which the New School Assembly persisted in adopting. Although almost a third of them had studied theology at Union Seminary in New York,[3] only Andrew Hunter Holmes Boyd, who had studied at Yale, could be labelled "New School" in the strictest doctrinal sense. His death shortly after the reunion probably removed from the scene a possible source of any doctrinal agitation or later embarrassment that may have arisen.

Finally, a most enduring contribution to the union was the acquisition of the *Christian Observer*. It was the only "institution" which the Southern Church received. Here it was not so much physical property which came with the union as it was a respected medium of religious journalism. Maryville College reverted to the New School; the funds raised for the United Synod's seminary in Virginia were probably invested in Confederate bonds, for no record of them has been found; and apart from a single missionary in Greece, the United Synod had little other tangible benevolent work. But the influence of the *Christian Observer*, together with the integrity of its editor, Amasa Converse, can scarcely be adequately estimated. In the next decade it led the fight for every organic union which the Southern Church experienced. The addition of this weekly independent religious paper, plus the contributions the addition of congregations and ministers effected, made the union with the United Synod the most significant one that the Southern Presbyterian Church ever consummated in the nineteenth century.

The war left the South prostrate. A third of the Presbyterian church edifices were destroyed. Others were left unattended or in poor repair. The wealth of the region, formerly invested in slaves and Confederate bonds, was reduced to a fraction of its antebellum worth. But from the union of these two branches of the Presbyterian Church emerged a Church that rose above the moral and political confusion and despair of the day as a tower beckoning people to her ministry and leadership. It molded a united Southern Presbyterianism which alone could have overcome the hurdles of discouragement and desolation.

NOTES

1. The only comprehensive statistics in tabulated form this writer has found were compiled by Joseph M. Wilson, editor of the *Presbyterian Historical Almanac and Annual Remembrancer* 9 (1867): 464-467. In statistical tables he listed 193 congregations "in connection with the [United] Synod at the time of union," and forty-three others listed in connection with the Church at one time or another. The largest number of churches ever connected with the United Synod at any one time was 233. Wilson's tables, however, have some glaring errors, the chief one being the inclusion of the

congregations of the Presbytery of District of Columbia as having been in connection with the United Synod.

2. Ibid., pp. 464-466. Wilson lists five categories of ministers who were in the United Synod: those who joined the Presbyterian Church in the United States (72); those who joined the New School (26); those who joined the Old School (9); those who died while in connection with the United Synod (12); and those who seemingly had no connection with any branch of the Presbyterian Church (24). These tables, also, reveal errors. For instance, A. H. H. Boyd is listed as having died while still in connection with the United Synod. He was entered on the Roll of Winchester Presbytery of the Southern Presbyterian Church in August 1865. He died in December. Of the twenty-four ministers Wilson listed as having died while in connection with the USS, the *Ministerial Directory of the Presbyterian Church, U. S., 1861-1941*, comp. E. C. Scott (Austin, Texas: Von Boeckmann-Jones Co., 1942) lists twelve as having been on the rolls of the Southern Church. Of the seventy-two Wilson listed as having united with the Southern Church, Scott does not list four in the *Directory*. These comparisons illustrate the difficulty one has in arriving at statistical accuracy. Wilson's total of the five categories is 155 ministers who were in connection with the USS at one time or another. The most rational statistics that I have found on the statistics of the United Synod at the time of union are from the *Free Christian Commonwealth* (19 April 1866): 165 churches, 110 ministers, and 11,448 members. This does not imply that these were the totals who entered the union, but merely the statistics *at the time of union*.

3. This figure was arrived at by compiling the seminaries attended by the ministers of the USS who entered the Southern Assembly, and whose names are listed in Scott, *Directory, 1941*. Of those listed, twenty-seven received their theological degrees from Union Seminary in New York, ten attended Princeton, seven attended Union Seminary in Virginia, six attended Maryville, four attended Lane, two attended Andover, and one attended Columbia Theological Seminary. Six studied theology privately, and fifteen had no formal seminary training.

16

The United Synod of the South: An Appraisal

In 1843 the New School in the South embraced six synods, eighteen presbyteries, 131 ministers, 172 churches, and 12,346 members. The number of communicants in the South constituted about 10 percent of the total in the New School Church. This figure never increased, but continued a gradual decline. This chapter assesses this movement which culminated in the emergence of the United Synod of the Presbyterian Church in the United States of America. It also attempts to explain the reasons for the failure of the New School movement in the South in general, the United Synod in particular, to grow numerically as did the New School counterpart in the North as well as the Old School Presbyterian Church. The causes for this failure are discussed under four major categories: demographic, ecclesiastical, heterogeneity, and historical.

DEMOGRAPHIC

The South was not noted as a region of large cities in the antebellum period. Yet the inability of the Southern New School to make much headway in what urban centers there were certainly must be considered a major factor in accounting for the inability to keep apace with other Presbyterian bodies.[1] Of the eleven "largest" cities in the South in the 1850 census, the New School had congregations in only six; and of the fifteen "large" cities, congregations were in only two. Successful efforts were made during these years to establish congregations in Nashville and Mobile, but these were counterbalanced by the inability to form congregations in Louisville and Lexington, Kentucky. The major urban southern Presbyterian pulpits were occupied by Old School preachers. In only three southern state capitals were New School congregations to be found--Richmond, Jackson, and Nashville--the last where a congregation was not established until 1857.

The major new church development was in the rural areas. In fact, the seminaries of the southern New School were located in out-of-the-way, isolated areas, unlike the northern New School schools which were situated in New York, Philadelphia, Cincinnati, and Auburn. The Maryville seminary served a very localized clientele. The attempt of the Synod of Kentucky to found a seminary in rural Woodford County is further indication of the inability, the hesitancy to penetrate the urban wall, for it was supposed that this school would be used for training Kentucky men for Kentucky pulpits--all located in small towns, villages, or open country sites. The venerable Thomas Cleland had trained some fifteen men for the ministry in his open-country New Providence Church. These men in turn entered rural pastorates.

The antebellum South was not only rural, but its population was scattered. The congregations for the most part tended to be small, serving as they did, not a farm-oriented rural area such as existed in the North, but a plantation-centered demography whose population lacked the density of the northern rural areas. Thus, the inability to get into the city meant that the southern New School had to be content with smaller congregations. In 1856, for instance, there were 249 churches in the six southern synods, not including the District of Columbia Presbytery. Only forty-four of the churches (17 percent) had 100 member or more. The average membership in all churches was 58.43. Entire southern presbyteries reported not one church with 100 members. Of the total membership reported that year, 6,806 members were in the forty-four congregations of 100+ members, giving them an average of 154.68, but only 37.38 average members for the other 205 congregations. Hence, 17 percent of the congregations contained 46.7 percent of the membership. Of the forty-four churches with 100 or more members, fifteen were located in East Tennessee.

The Southern New School was also demographically parochial. One could begin with Richmond, go across to the Shenandoah Valley at Winchester, go down the Valley in a southwesterly direction through East Tennessee to the Huntsville vale, and then skip over to the rich delta region around Jackson, Mississippi, and embrace the greater number of members, churches, and ministers. A closer examination of that geographical distribution reveals, however, that the churches were in clusters, not really distributed over a wide area. In Kentucky, for instance, all the churches in the Presbytery of Providence were found in just two contiguous counties. In the Presbytery of Newton (Mississippi), most of the churches were stretched along the railroad that extended from Columbus, Mississippi, to Mobile, Alabama. The Presbytery of Texas consisted of five small congregations clustered in what is now the Dallas-Fort Worth area. The East Tennessee Presbyteries of Holston, Union, and Kingston were located for the most part in the valley of the Holston-Tennessee Rivers.

Large areas of the South were bereft of any New School congregations. South Carolina, Florida, West Virginia, and Louisiana had no churches; North Carolina had churches in only two or three counties; in Kentucky the churches were located in the central part of the state on a line extending from Maysville down to the Barrens around Bowling Green; the western third of Tennessee had no churches; nor did the southeastern two-thirds of Alabama. In Georgia, two attempts to establish New School presbyteries failed. This geographical limitation marked the New School in the South, the presbytery in Texas and the two in Missouri being the only exceptions.

A third demographic aspect of the Church which must be considered was its ministerial leadership. In any movement leaders are valuable. But as they die, they must be replaced, or the institution will suffer dire consequences, whether the institution be commercial, educational, or ecclesiastical. In every instance, there were strong men in the various southern New School elements that protested the actions of 1837. These were men around whom the southern New School churches and presbyteries clustered. The learned, brilliant, and youthful A. H. H. Boyd of Winchester Presbytery is an example. His entire ministry was spent in that presbytery, from the time of his ordination shortly after the rift of 1837 until his agonizing death in December 1865. After his demise, no one rose to take his place.

Or consider the case of the Kentucky triumvirate: Joseph C. Stiles, Thomas Cleland, and Archer C. Dickerson. Around Stiles, the Presbytery of

Harmony had been organized; around Cleland, the Presbytery of Providence; and around Dickerson, the Presbytery of Green River. Stiles moved from Kentucky in the early 1840s, and no leadership emerged to replace him. He was a brilliant man: an active ecclesiastic, a powerful pulpiteer, an intelligent theologian, and an ideal "idea" man. He was apparently irreplaceable. The death of the aged Cleland in 1857 brought the demise of the Presbytery of Providence as well as the Synod of Kentucky. In 1838 Archer C. Dickerson had penned one of the most lucid statements yet found from a southern pen in which he explained his rationale for withdrawing from the Old School jurisdiction. But the continuous Old School pressures on him and his presbytery finally brought him to the place where he opted for reunion rather than carry on the fight. With his spirited leadership broken, no one from the ranks rose to claim his place. Thus the Presbytery of Green River folded its tents.

Further, very little leadership developed in the score of years following the exscision of 1837. Most of the leaders had surfaced prior to that incident--Frederick A. Ross, Isaac Anderson, William Hill, C. W. Howard--to name but a few. The southern element of the New School did not raise up an indigenous ministry. It continually called on its ministerial capital but did not replenish the resources which it was using up. For the most part, the southern New School/United Synod pens were dry. Few were the books they published; few the pamphlets they wrote. A handful of men in East Tennessee did publish on two different occasions the apologetic *Calvinistic Magazine*. Another East Tennessee group for a decade published the *Presbyterian Witness*, a weekly whose office wandered from Bristol to Knoxville until it finally folded. Thus, when the men in the United Synod reunited with the Old School in 1864, they entered the union as beloved pastors, devoted to their people. But only one would ever become a seminary professor, and the double-edged pen of Frederick A. Ross had lost its sharpness.

ECCLESIASTICAL

The ecclesiastical reasons for the failure of the Southern New School/United Synod can be placed into two categories: external and internal. The external are those factors which lay outside the Church, factors over which the Church had no control. The internal were matters related to the manner by which the Church handled its own affairs, wherein the Church failed to exert proper management.

One of the external factors that definitely hindered the Church was the large Old School opposition in the South. The Old School was a very able and competent opponent, an adversary that not only outnumbered the New School in the South, but that was composed of a corps of outstanding theologians, ministers, and ecclesiastics who were, and still are, recognized as leading Presbyterian lights in nineteenth-century Presbyterian history through both the war and the subsequent days of the Reconstruction of the Southern Presbyterian Church.

There was simply no one in the United Synod comparable to James Henley Thornwell, the magnetic Benjamin M. Palmer, the astute Charles C. Jones, the visionary John L. Girardeau, the statesman John N. Waddell, the versatile Robert L. Dabney, and a host of others--all cut from Presbyterian cloth. Ecclesiastics, preachers of the first order, together they formed a coterie of leadership which guided the Old School ship through the shoals of the 1840s and 1850s, steadied the helm during the war, and successfully tended to the battered ship of Church after Appomattox was a fact.

So prestigious were the pulpits of the Old School South that its churches experienced little difficulty in attracting outstanding graduates from Princeton and other northern seminaries. Further, the Old School had made peace with slavery. In the New School South, the odious presence of slavery discouraged men from the North who might otherwise consider laboring south of the Ohio. The two Old School seminaries in the South--Union Seminary at Hampden-Sydney, Virginia, and the one at the more urban setting at Columbia, South Carolina--produced scores of well-trained, theologically sound, sociologically acclimated graduates to fill its pulpits. This condition contrasted greatly to the New School seminaries at Maryville and Woodford County, which were incapable of meeting the churches' demands for ministers.

Southern Old Schoolmen were churchmen of the highest order. The Old School in 1837 set about to organize ecclesiastical boards under the direct, immediate control of the Church for carrying out the mission of the Church. Further, its members supplied funds for home mission sustentation, for new church development, for assisting young men preparing for the ministry. The New School, on the other hand, for a decade and a half stood hat in hand before such interdenominational groups as the American Home Missionary Society. The refusal of the New School to act as a responsible denomination did irreparable harm to the South.

Old School pastors and officers developed the grace of liberality among their people. Their church edifices were more sumptuous, their pastors better paid, their missionaries better supported. The Old School had learned to "give of their sons to bear the message glorious, give of their wealth to speed them on their way"--an attitude which the southern New School never nourished.

With the exception of the *Presbyterian Witness* and the *Christian Observer*, the other Presbyterian papers in the South were Old School, each in the hands of militant, competent Old School journalists-theologians. For a season the New School Synod of Kentucky endeavored to publish its own paper as a defense against the Old School onslaught in the Blue Grass state, but the Bardstown-published *Protestant and Herald*, edited by such scions as Nathan Rice and the Breckinridges, was too formidable an adversary.

In 1845, the Old School made its definitive statement on the issue of slavery. The New School, on the other hand, from 1840 until the withdrawal of the southern synods in 1857, annually agitated the subject. The constant bickering, the strident debates that issued at each Assembly, the continuous harangues from pulpits and in the New School papers--all certainly did not enhance the posture of the New School in the South. The voices of the southern men were scarcely audible amid the din and roar that accompanied the debates at each meeting of the Assembly. Forgotten was the fact that these men had moved deliberately into the ranks of the New School because of a principle; forgotten was the fact that nowhere in the doctrinal standards of the Church was slavery ever referred to as a sin or as a disqualification for church membership; rather, the exercises in ecclesiastical bloodletting seemed to the men from the South to have but a singular purpose: to humiliate them, to classify them as second-class Presbyterians, weak in numbers and equally weak in sensitivity over social issues.

Conditions were not thus in the Southern Old School. That element comprised a large percentage of the Old School membership, not a majority, but a strong minority. Further, the Old School had worked out its apologia for slavery. In the South, the facile pens of such men as Thornwell, Palmer, Girardeau, and Charles C. Jones produced masterpieces of the southern philosophical defense of the institution of slavery. It is not by chance that in its first General Assembly Southern Old Schoolmen proclaimed to the world that it was the mission of the newly-formed Presbyterian Church in the Confederate States of America to conserve the institution of slavery.[2] Antebellum southern Old School commissioners did not return from their annual peregrinations to the Assembly to defend their Assembly's latest pronouncements on slavery. Such, however, was not the fate of the southern New Schoolmen, who agonized year after year under increasingly antislavery, abolitionist northern-dominated legislation that the New School Assembly passed. Only Ross's *Slavery Ordained of God* represented the major published southern New School position on slavery.

Yet the New School did not always stand in the shadows of the Old. Where the southern New School seriously considered its mission, where it made a genuine, sincere effort to present a truly Presbyterian stance, it was frequently stronger than the Old School. The classic instance, of course, was in East Tennessee, where very few Old School congregations remained. The involvement of the southern New School in employing the "new measures" on the local scene helped congregations to grow. Even in those situations where the two denominations labored in the same community, and where they frequently used the same edifice, it was not at all uncommon for the New School segment to be the stronger numerically. But the weakness lay, nevertheless, in the overall condition throughout the South, coupled by the Church's inability to reach out and form new congregations concomitant with the total growth of the South.

One major factor in this lack of intensive home mission activity lay in the peculiar ecclesiasticism--or lack of it--in the New School Church. Following the Division of 1837, the Old School quickly adopted what existing formal ecclesiastical structures existed, and continued operating them as boards of the Church. The New School continued its policy of supporting the voluntary agencies, largely in conjunction with the Congregationalists, who had cooperated with the Presbyterians in the volunteer philosophy from the days of the Plan of Union of 1801. New School contributions went to the AHMS, as they had been doing for over a decade prior to the Division. The Congregationalists, however, had no churches in the South, and the powers that controlled the AHMS developed a gradual coolness toward home missionary activity in the South, solely because of slavery.

Newly commissioned home missionaries, usually fresh from the northern seminaries, and almost all of whom were northern-bred, were most reluctant to go south because of the possibility that the AHMS would not support them. There was also an administrative problem: did the missionary labor under the direction of the Church or the AHMS? The AHMS urged the latter position, much to the chagrin of the presbyteries. A cursory review of the number of missionaries laboring in the South under the umbrage of the AHMS reveals that only a handful of the total number were so geographically engaged. In the fiscal year 1856-1857, for instance, of a total of 974 missionaries who received support that year, six labored in North Carolina, one in Kentucky, and one in Tennessee. That year the AHMS voted to discontinue support to any missionary serving a church that had slaveholders on its roll. Thus, what had been a mere trickle of financial assistance was now finally cut off.

The New School's establishment of a denominationally controlled home missions program came too late to give effective assistance to the South. After the formation of the United Synod, a Committee of Domestic Missions was organized; but it scarcely had time to function before the war disrupted its program. The Southern Aid Society had been formed in 1853, composed of northern men who were disturbed and concerned over the financial plight of the southern wing of the New School. Although not all the funds of the SAS were sent exclusively to southern New School churches, a perusal of the *Fifth Annual Report* (1858) reveals that about 80 percent of the $8,890 distributed did go to support New School ministers or judicatories in the South. By the end of the first five years of operations, the SAS had contributed a total of $34,345 to home missions in the South. These funds greatly assisted the southern New School; however, the support came too late to give effective, long-range assistance.

Internally, the Southern New School faced ecclesiastical difficulties of gargantuan proportions. By far the most significant was the Church's poor track record in stewardship. Not only did the support of the local church suffer, but so also did the denomination's program after the United Synod was formed. Further, one must question the propriety of the SAS's pumping thousands of dollars into a program which the members themselves did not see fit to support.

The United Synod of the South: An Appraisal   299

A second internal ecclesiastical problem the Church confronted was its poor, if not somewhat belated, institutional development. Because the New School was a minority almost everywhere among southern Presbyterians, it was able to carry with it only the seminary and college at Maryville when the various judicatories withdrew in the 1830s and 1840s. All other Presbyterian institutions in the antebellum South were controlled by other Presbyterian bodies. It was not until after the formation of the United Synod in 1858 that any real effort was made by the southern New School elements to establish institutions worthy of the name.

Even then there was considerable waste of effort, particularly in the matter of the organization and location of the proposed United Synod seminary. As early as the Cassville Convention in 1840, Isaac Anderson of the Maryville seminary had proposed that the Convention entertain the invitation to make the seminary and college at Maryville the theological and literary institutions of the proposed sectional Church. Before that decade was through, the debacle of attempting to organize and operate the ill-fated seminary in Kentucky had been experienced. In spite of the adequate physical facilities at Maryville, the United Synod decided to raise funds for buildings and endowment of a seminary in Virginia. This proposal, cut short by the exigencies of the war and the subsequent merger with the Southern Presbyterian Church, was a foolish one. It simply disregarded what was already a very successful operation in Maryville. Duplication of effort on the one hand, refusal to recognize existing institutions on the other, led to an institutional maze which resulted in ecclesiastical confusion and horrible waste of sparse funds.

Perhaps the greatest internal difficulty which the southern New School confronted, however, was its decision to form the United Synod. In 1857 the southern delegates walked out of the New School Assembly over the antislavery agitation. This action placed the New School judicatories and ministers in the South in a perplexing quandary. For years they had maintained that the discussion of slavery did not belong in the Church courts, that it was a purely secular matter. A score of years earlier, they had withdrawn from the Old School in sympathy with the exscinded northern judicatories, which, they believed, had been cut off from the Church unfairly. In Missouri and Kentucky, the confusion following the 1857 Assembly created chaos rather than order. Before long, Kentucky lay in its ecclesiastical grave, and Missouri was greatly handicapped in its undertakings.

The United Synod at its organizational meeting had high aspirations for the future. It quickly passed legislation that prohibited the discussion of slavery in the Church. By taking such a stand, it hoped that it would draw other Presbyterians--Old School as well as disgruntled northern New School-men--into its ranks. The hope never materialized. Instead of some Old School congregations joining the United Synod, just the opposite occurred: some churches forsook the United Synod to go Old School. To add to the confusion, the United Synod overtured the Old School for union. This action was spurned. But the very fact that it was built into the agenda of the first meeting of the United Synod created considerable consternation within the ranks of the new Church.

Thus, the period of May 1857 to April 1858 was a time of turmoil, as sessions, presbyteries, even synods sought to assess their ecclesiastical relations. The first statistics of the United Synod reported four synods, fifteen presbyteries (including the Presbytery of District of Columbia, which was never officially connected with the Synod), 113 ministers, 197 churches, and 10,205 communicants--a loss of fifty-two churches and 4,346 members from the year before. These losses, due to the "times of troubles," were never made up by the United Synod.

The indecision of the United Synod to wait so long before getting organized could only have been costly. The Richmond Convention of August 1857, which set up the organizing meeting of the United Synod the following April, had been well attended. But for many delegates it was at best a look-see experience, an ecclesiastical window-shopping expedition. Many delegates returned home, not satisfied with what they had seen and heard. Had the Convention not proposed organic union with the Old School, perhaps things would have worked out better. After all, many in the southern New School were still smarting from the treatment accorded "Constitutional" Presbyterians a score of years earlier. Then when the proposed union was brought to the floor of the Old School Assembly in 1858, it was summarily turned down. The indecision over whether to unite with the Old School or take up the full work of a new Church proved very costly indeed.

HETEROGENEITY

At best, the New School was a congeries of diversity. Its leadership reflected this quandary. The numerous factors which led to the 1837 Division each had its own constituency and leaders within the group. Quite in contrast was the Old School. When the New School emerged after the controversy which extended over a year, the Old School was monolithically structured--doctrinally, ecclesiastically, socially--while the minority New School was composed of numerous sub-groups held together only by the experience of exscision. The only term adequate to describe the morass is "heterogeneity." This characteristic which marked the New School was the disdain of the Old.

New School heterogeneity was exhibited in numerous ways: doctrine, ecclesiastical functionalism, evangelistic procedures, abolitionism, interdenominational cooperation. In addition, there were those in the New School whose only grounds for being in the ranks were those of sympathy. The southern New School element fell into this latter category. Theologically, the men of the South were much closer to the Old School as a group than they were to men like Albert Barnes or Lyman Beecher. Socially and culturally, on the slavery issue they stood almost identically with the Old School, rather than with the abolition-raked ranks of the New School.

Treating its southern constituents a degree above ecclesiastical pariahs, the New School Assemblies never appointed men from the South to important committee positions. Only twice, in St. Louis and Washington, did the New School Assembly ever meet in slaveholding territory. Never was a man from the South invited to a college or theological faculty in a northern New School institution. The constant barrage of overtures regarding slavery from every corner of the North, the paucity of home missionary funds dispersed in the South, the contemptuous disdain by which northern men shunned the empty pulpits in the South, and the urbane, sophisticated manner that characterized the men at the North--all tended to make higher the walls that separated the two regions of the Church.

Nor were all hanging together in the South. For there was also a diversity there which tended to prevent the southern New School from experiencing ecclesiastical homogeneity. From the beginning, the major concentration of the southern New School was in East Tennessee. The ministers of that area differed from other New School clergy in two respects. For one thing, East Tennessee was not avidly proslavery. Antislavery forces had always been strong there. Thus, the New School element there, which considerably outnumbered the Old School, tended to support the New School sentiment on the abolition issue. It did deplore, however, the radicalism of the abolitionists as their policy developed in the late 1830s and 1840s. The second factor that set the East Tennessee ministers apart from their New School confreres in the South was their theological Hopkinsianism. One may well hazard the proposition that the major reason for the southern New School men to shun the college and seminary at Maryville was due to its Hopkinsian taint.

There was a certain geographical element that entered into this matter of heterogeneity. As one reads the documents relating to the southern New School in general, the United Synod in particular, one receives the impression that the concerns of one portion of the Church were not those of other portions. "What has Virginia to do with Texas?" may not have been specifically raised, but certainly the psychological mentality existed for raising such a question. More concretely, this frame of mind was unconsciously built into the constitution of the United Synod at its formation when various safeguards were added that would encourage this ecclesiastical frame of mind.

The supreme judicatory, for instance, would be a "general synod," with advisory capacity only, as the following statement from the Declaration of Principles indicates:

> According to the Constitution of the Presbyterian Church, the General Assembly is an advisory and judicial body. It possesses no legislative power in the proper acceptance of the term. It cannot enact laws that are binding on the lower judicatories. The Constitution expressly provides that all ecclesiastical rules or changes in the Constitution shall receive the approval of a majority of the Presbyteries before they can be obligatory upon the churches. This "United Synod," therefore, disclaims the right to legislate, or to make laws upon any subject that will be binding upon the lower judicatories, or upon any portion of the Presbyterian Church.

The practical effects of this attitude were seen, for instance, in the failure of congregations to support the missionary to Greece. This philosophy of church polity placed great emphasis on the role of the lower judicatories, especially the presbyteries. Thus, there was not the feeling of denominational unity, denominational cohesion, which must characterize a Church.

The end of the southern New School/United Synod came when it united with the Old School South in 1864. The union required some accommodation on the part of both groups. There is no question that southern Presbyterianism was greatly strengthened through it. The fact that the union was worked out through wartime exigencies stands as a tribute to the men who planned it and worked through its consummation. At the same time, it must be recognized that the United Synod brought into the union fewer churches, fewer ministers, and fewer members than it had claimed in 1843 when the first reliable souther New School statistics were available.

According to the most reliable sources, the United Synod at the time of union consisted of 110 ministers, 165 churches, and 11,488 communicants. In 1843 it claimed 131 ministers, 172 churches, and 12,346 communicants. In the twenty-one-year period the Church in the South had failed to gain in each category. Further, the entire Synod of Kentucky had been formed and lost during this period, and only one presbytery remained out of the entire synod in Missouri.

The entire New School had 1,263 ministers in 1843, 1,644 in 1864; 1,286 churches in 1843, 1,442 in 1864; and 120,645 members in 1843, 138,074 in 1864--and these figures for 1864 reflect the losses suffered by the 1857 withdrawal of the southern synods. In 1843, the Old School had 1,434 ministers, 2,265 in 1864; 2,092 churches in 1843, 2,626 in 1864; and 129,137 members in 1843 and 231,960 in 1864--and the figures for 1864 reflect the large losses the Old School suffered by the withdrawal of its southern presbyteries in 1861.[4]

These statistics point out that the other Presbyterian bodies gained in each category in the period 1843 to 1864 except the southern New School/United Synod.

HISTORICAL

There were also historical events that overpowered the United Synod. Two of these in particular will be elaborated upon: the Church's position on slavery and the Civil War. The major weakness of the United Synod in history was its formation on a platform with but a single plank: the issue of domestic slavery was not to be discussed on the floors or in the halls of the Church's judicatories. In spite of the optimism that such a platform would attract churches and even presbyteries in the North, such optimism was never rewarded with reality. A sect has often been defined as a religious group that emphasizes one doctrine or position out of harmony or balance with the rest of the teachings of normative religious expression. The issue may be the mode of baptism, tithing, form of government, the nature of the sacraments, but whatever it is, however it manifests itself, when it is extended to the degree that the total harmony of teaching and practice is distorted by this one belief or act, that group is a sect, not a Church.

In retrospect, one must question the wisdom of forming a Church on a one-plank platform such as marked the United Synod's effort to erect a Church on the platform of silence in respect to slavery. A score of years earlier, a similar psychosis had captured the southern New School, when it withdrew in sympathy with those who had been exscinded without trial, and for no other reason. For two decades following the decision, which was nomistic in its determination, southern New Schoolmen must have felt that they were not really a part of the larger body. They differed in theology, in the stance on abolitionism, in the total sociological position of the New School. But, sect-like, they maintained their fidelity to the New School, the issue of Constitutionalism overriding all other considerations.

To close their eyes to the issue of domestic slavery at this point in history was like people on the deck of a ship watching a tidal wave approaching while refusing to believe that it is possible that it has the power to destroy the vessel on whose decks they are standing. The very fact that in the short period between the Richmond Convention in August 1857, when the doctrine of silence on the issue of slavery was first propounded, and the formal organization of the United Synod in Knoxville the following April, witnessed the withdrawal of numerous ministers and congregations from the New School to go Old School, to say nothing of the demise of judicatories--these signals should have been heeded. They were not. And while the terms of the Old School for union in 1858 were unbending, at the same time one must ponder whether the alternative to launch a new ship with but a single mast was the sensible alternative. If history teaches nothing else, it demonstrates that a monistic solution to a complex problem is in the end vain and foolish.

A major error of the United Synod was its sect-like approach to its origin, compounded by the destructive force of the war which simply overwhelmed the young Church before it was firmly established. For the war prevented the "best laid plans" of the new Church from materializing. Hardly three years had passed from the time the Church was formed before it was caught up in the maelstrom which engulfed the South. The Synod could not meet in 1862 because so many of the commissioners were behind Federal lines. Its last meeting had to be changed both in time and place because of similar conditions. By the end of 1863, the constituent presbyteries in the Synod of Mississippi were cut off from the rest of the presbyteries in the United Synod.

The political confusion which prevailed between the 1860 and 1861 meetings contributed greatly to the Church's difficulties. The Old School in the South was not as greatly affected because it was well-rooted ecclesiastically, theologically, functionally. It was prepared for the exigencies the war created. Its leadership was mature. Its churches were well-established. For decades nothing had disturbed their calm. The Old School entered the war with confidence. Throughout the years of conflict, it experienced despair but never defeat. It emerged from the War "bloody but unbowed." Its institutions, though largely in ruins, were still intact. Its leadership was thin, but still viable.

The storm of war hit the United Synod like a hurricane attacking freshly planted tomato vines. Hardly had the roots been set when the onslaught began. The buds of planning were whipped from the stem, and the fruit never appeared. Chaos came from every corner. The ambitious hopes for the seminary never materialized. The well-devised plans for home missions hardly left the drawing board. The war seemed to capsulate those decades when the southern New School and then the United Synod held out their hands for gifts from the North. Those gifts were no longer forthcoming. The Church had failed to develop responsible stewardship. The financial burdens, which the twin foes of the battlefield and inflation developed, became increasingly weighty and burdensome.

Thus, the overture for union which came from the Old School arrived at a most propitious time. By 1863, when the Old School offered its hand, only the most naive could fail to see the ultimate course of the war. And by the time the United Synod assembled in 1864 to act upon the formal proposition, less than a year would be given the Confederacy to act out its drama. The little handful which met in Lynchburg in August 1864 to consider the altered Plan of Union represented but a fraction of those who had met with such optimism just six years earlier in Knoxville to launch the new Church. They really had no alternative but to accept the gracious hand which had been extended them. Indeed, the war had taken its toll on the infant Church.

NOTES

1. For an in-depth study of this thesis, see Harold M. Parker, Jr., "The Urban Failure of the Southern New School Presbyterian Church," *Social Science Journal* 14 (1977): 139-148; reprinted in idem, *SSPH*, pp. 180-189.

2. For the text of the "Address to All the Churches of Jesus Christ throughout the Earth," see GAPCCSA, *Minutes* (1861), pp. 51ff.; W. A. Alexander, *A Digest of the Acts and Proceedings of the General Assembly of the Presbyterian Church in the United States* . . . . (Richmond: Presbyterian Committee of Publication, 1888), sect. 611; Robert Ellis Thompson, *A History of the Presbyterian Churches in the United States*, 2nd ed., The American Church History Series, ed. Philip Schaff (New York: Charles Scribner's Sons, 1900), pp. 388-406. An abbreviated form is found in Maurice W. Armstrong, Lefferts A. Loetscher, and Charles A. Anderson, eds., *The Presbyterian Enterprise: Sources of American Presbyterian History* (Philadelphia: Westminster Press, 1956), pp. 212-218.

3. See Appendix "B" Declaration of Principles of the United Synod."

4. Statistics taken from appropriate tables in Herman C. Weber, *Presbyterian Statistics through One Hundred Years 1826-1926: Tabulated, Visualized, and Interpreted* ([Philadelphia]: The General Council, Presbyterian Church in the U. S. A., 1927).

Appendix A
Address of Protest

This protest was written by the Southern New School delegates to the 1857 New School Assembly, meeting at Cleveland. It presents the reasons for calling the Washington (Richmond) Convention held later that year.

DEAR BRETHREN:--The undersigned, members of the General Assembly now in session in Cleveland, Ohio, are constrained to address you with reference to the state of our beloved Church, and to indicate the course which should be pursued by all who adhere to the principles of our Constitution, as interpreted by its framers, and as practically acknowledged during the almost entire period of our history as a church.

The action of the present Assembly on the subject of Slavery, especially when considered in connection with the spirit and manifest purpose of several of the Western Synods, has impressed us with the belief that peace and harmony can no longer prevail amongst us; that the Assembly, as at present constituted, instead of being a bond of union between different sections of the church, will continue to be the theatre of strife and discord; and that the glory of God, the welfare of our churches, and the good of the country demand a separation of the discordant elements, and the existence of another Assembly, in which the agitation of the Slavery question will be unknown.

We had hoped that our brethren who have been disposed to introduce this subject into the General Assembly would ere this have been convinced that no good could result to the Church from this agitation--that it was alienating brethren of a common Christian faith, and was calculated to render the condition of the slave more undesirable, and to sunder the ties that bind our union together. In this regard we have been sadly disappointed. In consequence of the political agitation on the subject, and of the pressure brought to bear upon them by Congregational Churches holding the most ultra abolition sentiments, many of our Western Presbyteries have become more urgent in demanding progressive action of the Assembly. They have desired the Assembly to express its views of the sin of slave-holding so clearly, that they can be made the basis of discipline by the Courts of the Church. This action has now been virtually taken by the Assembly. It has avowed that the relation of master and servant--which necessarily involves the idea of property in the services of the latter--is a sin in the sight of God, an offence in the sense in which the term is used in the Constitution of the Church. This declaration has been made, although confessedly there is not the most remote allusion to slave-holding in our standards, and also with the knowledge of the fact that when our Constitution was adopted, twelve out of the thirteen States were slave-holding States, and many of those who composed the Assembly of 1789, if not slaveholders themselves, were the representatives of Presbyteries in which were churches whose members were slave-holders. We regard this action of the General Assembly as a palpable violation of the spirit and letter of the Constitution of the Church. The principle involved in it, if carried into practice, would convert the highest judicatory of the Church into an ecclesiastical despotism as tyrranical as that which has distinguished the Church of Rome. It makes the Assembly not only the interpreter of law in an irregular way, but also the supreme legislature of the Church--a position which has been always repudiated by the Presbyterian Church.

Apart, therefore, from the disastrous consequence resulting from the agitation of the subject of Slavery in the General Assembly--

destroying, as it does, our peace, keeping us in a state of excitement unfavourable to spiritual growth, and paralyzing our efforts to advance the cause of the Redeemer through the channel of our admirable system of government--we consider that the Assembly has so far departed from the Constitution of the Church as to render our adherence to it undesirable and impossible. Having protested repeatedly against this agitation, and finding that our brethren are determined to continue it, we have deliberately and prayerfully come to the conclusion that, however painful it may be to us, the good of the Church and of the country required a separation from them. We shall hold our brethren who have disturbed our peace, by the introduction of this vexed question into our judicatories, as alone responsible for the consequences of this division.

With these convictions as to the necessity of a separation from our once united and beloved Zion, the only question that remains for us now to settle, pertains to the mode of separation. The undersigned are satisfied that but one course is left to us--and that is, to invite all Constitutional Presbyterians in the land, who are opposed to the agitation of Slavery in the General Assembly, to unite in an organization in which this subject shall be utterly eschewed. We do not restrict our invitation to the Southern Churches. We wish to have a National Church--that is, a Church, the constituent parts of which will come from every section of the Union. Holding to the same Confession of Faith, we shall have a common basis as to doctrine and government--and an understanding that, however, we may differ in our views respecting Slavery, the subject is never to be introduced into the Assembly either by Northern or Southern men, unless, indeed judicial cases are brought up regularly from the lower courts. In the judgment of the undersigned, this course is our only alternative. There is so much of the same abolition spirit pervading other Churches that adhere to the same standards of Faith, that we could not expect peace on this subject by uniting with them. We are persuaded that, although this question may be suppressed in their judicatories for a while, the abolition spirit exists to such an extent as to threaten their dismemberment. The result may be that the disturbing elements of the different branches of the Presbyterian Church may be united in one body, and that the conservative portions of the same may ultimately be brought together, and thus prove more efficient in promoting the cause of the Redeemer, and in diffusing through the land a truly national spirit. At present, however, the union of these Churches would not afford relief to those who are wearied of this Slavery agitation. We are desirous of forming an organization where we shall not be liable to another division from this exciting subject.

The undersigned, therefore, would invite all Presbyterians, from all sections of the country, to meet in Convention in the city of Washington, on the 27th day of August, 1857, for the purpose of consultation, and of organizing a General Assembly, in which it will be distinctly understood, the subject of Slavery will not be introduced. [The place for the meeting of the proposed Convention was afterwards changed to Richmond, Va.--in the United Presbyterian Church.] We propose this course, instead of organizing an Assembly at once, as being due to the Presbyteries we represent. We would suggest that the Presbyteries be called together as soon as possible; and that, while the Presbyteries appoint their delegates to the Convention in the usual proportion, it is desirable that as many ministers and elders should attend the Convention as can do so. We suggest, also, that in case any of: the Presbyteries desiring to be connected with this new Assembly, should find it impossible to be represented in the Convention, it would be important that the Convention should be informed of their action.

Praying that God may overrule the distractions of Zion for his own glory, and that we may be guided in this crisis of our history by his unerring counsel, we subscribe ourselves your brethren in Christ,

FREDERICK A. ROSS, D.D.	MICHAEL S. SHUCK.
GEORGE PAINTER.	ISAAC W. K. HANDY.
WILLIAM B. CALDWELL.	JAMES G. HAMNER, D.D.
JOHN B. LOGAN.	HENRY MATTHEWS.
ROBERT P. RHEA.	PEACHY R. GRATTAN.
ARCHER C. DICKERSON.	GEORGE W. HUTCHINS.
THOMAS H. CLELAND.	ELIJAH A. CARSON.

FINCELIUS R. GRAY.

Address of Protest

The undersigned, though not members of the General Assembly now in session in Cleveland, have been present during its discussion of Slavery. Being fully convinced that there is no prospect of the cessation of this agitation in the Assembly, and that the action taken is a violation of the Constitution of the Church, we cordially unite in the above invitation.

A. H. H. BOYD, D.D.   GEORGE M. CRAWFORD.

Appendix B
Declaration of Principles of the United Synod

Whereas, In the Providence of God, we, the representatives of Presbyteries heretofore in connection with the General Assembly of the Presbyterian Church in the United States of America, have been constrained by a regard to our conviction of duty to ourselves, to the Church of Christ, and to our entire country, to withdraw from said General Assembly, and to form a separate ecclesiastical judicatory, under the name of the United Synod of the Presbyterian Church in the United States of America, to be possessed of powers similar to those recognized in the Confession of Faith as belonging to the General Assembly; and *Whereas,* It seems to be necessary, in order to avoid misapprehensions of our position, both now and hereafter, that we should place upon permanent record, a statement of the principles which have governed us in forming a separate organization; therefore--

Resolved, That this "United Synod" make the following *Declaration of Principles*, as in their judgment, in accordance with the Word of God, and the Constitution of the Presbyterian Church, and as essential to the peace, unity and permanent prosperity of the Presbyterian Church in this land.

1. We declare our agreement in, and approbation of, the Westminster Confession of Faith, with the Larger and Shorter Catechisms of the Westminster Assembly, as containing the system of doctrine taught in the Holy

Scriptures; and also our adherence to the Form of Government and Book of Discipline of the Presbyterian Church in these United States.

In thus adopting the Westminster Confession of Faith as containing the system of doctrine taught in the Holy Scriptures, we adopt it in the sense in which we believe the fathers of the American Presbyterian Church received it, to wit: not as requiring an agreement in sentiment with every opinion expressed in said Confession, but a belief in the fundamental doctrines of Christianity, and in the doctrines which distinguish the Calvinistic system from the Pelagian, Socinian, Arminian, and other systems of Theology. This system we understand to include the following doctrines, viz: the Trinity; the Incarnation and Supreme Deity of Christ; the Fall and Original Sin; Atonement; Justification by Faith; Personal Election; Effectual Calling; Perseverance of the Saints; Eternal Happiness of the righteous, and Eternal Punishment of the wicked. Whilst various modes of stating and explaining these truths may be adopted, yet when they are received according to the usual way of interpreting language, and as they have been understood by the great body of the Presbyterian Church in this country, from the period of the adoption of the Westminster Confession, in 1729, to the present day, the requisitions of the Confession of Faith are complied with, and all such persons are to be regarded as having received as their doctrinal creed this system of doctrines taught in the Holy Scriptures.

2. It is a fundamental principle of the Constitution of the Presbyterian Church, that no judicatory, or minister, or private member, can be censured or condemned, or excluded from church privileges, by any court of the church, for doctrinal sentiments expressed, or for practices that the court may regard as sinful and inconsistent with the requirements of the Confession of Faith, without a process of trial, such as is prescribed in said Constitution. To censure or condemn individuals or judicatories, for heresy or crime, is a judicial act; and if a court of the church has the constitutional right, in any case, to condemn or cut off from the church, members or judicatories, for heresy or crime, *without trial* it can be exercised whenever, in their judgment, said members or judicatories are

guilty of teaching heresy or practicing immorality; and thus the Constitution would not only be inconsistent with itself, but it would sanction the violation of the principles of common justice, which are recognized in every civilized country in the world.

3. According to the Constitution of the Presbyterian Church, the General Assembly is an advisory and judicial body. It possesses no legislative power in the proper acceptance of the term. It cannot enact laws that are binding upon the lower judicatories. The constitution expressly provides that all ecclesiastical rules or changes in the Constitution shall receive the approval of a majority of the Presbyteries before they can be obligatory upon the churches. This "United Synod," therefore, disclaims the right to legislate, or to make laws upon any subject that will be binding upon the lower judicatories, or upon any portion of the Presbyterian Church.

4. In virtue of their advisory capacity, the different judicatories of the Presbyterian Church can testify against what they regard as heresies or immoralities prevailing in the community. But they have no power to bear their testimony against judicatories, or ministers, or private members of the church, for teaching heretical sentiments, or practicing immoralities. The testifying and judicial powers of church judicatories are distinct. They cannot perform a *judicial* act in their *advisory* capacity. To *individualize*, in the form of testimony, judicatories, or ministers, or private members, as guilty of heresy or immorality, is assuming their guilt, without proof or trial. This "United Synod," therefore, whilst they recognize the right of the judicatories of the church, in a *judicial* capacity, to prosecute ministers and private members for heresy and crime, in the way prescribed by the Book of Discipline, affirm that it would be a palpable violation of the spirit and letter of the Constitution of the Presbyterian Church, for any judicatory in its advisory capacity to bear its testimony against other judicatories, or ministers, or private members, for supposed heresy or crime, and without such a judicial process as is specified in the Book of Discipline.

5. In the judgment of this "United Synod," nothing can be made the basis for discipline in

the Presbyterian Church, which is not *specifically referred to in the Constitution of the Church as crime or heresy. The Westminster Confession of Faith, with the Larger and Shorter Catechisms, contains what we believe to be essential to truth and morality. Presbyterians profess to be governed by Constitutional law* as it is developed in the Confession of Faith, and not by the opinions of a Session, or Presbytery, or Synod, or General Assembly, further than they act in a judicial capacity with respect to matters distinctly referred to in said Confession. A departure from this principle and a recognition of the right of an ecclesiastical judicatory to decide what is heresy or crime, when there is no allusion in the Confession of Faith to that which is so regarded, would be tantamount to making the judicatory, instead of the Confession of Faith, the standard of truth and morality, and as the decision of one judicatory cannot bind another, there might be as many different opinions in reference to the supposed heresy or crime, as there are judicatories in the Church. This "United Synod," therefore, deny the right of any judicatory of the Presbyterian Church to make anything a subject of discipline which, according to the usual mode of interpreting language, and the manifest intent of the framers of the Confession, is not *specifically* referred to in the Constitution of the Church.

6. As slaveholding, or the relation between master and slave, is not referred to in the Confession of Faith, either directly or indirectly, as an offence, it cannot, *in itself considered*, in any case, be made the basis of discipline in the Presbyterian Church. At the same time, we declare the right of the Church Courts to take cognizance, in their judicial capacity, of cruelties practised in this and other relations in life. The Confession of Faith gives to Church judicatories the power to discipline members of the Church for cruelties, whether they occur in the parental or any other relation, implying in the language of the Confession, superiors and inferiors.

7. Inasmuch as slaveholders were admitted into the Churches organized by the Apostles, and as neither Christ nor his Apostles intimated that the slaveholding relation was a sin, although they lived in the midst of the institution, and enjoined upon masters to treat

their slaves with kindness, it follows necessarily, that a Church Court that makes slaveholding, *in any case*, a bar to communion, is usurping authority that belongs only to the Great Head of the Church. Such a Court would be legislating where Christ has not legislated. It would be prescribing terms of membership which the Son of God himself did not prescribe, notwithstanding he was surrounded by slaveholders. This Synod denies that any ecclesiastical judicatory has the power to make terms of membership which neither Christ nor his Apostles recognized, when placed in similar circumstances as respects the existence of the slaveholding relation.

8. Inasmuch as neither the Saviour nor his Apostles intimated that the slaveholding relation was sinful, and as they did not attempt to remove slaveholders from the church by legislation or by testifying against it; and further, as the system of slavery is an institution of the State, its continuance or abolition depending entirely upon the will of the State, irrespective of the views and decisions of church courts, it is the opinion of this Synod that the discussion or agitation of slavery in the judicatories of the Church, except so far as respects the moral and religious duties growing out of the relation of master and slave, is inappropriate to said judicatories. This Synod representing Presbyteries that have withdrawn from their former ecclesiastical connection, because of the repeated and unconstitutional action on slavery by the General Assembly, therefore declares, that, under the present Constitution of the Presbyterian Church, the agitation of slavery in any of our judicatories, further than pertains to the moral and religious duties arising from the relation, would be inconsistent with the design of our withdrawal from our former connection, and in forming a separate organization. Whilst, then we propose no alteration of the Constitution of the Presbyterian Church, believing that as it now stands the spirit of it is against the agitation of slaveholding in the Church, we express the opinion that those who unite with us, or who may come after us, will be under a moral obligation, so long as the Constitution remains as it is, to exclude slavery, the agitation of which has already divided three large denomina-

tions in this country, as a subject of discussion from the Church Courts.

9. Entertaining the above views, and disclaiming all responsibility for, and endorsement of the actions, resolutions, and testimonies of past General Assemblies of the Presbyterian Church, whereby suspicions and doubts of the good standing and equal rights and privileges of the slaveholding members of the Church, or implications or charges against their Christian character, have been either implied or expressed, this "United Synod" is organized. And to avoid any misapprehensions of our position, we hereby express the wish that Presbyteries *from every section of the Union*-- who adopt the Westminster Confession of Faith as their system of doctrine, and adhere to its Form of Government and Book of Discipline, and who, whatever may be their opinion of slavery as a civil institution, believe that the relation of master and servant should be no bar to membership in the Church of Christ, and that the agitation of the question of slavery, further than pertains to the performance of the duties which the Scriptures state as imposed upon the master and slave, is inappropriate to the function of the Church, and therefore ought not to be introduced into the Church Courts-- should unite with our body, and thus aid in the diffusion of the truths of our common Christianity, free from an agitation that has already resulted in the dismemberment of several evangelical Churches.

Appendix C

Proposed Terms of Union With the Old School Assembly by the United Synod of the South

Whereas, This Synod believe that a union between Christian brethren who adopt the same standards of faith and practice, when it can be effected without compromising vital principles, is always desirable; and *Whereas*, The sentiment exists among members of our churches that a union between this Synod and the Old School General Assembly might be effected upon terms honourable to both parties; and *Whereas*, The Convention of ministers and laymen held in Richmond, Va., in August, 1857, for the purpose of consulting as to the wisest course to be pursued by those who felt aggrieved by the abolition action of the General Assembly at Cleveland, Ohio, in May, 1857, recommended to this Synod, when organized, to appoint a Committee to confer with one from the Old School Assembly, (if they should think proper to appoint a Committee for the purpose,) with reference to a union of these two branches of the Presbyterian Church; therefore--

1. *Resolved*, That a Committee of two be appointed to confer with a Committee of the Old School Assembly, in the event of that body appointing one for the purpose, with reference to a union of the two bodies.

2. *Resolved*, That Rev. C. H. Read, D. D., and Rev. M. M. Marshall be said Committee, and that Rev. A. H. H. Boyd, D. D., and Rev. Robt. McLain be alternates.

3. *Resolved*, That said Committee be directed to propose to the Committee appointed

by the General Assembly the following terms of union, as indispensible to an honourable union on our part:

First. We agree to unite as ecclesiastical bodies by declaring, as this Synod now does, our approval of the Westminster Confession of Faith, and Larger and Shorter Catechisms, as an orthodox and excellent system of christian doctrine--and also our adherence to the plan of Worship, Government, and Discipline contained in the Westminster Directory.

Second. Both parties agree in declaring it to be a fundamental principle in the Presbyterian Church, that no judicatory of the Church can, *for any cause whatever*, by an act of legislation, constitutionally condemn, or exclude from the Church other judicatories, or ministers, or private members, without a process of trial, such as is prescribed in the Constitution of the Presbyterian Church.

Third. Both parties agree that it is consistent with the requirements of the Westminster Confession of Faith, to receive said Confession according to the Adopting Act of 1729, to wit: as containing all the essential truths of Christianity, and also the doctrines that distinguish the Calvinistic from the Pelagian, Socinian, and Arminian systems of Theology. We agree, likewise, in believing that this system of doctrine includes the following truths, viz: the Trinity; the Incarnation and Deity of Christ; the Fall and Original Sin; Atonement; Justification by Faith; Personal Election; Effectual Calling; Perseverance of the Saints; the Eternal Happiness of the righteous, and Eternal Punishment of the wicked.

Fourth. Both bodies agree in declaring that slaveholding, or the relation of master and slave, cannot, *in any case*, be a bar to membership in the Church of Christ. And whilst they admit the right of the judicatories of the Church to take cognizance, in the way prescribed in the Constitution, of cruelties practised in the relation, they hereby declare the opinion that, as the continuance or abolition of the system of slavery in this country belongs exclusively to the State, the discussion or agitation of slavery, further than pertains to the moral and religious duties arising from the relation, is inappropriate to the functions of Church judicatories.

Fifth. It is further agreed that in effecting the union, the Presbyteries connected with this Synod shall be united as Presbyteries, and without an examination of their ministers with the Synods belonging to the General Assembly to which, because of their geographical limits, they should be attached, excepting that the Synod of Tennessee and the North Alabama Presbytery shall retain their name, and occupy their present territory.

Sixth. In the event of the General Assembly agreeing to the above terms, the Committee of Synod are directed to communicate the fact to the Presbyteries in connection with the Synod, and the Presbyteries are hereby requested by the United Synod to take action upon the terms of union agreed upon by the Committees of Synod and the General Assembly, and to send a copy of their minutes to the United Synod that will meet in Lynchburg on the third Thursday in May. 1859.

Seventh. The Committee appointed by this Synod to confer with a Committee of the General Assembly, are hereby directed to attend the meeting of the Assembly in New Orleans in May next, and present the preamble and first two resolutions adopted by this Synod as their authority for requesting a conference with a Committee appointed by the General Assembly, to the General Assembly which will then be in session in that city. And if no member of the Committee should be able to attend the meeting of the Assembly in New Orleans, they are directed to send a copy of the preamble and first two resolutions to the Moderator of the Assembly, and request that body, if they should think proper to appoint a Committee for the purpose above specified, to designate a time immediately after the adjournment of the Assembly for a conference of the Committees. The Committee of this Synod are requested, in the event of a conference being had with a Committee of the Old School Assembly, to publish, as soon as practicable, the result of their consultations.

Eighth. That in the event no union is agreed to, the Committee be directed to propose to the General Assembly the establishment of a mutual correspondence in the future between us as ecclesiastical bodies.

Selected Bibliography

PRIMARY SOURCES

Bowling Green, Kentucky, Presbyterian Church, "Minutes," 1819-1858, Kentucky Library and Museum, Bowling Green, Kentucky.
Central Texas Presbytery, "Minutes," 1865-1871, PHF.
Holston Presbytery [NS], "Minutes," 1838-1860, PHF; 1865--, Tusculum College Library, Tusculum, Tennessee.
Holston Presbytery, [USS], "Minutes," 1860-1865, PHF.
Holston Presbytery, [PCUS], "Minutes," 1865-1870, PHF.
Huntsville, Alabama, First Presbyterian Church, microfilm "Minutes," Huntsville, Alabama, Public Library.
Indiana, Synod of [NS], typed "Minutes," 1838-1869, PHF.
"Minutes of the New School Synod of Kentucky, Beginning with Convention & Ending with United Presbytery of Kentucky, 1840-1858," typewritten copy by E. E. Smith, PHF.
Mississippi, Synod of [NS], "Minutes," 1845-1860, Department of Archives and History, Jackson, Mississippi.
Mississippi, Synod of [OS], "Minutes," 1835-1844, Department of Archives and History, Jackson, Mississippi.
Mississippi, Synod of [USS], "Minutes, 1857-1866, Department of Archives and History, Jackson, Mississippi.

Missouri, Synod of [NS], "Minutes," Murrell Memorial Library, Missouri Valley College, Marshall, Missouri.
Morganton Presbytery, "Minutes," 1836-1840, PHF.
Muhlenburg Presbytery, "Minutes," 1832-1846, Lucy Stites Barrett Library, LPTS.
Nashville, Synod of, "Minutes," 1851-1867, PHF.
Newton Presbytery [NS], "Minutes," 1851-1864, PHF.
North Alabama Presbytery [also known as Richland Presbytery], "Minutes," 1840-1871, PHF.
North Carolina, Synod of, "Minutes," 1829-1840, PHF.
Osage Presbytery, "Minutes," 1865-1869, Murrell Memorial Library, Missouri Valley College, Marshall, Missouri.
Presbyterian Church in the Confederate States of America, *Minutes*, 1861-1864.
Presbyterian Church in the United States, *Minutes*, 1865-1875.
Presbyterian Church in the United States of America [NS], *Minutes*, 1838-1869.
Presbyterian Church in the United States of America [OS], *Minutes*, 1837-1869.
Providence Presbytery, "Minutes," 1840-1857, Lucy Stites Barrett Library, LPTS.
Second Presbyterian Church, Knoxville, Tennessee, "Session Minutes," 1841-1870, in church archives.
Texas, Synod of, "Minutes," 1851-1871, PHF.
Transylvania Presbytery, typewritten "Minutes," vol. 8, PHF.
Union, Presbytery of, typewritten "Minutes," 1829-1874, McClung Room, Lawson McGhee Library, Knoxville, Tennessee.
United Synod of the Presbyterian Church in the United States of America, *Minutes*, 1858-1863.
Ibid., "Minutes," 1858-1860 (partial), PHF.
Virginia, Synod of [OS], *Minutes,* 1862-1864., PHF.
West Tennessee, Presbytery of [NS], "Minutes," 1840-1857, PHF.
West Tennessee, Presbytery of [OS], "Minutes," 1832-1852, PHF.

EDITED WORKS AND ANTHOLOGIES

Alexander, W. A. *A Digest of the Acts and Proceedings of the General Assembly of the Presbyterian Church in the United States, from its Organization to the Assembly of 1887, Inclusive, with Certain Historical and Explanatory Notes*. Richmond: Presbyterian Committee of Publication, 1888.

Armstrong, Maurice W., Loetscher, Lefferts A., and Anderson, Charles A., eds. *The Presbyterian Enterprise: Sources of Presbyterian History.* Philadelphia: Westminster Press, 1956.

Baird, E. Thompson, ed. *Distinctive Principles of the Presbyterian Church in the United States, Commonly Called the Southern Presbyterian Church, As Set Forth in the Formal Declarations and Illustrated by Extracts from Proceedings of the Assembly, from 1860 to 1870; and Explanatory Remarks*, 3rd ed. Richmond: Committee of Publication, 1870.

Baird, Samuel J., comp. *A Collection of the Acts, Deliverances, and Testimonies of the Supreme Judicatory of the Presbyterian Church: from its Origin in America to the Present Time. With Notes and Documents Explanatory and Historical: Constituting a Complete Illustration of her Polity, Faith, and History.* Philadelphia: Presbyterian Board of Publication, 1856.

Beecher, Willis J. *Index of Presbyterian Ministers Containing the Names of All the Ministers of the Presbyterian Church in the United States of America with References to the Pages on which those Names are Found in its Records and Minutes from A. D. 1706 to A. D. 1881.* Philadelphia: Presbyterian Board of Publication, 1883.

Form of Government, of the Presbyterian Church, in the United States of America; and the Directory for the Worship of God, As Amended and Ratified by the General Assembly at Their Sessions in May, 1821. Elizabeth-town, N. J.: Mervin Hale, 1822.

Mode, Peter G. *Source Book and Bibliographical Guide for American Church History.* Menasha, Wisconsin: George Banta Publishing Co., 1921.

Moore, W. E. *A New Digest of the Acts and Deliverances of the General Assembly of the Presbyterian Church in the United States of America [NS]. Compiled by Order and Authority of the General Assembly.* Philadelphia: Presbyterian Publication Committee; New York: A. D. F. Randolph, 1861.

Register of the Appointment of Chaplains. Chap. I., vol. 132, Record Group 109: War Department Collection of Confederate Records. Microfilm. Washington: National Archives and Records Service.

Robinson, Edgar Sutton. *The Ministerial Directory of the Ministers in "The Presbyterian Church in the United States" (Southern) and in "The

324 Selected Bibliography

Presbyterian Church in the United States of America" (Northern), Together with a Statement of the Work of the Executive Commmittees and Boards of the Two Churches, with the Names and Location of Their Educational Institutions and Church Papers. Vol. 1. Oxford, Ohio: Ministerial Directory Co., 1898.

Scott, E. C., comp. *Ministerial Directory of the Presbyterian Church U. S. 1861-1941.* Austin: Von Boechamann-Jones, 1942.

-------. *Ministerial Directory of the Presbyterian Church U. S. 1861-1941 Revised and Supplemented 1942-1950.* Atlanta: Hubbard Printing Co., 1950.

Sweet, William Warren. *Religion on the Frontier, 1783-1850,* 4 vols. Chicago: University of Chicago Press, 1939.

NEWSPAPERS, MAGAZINES AND ANNUAL REPORTS

American Board of Commissioners for Foreign Missions. *Annual Report.*
American Education Society. *Annual Report.*
American Home Missionary Society. *Annual Report.*
Calvinistic Magazine, vols. 1-5 (1827-1831); vols. 1-5 (1846-1850).
Central Presbyterian, 1857-1865.
Christian Observer, 1835-1866.
Minutes of the Auburn Convention, Held August 17, 1837, to Deliberate upon the Doings of the Last General Assembly in Relation to the Synods of Western Reserve, Utica, Geneva and Genesee and the Third Presbytery of Philadelphia. Auburn: Published by the Convention, Oliphant and Skinner, Printers, 1837.
Minutes of the Southern and South-Western Presbyterian Convention, Held at Cassville, Ga. October, 1840. Charleston: B. B. Hussey, 1840.
Missouri Presbyterian Recorder, 1855-1856.
Presbyterian Witness, 1850-1860.
Protestant and Herald, 1839-1845.

ARTICLES

Adams, James Luther. "The Voluntary Principle in the Forming of American Religion." In *The Religion of the Republic,* ed. Elwyn A. Smith. Philadelphia: Fortress Press, 1971, pp. 217-246.
[Alexander, Archibald]. "The Present Conditions and Prospects of the Presbyterian Church." *Biblical*

Repertory and Theological Review 4 (1832): 28-47.
Anderson Charles A., ed. "Presbyterians Meet the Slavery Problem." *JPHS* 29 (1951): 9-40.
"Autobiography of the Rev. Amasa Converse." *JPH* 43 (1965): 197-218, 254-263.
Banner, Lois. "Presbyterians and Voluntarism in the Early Republic." *JPH* 50 (1972): 187-205.
Brackett, William O., Jr. "The Rise and Development of the New School Presbyterian Church in the U. S. A. to the Reunion of 1869." *JPHS* 13 (1928): 117-174.
Daniel, W. Harrison. "English Presbyterians, Slavery and the Crisis of the 1860s." *JPH* 58 (1980): 50-62.
Davis, David Brion. "The Emergence of Immediatism in British and American Antislavery Thought." *MVHR* 49 (1962): 209-230.
Drury, Clifford M. "Missionary Expansion at Home." In *They Seek a Country: The American Presbyterians. Some Aspects,* ed. Gaius Jackson Slosser. New York: Macmillan, 1955, pp. 165-190.
Ferm, Robert L. "Jonathan Edwards the Younger and the Plan of Union of 1801." *JPH* 42 (1964): 286-292.
Garrison, Winfred Ernest. "Interdenominational Relations in America before 1837." *Papers of the American Society of Church History*, 2nd. ser., 9 (1934): 57-94.
Griffin, Clifford S. "The Abolitionists and the Benevolent Societies, 1831-1861." *Journal of Negro History* 44 (1959): 195-216.
-------. "Religious Benevolence as Social Control, 1815-1860." *MVHR* 44 (1957): 423-444.
Hammond, John L. "Revival Religion and Antislavery Politics." *American Sociological Review* 39 (1974): 175-86.
Heiskell, C. W. "Pioneer Presbyterianism in Tennessee." In *Pioneer Presbyterianism in Tennessee: Addresses Delivered at the Tennessee Exposition on Presbyterian Day, October 28, 1897.* Richmond: Presbyterian Committee of Publication, 1898, pp. 9-35.
Highsaw, Mary Wagner. "A History of Zion Community in Maury County, 1806-1860." *Tennessee Historical Quarterly* 5 (1946): 3-34, 110-140, 222-233.
Hill, John B. "Home Missions in Missouri." *JPHS* 29 (1951): 237-256.
-------. "Timothy Hill Reports on Slavery." *JPHS* 29 (1951): 22-39.
Horton, Douglas. "The Plan of Union of 1801 in the

United States." *Reformed and Presbyterian World* 26 (1961): 246-252.

Howard, Victor B. "The Southern Aid Society and the Slavery Controversy." *CH* 41 (1972): 208-224.

Johnson, Thomas Cary. "A Brief Sketch of the United Synod of the Presbyterian Church in the United States of America." *Papers of the American Society of Church History* 8 (1897): 1-38.

Kuhns, Frederick. "Slavery and Missions in the Old Northwest." *JPHS* 24 (1946): 205-222.

Kull, Irving Stoddard. "Presbyterian Attitudes Toward Slavery." *CH* 7 (1938): 101-114.

Lewitt, Robert T. "Indian Missions and Antislavery Sentiment: A Conflict of Evangelical and Humanitarian Ideals." *MVHR* 50 (1963): 39-55.

Lloyd, Ralph Waldo. "Some History of the Three Synods of Tennessee, Alabama, and Mississippi." *JPHS* 23 (1945): 143-149.

Loetscher, Lefferts A. "The Problem of Christian Unity in Early Nineteenth Century America." *CH* 32 (1963): 3-16.

Lyons, John F. "The Attitude of Presbyterians in Ohio, Indiana and Illinois toward Slavery, 1825-1861." *JPHS* 11 (1921): 69-82.

MacCormac, Earl R. "The Development of Presbyterian Missionary Organizations: 1790-1870." *JPH* 43 (1965): 149-173.

--------. "An Ecumenical Failure: The Development of Congregational Missions and its Influence upon Presbyterians." *JPH* 44 (1966): 266-285.

--------. "Missions and the Presbyterian Schism of 1837." *CH* 32 (1963): 32-45.

McLoughlin, William G. "Indian Slaveholders and Presbyterian Missionaries, 1837-1861." *CH* 42 (1973): 535-551.

Martin, Asa Earl. "The Anti-slavery Societies of Tennessee." *Tennessee Historical Magazine* 1 (1915): 216-281.

Mead, Sydney E. "Denominationalism: The Shape of Protestantism in America." *CH* 23 (1954): 291-320.

Morrow, Ralph E. "The Proslavery Argument Revisited." *MVHR* 48 (1961): 79-94.

Mounger, Dwyn Mecklin. "Samuel Hanson Cox: Anti-Catholic, Anti-Anglican, Anti-Congregational Ecumenist." *JPH* 55 (1977): 347-361.

Oliphant, J. Orin. "The American Missionary Spirit, 1828-35." *CH* 7 (1938): 125-137.

Opie, John. "Finney's Failure of Nerve: The Untimely Demise of Evangelical Theology." *JPH* 51 (1973): 155-173.

Orr, Horace E. "One Hundred Years of the New Prospect Presbyterian Church, Knox County, Tennessee, 1834-1934." *East Tennessee Historical Society's Publications* 7 (1935): 50-63.

Parker, Harold M., Jr. "The Cassville Convention: Aborted Birth of a Southern Presbyterian Church." *Historian* 42 (1980): 612-630.

-------. "The Independent Presbyterian Church and Reunion in the South, 1813-1863." *JPH* 50 (1972): 89-110.

-------. "The New School Presbyterian Disruption in North Carolina." *Iliff Review* 32 (1975): 51-63.

-------. "A New School Presbyterian Seminary in Woodford County." *Register of the Kentucky Historical Society* 74 (1976): 99-111.

-------. "The New School Synod of Kentucky." *Filson Club History Quarterly* 50 (1976): 52-89.

-------. "A School of the Prophets at Maryville." *Tennessee Historical Quarterly* 34 (1975): 72-90.

-------. "Southern Presbyterian Ecumenism: Six Successful Unions." *JPH* 56 (1978): 91-106.

-------. "The Urban Failure of the Southern New School Presbyterian Church." *Social Science Journal* 14 (1977): 139-148.

Peel, Albert. "Co-operation of Presbyterians and Congregationalists: Some Previous Attempts." *Transactions of the Congregational Historical Society* 12 (1933-1936): 147-163.

Posey, Walter Brownlow. "The Slavery Question in the Presbyterian Church in the Old Southwest." *Journal of Southern History* 15 (1949): 311-324.

Potts, David B. "American Colleges in the Nineteenth Century: From Localism to Denominationalism." *History of Education Quarterly* 11 (1971): 363-380.

Reed, R. C. "Presbyterians. VIII In the United States and Canada: 2 Presbyterian Church in the United States." *New Schaff-Herzog Encyclopedia of Religious Knowledge*, s.v.

Rogers, Tommy W. "Dr. Frederick A. Ross and the Presbyterian Defense of Slavery." *JPH* 45 (1967): 112-124.

Smith, Elwyn A. "The Role of the South in the Presbyterian Schism of 1837-38." *CH* 29 (1960): 44-63.

-------. "The Voluntary Establishment of Religion." In *The Religion of the Republic*, ed. Elwyn A. Smith. Philadelphia: Fortress Press, 1971, pp. 154-182.

"The Southern Apostasy." *New Englander* 12 (1854): 627-662.

Spence, T. H., Jr. "Southern Presbyterian Reviews." *Union Seminary Review* 56 (1945): 93-109.
Staiger, C. Bruce. "Abolitionism, and the Presbyterian Schism of 1837-1838." *MVHR* 36 (1949): 391-414.
Stearns, Jonathan F. "Historical Review of the Church (New School Branch) Since 1837." In *Presbyterian Reunion: A Memorial Volume. 1837-1871*. New York: De Witt C. Lent & Co.; Chicago: Van Nortwick & Sparks, 1870, pp. 50-102.
Thompson, Ernest Trice. "The First Years." In *"The Days of Our Years" 1812-1962: The Historical Convocations Held April 24-27, 1962 as a Feature of the Celebration of the Sesquicentennial of Union Theological Seminary in Virginia*. Richmond: n.p., 1962, pp. 7-20.
———. "Presbyterians North and South--Efforts Toward Reunion." *JPH* 43 (1965): 1-15.
Thompson, J. Earl, Jr. "Lyman Beecher's Long Road to Conservative Abolitionism." *CH* 42 (1973): 89-109.
Thornwell, James Henley. "Report on the Subject of Slavery." *JPHS* 29 (1951): 137-142.
Welsh, Edward Burgett. "Chillicothe: A Distinguished Rural Presbytery." *JPHS* 23 (1945): 137-142.
———. "Wrestling with Human Values: The Slavery Years." In *They Seek a Country: The American Presbyterians. Some Aspects*, ed. Gaius Jackson Slosser. New York: Macmillan, 1955, pp. 210-233.
Wentz, Abdel Ross. "Permanent Deposits of Sectionalism in American Christianity.": *Lutheran Church Quarterly* 9 (1936): 27-38.
Whatley, George C., III. "The Alabama Presbyterian and His Slave." *Alabama Review* 13 (1960): 40-51.
Wilson, Samuel Tyndale. "New Market Students at Maryville College." *JPHS* 12 (1927): 399-414.
Woodworth, R. B. "The History of Winchester Presbytery (with Particular Reference to Evangelism)." In *Diamond Jubilee Presbyterian Church in the United States*. Pulaski, Virginia: B. D. Smith & Bros., [1936], pp. 3-21.

BOOKS AND PAMPHLETS

Address of the Executive Committee of the American Tract Society to the Christian Public: Together with a Brief Account of the Formation of the Society, Its Constitution and Officers. New York: D. Fanshaw, 1825.

Selected Bibliography 329

Ahlstrom, Sydney E. *A Religious History of the American People.* New Haven/London: Yale University Press, 1972.
Alexander, J. E. *A Brief History of the Synod of Tennessee, From 1817 to 1887.* Philadelphia: MacCalla & Co., 1890.
American Tract Society. *Publications of the American Tract Society,* vol. 1 New York: American Tract Society, circa 1826.
Armstrong, George D. *The Christian Doctrine of Slavery.* New York: Charles Scribner; Norfolk: J. D. Ghiselin, Jr., 1857.
Atkins, Gaius Glenn, and Fagley, Frederick L. *History of American Congregationalism.* Boston and Chicago: Pilgrim Press, 1942.
Bachman, Robert L. *Historical Sermon, Preached by the Pastor, Rev. Robert L. Bachman, D. D., in the Second Presbyterian Church, Knoxville, Tennessee, September 23, 1906.* Knoxville: Gaut-Ogden Co., n.d.
Bacon, Leonard Woolsey. *A History of American Christianity.* American Church History Series, ed. Philip Schaff. New York: Charles Scribner's Sons, 1918.
Baird, Samuel J. *A History of the New School and of the Questions Involved in the Disruption of the Presbyterian Church in 1838.* Philadelphia: Claxton, Remsen & Haffelfinger, 1868.
Barnes, Albert. *The Church and Slavery,* 2nd ed. Philadelphia: Parry & McMillan, 1857.
Barnes, Gilbert Hobbs. *The Antislavery Impulse 1830-1844.* Gloucester, Mass.: Peter Smith, 1957.
Barney, William L.*Flawed Victory: A New Perspective on the Civil War.* New Perspectives in American History Series, ed. James P. Shenton. New York and Washington: Praeger, 1972.
-------. *The Road to Secession: A New Perspective on the Old South.* New Perspectives in American History Series, ed. James P. Shenton. New York and Washington: Praeger, 1972.
Beard, Augustus Field. *A Crusade of Brotherhood: A History of the American Missionary Association.* Boston: Pilgrim Press, 1909.
Belcher, Joseph. *The Religious Denominations in the United States: Their History, Doctrine, Government and Statistics. With a Preliminary Sketch of Judaism, Paganism and Mohammedanism.* Philadelphia: John E. Potter; Indianapolis: Stearns & Spicer; Memphis: J. G. Clarke, 1856.
Bennett, William W. *A Narrative of the Great Revival which Prevailed in the Southern Armies during the Late Civil War between the States of the*

Federal Union. Philadelphia: Claxton, Remsen & Haffelfinger, 1877.

[Birney, James Gillespie.] *The American Churches, The Bulwarks of American Slavery*, 2nd American ed. Newburyport: Charles Whipple, 1842.

Bratton, Mary Elizabeth Kinnier. *Our Goodly Heritage: A History of the First Presbyterian Church of Lynchburg, Virginia, 1815-1940*. Lynchburg, L. P. Bell, n.d.

Cash, W. J. *The Mind of the South*. New York: Alfred A. Knopf, 1941.

Channing, William E. *Slavery*, 3rd ed., rev. Boston: James Munroe and Co., 1836.

[Cincinnati Presbytery.] *One Hundred and Fifty Years of Presbyterianism in the Ohio Valley 1790-1840*. Cincinnati: n.p., 1941.

Clark, Blanch Henry. *The Tennessee Yeomen 1840-1860*. Nashville: Vanderbilt University Press, 1942.

Cogswell, Robert E. *Written on Many Hearts: The History of the First Presbyterian Church Shelbyville, Bedford County, Tennessee 1815-1865*. Nashville: Parthenon Press, n.d.

Cole, Charles C., Jr. *The Social Ideas of the Northern Evangelists 1826-1860*. No. 580 Columbia Studies in the Social Sciences. Edited by the Faculty of Political Science of Columbia University. New York: Columbia University Press, 1954.

Committee of Peoria Presbytery. *The History of the Presbytery of Peoria and its Churches, From 1828 to 1888*. Peoria: H. S. Hill Printing Co., 1888.

Craven, Avery O. *Civil War in the Making, 1815-1860*. Baton Rouge: Louisiana State University Press, 1959.

Crawford, G. S. W. *The History of Maryville College. An Address Delivered before the Annual Meeting of the Alumni, Thursday, May 25th, 1876*. Maryville: College Printing Office, 1876.

Crocker, Zebulon. *The Catastrophe of the Presbyterian Church in 1837, Including a Full View of the Recent Theological Controversies in New England*. New Haven: B. & W. Noyes, 1838.

Cross, Whitney R. *The Burned-over District: Social and Intellectual History of Enthusiastic Religion in Western New York, 1800-1850*. Ithaca: Cornell University Press, 1950.

Davidson, Robert. *History of the Presbyterian Church in the State of Kentucky; with a Preliminary Sketch of the Churches in the Valley of Virginia*. New York: Robert Carter, 1847.

Dorchester, Daniel. *Christianity in the United States: From the First Settlement down to the Present Time*. New York: Phillips & Hunt; Cincinnati: Cranston & Stowe, 1888.
Doyle, Sherman H. *Presbyterian Home Missions: An Account of the Home Missions of the Presbyterian Church in the U. S. A.* Philadelphia: Presbyterian Board of Publication and Sabbath-School Work, 1902.
Drury, Clifford Merrill. *Presbyterian Panorama: One Hundred and Fifty Years of National Missions History*. Philadelphia: Board of Christian Education, Presbyterian Church in the United States of America, 1952.
Dumond, Dwight Lowell. *Antislavery Origins of the Civil War in the United States*. 1939. Reprinted, Ann Arbor: University of Michigan Press, 1959.
Eaton, Clement. *The Growth of Southern Civilization, 1790-1860*. The New American Nation Series. Ed. Henry Steele Commager and Richard B. Norris. New York: Harper & Row, 1963.
--------. *A History of the Old South*, 2nd ed. New York: Macmillan; London: Collier-Macmillan, 1966.
--------. *A History of the Southern Confederacy*. New York: Free Press, 1965.
Elsbree, Oliver Wendell. *The Rise of the Missionary Spirit in America, 1790-1815*. Williamsport, Va.: The Williamsport Printing and Binding Co., 1928.
Filler, Louis. *The Crusade against Slavery 1830-1860*. New American Nation Series. Ed. Henry Steele Commager and Richard B.d Morris. New York: Harper & Row, 1960.
Finney, Charles G. *Lectures on Revivals of Religion*. New York: Leavitt, Lord & Co.; Boston: Crocker & Brewster, 1835.
Foote, William Henry. *Sketches of Virginia, Historical and Biographical*. 2nd series, 2nd ed., rev. Philadelphia: J. B. Lippincott, 1856.
Fowler, P[hilemon] H. *Historical Sketch of Presbyterianism within the Bounds of the Synod of Central New York*. Utica: Curtiss & Childs, 1877.
Fox, Early Lee. *The American Colonization Society, 1817-1840*. Baltimore: Johns Hopkins, 1919.
Galbraith, R. C., Jr. *History of the Chillicothe Presbytery, From its Organization in 1799 to 1889*. Chillicothe, Ohio: Scioto Gazette Book and Job Office, 1889.

Gallaher, James. *The Western Sketch-Book*. Boston: Crocker & Brewster; New York: W. M. Dodd; Philadelphia: William L. Martien, 1850.

Gillett, E. H. *History of the Presbyterian Church in the United States of America*. 2 vols. Philadelphia: Presbyterian Publication Committee, 1864.

Goodykoontz, Colin Brummitt. *Home Missions on the American Frontier: With Particular Reference to the American Home Missionary Society*. Caldwell, Idaho: Caxton Printers, Ltd., 1939.

Griffin, C. S. *The Ferment of Reform, 1830-1860*. The Crowell History Series. Ed. John Hope Franklin and Abraham Eisenstadt. New York: Thomas Y. Crowell, 1967.

Handy, Robert E. *A Christian America: Protestant Hopes and Historical Realities*. New York: Oxford University Press, 1971.

--------. *The Protestant Quest for a Christian America 1830-1890.*. Facet Books: Historical Series. Philadelphia: Fortress Press, 1967.

Hedrick, Charles Embury. *Social and Economic Aspects of Slavery in the Transmontane prior to 1850*. No. 46 George Peabody College for Teachers Contributions to Education. Nashville: George Peabody College for Teachers, 1927.

Hesseltine, William B. *The South in American History*. 2nd ed. Englewood Cliffs, New Jersey: Prentice-Hall, 1960.

Hill, John B. *Presbyterianism in Missouri*. n.p.: n.p., ca. 1900.

--------. *The Presbytery of Kansas City and Its Predecessors 1821-1901: Historical Sketches and Statistical Matter*. Kansas City: Burd & Fletcher Printing Co., 1901.

Historical Sketch of the Synod of Ohio (N. S.) From 1838 to 1868. Cincinnati: Elm Street Printing Co., 1870.

Howe, George. *History of the Presbyterian Church in South Carolina*. 2 vols. Columbia: Duffie and Chapman, 1870; Walker, Evans and Cogswell, 1883.

Hudson, Winthrop. *American Protestantism*. The Chicago History of American Civilization Series. Ed. Daniel J. Boorstin. Chicago and London: University of Chicago Press, 1961.

Hume, John F. *The Abolitionists: Together with Personal Memories of the Struggle for Human Rights 1830-1864*. New York: G. P. Putnam's Sons, 1905.

Jenkins, William Sumner. *Pro-Slavery Thought in the Old South*. Chapel Hill, North Carolina: University of North Carolina Press, 1935.

Johnson, Thomas Cary. *The Life and Letters of Robert Lewis Dabney*. Richmond: Presbyterian Committee of Publication, 1903.

Jones, Charles C. *A Catechism of Scripture Doctrine and Practice for Families and Sabbath-Schools Designed also for the Oral Instruction of Coloured Persons*. 3rd ed. Philadelphia: Presbyterian Board of Publication, 1852.

Kuhns, Frederick Irving. *The American Home Missionary Society in Relation to the Antislavery Controversy in the Old Northwest*. Billings, Montana, n.p., 1959.

Little, D. D. *History of the Presbytery of Columbia Tennessee*. Columbia: Maury Democrat, 1928.

Lloyd, Ralph Waldo. *Maryville College: A History of 150 Years, 1819-1969*. Maryville: Maryville College Press, 1969.

McLoughlin, William O., Jr. *Modern Revivalism: Charles Grandison Finney to Billy Graham*. New York: Ronald Press, 1959.

McPherson, Edward. *The Political History of the United States of America during the Great Rebellion*. 3rd ed. Washington: Solomon and Chapman, 1876.

Marsden, George M. *The Evangelical Mind and the New School Presbyterian Experience: A Case Study of Thought and Theology in Nineteenth-Century America*. New Haven and London: Yale University Press, 1970.

Marshall, James Williams. *The Presbyterian Church in Alabama*. Ed. Robert Strong. The Presbyterian Historical Society of Alabama, 1977.

Miller, George. *Missouri's Memorable Decade: 1860-1870. An Historical Sketch, Personal--Political--Religious*. Columbia, Missouri: E. W. Stephens, 1898.

Morris, Edward D. *The Presbyterian Church New School 1837-1869: An Historical Review*. Columbus, Ohio: Champlin Press, 1905.

Murray, Andrew E. *Presbyterians and the Negro--A History*. Philadelphia: Presbyterian Historical Society, 1966.

Nevin, Alfred, ed. *Encyclopaedia of the Presbyterian Church in the United States of America: Including the Northern and Southern Assemblies*. Philadelphia: Presbyterian Encyclopaedia Publishing Co., 1884.

Nye, Russell Blain. *The Cultural Life of the New Nation, 1776-1830.*. New American Nation Series. Ed. Henry Steele Commager and Richard B. Morris. New York: Harper & Bros., 1960.

Olmstead, Clifton E. *History of Religion in the United States*. Englewood Cliffs, New Jersey: Prentice-Hall, 1960.
Parker, Harold M., Jr. *Studies in Southern Presbyterian History*. Gunnison, Colorado: B. & B. Printers, 1979.
Patterson, Caleb Perry. *The Negro in Tennessee, 1790-1865*. University of Texas Bulletin No. 2205, February 1, 1922. Austin: University of Texas, 1922.
Patton, Jacob Harris. *A Popular History of the Presbyterian Church in the United States of America*. New York: R. S. Mighill and Co., 1900.
[Peters, Absalom]. *A Plea for Voluntary Societies, and a Defence of the Decisions of the General Assembly of 1836, Against the Strictures of the Princeton Reviewers and Others*. New York: John S. Taylor, 1837.
Posey, Walter Brownlow. *The Presbyterian Church in the Old Southwest 1778-1838*. Richmond: John Knox Press, 1952.
Red, William Stuart. *A History of the Presbyterian Church in Texas*. [Austin]: Steck Co., 1936.
Robinson, John J. *Memoir of Rev. Isaac Anderson, DD., Late President of Maryville College, and Professor of Didactic Theology*. Knoxville: J. Addison Rayl, 1860.
Ross, Charles C., ed. and comp. *The Story of Rotherwood from the Autobiography of Rev. Frederick A. Ross, D. D.* Knoxville: Bean, Waters, & Co., 1923.
Ross, Fred[erick] A. *Slavery Ordained of God*. Philadelphia: J. B. Lippincott, 1859.
Rothrock, Mary U., ed. *The French Broad-Holston Country: A History of Knox County, Tennessee*. Knoxville: East Tennessee Historical Society, 1946.
Rudolph, L. C. *Hoosier Zion: The Presbyterians in Early Indiana*. New Haven and London: Yale University Press, 1963.
Sanders, Robert Stuart. *Presbyterianism in Versailles and Woodford County, Kentucky*. Louisville: Dunne Press, 1963.
Sellers, James Benson. *Slavery in Alabama*. Birmingham: University of Alabama Press, 1950.
Silver, James W. *Confederate Morale and Church Propaganda*. New York: W. W. Norton & Co., The Norton Library, 1967.
Simkins, Francis Butler. *A History of the South*. 3rd ed. New York: Alfred A. Knopf, 1963.
Simms, Henry H. *Emotion at High Tide: Abolition as a

Controversial Factor, 1830-1845. Richmond: William Byrd, 1960.
Slosser, Gaius Jackson, ed. *They Seek a Country: The American Presbyterians. Some Aspects.* New York: Macmillan, 1955.
Smith, Elwyn Allen. *The Presbyterian Ministry in American Culture: A Study in Changing Concepts, 1700-1900.* Philadelphia: Westminster Press, 1962.
Smith, Gerrit. *A Letter of Gerrit Smith to Rev. James Smylie of the State of Mississippi.* New York: American Anti-Slavery Society, 1837.
Smith, Morton Howison. *Studies in Southern Presbyterian Theology.* Jackson, Mississippi: Presbyterian Reformation Society; Amsterdam: Drukkerij en Uitgever ij Jacob van Campen, 1962.
Smith, Timothy L. *Revivalism and Social Reform in Mid-Nineteenth Century America.* New York and Nashville: Abingdon Press, 1957.
Smylie, James. *A Reply to a Letter from the Presbytery of Chillicothe, to the Presbytery of Mississippi, on the Subject of Slavery.* Woodville, Miss.: Wm. A. Norris and Co., 1836.
Southern Aid Society: And Its Constitution, and Address to the Christian Public, Together with Some Notice of the Convention which Resulted in its Formation, and Extracts from its Correspondence New York: Day Book Female Typesetting, 1854.
Sprague, William B. *Lectures on Revivals of Religion.* New York: J. P. Haven and J. Leavitt, 1832.
Stacy, James. *A History of the Presbyterian Church in Georgia.* Elberton, Georgia: Star Press, ca. 1912.
Stampp, Kenneth M. *The Peculiar Institution: Slavery in the Ante-Bellum South.* New York: Alfred A. Knopf, 1956.
Stiles, Joseph C. *Speech on the Slavery Resolutions Delivered in the General Assembly which Met in Detroit in May Last.* Washington: Jno. T. Towers, 1850.
Stringfield, E. E. *Presbyterianism in the Ozarks: A History of the Work of the Various Branches of the Presbyterian Church in Southwest Missouri.* n.p.: n.p., 1909.
Sweet, William Warren. *The American Churches: An Interpretation.* New York and Nashville: Abingdon-Cokesbury Press, 1947.
--------. *Religion in the Development of American*

Culture 1765-1840. New York: Charles Scribner's Sons, 1952.
———. *Revivalism in America: Its Origin, Growth and Decline.* New York: Charles Scribner's Sons, 1944.
———. *The Story of Religion in America.* Enlarged ed. New York and London: Harper & Bros., 1939.
Taylor, Nathaniel W. *Concio ad Clerum: A Sermon.* New Haven: Hezekiah Howe, 1828.
Tewksbury, Donald G. *The Founding of American Colleges and Universities before the Civil War: With Particular Reference to the Religious Influences Bearing upon the College Movement.* Teachers College, Columbia University Contributions to Education, No. 543. New York: Teachers College, Columbia University, 1932.
Thompson, Ernest Trice. *The Changing South and the Presbyterian Church in the United States.* Richmond: John Knox Press, 1950.
———. *Presbyterians in the South.* 3 vols. Richmond: John Knox Press, 1963-1973.
———. *The Spirituality of the Church: A Distinctive Doctrine of the Presbyterian Church in the United States.* Richmond: John Knox Press, 1961.
Thompson, Robert Ellis. *A History of the Presbyterian Churches in the United States.* 2nd ed. American Church History Series. Ed. Philip Schaff. New York: Charles Scribner's Sons, 1900.
Turner, Frederick Jackson. *The United States 1830-1850: The Nation and its Sections.* New York: W. W. Norton & Co., 1935.
Tyler, Alice Felt. *Freedom's Ferment: Phases of American Social History to 1860.* Minneapolis: University of Minnesota Press, 1944.
Vander Velde, Lewis G. *The Presbyterian Churches and the Federal Union 1861-1869.* Harvard Historical Studies. Cambridge: Harvard University Press, 1932.
Walker, Williston. *A History of the Congregational Churches in the United States.* 6th ed. American Church History Series. Ed. Philip Schaff. New York: Charles Scribner's Sons, 1903.
Weeks, Louis B. *Kentucky Presbyterians.* Atlanta: John Knox Press, 1983.
Weisberger, Bernard A. *They Gathered at the River: The Story of the Great Revivalists and Their Impact on Religion in America.* Boston and Toronto: Little, Brown and Co., 1958.
Wilson, Howard McKnight. *The Lexington Presbytery Heritage: The Presbytery of Lexington and Its Churches in the Synod of Virginia Presbyterian*

Church in the United States. Verona, Virginia: McClure Press, [1971].
Wilson, Samuel Tyndale. *A Century of Maryville College, 1819-1919: A Story of Altruism*. Maryville, Tennessee: Directors of Maryville College, 1916.
────. *Isaac Anderson: Founder and First President of Maryville College: A Memorial Sketch*. Maryville: n.p., 1932.
────. *Thomas Jefferson Lamar: A Memorial Sketch*. Maryville, Tennessee: n.p., 1920.
Wood, James. *Old and New Theology, or An Exhibition of Those Differences with Regard to Scripture Doctrines, which have Recently Agitated and Now Divided the Presbyterian Church*. Philadelphia: Presbyterian Board of Publication, 1845.
Woods, H[enry]. *The History of the Presbyterian Controversy with Early Sketches of Presbyterianism*. Louisville: N. H. White, 1843.
Woodworth, Robert Bell. *A History of the Presbyterian Church in Winchester, Virginia, 1780-1949, Based on Official Documents*. Winchester, Virginia: Pifer Printing Co., 1950.

THESES AND DISSERTATIONS

Akers, John N. "Slavery and Sectionalism: Some Aspects of Church and Society Among Presbyterians in the American South, 1789-1861." Ph.D. dissertation, University of Edinburgh, 1973.
Foreman, Kenneth Joseph, Jr. "The Debate on the Administration of Missions Led by James Henley Thornwell in the Presbyterian Church 1839-1861. Ph.D. dissertation, Princeton Theological Seminary, 1977.
Hash, Judith Haws. "A History of the First Presbyterian Church of Jonesboro, Tennessee." M.A. thesis, East Tennessee State University, 1965.
Howard, Victor B. "The Anti-Slavery Movement in the Presbyterian Church, 1835-1861." Ph.D. dissertation, Ohio State University, 1961.
Lewis, Frank Bell. "Robert Lewis Dabney." Ph.D. dissertation, Duke University, 1946.
Martin, Faybert. "The Presbyterian and Methodist Churches and Slavery. A Study of Source Materials Showing the Relation of the Presbyterian And Methodist Churches to Slavery." M.A. thesis, Y. M. C. A. Graduate School, 1931.
Taylor, Hubert Vance. "Slavery and the Deliberations of the Presbyterian General Assembly, 1833-

1838." Ph.D. dissertation, Northwestern University, 1964.
Watkin, Robert Nuckols, Jr. "The Forming of the Southern Presbyterian Minister: From Calvin to the American Civil War." Ph.D. dissertation, Vanderbilt University, 1969.

MISCELLANEOUS UNPUBLISHED MATERIALS

MS "Agreement between Sessions of the Two Churches of the Presbyn. Church in Bow. Green Ky." Western Kentucky Library, Bowling Green, Ky.
Alexander, J. E. "A Historical Sketch of Timberridge Presbyterian Church." Typed copy in McClung Room, Lawson McGhee Library, Knoxville, copied from Greeneville, Tennessee, *Democrat*, 26 January 1888.
MS "Biographical Sketches of the Lives of the Deceased Members of the Synod of Kentucky prepared by order of Synod. Commenced in 1858." Ernest Miller White Library, LPTS.
Chadwick, Mrs. W. D. "Diary of Civil War Days in Huntsville, Ala." A series of undated articles reprinted in the *Huntsville Times,* and in a scrapbook in the Huntsville Public Library.
Dickerson, Archer C. MS "An Expression of the Views of the Pbn Church at Bowling-green, Ky., relative to the late Dismemberment of the Pbn Ch in the U.S." Western Kentucky Library, Bowling Green, Ky.
Duncan, Kate Clagett. "Divided Way: The Story of the Presbyterian Church of Bowling Green, Kentucky." Typed MS, ca 1960, Western Kentucky Library, Bowling Green.
Grafton, C. W. "History of the Mississippi Synod Presbyterian Church." Microfilm of typed MS, 1927, Department of Archives and History, State of Mississippi, Jackson, Mississippi.
McGeachy, Neill Roderick. MS "Men and Mission: A History of the Presbytery of Concord Synod of North Carolina from 1795 to--." PHF.
Nankivell, J. R. Typed "Short History of Mars Hill Presbyterian Church, November 1823--November 1923." McClung Room, Lawson McGhee Library, Knoxville.
"Resolutions of Synod (O. S.) Respect. of B. G. Church on Mr. Dickerson's [illegible] Petition for Ch Meeting." Western Kentucky Library, Bowling Green.
Rodes, Jno. B. "The Story of Bowling Green, Kentucky

and the First Presbyterian Church." Typed MS, 1939. Western Kentucky Library, Bowling Green.
Ross, F[rederick] A[ugustus]. "Autobiography of Rev. F. A. Ross, D. D. in Letters to a Lady of Knoxville, East Tennessee, including an account of his Life in Virginia and Huntsville to the time of his death in 1883." Typed copy in the Huntsville Public Library, Huntsville, Alabama.
Smith, Edward Everett. "Western Kentucky Presbyterian History." Typed MS, PHF.
Tenney, Levi, et al. "History of Central Texas Presbytery, 1854-1938." Typed MS, PHF.
"United Church, Lebanon, Kentucky." MS in Local Church History Program, PHF.
"History of Zion Church 1806-1858." Typed MS. Historical Records Project Official Project No. 465-44-3-115 Copied under Works Progress Administration, Sept 8, 1938. Tennessee: Records of Maury County. Copy in McClung Room, Lawson McGhee Library, Knoxville, Tennessee.
"Zion Church." MS in Local Church History Program, PHF.

Index

Abolitionists, 96-97, 279-280
Adger, J. B., 256-259
Alexander, Archibald, 12, 13, 26
"Address to Christians Throughout the World," 243-244
American Board of Commissioners for Foreign Missions, 4; opposition to slavery, 96-98
American Education Society, 4, 32, 101.
American Home missionary Society, 55, 58, 69; New School severs tie with, 82, 141; no longer supports slaver®holding churches, 83, 93n; relations in South, 84-86
American Sunday School Union, 30
Anderson, Isaac, 32, 103, 118, 161, 294, 299; Hopkinsian, 10, 32, 101
Anti slavery legislation, 296-297.
Apolitical nature of the Church, 16, 38, 115

Associate Reformed Synod of the South, 249, 287
Auburn Declaration, 251

Bachman, Jonathan W., 237, 274-75, 287
Baird, E.T. 249; opposed USS-OS union, 255, 260, 269.
Balch, Hezekiah, 31, 102
Barnes, Albert, 10, 12, 301; wrote commentary on Slavery legislation, 113-132
Baxter, George A., 27, 36, 37.
Belated institutional development, 299
Benevolent programs, lack of support for, 231
Blackburn, Gideon, 32
Board of Church Extension (NS), 185-187
Board of Domestic and Foreign Missions (USS), 179
Bourne, George, 112

Boyd, Andrew Hunter Holmes: biography, 201-202; favored stand of USS on slavery, 216; hostage during Civil War, 234-35, 260; leader in the USS 177-181, 210-212; pastor, 57, 293; theology, 10, 169, 264, 288
Breckinridge, Robert J., 181
Brown, Thomas, 196, 276-277, 278
Bullard, Artemas, 86

Caldwell College, 180
Caldwell, George, 236-238
Calvinistic Magazine, 33,103,294
Candidates for ministry: lack of during war, 236
Cassville Convention, 27, 47, 95, 102, 115, 299
Christian Observer, 104, 210-211, 254, 275-276, 289, 296; moved to Richmond, 228
Church Erection Fund, 86-88, 129, 183-84
Cities
  Augusta, Ga., 249
  Charlotte, N. C., 256
  Dalton, Ga., 234
  Kansas City, Mo., 273
  Knoxville, Tn., 241, 266-270, 280
  Leesburg, Va., 235
  Lynchburg, Va., 254
  Maryville, Tn., 10; abolition center, 35
  New Market, Tn., 276-77
  Richmond, Va., 223, 231
Civil War, Battles
  Antietam, 243
  Gettysburg, 243
  Shiloh, 229, 239
  Stone's River, 240
  Vicksburg, 243
  Effects on students, 236
  Identified with God's plan, 222
  Blocks spiritual growth, 232
  Early impact on USS, 231, 305
Cleland, Thomas: death, 161, 168, 190; defends slavery, 158; favors union with OS; leader in Providence Presbytery, 46, 293-94
Committee on Church Erection (USS), 180
Committee on Church Extension (NS), 80
Committee on Education (USS), 213
Committee on Education for Ministry (NS), 81
Committee on Home Missions (NS), 82
"Concio ad Clerum," 9, 12
Confederate army, a field for evangelism, 232-34, chaplains, 232
Confessional standards, 7, 8
Congregational Church, 5, 9; NS cooperation with, 80
Congregations
  Athens, Tn., Mars Hill, 273-276
  Bowling Green, Ky., (OS), 46, 189
  Greeneville, Tn., 274
  Huntsville, Al., 214
  Jonesboro, Tn., 159, 196
  Knoxville, Tn., Second Church, 32, 159, 177, 237
  Shiloh, 280
  Lynchburg, Second Church, 210
  Maryville, Tn., New Providence Church, 235

Mobile, Al., NS Church, 63
Nashville, NS Church, 59, 225
New Prospect, Tn., 237
New Providence Church (Ky.), 46
Philadelphia, Pa., First Church, 10; Seventh Church, 37
Portsmouth, Va., 234
Richmond, Va., First Church, 38; United Church, 162
Shelbyville, Tn., 59
Salem Church (Tn.), 227
Timber Ridge, Tn., 196-197, 274
Versailles, Ky., 46
Wytheville, Va., 232
Converse, Amasa 81, 164; biography, 202-203; editor of *Christian Observer*, 37; joins USS, 289; moderate, 125; role in Civil War, 228-231; sympathetic to NS in South, 104; USS Moderator, 260
Cox, Samuel A., 74, 95, 114, 124
Cumberland Presbyterian Church, 249, 270, 287

Dabney, Robert L., advocate of OS-USS union in 1864, 235, 249-251, 254, 257-266; OS theologian, 295
Denomination, NS emergence into, 78-84
Detroit Resolutions, text, 121; impact, 122
Dickerson, Archer C.: at Richmond Convention, 166, 169; NS leader in Ky., 46, 67-68, 189, 293-294; prescribes for pioneer preachers, 105
Division of 1837, causes: doctrinal, 7-11; Plan of Union of 1801, 3-5; revivalism, 11-13; slavery, 13-17, 111; voluntary agencies, 5-7
Domestic Missionary Society of Virginia, 55
Domestic Society of Richmond, 55

Eagleton, George E., 204, 232, 236
East Tennessee: abolition stance, 227; church conditions during Civil War, 228, 240-41; little slavery in, 35; pro-Union sentiment, 222, 227, 269; religious background, 28-36; homogeneity, 101, 103
Elective affinity, 10, 32
Emancipation Proclamation, 243
English Presbyterians, 1
Evangelism, cause for 1837 schism, 11-13; NS concept of, 112
Excision Acts, 250

Farmville Convention, 16, 40-41
Free Presbyterian Church, 85, 116
Fugitive Slave Law, 122

Gardiner Spring Resolutions, 250
General Assemblies: 1818, 112, 126
1836, 15, 26
1837, 1, 38, 95, 112
NS 1838, 2, 17
NS 1839, 113
NS 1840, 114
NS 1843, 115-116
NS 1846, 61, 65, 78, 116-120

NS 1847, 78, 82, 120
NS 1849, 120
NS 1850, 121-122
NS 1852, 80, 87, 122
NS 1853, 86, 123-24, 126-27
NS 1854, 126
NS 1855, 128-29
NS 1856, 130-32
NS 1857, 157-58, 195, 198, 253, 299
NS 1865, 274
OS 1858, 181-83, 210, 263-64, 300
USS 1858, 177-183
USS 1859, 210-14
USS 1860, 214-17
USS 1861, 223-26
USS 1863, 241-43
USS 1864, 260-61
PCCSA 1861, 249-250
PCCSA 1863, 254
PCCSA 1864, 256-260
Girardeau, John L., 295-96
Grace of liberality lacking, 218
Greeneville College, 31-32
Growth, hindrances to, 218-219

Handy, I. H. K., 204, 234
Hannibal Convention, 45, 64-66
Heterogeneity, 160, 301-303
Hill, Timothy, 185-89, 199
Hill, William, 27, 36, 37, 294
Hopkins, Samuel, 31
Hopkinsianism: 8, 102, 302; influence in East Tennessee, 31-35
Howard, Charles W., 47, 294

Independent Presbyterian Church, 249, 254

Jackson, Thomas J., 232

Johnson, Andrew, 227
Jones, Charles C., 69n.7, 217, 295-96

Kalopothakes, Michael, 180, 237-38, 287
King, Samuel A., 199, 287; biography, 203
King, William M., 64, 69, 103, 203
Knox County, Tennessee, 227

Lamar, Thomas, 273
Levere, G. W., 276, 280
Lincoln, Abraham, 227, 243, 270
Loyalists in South, 269-270

Macedonia Seminary (Woodford Co.), 68-69, 102-103
Marshall, M. M., 162, 166, 168
Martin, James H., 159, 237, 272
Maryville College, 100, 180, 242; closed during Civil War, 235, 278
Maryville Seminary, 58, 295, 302. See also South-Western Seminary
Maynard, Horace, 162
McGuffey, William H., 254
Middle Judicatories. See Presbyteries and Synods
Missouri Home Missionary Society, 45
Morrison, L. R., 279
Morrison, Levi, 29
Murfreesboro Convention, 98-100, 125-126, 137n

Nelson, David, 76, 103
New divinity, 31. See also New England

School, New Haven Theology
New England School, 257. See also New divinity, New Haven theology
New Haven theology, 7, 9. See also New divinity and New England School
New Measures, 12-13
NS boards, 298
NS theology, 3; heterogeneous, 75-77
NS post war, 273-280
Newton, Alexander, 64, 65, 104
North Alabama College, 180

Oberlin theology, 12
Old Light-New Light controversy, 1
OS: Conservative position, 3; first time term used, 2
OS: differences, 73-74; division, 1-17
OS: opposition to USS, 295-97; proslavery stance, 296-97
OS--South, 222-223; proposed union with USS, 179, 181-82, 249-268
OS-NS reunion in the North, 281

Palmer, Benjamin, 181, 256-260, 295-96
Piedmont Institute, 180
Plan of Union (1801): 113; factor in division of 1837, 3-5; repudiated by NS, 80
Plan of Union (1858, proposed), 179-182, 252
Plan of Union (1864): 249-268, 255; debate on, 256-261; proposed, 241-42; results, 249-268
Plumer, William Swan, 12, 13, 38; editor of *Watchman of the South*, 38
Pope, Fielding, 235, 272
Population sparsity in South, 104-105
Pre-Assembly convention (1838), 39
Presbyterian, The, 169, 170, 181-82
Presbyterian Church in the Confederate States of America: 104, 249; proposed union with USS, 241-242
Presbyterian Sentinel, 68, 104
Presbyterian Witness: 104, 169, 296; began as reaction to NS Assembly of 1850, 122
Presbyteries
  Abingdon (OS), 32, 33, 37
  Amite (OS), 43
  Austin (NS), 281
  Bethel (OS), 249, 254
  Central Mississippi (OS), 263
  Champlain (NS), 127-128
  Charleston Union (OS), 27, 47
  Chattahoochee (NS), 47
  Clinton (NS/USS), 61
  Clinton (OS), 43, 104
  District of Columbia (NS), 37, 168, 195
  East Alabama (OS), 256
  East Hanover (OS), 38, 254
  Etowah (NS), 46-47
  Franklin (NS), 122
  French Broad (NS), 41
  Green River (NS), 46, 66, 294
  Hanover (NS/USS), 39, 56-57, 164, 234, 242, 260

Harmony (Ky), (NS/USS), 46, 87, 128, 294
Harmony (Mo), (NS), 45
Holston (NS), 33, 41, 76, 85, 196-97, 237, 260, 271, 273-75, 281
Hopewell (OS), 46-47
Kingston (NS/USS), 260, 271, 273, 281
Lexington, South (USS), 46, 61, 184-89, 198-99, 224-25
Louisiana (OS), 43
Mississippi (OS), 15, 43, 93n
Missouri (OS), 45
Montgomery (OS), 38
Nashville (NS), 281
New Orleans (NS), 281
New River (NS/USS), 38, 232, 260, 273
Newton (NS/USS), 61, 63, 125, 168, 223-24, 293
North Alabama (NS/USS), 58, 197-98, 231, 241-42
North Alabama (OS), 42
Osage (NS/USS), 105, 184-89, 191, 223, 239, 273-79
Philadelphia, Third (NS), 10, 128
Piedmont (NS/USS), 260
Pittsburgh (OS), 78
Providence (NS), 46, 168, 293-94
Richland (NS), 168
St. Charles (NS), 45
St. Louis (NS), 45, 186-87
Shiloh (NS/USS), 42, 58-60, 170
South Alabama (OS), 255-56
South Carolina (OS), 256
Texas (NS), 63-64, 199, 239, 262, 293
Tuscaloosa (OS), 256
Union (NS/USS), 30, 32, 41, 58-60, 74, 159, 196, 200, 228, 232, 271-73, 281
West Hanover (OS), 38
West Tennessee (NS/USS), 58-60
West Tennessee (OS), 42, 197-98
Winchester (NS), 38, 160, 260, 262, 293
Princeton Seminary, 12, 33, 102
Princeton theology, 17
Proposed USS Seminary, 183, 225-26, 242
Protestant and Herald, 116, 296

Read, Charles H., 99; chaired Richmond Convention, 166; his hope in God, 230; leader in USS, 204; Moderator of USS, 210; pastor, 233
Reconstruction by New School, 271-280
Religious papers: morale factor in Civil War, 228-230
Revivals, revivalism: factor in 1837 division, 11-13
Rhea, Samuel A., 180, 238, 274
Richmond Convention: 162-67, 196, 300; reaction to, 167-170
Robinson, John J.: 214, 272, 278; biography, 203
Roby, William D., 56
Ross, Frederick Augustus: author of *Slavery Ordained of God*, 33, 103, 294; biography, 200; manumitted slaves, 35; opposed Excision Acts, 33-35; orthodoxy questionable, 76, 169; protested

actions of NS in 1857, 124; supporter of Sabbath Schools, 224
Russell, Robert Young, 266n.31

Sabbath Schools in war, 224
Sawyer, Samuel, 274
Scotch-Irish Presbyterians, 1, 28-29, 31
Secession (political), 226
Slavery in division of 1837, 13-17
Slavery debate halted growth in NS South, 111
Slavery issue as USS monistic approach, 303-305
Slavery legislation in NS, 113-132
Slaves: education of, 217; evangelism of, 217-218, 224; preaching to, 180; religious instruction, 56-57
Smylie, James, 43
Southern Aid Society: assistance to southern churches, 298; assistance withdrawn during war, 224; board of directors, 98-99; formation in 1853, 62; purpose of, 86-87
Southern Christian Sentinel, 27
Southern Old School, 225. See also Presbyterian Church in Confederate States of America
Southern Presbyterian theological purism questioned, 263-264, 288
Southern Religious Telegram, 37
South-Western Theological Seminary, 33, 100-103. See also Maryville Seminary

Spirituality of the Church, 95. See also apolitical nature of the Church
States
 Georgia, 46-47
 Maryland, 227
 Missouri, 223
 New York, 12
 South Carolina, 47
 Tennessee, 227. See also East Tennessee
Statistics: difficulty in finding accurate, 282, nn. 8, 17, 283n., 19, 287; USS (1857), 181, 289n.1, 290n.2; (1864), 303
Stewardship deficiency, 225
Stiles, Joseph C.: biography, 202, 233-34; leader in Synod of KY (NS), 46, 293-94; member, Joint Committee of Plan of Union (1864), 254, 266n.30; professor of proposed USS seminary, 212; Sec. of SAS, 98; USS evangelist, 232, 236
Subscription, 4, 7, 10
Synods
 Carolina (OS), 32
 Genesee (NS), 5
 Geneva (NS), 5
 Indiana (NS), 116
 Kentucky (NS), 46, 66-69, 102, 104, 116, 165, 168, 169, 171, 189-190, 195
 Kentucky (OS), 190, 288
 Mississippi (NS/USS), 43-44, 60-64, 121-22, 129, 165, 198, 238
 Mississippi (OS), 43-44
 Missouri (NS), 45-46, 64-66, 86, 119,

184-189, 195, 198-99, 278-79
Missouri (OS), 45-46, 288
Nashville (OS), 165
Pennsylvania (NS), 56, 195
Pittsburgh (OS), 2
South Carolina (OS), 249, 256
Tennessee (NS/USS), 28-36, 57-58, 168, 195-196, 226, 274-76, 281
Texas (OS), 262
Utica (NS), 5
Virginia (NS/USS), 36-41, 55-57, 119, 157, 164, 195, 235, 240, 261-62
Virginia (OS), 164
Western Reserve (NS), 5, 15
Western Synod of the Carolinas (Proposed), 36
West Tennessee (NS/USS), 58-60, 195, 197-98
West Tennessee (OS), 41

Tappan, Arthur, 84
Taylor, Nathaniel W., 9, 12
Tennessee Constitutional Convention (1834), 31
Tennessee Valley, 29, 47
Theological education in America, 100
Thompson, Ernest Trice, 270
Thornwell, James Henley, 168, 295, 296
Triennial Assemblies (NS), 77-78, 114
Tucker, John Randolph, 166, 168, 205, 260

Union Sympathizers in East Tennessee, 227-28
Union Theological Seminary in Virginia, 37, 100, 295
USS: Clergy persecuted in Civil War, 234-36; congregations geographically located, 292-93; leading clergy, 200-204; small churches, 292; Urban churches, 291-92
Unity of the NS: its importance, 113
University of Virginia, 225

Voluntary societies: decline of interest in, 80; factor in division of 1837, 5-7
Waddell, J. N., 249, 295
Watchman of the South, 36
Weld, Theodore, 12, 14
Wells, Rufus, P., 274-76
Western Missionary Society, 78
Western North Carolina, 28, 35, 196
Western Tennessee, 30
Westminster Standards, 179
Woodford County Seminary, 295. See also Macedonia Seminary

Yeoman farmers, 31

Zivley, J. H., 203

Presbyterian Historical Society Publications

Vol. I. *The Presbyterian Enterprise* by M. W. Armstrong L. A. Loetscher and C. A. Anderson (Westminster Press, 1956; Paperback reprinted for P.H.S., 1963 & 1976)

II. *Presbyterian Ministry in American Culture* by E. A. Smith (Westminster Press, 1962)

III. *Journals of Charles Beatty, 1762-1769,* edited by Guy S. Klett (Pennsylvania State University Press, 1962)

IV. *Hoosier Zion, The Presbyterian in Early Indiana* by L. C. Rudolph (Yale University Press, 1963)

V. *Presbyterianism in New York State* by Robert Hastings Nichols, edited and completed by James Hastings Nichols (Westminster Press, 1963)

VI. *Scots Breed and Susquehanna* by Hubertis M. Cummings (University of Pittsburgh Press, 1964)

VII. *Presbyterians and the Negro—A History* by Andrew E. Murray (Presbyterian Historical Society, 1966)

VIII. *A Bibliography of American Presbyteranism During the Colonial Period* by Leonard J. Trinterud (Presbyterian Histoical Society, 1968)

IX. *George Bourne and "The Book and Slavery Irreconcilable"* by John W. Christie and Dwight L. Dumond (Historial Society of Delaware and Presbyterian Historical Society, 1969)

X. *The Skyline Synod: Presbyterianism in Colorado and Utah* by Andrew E. Murray (Synod of Colorado/Utah, 1977)

XI. *The Life and Writings of Francis Makemie,* edited by Boyd S. Schlenteher (Presbyterian Historical Society, 1971)

XII. *A Younger Church in Search of Maturity: Presbyterianism in Brazil from 1910 to 1959* by Paul Pierson (Trinity University Press, 1974)

XIII. *Presbyterians in the South,* vols. II and III, by Ernest Trice Thompson (John Knox Press, 1973

XIV. *Ecumenical Testimony* by John McNeill and James H. Nichols (Westminster Press, 1974)

XV. *Iglesia Presbiteriana: A History of Presbyterians and Mexican Americans in the Southwest* by R. Douglas Brackenridge and Francisco O. Garcia Treto (Trinity University Press, 1974; 2nd edition, 1987)

XVI. *The Rise and Decline of Education for Black Presbyterians* by Inez M. Parker (Trinity University Press, 1977)

XVII. *Minutes of the Presbyterian Church in America, 1706-1788* edited by Buy S. Klett (Presbyterian Historical Society, 1977)

XVIII. **Eugene Carson Blake, Prophet with Portfolio* by R. Douglas Brackenridge (Seabury Press, 1978)

XIX. *Prisoners of Hope: A Search for Mission 1815-1822* by Marjorie Barnhart (Presbyterian Historical Society, 1980)
XX. *From Colonialism to World Community: The Church's Pilgrimage* by John Coventry Smith (Geneva Press, 1982)
XXI. *Facing the Enlightenment and Pietism: Archibald Alexander and the Founding of Princeton Theological Seminary* by Lefferts A. Loetscher (Greenwood Press, 1983)
XXII. *Presbyterian Women in America: Two Centuries of a Quest for Status* by Lois A. Boyd and R. Douglas Brackenridge (Greenwood Press, 1983)
XXIII. *Kentucky Presbyterians* by Louis B. Weeks (John Knox Press, 1983)
XXIV. *Merging Mission and Unity* by Donald Black (Geneva Press, 1983)
XXV. *Gilbert Tennent, Son of Thunder* by Milton J. Coalter, Jr. (Greenwood Press, 1986)

*Out of print

About the Author

HAROLD M. PARKER, JR., is former Chairman of the Graduate Council, past Chairman of the Division of Social Sciences, and Emeritus Professor of History at Western State College of Colorado, Gunnison. The author of *Oldest Church on the Western Slope, Sermons on the Minor Prophets,* and *Studies in Southern Presbyterian History,* Mr. Parker is also the compiler of *Bibliography of Published Articles on American Presbyterianism, 1901-1980* (Greenwood Press, 1985). His articles have appeared in the *Iliff Review, The Historian,* the *Journal of Presbyterian History, Maryland Historical Magazine, Filson Club Historical Quarterly, Tennessee Historical Quarterly, Register of the Kentucky Historical Society, The Social Science Journal,* and the *Jewish Quarterly Review.*